Shaping the Campus Conversation on Student Learning and Experience:

ACTIVATING THE RESULTS OF ASSESSMENT IN ACTION

Edited by Karen Brown, Debra Gilchrist, Sara Goek, Lisa Janicke Hinchliffe, Kara Malenfant, Chase Ollis, and Allison Payne

Association of College and Research Libraries
A division of the American Library Association
Chicago, Illinois 2018

12\28\20

Table of Contents

Preface

The Association of College and Research Libraries' (ACRL) Assessment in Action (AiA) was a multiyear professional development program, funded in part by the Institute of Museum and Library Services (IMLS) and in partnership with the Association for Institutional Research and the Association of Public and Land-grant Universities, that ran from 2013 to 2016. It has been central to the ACRL Value of Academic Libraries initiative by involving over 200 higher education institutions, generating evidence of library impact, and advancing library leadership and evidence-based advocacy. This publication provides, in a single and comprehensive work, the story of AiA—the context surrounding its development, findings of the team-based assessment projects, insights about the program results, reflections about its impact, and recommendations for future directions. While each chapter can stand on its own, the publication also captures a full picture of all aspects of the program. Some repetition of content occurs to facilitate both of these goals.

Contents*

Introduction

The introduction, titled "The Assessment in Action Program: A Cornerstone of the Value of Academic Libraries Initiative," provides a brief overview of the program's development and considers its context with the association's various assessment activities.

Section 1: Results

The chapters in section 1 present notable outcomes of the program, including evidence about library impact on student learning and success, findings about the importance of a collaborative approach to assessment, and demonstrations of library leadership.

---

* Please note that chapters 3, 4, 5, 6, 16, and Appendix B were first published elsewhere and this book reproduces their original formatting and editorial conventions.

Section 2: Reflections

The AiA program was designed to produce results that promote meaningful actions and sustainable changes around student academic outcomes. The chapters in section 2 consider the ongoing effectiveness of the AiA program and include reflections by nine AiA librarians who led campus projects, observations by the program facilitators about librarian learning and assessment work, recommendations for leveraging features of the AiA approach to collaborate with campus stakeholders, and a consideration of the AiA program within the context of ACRL's ongoing activities to build the profession's capacity for assessment.

- *Chapter 7, "A Stone Soup Approach to Building Large-Scale Library Assessments,"* discusses the library's assessment activities at Grand Valley State University library, which is documenting its contributions to student retention.
- *Chapter 8, "Filling In the Potholes: Providing Smooth Pathways for Successful Library Instruction for First-Year Students,"* describes the impact of the Tulsa Community College AiA project on campus-wide curriculum development work, particularly a greater emphasis on standardizing learning outcomes across library instruction in the English and writing courses.
- *Chapter 9, "Building Campus Partnerships and Improving Student Success Through a Collaborative Drop-in Tutoring Service,"* considers the multiple ways that the library's tutoring service has strengthened relationships with students on the Eastern Mennonite University campus.
- *Chapter 10, "Becoming Part of the Conversation through Assessment of Undergraduate Library Internships,"* explores the library's contribution to high-impact educational practices at Gettysburg College through its library internship program.
- *Chapter 11, "Positively Impacting the Library Experience of Aboriginal and International Students,"* explains how the foundational work of the University of Alberta AiA project provided a context for creating a scalable Personal Librarian program that expanded from academic support for Aboriginal students to engagement with international students.
- *Chapter 12, "You Spin Me Right Round (Like a Record)—Or, Does the Assessment Loop Ever Truly 'Close'?"* describes the increasing role of the University of Massachusetts Boston librarians as consultants to faculty who handle aspects of information literacy instruction.
- *Chapter 13, "Don't Wait for Them to Come to You: Partnering with Student Support Services,"* highlights the importance of collecting data to document library impact and describes new library partnerships with academic and student services at the University of Nebraska Omaha.
- *Chapter 14, "Assessing Information Literacy for Transfer Student Success,"* considers the ongoing impact of the AiA project at the University of North Carolina at Greensboro on expanding the library's collaboration with other campus units to improve services and resources for transfer students.
- *Chapter 15, "Opening Doors for Libraries on Campus and Beyond,"* explains how AiA increased awareness of the library and the importance of information literacy efforts to general education on the Boston University campus and has spurred new collaborations with other higher education institutions.
- *Chapter 16, "Professional Development for Assessment: Lessons from Reflective Practice,"* synthesizes a conversation with five AiA program facilitators about the importance of outcomes, alignment, leadership, results, and perseverance in relation to learning about assessment.

Section 3: Advancing Assessment to the Future

The two chapters in section 3 look to the future by considering the important contributions of the AiA program to ACRL's Value of Academic Library Initiative and new directions for advancing academic library assessment.

- *Chapter 17, "Assessing for Alignment: How to Win Collaborators and Influence Stakeholders,"* presents recommendations for adapting the AiA approach to advance three key priority areas at institutions: communication, collaboration, and institutional mission and alignment.
- *Chapter 18, "Conclusion: Reflecting on the Past, Looking to the Future,"* recaps the significance of the AiA program as a cornerstone of the ACRL Value of Academic Libraries initiative and looks to ACRL's continued influence in building a broad and inclusive community of practice around assessment and library leadership.

Appendices

Eleven appendices provide supporting material about the planning activities leading up to the implementation of AiA, information about the participating institutions and program contributors, an overview of professional development and project design elements, periodic reports to IMLS, a list of publications and presentations related to AiA, and documents that recommend strategic directions for academic library assessment work.

Intended Audiences

The book is intended to appeal to different audiences and meet a variety of needs within the library profession and the higher education community.

- Academic librarians who are new to assessment or work at libraries with limited assessment activity will find the planning and implementation overviews and the project design elements covered in the annual analyses of chapters 3, 4, and 5 and appendix J useful. The reflective essays of chapters 7–15 provide insightful behind-the-scenes looks at coordinating assessment activities.
- For those libraries that already have an ongoing assessment program and are looking for new directions or ideas for expanding their efforts, chapter 17 presents a summary of multiple ways that academic libraries can demonstrate contributions to students' academic outcomes and suggests priority areas for future assessment and research. Nine AiA librarian team leaders recount in chapters 7–15 their experiences with sustaining their initial assessment work and expanding it in new directions.
- If you are looking to make a case to your campus administrators about library impact on student learning and success, the overview of key AiA findings in chapter 1 and the ACRL Value of Academic Libraries Statement in chapter 6 present succinct summaries.
- Campus assessment officers and higher education administrators may be most interested in the high-level summary of the AiA project in chapter 1; the discussion of cross-campus collaboration presented in chapter 2; the recommendations from several campus provosts in chapter 17 about assessment alignment, collaboration, and communication; and appendix H, which lists participating institutions by regional accrediting agency. The individual project reports of the participating institutions are available online at https://apply.ala.org/aia/public.
- Library and information science faculty and scholars may find the insights of the AiA program facilitators in chapter 16, the suggested areas of research critical to higher education

covered in chapter 17, and the synthesis of conversations with representatives at twelve higher education organizations outside the library profession in appendix K of greatest interest.

In Appreciation

The editorial team for this book wishes to acknowledge all of the contributors to the chapters, participants in the AiA program, and leaders in ACRL and partner associations and IMLS. Without your work, the AiA program and its outcomes would not exist.

The Assessment in Action Program

A Cornerstone of the Value of Academic Libraries Initiative

Mary Ellen K. Davis and Cheryl A. Middleton

In the Beginning

ACRL has a long history of helping academic libraries demonstrate their contributions to their institutions, dating back to the early 1980s when ACRL created an Ad Hoc Committee on Performance Measures that issued an RFP and selected Dr. Nancy Van House to develop a manual on assessment.[1]

More recently, in September 2012, ACRL was awarded a National Leadership Demonstration Grant by the Institute of Museum and Library Services (IMLS) for the program Assessment in Action: Academic Libraries and Student Success (AiA), the subject of this book. A cornerstone of ACRL's Value of Academic Libraries initiative, AiA was undertaken in partnership with the Association for Institutional Research (AIR) and the Association of Public and Land-grant Universities (APLU). The grant supported the design, implementation, and evaluation of a program to strengthen the competencies of librarians in campus leadership and data-informed advocacy.

The genesis of AiA can be traced to ACRL's Value of Academic Libraries initiative, first launched in 2009. After an open call for proposals, ACRL selected Megan Oakleaf to prepare a comprehensive review of the quantitative and qualitative literature, methodologies, and best practices currently in place for demonstrating the value of academic libraries. The subsequent 2010 report, *The Value of Academic Libraries: A Comprehensive Research Review and Report,*[2] represents a seminal work on the subject and set a direction for the association via its recommendation that ACRL, "create a professional development program to build the profession's capacity to document, demonstrate, and communicate library value in alignment with the mission and goals of their colleges and universities."

To understand how to shape such a professional development program, ACRL convened two planning summits in 2011, supported by an IMLS Collaborative Planning Grant (read more in appendix B, "Connect, Collaborate, and Communicate: A Report from the Value of Academic Libraries Summits"). Through these summits, ACRL sought advice from a broad range of stakeholders: senior librarians, chief academic administrators, and institutional researchers from twenty-two postsecondary institutions, along with fifteen representatives from higher education organizations, associations, and accreditation bodies. The challenging work and deep thinking of those participants led us to the design of the AiA program.

Through AiA, librarian-led teams carried out assessment projects over fourteen months at their community colleges, colleges, and universities. The projects examined the impact of the library (instruction, reference, collections, space, and more) on student learning and success, evident through measures such as assignment or course grades, rubric scores relative to achieving learning outcomes, graduation rates, and so on. Over the course of the three-year program, teams from more than two hundred institutions participated in AiA. They represent all types of institutions from forty-one states, the District of Columbia, four Canadian provinces, and Australia.

This book serves to commemorate the important work completed during the AiA program, as well as to document and reflect on program outcomes. The program budget, nearly $400,000 between the IMLS grant and ACRL's in-kind contribution, represented a significant investment for ACRL. The program design reflects our strong commitment to the principle that partnering with others on campus to ask and answer important questions about student learning yields stronger, more actionable information than going it alone. Collaboration ultimately not only improves our ability to help students succeed, but also creates a deeper understanding of how the library is a valuable educational partner on campus.

Exploring *Shaping the Campus Conversation on Student Learning and Experience* and Spurring Conversations about Library Contributions

Section 1 pulls together in one place important research about the program to spur conversations about the contributions of libraries on campus. It reprints three important pieces that synthesize the results of the AiA team projects during each of the program's three years. While these have been available in PDF format on the ACRL website, publishing here provides lasting access as well as convenience for the reader. These reports are: chapter 3, "Academic Library Contributions to Student Success: Documented Practices from the Field"; chapter 4, "Documented Library Contributions to Student Learning and Success: Building Evidence with Team-Based Assessment in Action Campus Projects"; and chapter 5, "Academic Library Impact on Student Learning and Success: Findings from Assessment in Action Team Projects." As a framework for these three pieces, chapter 1 provides a "mega" executive summary of the AiA program results in light of the 2011 summit recommendations. By synthesizing the results across all three years of the AiA program, this chapter is particularly useful for librarians in talking with stakeholders about the contributions that a library can make to an institution.

Section 1 also includes a chapter that draws out lessons from AiA about collaborative assessment. Written for a broad higher education audience and first published as an occasional paper in November 2017 by the National Institute for Learning Outcomes Assessment, chapter 2, "Creating Sustainable Assessment through Collaboration: A National Program Reveals Effective Practices," focuses on the collaborative assessment practices guiding AiA teams that resulted in campus-wide benefits. As the chapter authors explain, higher education leaders have long expressed concerns about the lack of collaboration on campus, while at the same time noting the pivotal role such cooperation plays in promoting student learning. While many have observed that assessment is often a solo activity, changes based on assessment are often a department-wide decision. This chapter explains how a collaborative approach to assessment, with a team of diverse stakeholders, will more likely overcome the challenges of taking action to improve student learning. The analysis relates findings from AiA team experiences to a selected body of literature on organization development, leadership, and change to draw out lessons that can be applied more broadly within higher education institutions.

The first section concludes with an outreach resource; chapter 6, "Value of Academic Libraries Statement," authored by the ACRL Value of Academic Libraries Committee and approved by the

ACRL Board of Directors in June 2016. It articulates the various ways academic libraries provide direct and indirect value to institutions of higher education. This statement, asserting the essential role that academic libraries play, should be used by librarians to develop their own talking points about the contributions their libraries make to student success:

> "Academic libraries are one of the few units in a modern institution of higher education that can provide an impact on all realms of institutional importance, from student enrollment to faculty productivity to institutional reputation, while balancing services and resources for all constituency groups and stakeholders in higher education."

We encourage readers to use the chapters in section 1 to spur conversations about the role and contributions of the library on campus.

Reflections on Assessment and ACRL's Work

Section 2 examines how perceptions about the library and its role may have changed as a result of the AiA projects. Nine chapters by AiA librarian team leaders analyze the ongoing impact of their work. To secure these contributions, an open call for proposals was issued to all AiA team leaders, asking for essays that would describe the positive outcomes that occurred for the team leaders and their libraries because of their participation in AiA. These authors were directed to focus their reflective essays less on each assessment project itself, and more on what happened with their relationships with people in other units outside the library and what changed in terms of the behaviors or perceptions of others on campus. While not every AiA project necessarily led to the deep kinds of impact described by these nine teams, we believe these case studies provide useful insights into the promise of a library undertaking this kind of work. These reflective essays connect the projects with the authors' current status: which pieces they built on, which relationships they cultivated, and how they made change happen. Not only do these essays describe what the impact was, they also focus on why it is important and how it was used to further the campus recognition of the library's work in supporting students.

For a different reflective viewpoint, chapter 16, "Professional Development for Assessment: Lessons from Reflective Practice," shares the perspective of the AiA design/facilitation team. This chapter, first published as an article in the *Journal of Academic Librarianship* and reprinted with permission, takes stock of their experiences teaching AiA team leader librarians about assessment and describes how this work inspired, challenged, and helped them grow in their own assessment work.

Advancing Assessment to the Future

Section 3 takes a prospective look at ways for academic librarians to continue leveraging assessment to progress and ACRL's continued support of the profession in this work. In chapter 17, "Assessing for Alignment: How to Win Collaborators and Influence Stakeholders," a team at OCLC Research describes their findings about how academic libraries can contribute to student learning and success to advance their institutional missions and goals in these areas. After an open request for proposals to develop an action-oriented research agenda that would update the 2010 *Value of Academic Libraries* report and examine how academic libraries can contribute to student learning and success as well as demonstrate these contributions, ACRL selected the proposal from OCLC Research. ACRL published the report entitled *Academic Library Impact: Improving Practice and Essential Areas to Research*[3] in September 2017. In developing the report, the project team analyzed a total of 535 documents published between 2010 and 2016, including the AiA project descriptions. They found notable differences and areas of strength in the approach taken by AiA teams over other approaches to assessment and research about library impact on student learning and success. The OCLC Research team was invited to contribute a chapter to this book, and they have identified how researchers and professionals can leverage the AiA approach to advance three key priority areas: communication, collaboration, and institutional mission alignment and strategy. This chapter identifies effective practices to implement those aspects of the AiA approach.

The final chapter, a conclusion by Lisa Janicke Hinchliffe, presents a unique viewpoint. Hinchliffe was ACRL president (2010–11) when the ACRL Board of Directors defined the Value of Academic Libraries initiative as one of its strategic goals, and she went on to co-chair the Value of Academic Libraries Committee (2011–13). Due to her experience with the initiative, she was selected as a co-lead designer of AiA. In this chapter, she reflects on the themes of communication, collaboration, and connection and how they related to the ongoing development of an assessment/value community of practice.

ACRL's Next Steps

This book paints a vivid picture of the thinking that went into creating the AiA program, the results of the individual projects, the impact on participating teams, and the broader importance to the profession. Although the grant funding has ended, ACRL has adapted the AiA program to meet the needs and capacity of our community. In 2017, ACRL launched a new day-long workshop that builds on the AiA curriculum with a focus on strategic and sustainable assessment. Academic librarians can now bring this and other ACRL RoadShow Traveling Workshops to their institutions, chapters, or consortia.

Additionally, ACRL is creating new professional development offerings and programs to stimulate assessment activities. A program of travel scholarships, announced in October 2017, supports librarians in presenting their work about the impact of academic libraries at higher education conferences or disciplinary conferences where they will reach a wide audience. Also, a program for small research grants was announced in January 2018 so that scholars and practitioners can undertake research in the priority areas indicated by ACRL's September 2017 report, *Academic Library Impact: Improving Practice and Essential Areas to Research.*[4] We encourage all academic librarians to apply these findings and develop assessments that result in meaningful impacts on their own campuses. Use these assessments to better tell the story of the positive contributions libraries are making. And we encourage all librarians to embrace the strategies and principles inherent in the AiA project's design—developing relationships with stakeholders across campus, partnering with faculty and other stakeholders to develop action-based research, and relating assessments to campus priorities.

Biographies

Mary Ellen K. Davis is the Executive Director of the Association of College and Research Libraries (ACRL). She represents more than 10,000 members to the higher education community and has advanced ACRL's stands on scholarly communication, information literacy, assessment, and new roles for academic librarians through presentations, conversations, papers, and collaborative activities, including grants. She works closely with the ACRL Board of Directors on strategic planning and governance and with the Budget & Finance Committee. Mary Ellen served in various capacities at ACRL including chief operating officer, editor of *C&RL News*, and professional development program manager before becoming the executive director in 2001. She has an MS in library and information science from the University of Illinois at Urbana-Champaign and an MA in education from Central Michigan University, where she worked as a reference and instruction librarian; email mdavis@ala.org.

Cheryl A. Middleton, 2017/18 ACRL President, is an Assistant Professor and the Associate University Librarian for Research & Scholarly Communication at Oregon State University Libraries and Press (OSULP). She earned her MLIS from Louisiana State University and graduated Beta Phi Mu. She holds a BS in General Science from Oregon State University. Her research interest included examining the current information eco-system and its impacts on library services to enhance research and learning. Her publications include "Magical Thinking: Moving Beyond Natural Bias to Examine Core Services" in *Letting Go of Legacy Services: Library Case Studies* (2014); co-authorship of "Management of Library Course Reserves and the Textbook Affordability Crisis," *Journal of Access Services* (2009); and co-authorship of "Student Strategies for Coping with the High Cost of Textbooks and the Role of Academic Library Course Reserves," *portal: Libraries and the Academy* (2009); email cheryl.middleton@oregonstate.edu.

Notes

1. Nancy A. Van House, *Measuring Academic Library Performance* (Chicago, IL: American Library Association, 1990).
2. Association of College and Research Libraries. *Value of Academic Libraries: A Comprehensive Research Review and Report*. Researched by Megan Oakleaf. (Chicago: Association of College and Research Libraries, 2010). Available at http://www.ala.org/acrl/sites/ala.org.acrl/files/content/issues/value/val_report.pdf.
3. Association of College and Research Libraries. *Academic Library Impact: Improving Practice and Essential Areas to Research*. Prepared by Lynn Silipigni Connaway, William Harvey, Vanessa Kitzie, and Stephanie Mikitish of OCLC Research. (Chicago: Association of College and Research Libraries, 2017). Available at http://www.ala.org/acrl/sites/ala.org.acrl/files/content/publications/whitepapers/academiclib.pdf.
4. Ibid.

Results

Over the course of the immersive three year Assessment in Action (AiA) program, ACRL compiled and reported on the results of over 200 unique team-based projects from a diverse spectrum of higher education institutions. These results highlight the myriad ways in which libraries contribute to student learning and success and add to our collective knowledge of effective library practices. The profession now benefits from the vast array of assessment methods and tools the AiA teams have used to investigate library impact over the course of the program. Academic libraries are encouraged to adapt the findings from these projects to their own unique institutional contexts to develop and strengthen high-quality, collaborative assessment programs.

The AiA program's direct impact extends beyond revealing evidence of and communicating the library's pivotal role in student learning and success. As a result of participating in the program, team leaders saw significant growth in their personal and professional leadership competencies. A strong and supportive community of practice around academic library assessment has emerged and continues to develop. Finally, participants and project teams continue to contribute to the profession through further scholarly literature and presentations, which have been captured in the "Assessment in Action Comprehensive Bibliography" at the end of this book (see appendix I).

Chapter 1 looks across all three years of the AiA program to provide a broad overview and highlight significant results of the program. Chapter 2, "Creating Sustainable Assessment through Collaboration: A National Program Reveals Effective Practices," is intended for a broad higher education audience and draws out lessons from the program results related to collaborative assessment. Full reports from each year of the program, previously available only in electronic format, expand on the overview by highlighting several projects from a variety of institutions. And finally, the ACRL "Value of Academic Libraries Statement" articulates the essential roles academic libraries play in their institutions.

CHAPTER 1

Evidence of Academic Library Impact on Student Learning and Success

Key Outcomes and Compelling Findings of Assessment in Action

Karen Brown, Dominican University

Introduction

Academic librarians have increasingly recognized the need to be part of the larger national dialogue about higher education effectiveness and quality. In response to this need, the Association of College and Research Libraries (ACRL) Value of Academic Libraries initiative was launched publicly with the release of *The Value of Academic Libraries: A Comprehensive Research Review and Report*. The report recommended that ACRL create a professional development program to build the profession's capacity to document, demonstrate, and communicate library value in alignment with institutional goals.

A 2011 Institute of Museum and Library Services (IMLS) National Leadership Collaborative Planning Grant provided funding for ACRL to partner with three influential higher education groups experienced with education assessment and institutional effectiveness—the Association for Institutional Research, the Association of Public and Land-grant Universities, and the Council of Independent Colleges—to plan and carry out two national summits for discussions about library impact. "Demonstrating Library Value: A National Conversation" (November 29–December 1, 2011) brought together representatives from a broad spectrum of twenty-two postsecondary institutions, including senior librarians, chief academic administrators, and institutional researchers, as well as fifteen representatives from higher education organizations and associations. Broad themes about the dynamic nature of higher education assessment emerged from the discussions and collaborative work at the summits and provided a context for recommendations on leveraging collaborative efforts with campus stakeholders, investigating and articulating various dimensions of library impact, and building the profession's capacity to document and communicate library value. The ACRL program, Assessment in Action: Academic Libraries and Student Success (AiA), funded in part by a grant from IMLS, was designed and planned in response to these recommendations. This chapter draws from the analyses of results published annually during the AiA program to highlight key findings about academic library contributions to student learning and success and synthesizes results of AiA in light of the summits' proposed strategic actions for advancing the profession's work around library impact.

Findings about Academic Library Contributions to Student Academic Outcomes

Over 200 postsecondary institutions participated in the AiA program between 2013 and 2016. At each AiA institution, a campus assessment team, consisting of a librarian and at least two people from other departments or units, planned and implemented a project about library impact that aligned with its institutional priorities about student academic outcomes. The AiA campus teams found that student learning and success encompass a multitude of possible outcomes, and they needed to break apart the complex and interrelated aspects of learning to investigate library impact on specific academic outcomes. In addition, the various library factors that might be investigated could have different types of impact on students' academic experiences. The primary learning outcomes and library factors considered in the AiA projects are summarized in tables 1.1 and 1.2.

COMPELLING FINDINGS

- Students benefit from library instruction in their initial coursework.

- Library use increases student success.

- Collaborative academic programs and services involving the library enhance student learning.

- Information literacy instruction strengthens general education outcomes.

- Library research consultations boost student learning.

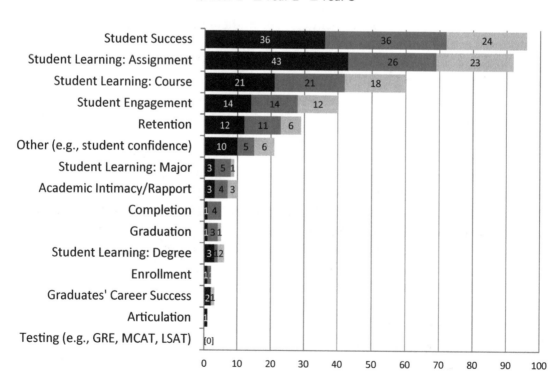

TABLE 1.1

The number of AiA projects that investigated the listed academic outcome.

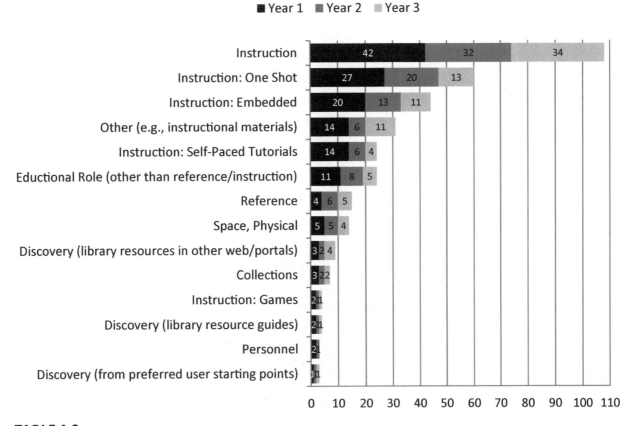

TABLE 1.2
The number of AiA projects that assessed the listed library factor.

Compelling Findings

Demonstrations of positive connections between the library and aspects of student learning and success in five areas that emerged from the AiA team projects are particularly noteworthy. These findings, which come from over 200 projects conducted at different types of institutions, indicate multiple ways that libraries contribute to students' academic outcomes. The assessment findings highlight effective library practice, and libraries that engage in these five practices can anticipate positive contributions to students' academic experiences.

- *Students benefit from library instruction in their initial coursework.* Academic libraries typically place a high priority on information literacy instruction for first-year students to provide them with a common set of competencies for their undergraduate studies. The assessment findings from numerous AiA projects that focused on information literacy initiatives for freshmen and new students underscore that students who receive this instruction perform better in their initial courses than students who do not.
- *Library use is related to student success.* Several AiA studies point to positive connections between students' use of the library and academic success. The analysis of multiple data points (e.g., circulation, library instruction session attendance, online database access, study room use, interlibrary loan) frequently showed that students who used the library in some way achieved higher levels of academic success represented by GPA, course grades, and persistence compared with their peers who did not use the library.

- *Collaborative academic programs and services involving the library enhance student learning.* To provide more comprehensive and integrated approaches to academic support for students, libraries are finding that partnerships with other campus units, such as the writing center, academic enrichment, and speech lab, are yielding promising benefits. Although campuses vary widely in the types of academic support they provide, the AiA teams at several institutions that investigated collaborative approaches documented positive benefits for students, such as higher grades, academic confidence, and persistence from one term to the next.

- *Information literacy instruction strengthens general education outcomes.* The general education curriculum at most colleges and universities is designed to reach all undergraduate students with a broad liberal arts and science learning experience that revolves around a core set of institutionally defined proficiencies and academic outcomes. A focus on inquiry and problem solving for students' personal and professional lives and attention to significant social questions typically frame the courses and learning activities. Some AiA projects studied the library's impact on this aspect of a student's academic learning and found connections between library instruction and students' achievement of institutional core competencies and general education outcomes. The project findings demonstrated multiple ways that information literacy contributes to inquiry-based and problem-solving learning, including effective identification and use of information, critical thinking, ethical reasoning, and civic engagement.

- *Library research consultations boost student learning.* Several AiA projects that assessed one-on-one or small-group reference and research assistance with a librarian demonstrated positive associations with academic success, as documented by such factors as student confidence, GPAs, and improved achievement on course assignments. At some institutions, consultation services provide opportunities for customized, focused instruction, and at other institutions, the library offers research consultation services off site from the library and may use a new service design.

Because the findings derive from action research, the results reflect "on the ground" practices unique to each campus and its institutional campus priorities, and the findings do not attempt to provide causal explanations of library impact. While the AiA project findings may not be generalizable (as one would expect of social science research from a positivist perspective), the assessment results can be adapted to other academic settings with care and consideration to local context.

Promising Areas of Impact

The AiA projects generated evidence of library impact in other areas as well. Investigations in four areas point to evidence of promise. The assessment of library impact in these areas, however, tends not to have been investigated as extensively as those noted above, or the findings may not be as consistently strong. Even so, the growing number of studies in these four areas have yielded promising results about positive connections between the library and students' academic success and experiences.

- *The library contributes to improved student retention.* At most higher education institutions, student retention is designated as a high priority, and the campus library's contributions to this priority are receiving attention and recognition as a result of assessment studies that investigate this connection. Determining retention rates can include different measures, but the focus is typically on a student's continued progress from one semester to the next or a student's persistence toward degree completion. Some AiA projects investigated how library instruction contributes to improving an institution's student retention and academic persistence. Even though the complexity of factors and influences that may affect students' progress from one semester to the next or their persistence toward degree completion is considerable and determining reliable methods for assessing such progress is challenging, the results of these AiA projects show promising associations of the library to student retention and persistence.

> **PROMISING AREAS OF IMPACT**
>
> - The library contributes to improved student retention.
>
> - Library instruction adds value to a student's long-term academic experience.
>
> - The library promotes academic rapport and student engagement.
>
> - Use of library space relates positively to student learning and success.

- *Library instruction adds value to a student's long-term academic experience.* First-year courses that all freshmen take provide excellent opportunities for the library to reach a majority of students and present core information literacy instruction that serves as a foundation for their subsequent coursework. Many academic libraries are increasingly looking at the impact of this instruction as students move through their academic studies. In addition, the development and assessment of library instruction provided after the first year is receiving attention, particularly when information literacy competency is designated as one of the college's or university's core proficiencies. As students progress in their studies, library instruction usually needs to use a scaffolded approach to teach more specialized research strategies or discipline-specific content. A number of AiA campus teams investigated the value of information literacy competencies as students move through their academic programs and complete upper-level courses, and the benefits associated with library instruction beyond a student's first year were noted.

- *The library promotes academic rapport and student engagement.* Academic rapport can influence student motivation, academic engagement, and enjoyment of courses and learning in general. Faculty and staff being available, being responsive, interacting and showing an interest in students, and understanding that students encounter personal problems that may affect their academic work are all attributes that foster academic rapport. Some AiA teams assessed how the library might contribute to a student's sense of academic rapport with a college or university. While academic rapport encompasses multiple attributes, the findings of these AiA projects exemplify different ways that these various factors can be investigated to assess the library's impact on a student's sense of connection with his or her institution and the types of contributions the library might make to enhancing academic rapport.

- *Use of library space relates positively to student learning and success.* Several AiA campus teams also investigated the function of library space and its potential impact on students' academic experience. Some aspects of this impact area that were studied included the location of service points in relation to students' study preferences and learning needs and the configuration of the facility's space, furniture, and technology in relation to fostering academic and social community among students. Many of the AiA project teams with this inquiry focus recorded positive connections between aspects of library space configuration and use and student academic engagement, collaborative learning, and a student's sense of academic community.

The annual AiA synthesis reports, which are presented as chapters 3, 4, and 5, provide a full discussion of these compelling findings and promising areas and include descriptions of sample campus projects.

Building Professional Capacity for Assessment

The findings about library contributions to student learning and success were generated by the institutional teams that participated in the AiA program initiative, which was designed with three overarching goals in mind:

- Develop academic librarians' professional competencies needed to document and communicate the value of the academic library in relation to an institution's goals for student learning and success.
- Strengthen collaborative relationships with higher education stakeholders, including campus faculty, academic administrators, and assessment officers.
- Contribute to higher education assessment by creating approaches, strategies, and practices that document the contribution of academic libraries.

These goals encompass recommendations from the summits about strengthening the competencies of librarians in assessment, campus leadership, and data-informed advocacy about library impact. Several features of the AiA program design, which are described below, were central to advancing the profession's capacity for assessment work.

Participation by a Diverse Array of Higher Education Institutions

The mission, academic priorities, and campus culture vary from institution to institution. During the initial planning for the AiA program, it quickly became apparent that a single generic approach to assessment was not realistic; multiple approaches were needed to be responsive and take into consideration different higher education settings. AiA institutions were selected through a competitive process designed to ensure representation from a wide spectrum of geographic regions and higher education institutions, and over 200 postsecondary institutions of all types participated in the AiA program between 2013 and 2016 (see table 1.3).

INSTITUTION TYPE	YEAR 1	YEAR 2	YEAR 3	TOTAL
Associate's Colleges	10	13	3	26
Baccalaureate Colleges	7	15	10	32
Master's Colleges and Universities	32	11	18	61
Doctoral/Research Universities	6	4	2	12
Research Universities (High/Very High Research Activity)	18	23	21	62
Tribal Colleges	1	1	0	2
Special Focus Institutions (medical, culinary, theological seminary)	1	6	1	8
TOTAL	75	73	55	203

TABLE 1.3
Types of institutions for teams selected into the AiA program, Years 1–3.

The institutions are represented by a variety of different accrediting bodies, including US regional, specialized, Canadian, and Australian (see table 1.4).

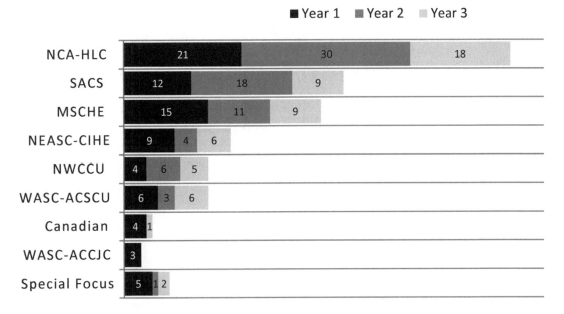

TABLE 1.4
The accreditation agencies of institutions selected into the AiA program, Years 1–3.

At each AiA institution, the lead librarian collaborated with the campus team members to design and implement a project that focused on assessing the possible connection between an aspect of the library's services, resources, or practices and its impact on student learning and success. As a result, a variety of assessment approaches, methods, and tools were developed by the AiA teams over the three program years. Many of the project approaches are replicable or contain elements that can be customized to a college's or university's unique institutional context, providing the academic library profession with multiple ways to assess student learning and success in relation to library services, resources, and practices.

Immersive Professional Development Experience

The librarians participated in an immersive professional development program during the fourteen months that they worked with their campus teams to investigate library impact. The professional development integrated blended learning, peer-to-peer collegial relationships, and action learning projects to create a dynamic, authentic learning experience. Unlike traditional educational models that spotlight an instructor's central role as the "sage on the stage" with primary authority and content expertise, the blended learning approach emphasized the facilitative role of instructors (i.e., "guide on the side"). Learners worked collaboratively in face-to-face workshops, webinars, and asynchronous online environments to develop and share assessment strategies, content, and products. These activities emphasized skill building through collaborative problem solving and bridging theory to practice.

Although ACRL has a long history of initiating and sponsoring innovative training, an approach that focused on blended, peer-to-peer learning was a new model. AiA also differed from other ACRL training by involving librarians in a year-long series of activities that merged learning with real-world application and the opportunity for reflective practice. The emphasis on action learning led to a deeper understanding of what happens when new knowledge and skills are applied in practice.

Essential Competencies for Academic Library Assessment

During the 2011 summits, participants emphasized that effective assessment practices require a set of core competencies, including planning and implementing outcomes-based assessment, data gathering and analysis, communication, and leadership. The AiA program provided an opportunity to create learning activities for librarians to develop and use these competencies as they worked with their campus teams to plan and carry out assessment projects. The team librarians also noted important skill sets in their project reports that informed the program's learning activities in each subsequent year. The AiA program focused on four broad competency areas: action research; data gathering, analysis, and interpretation; leadership and evidence-based advocacy; and communicating library impact.

ACTION RESEARCH

The AiA librarians learned to use an action research approach to design and conduct team-based assessment projects. Action research, which emphasizes improving practice through systematic investigation of a question grounded in institutional context, engaged the librarians in an immersive process of ongoing interaction with one another and collaboration with their team members. The librarians led the planning and implementation of assessment activities that related directly to their campus's academic priorities, creating opportunities for substantive conversations with campus stakeholders about student learning and resulting in meaningful findings that informed decision-making about library programs and practices.

> *The project illuminated the importance of closing the assessment cycle by reporting results and making decisions based on those results.*
>
> —*AiA librarian team leader, Webster University*

DATA GATHERING, ANALYSIS, AND INTERPRETATION

Each AiA campus team formulated an inquiry question that provided a framework for its assessment project by positing a relationship between the library and student learning or success outcomes. The questions also indicated the type of data needed to measure library factors and academic outcome attributes and the methods most appropriate for collecting the data. Depending on the question, the collection of data may have involved direct or indirect measures of student learning or success. The assessment methods selected by the teams also varied. While some teams focused on quantitative methodologies (e.g., comparison of circulation statistics with GPA), other teams used qualitative approaches (e.g., reflection essays). Many teams decided to use more than one assessment method to investigate possible impact, resulting in a mixed-methods approach that could expand and enrich their findings (see table 1.5).

ASSESSMENT METHODS AND TOOLS[a]	YEAR 1	YEAR 2	YEAR 3
Survey	41	31	28
Rubric	40	26	19
Pre- and Post-test	23	23	14
Other (e.g., correlational analysis, content analysis, ethnographic)	20	15	13
Interviews	13	7	4
Observation	10	9	4
Focus Group(s)	10	6	4
a. The totals on the table columns do not equal 74, 64, 52, or 190 (i.e., the number of AiA teams completing the program and reporting in Year 1, Year 2, and Year 3, respectively) because many teams used more than one assessment method and/or type of measure.			

TABLE 1.5
Assessment methods and tools used by AiA teams, Years 1–3

The numerous methods and tools that the AiA teams used to investigate library impact over the three-year program yielded a wide array of approaches for libraries to consider for assessment initiatives. These approaches move the profession's understanding of library value from assumptions or anecdotal observations about library impact to systematic methods for data collection, analysis, and interpretation.

> *In the past, the library had only "we think" and "we feel" anecdotal student success contributions—we could be qualitative about ourselves, reflectively, but had little data to support these statements. Now we have some and will continue growing that pool of data from our various services, so that we can analyze and contribute further to assessment activities.*
>
> *—AiA librarian team leader, Colorado Mesa University*

LEADERSHIP AND EVIDENCE-BASED ADVOCACY

In each of the three years of the AiA program, the librarians commented in their project reports that their leadership competence grew as a result of the theory-to-practice professional development activities. This process strengthened three leadership qualities in particular:

- *Understanding of institutional context:* The librarians learned strategies to align the library's assessment activities with institutional priorities. They led their campus team through an assessment project that focused on a question that was important to the institution and that had shared interest among the team members. The collaborative approach used by the AiA teams often generated campus-wide synergy around assessment, and many of the lead librarians expanded their knowledge of and participation in institutional assessment activities.

> *The main takeaway from our involvement with AiA has been assessing what we value, not just valuing what we assess. We understand now that the context matters and librarians need to pay close attention to institutional values and how can we add value to them.*
>
> *—AiA librarian team leader [reflective report comment]*[1]

- *Facilitating the dynamic nature of assessment*: The librarians developed leadership skills that anticipated and were responsive to the dynamic nature of organizational cultures and practices. The team-based approach required collaboration throughout the assessment design, implementation, and analysis phases, a process that was iterative and generative as discussions took place. For many librarians, leadership competencies were required to navigate multiple tasks and dimensions of the project as it changed over the fourteen-month period. Even mistakes provided opportunities to learn and improve.

> *Having gone through the process of the AiA project, I am better versed at planning out assessment projects. I have a stronger base of experience to refer to when creating a research question and gathering meaningful data. I also feel that the process of failure and reaching dead ends in my AiA project helped me become more creative in using failure to create knowledge. I realize that data cannot tell the whole story, which helps me understand the type of questions I can ask that could be reasonably answered in a data project.*
>
> *—AiA librarian team leader [reflective report comment]*

Since the projects were designed to inform decision-making and to improve programs and practices, the likelihood of change, which is naturally dynamic and fluid, was built into the process. Through the professional development and campus team project activities, the librarians learned to negotiate strategically and navigate this evolving and often ambiguous process.

- *Embracing professional and personal growth*: As the librarians led their campus teams, they honed their leadership skills and recognized significant growth at personal and professional levels. The librarians positioned themselves as contributing members of the broader campus environment, and they saw their influence on the academic work of the institution. Leading a team-based assessment project also increased the librarians' competence to propose action steps based on evidence and implement changes in library instruction programs, services, and practices. As they made decisions based on project findings, they expanded their capacity to advocate for, lead, and initiate change.

> *I think this project has granted me some authority on campus and among our library staff that I didn't have previously—I feel more comfortable being able to approach faculty with ideas and be an advocate and representative of the library now that I've led a project that involved professionals from all over campus.*
>
> *—AiA librarian team leader [reflective report comment]*

COMMUNICATING LIBRARY IMPACT

Communication skills, as demonstrated by facilitation, collaboration, and presentations, were also strengthened during the fourteen-month project period. The librarians, for example, facilitated a group process that required communication of a shared vision and delegation of a procedure for carrying out the assessment. The facilitation also necessitated an understanding of interpersonal communication, small-group dynamics, and collaboration to move the project forward. Once the project findings were completed, the librarians considered the various campus constituent groups that would benefit from learning about the results, and they initiated conversations and delivered presentations to communicate the project outcomes and propose evidence-based actions.

Partnerships and Library Assessment

The AiA program has advanced awareness, understanding, and collaboration among campus constituent groups and higher education stakeholders around the issue of library impact. The AiA Grant Advisory Team, for example, included ACRL leaders, grant partners, and representatives from higher education organizations who participated in the collaborative planning grant summits, including the Association of Institutional Research and the Association of Public and Land-grant Universities.

The multiple perspectives represented on the AiA campus teams promoted a collaborative approach to assessing the library's impact on student learning and success on the campuses of the participating institutions. The project teams, led by a librarian, typically included teaching faculty and administrators from such departments as the assessment office, institutional research, the writing center, academic technology, and student affairs. In their project reports, the librarians frequently noted the benefits of having different perspectives brought into the team discussions. Through these discussions, the librarians developed a fuller understanding of the priorities and functions of other campus units. Likewise, the librarians reported that team members gained an awareness of the library, particularly in terms of its contribution to student learning and success.

> This project is one of the first that the library has undertaken to track the impact of our information literacy instruction services. In that regard, the simple acts of collecting, studying, and reporting data to our colleagues throughout the college are huge steps for us—it's a way of communicating to other stakeholders that we take student learning seriously and want to be active participants in facilitating student success and retention.
>
> —AiA librarian team leader, NorthWest Arkansas Community College

The AiA program also fostered networking among the team librarians, which has been sustained beyond the AiA activities. Many of the librarians have presented about their AiA experience and ongoing assessment work at conferences, written journal articles, or prepared book chapters, as documented by the growing Assessment in Action bibliography (see appendix I). While the library profession is learning more about assessment through these presentations and publications, the broader higher education community is also more informed about academic library contributions to student learning and success through presentations about the AiA program at such conferences as the Assessment Institute, Association for the Assessment of Learning in Higher Education, Conference on Higher Education Pedagogy, and the Canadian Writing Centres Conference. As a result, the library is increasingly recognized within the wider postsecondary education community as integral to advancing the academic success of students at higher education institutions.

> *Most importantly, I've identified AiA participants, both in and outside my co-hort, working on assessment activities similar to ours. I feel I have a network of people I can collaborate and brainstorm with.*
>
> —*AiA librarian team leader [reflective report comment]*

Leverage ACRL Resources

The AiA program has created opportunities to leverage and expand ACRL tools and resources designed to advance assessment work at higher education institutions. For example, *The Standards for Libraries in Higher Education,* which uses an outcomes-based approach to guide librarians in their role as educational partners on campuses, became an important framework for many of the AiA librarians as they designed their assessment projects in collaboration with campus stakeholders. During the second year of the AiA program, the draft ACRL *Framework for Information Literacy for Higher Education* was introduced, discussed within the academic library profession, revised, and eventually accepted by the ACRL Board of Directors. Several campus teams included the *Framework* in their projects and used elements of it to assess student learning. The results of these studies reveal new findings about the complexities of student learning and the potential impact of information literacy instruction on students' academic success.

ACRL has also developed new resources that augment the approaches and findings of the AiA program and academic library assessment in general. *Academic Library Impact: Improving Practice and Essential Areas to Research* (2017), developed for ACRL by OCLC Research, investigates how libraries can increase student learning and success and effectively communicate their value to higher education stakeholders. The publication identifies priority areas and suggests specific actions for academic librarians and administrators to take in developing and assessing programs, collections, and spaces focused on student learning and success. It includes effective practices, calls out exemplary studies, and indicates where more inquiry is needed, with proposed research designs. Chapter 17 of this book, "*Assessing for Alignment: How to Win Collaborators and Influence Stakeholders*" by the OCLC Research team, identifies how researchers and professionals can adapt the AiA approach to advance three key priority areas at their institutions: communication, collaboration, and institutional mission and alignment.

To support ongoing professional development for librarians to build their assessment skills and competencies, but in a format that does not require a year-long commitment, ACRL now offers a daylong workshop, "*Assessment in Action: Demonstrating and Communicating Library Contributions to Student Learning and Success.*" This workshop, introduced in 2017, is one of six of ACRL's popular *RoadShow Traveling Workshops* and focuses on identifying institutional priorities and campus partners, designing assessment activities grounded in action research, and preparing a plan for communicating the assessment results.

The AiA lead librarians were members of a learning community throughout the project. Sharing ideas, providing critical feedback, and lending general support were critical to the success of most of the projects. The librarians were working toward shared goals and pursuing inquiry through a collective learning experience. The AiA learning community fostered a dynamic, active form of learning among colleagues that combined small-group engagement in problem solving through questioning, testing assumptions about practice, and reflecting about what was learned. In the process, a "community of practice" emerged and continues to grow as ACRL expands resources and opportunities for assessment work on campuses.

I felt a part of a community of practice, thrust into a unique experience, all trying to find our way and learning from one another.

—AiA librarian team leader [reflective report comment]

Conclusion

The assessment findings of over 200 AiA campus projects address numerous aspects of student learning and success, and they document library contributions to students' academic experiences in key areas. The projects also demonstrate multiple ways that academic librarians can engage and lead campus representatives in assessment initiatives. Numerous methods and tools that can be replicated or adapted to a wide variety of higher education settings and contexts have emerged from the assessment work of the teams. As a result, academic librarians are leveraging and expanding their role in assessment work on their campuses. The AiA program has also promoted awareness, understanding, and collaboration among higher education stakeholders around issues of library impact in the wider postsecondary education community.

Biography

Karen Brown is a professor at Dominican University (River Forest, Illinois) in the School of Information Studies and teaches in the areas of assessment, collection management, foundations of the profession, and literacy and learning. Prior to joining Dominican University's faculty in 2000, she developed and coordinated continuing education programs for the Chicago Library System, one of Illinois's former regional library systems. She has also held positions focusing on collection development, reference, and instruction at the University of Wisconsin, the University of Maryland, Columbia University, and Bard College. She holds a PhD in media ecology from New York University and master's degrees in library science and adult education from the University of Wisconsin. Reach her at kbrown@dom.edu.

Notes

1. Each AiA librarian was asked to complete a reflective report about their project and, while the individual reports are kept confidential, aggregate and anonymous comments from the reports contributed to the annual analysis publications.

CHAPTER 2

Creating Sustainable Assessment through Collaboration:

A National Program Reveals Effective Practices[1]

Kara J. Malenfant

Senior Strategist for Special Initiatives
Association of College and Research Libraries, a division of the American Library Association
50 East Huron Street, Chicago, Illinois 60611
kmalenfant@ala.org

Karen Brown

Professor
School of Information Studies
Dominican University
7900 West Division Street, River Forest, Illinois 60305
kbrown@dom.edu

Biography of the Authors

Kara J. Malenfant is a senior staff member at the Association of College and Research Libraries (ACRL, a division of the American Library Association), where she coordinates government relations advocacy and scholarly communication activities and is the lead staff member on the Value of Academic Libraries initiative and Assessment in Action program. She provides consulting services on organization development and use of ACRL's standards for libraries in higher education. Kara began her position at ACRL in fall of 2005 after working for six years at DePaul University Libraries in Chicago. A former Peace Corps volunteer, she holds a PhD in leadership and change from Antioch University and a master's degree in library science from the University of Illinois at Urbana-Champaign.

Karen Brown is a professor at Dominican University (River Forest, Illinois) in the School of Information Studies and teaches in the areas of assessment, collection management, foundations of the profession, and literacy and learning. Prior to joining Dominican University's faculty in 2000, she developed and coordinated continuing education programs for the Chicago Library System, one of Illinois's former regional library systems. She has also held positions focusing on collection development, reference, and instruction at the University of Wisconsin, the University of Maryland, Columbia University, and Bard College. She holds a PhD in media ecology from New York University and master's degrees in library science and adult education from the University of Wisconsin.

Paper Abstract

Meaningful and sustained assessment is best achieved when a campus unit takes a collaborative leadership role to work with other departments, offices, and groups. Simply developing and implementing assessment in isolation and for the unit itself is not enough. While the value of collaboration among diverse campus constituents is widely recognized, it is not easily achieved. This occasional paper synthesizes the results of the program Assessment in Action: Academic Libraries and Student Success (AiA) by the Association of College and Research Libraries, which involved over 200 campus teams led by librarians.[2] Five particularly compelling AiA findings are the positive connections documented between various functions of the library and aspects of student learning and success: (1) Students benefit from library instruction in their initial coursework; (2) Library use increases student success; (3) Collaborative academic programs and services involving the library enhance student learning; (4) Information literacy instruction strengthens general education outcomes; and (5) Library research consultations boost student learning. These findings emerged from an assessment process grounded in collaborative planning, decision-making, and implementation. In this paper, we describe the collaborative practices advanced by the AiA program and explain how these practices promote assessment aligned with institutional priorities, encourage common understanding among stakeholder groups about attributes of academic success, produce meaningful measures of student learning, create a unified campus message about student learning and success, and focus on transformative and sustainable change. This paper asserts that the AiA experience serves as a framework for designing assessment approaches that build partnerships and generate results for improving student learning and success through action research, and that the program results demonstrate how libraries contribute to fostering broad student outcomes essential to contemporary postsecondary education. The assessment practices that emerged from the AiA projects can be implemented in a variety of institutional settings and with varying campus priorities.

Foreword

When the Association of College and Research Libraries (ACRL) convened the *Value of Academic Libraries (VAL) Summits* in 2011, the sense of potential and possibilities gave an excitement to the conversations that was thrilling and perhaps a bit daunting as well. Participants identified many opportunities to investigate and communicate the impact of academic libraries on student learning and success. They also, however, made clear that this work would require not only developing librarian capacity but also building campus partnerships to carry out the assessment projects.

Six years later, the results of ACRL's efforts have far exceeded what we had dared dream. This NILOA Occasional Paper tells the story of the strategies and benefits of collaborative assessment through an analysis of one of ACRL's VAL programs, *Assessment in Action: Academic Libraries and Student Success.*

Through the *Assessment in Action (AiA)* program, academic libraries have established compelling evidence of the impact of library programs and services on student learning and success. That evidence base is now the foundation of a formal research agenda for ACRL as well as related advocacy programs. In addition, the design of AiA established the components of a successful approach to professional development that equips librarians with assessment and leadership skills and strategies as well as joining them with what has become a thriving, self sustaining, and volunteer-led community of practice. And, most importantly for this publication, through AiA, ACRL has documented factors that foster collaborative assessment and the resulting benefits, which can serve as a model for other integrative assessment programs.

As Kara and Karen observe, while the value of collaboration for assessment is widely recognized in higher education, collaborative assessment that achieves meaningful and sustained change is not easily achieved. Varying cultures, organizational structures, and reward systems as well as competing priorities are just some of the factors that can act as barriers to developing an integrated approach to assessment that is aligned with institutional priorities and mission.

Higher education leaders who want to move their institutions toward more collaborative approaches to assessment will find pragmatic guidance in Kara and Karen's analysis of AiA, particularly with respect to the strategies for supporting and promoting successful assessment teams. AiA revealed that institutional administrator support is critical for success as well as careful attention to team leadership and membership, skills, and knowledge, and alignment with institutional priorities. AiA also demonstrated that academic librarians are uniquely positioned on campus to serve as bridges across various institutional divides, including those gaps between and among academic and student services, managerial and faculty cultures, and disciplinary and general education programs. Leveraging the unique nature of the library as an academic commons for situating shared discussions about student learning and success is a smart strategy for catalyzing campus-wide commitment and engagement with assessment and sustaining organizational transformation.

I was the President of ACRL when the *Value of Academic Libraries Initiative* was established as a strategic priority. It is with great pride that I can today share the results of the AiA program and its contributions to academic librarianship and to higher education more generally. Transforming academic libraries transforms higher education and we will continue to build on the strong foundation that is AiA.

Lisa Janicke Hinchliffe

Professor, University Library, University of Illinois at Urbana-Champaign
President, ACRL, 2010–2011

Table of Contents

Introduction

The Association of College and Research Libraries' (ACRL's) Value of Academic Libraries Initiative has flourished since its inception in 2010 with the publication of *Value of Academic Libraries: A Comprehensive Research Review and Report*.[3] The program Assessment in Action: Academic Libraries and Student Success (AiA) is a cornerstone of that success, supporting more than 200 campus teams as they investigated the impact of the academic library on student learning and success. The teams of diverse campus stakeholders participated from 2013 to 2016 (seventy-five in the first year, seventy-three in the second year, and fifty-five in the third year) and represented all types of higher education institutions from forty-one states, the District of Columbia, four Canadian provinces, and Australia. Funded through a National Leadership Demonstration Grant by the US federal agency the Institute of Museum and Library Services, AiA was undertaken in partnership with the Association for Institutional Research and the Association of Public and Land-grant Universities. The grant supported the design, implementation, and evaluation of campus-based projects with the overarching goals of strengthening the competencies of librarians in campus leadership and data-informed advocacy, fostering collaborative campus relationships around assessment, and building an evidence base about the impact of academic libraries on student learning and success as well as documenting effective assessment practices and strategies.

This paper focuses on the collaborative assessment practices that guided the teams and resulted in campus-wide benefits. For years, higher education leaders have bemoaned the lack of collaboration across academic and student affairs units and noted the pivotal role such cooperation plays in promoting student learning. As Kellogg explains, "The entire academic community must work together to place more of an emphasis on student learning and to create a seamless learning environment between in- and out-of-class experiences for students."[4] Banta and Kuh specifically point to the need for better collaboration between academic and student affairs professionals in terms of assessment[5] and identify three obstacles to collaboration between faculty and student affairs staff: cultural-historical, bureaucratic-structural, and institutional leadership.[6] Academic librarians, we believe, are uniquely situated to bring together and bridge the academic and student affairs sides of the house.[7] They focus their programmatic and service efforts on the intellectual development of students, and they care deeply about the life of the mind, while striving to run efficient, effective operations. They straddle what Bergquist and Pawlak call the "twin pillars" of contemporary higher education in the United States—collegial culture on the one hand and managerial culture on the other.[8] Librarians are well versed in collaborative work, having broad involvement in multiple facets of higher education. They are poised to play a convening role at the crossroads of disciplines and between academic and student affairs.[9]

Furthermore, findings from the Wabash National Study of Liberal Arts Education put into high relief the tremendous challenge of translating evidence from assessment into improvements in student learning. Blaich and Wise found, "Assessment data has legs only if the evidence collected rises out of extended conversations across constituencies about (a) what people hunger to know about their teaching and learning environments and (b) how the assessment evidence speaks to those questions."[10] There is widespread recognition that it is incredibly hard to get meaningful action and results in using assessment findings to improve student learning. The American Association of State Colleges and Universities 2016 Academic Affairs Winter Meeting, for example, focused on factors that contribute to student success. The conference description highlighted this challenge: "A growing body of research suggests that we know a great deal about the most promising practices to dramatically increase student success. Yet student success efforts on too many campuses remain piecemeal, disconnected, or idiosyncratic. We don't have a knowledge problem. We have an implementation problem."[11]

The AiA program was designed with the belief that a collaborative approach to assessment, with a team of diverse stakeholders, will more likely overcome the challenges of taking action to improve student learning. In this paper, we relate the AiA findings and team experiences to a selected body of literature on organization development, leadership, and change to draw out lessons that can be applied more broadly to higher education institutions seeking to improve students' learning and success through an assessment process that involves multiple campus representatives. This paper makes a contribution to the literature about higher education assessment by sharing the program's findings about practices that support and foster collaborative assessment and describing the benefits gained with this approach.

Brief Overview of "Assessment in Action" Program Design

Three primary goals framed the AiA program activities:

1. Develop academic librarians' professional competencies needed to document and communicate the value of the academic library in relation to an institution's goals for student learning and success.
2. Strengthen collaborative relationships with higher education stakeholders, including campus faculty, academic administrators, and assessment officers.
3. Contribute to higher education assessment by creating approaches, strategies, and practices that document the contribution of academic libraries.

Higher education institutions applied for the program through a competitive process. The program design required that the campus library take the lead, and the application included naming a librarian team leader and team members, securing letters of support from the library director and chief academic officer, and proposing an area of assessment inquiry that clearly related to a campus priority. The assessment areas needed to consider some aspect of the library, such as collections, space, instruction, or reference, in relation to a facet of either student learning, at the course, program, or degree level, or a feature of student success, for example, retention, completion, or persistence. In addition to a librarian leader, each team had to consist of at least two representatives from other campus departments or units—this could be a faculty member, student affairs representative, institutional researcher, assessment officer, or academic administrator. The AiA program provided direct support through blended in-person and online professional development for the librarian team leaders, during which they led campus teams in planning and implementing an assessment project over a fourteen-month period.

Team leaders and members presented the results of their assessment projects in poster sessions at the American Library Association annual conferences. Each of the AiA teams was also asked to submit a final project descriptive report, which includes an abstract and image of the conference poster. These reports are available in an online collection with an interface for filtering results based on institution type, geographic location, enrollment, accreditation body, team member role, and library staffing levels, among other criteria.[12] In addition to the individual project reports, for each of the three years of the AiA program, ACRL produced a synthesis of the findings.[13] These findings comprise a body of evidence about the impact of academic libraries on student learning and success but also about effective practices in library leadership and campus collaboration on assessment. For more on the design of AiA program, see Appendix A: Assessment in Action Program Design.

Compelling Evidence for Academic Library Contributions to Student Learning and Success

The collaborative process resulted in an extensive collection of methods and tools used by the campus teams during the three-year AiA program to identify and assess practices that contribute to students' academic outcomes. It's important to note that the AiA approach to assessment merged inquiry with practice, using an action research framework. The projects emphasized improving academic practices through systematic investigation of a question grounded in institutional context. While the project findings may not be generalizable, as you would expect of social science research from a positivist perspective, they do tell a strong story about the multiple ways that academic libraries are contributing to student learning and success. In addition, the AiA methods and tools can be adapted to other settings with care and consideration of local context. The collaboration that occurred among campus partners in each assessment project is reflected in and integral to the significance of these findings. A September 2017 ACRL report about the impact of libraries on student learning and success further spotlights the importance of collaborative assessment present in AiA. The report authors looked broadly across the scholarly and practice based literature to analyze 535 library and higher education documents from 2010 to present—including AiA project reports—and noted that the AiA projects serve as exemplars:

> ## ACADEMIC LIBRARY CONTRIBUTIONS TO STUDENT LEARNING AND SUCCESS
>
> Findings from over 200 assessment projects, conducted by teams of diverse campus stakeholders, tell a strong story about the multiple ways that academic libraries contribute to student learning and success:
>
> 1. Students benefit from library instruction in their initial coursework.
>
> 2. Library use is related to student success.
>
> 3. Collaborative academic programs and services involving the library enhance student learning.
>
> 4. Information literacy instruction strengthens general education outcomes.
>
> 5. Library research consultations boost student learning.

> Collaboration is an important theme because of the academic library's primary mission as a research and teaching support unit. The AiA projects explicitly required librarians to collaborate with at least two people outside the libraries…. The primary mission of the academic library is to support an institution's research and teaching, which necessitates collaboration with other educational stakeholders. Such collaboration includes all librarian efforts to work with those inside and outside their institution to influence student learning and success outcomes.[14]

Particularly noteworthy in the AiA collaborative projects are the positive connections documented between the library and aspects of student learning and success in five areas.

1. Students benefit from library instruction in their initial coursework.

Academic libraries typically place a high priority on information literacy instruction for first-year students to provide them with a common set of competencies for their undergraduate studies. The assessment findings from numerous AiA projects that focused on information literacy initiatives for freshmen and new students underscore that students receiving this instruction perform better in their initial courses than students who do not.

2. Library use is related to student success.

Several AiA studies point to positive connections between students' use of the library and academic success. The analysis of multiple data points (e.g., circulation, library instruction session attendance, online database access, study room use, interlibrary loan) frequently shows that students who used the library in some way achieved higher levels of academic success represented by GPA, course grades, and persistence compared with their peers who did not use the library.

3. Collaborative academic programs and services involving the library enhance student learning.

To provide more comprehensive and integrated approaches to academic support for students, libraries are finding that partnerships with other campus units, such as the writing center, academic enrichment, and speech lab, are yielding promising benefits. Although campuses vary widely in the types of academic support they provide, the AiA teams at several institutions that investigated collaborative approaches documented positive benefits for students, such as higher grades, academic confidence, and persistence from one term to the next.

4. Information literacy instruction strengthens general education outcomes.

The general education curriculum at most colleges and universities is designed to reach all undergraduate students with a broad liberal arts and science learning experience that revolves around a core set of institutionally defined proficiencies and academic outcomes. A focus on inquiry and problem solving for students' personal and professional lives and attention to significant social questions typically frame the courses and learning activities. Some AiA projects studied the library's impact on this aspect of a student's academic learning and found connections between library instruction and students' achievement of institutional core competencies and general education outcomes. The project findings demonstrate multiple ways that information literacy contributes to inquiry-based and problem-solving learning, including effective identification and use of information, critical thinking, ethical reasoning, and civic engagement.

5. Library research consultations boost student learning.

Several AiA projects that assessed one-on-one or small-group reference and research assistance with a librarian demonstrated positive associations with academic success, as documented by such factors as student confidence, GPAs, and improved achievement on course assignments. At some institutions, consultation services provide opportunities for customized, focused instruction, and at other institutions, research consultation services are offered off site from the library and may use a new service design.

Having overall consistent assessment findings and evidence of effective practice that yields positive library impact in these five areas—across a body of over 200 projects—is strong in part because of the variation. Each setting is different; each library program and service differed in its design and implementation as appropriate for the local context; student characteristics and backgrounds differ in some ways; and a variety of methods were used to document the library impact on students.[15] Because the findings are derived from action research, which is situated in authentic institutional contexts, the results reflect "on the ground" practices in terms of resources available and campus priorities.

Additional findings from the AiA projects suggest four other promising areas of inquiry about the impact of the library. While these impact areas may not have been studied as extensively as the five areas discussed above, the assessment results do build evidence for positive connections between the library and students' learning and success.

- *The library contributes to improved student retention.*
  At most higher education institutions, student retention is designated as a high priority, and the campus library's contributions to this priority are receiving attention and recognition as a result of assessment studies that investigate the connection. Determining retention rates can include different measures, but the focus is typically on a student's continued progress from one semester to the next or a student's persistence toward degree completion. Some AiA projects investigated how library instruction contributes to improving an institution's student retention and academic persistence. Even though the complexity of factors and influences that may affect students' progress from one semester to the next or their persistence toward degree completion is considerable and determining reliable methods for assessing such progress is challenging, the results of these AiA projects show promising associations of the library to student retention and persistence.

- *Library instruction adds value to a student's long-term academic experience.*
  First-year courses that all freshmen take provide excellent opportunities for the library to reach a majority of students and present core information literacy instruction that serves as a foundation for their subsequent coursework. Many academic libraries are increasingly looking at the impact of this instruction as students move through their academic studies. In addition, the development and assessment of library instruction provided after the first year is receiving attention, particularly when information literacy competency is designated as one of the college's or university's core proficiencies. As students progress in their studies, library instruction usually needs to use a scaffolded approach to teach more specialized research strategies or discipline-specific content. The value of information literacy competencies as students move through their academic programs and complete upper-level courses was investigated by a number of AiA campus teams, and benefits associated with library instruction beyond a student's first year were noted.

- *The library promotes academic rapport and student engagement.*
  Academic rapport can influence student motivation, academic engagement, and enjoyment of courses and learning in general. Faculty and staff availability, responsiveness, interacting and showing an interest in students, and understanding that students encounter personal problems that may affect their academic work are all attributes that foster academic rapport. Some AiA teams assessed how the library might contribute to a student's sense of academic rapport with a college or university. While academic rapport encompasses multiple attributes, the findings of these AiA projects exemplify different ways that these various factors can be investigated to assess the library's impact on a student's sense of connection with his or her institution and the types of contributions the library might make to enhancing academic rapport.

- ***Use of library space relates positively to student learning and success.***
  Several AiA campus teams also investigated the function of library space and its potential impact on students' academic experience. Some aspects of this impact area that were studied included the location of service points in relation to students' study preferences and learning needs and the configuration of the facility's space, furniture, and technology in relation to fostering academic and social community among students. Many of the AiA project with this inquiry focus recorded positive connections between aspects of library space configuration and use and student academic engagement, collaborative learning, and a student's sense of academic community.

The assessments completed by the AiA teams demonstrate the library's promising connection to desirable academic experiences and also help all of us in higher education better understand how the contemporary academic library contributes to fostering the kind of broad student learning outcomes that are increasingly seen as essential in postsecondary education. The AiA findings, yielded by systematically and carefully studying what is actually happening at the institutional level on local campuses, reveal an alignment of academic libraries with the interests of the broader higher education landscape. As Wehlburg notes, "Many institutional mission statements include items that are not specific to an academic discipline and, indeed, may not be focused within a specific department."[16] Public opinion research shows these cross-disciplinary, far-reaching academic outcomes are among the intellectual and practical skills that employers prize most and typically include critical thinking and analytic reasoning, complex problem solving, information fluency, and civic and global awareness and engagement.[17] They are skills that reflect integrative learning experience, and the assessment of these experiences is likely best when it's collaborative, involving multiple campus constituents.

A Commitment to Action

AiA was designed to support collaborative teamwork to identify important questions about library impact on student learning and success, design assessments that would reveal information about library contributions, and take action based on what was discovered. The action research framework of AiA challenged the teams to go beyond library use and satisfaction and to examine questions of impact and outcomes. It was understood that not *all* projects would likely demonstrate that there is in fact a library impact; however, there was a belief that developing and implementing a project as part of the AiA program would foster learning, spur action, and build capacity for continued collaborative work at each institution. An overarching goal in the AiA program design was that each project would be change-centric, and we kept the focus on "action" throughout.

We described AiA to prospective applicants as "team-based" and "collaborative," believing such an approach would generate and yield the action we were seeking (in terms of both growth and development of team members and improvements to practice that increase positive student outcomes). Lattuca and Creamer's description of faculty collaboration as "a social inquiry practice that promotes learning" resonates with the AiA project design.[18] They place an emphasis on the interaction and relational dynamics that occur during a collaborative process and an "inquiry practice" that merges scientific and artistic explorations to advance knowledge and the co-construction of knowledge for ongoing renewal and change. This notion of inquiry practice, with its emphasis on iterative knowledge construction to support meaningful and authentic change, is consistent with the action research approach of AiA.

As noted earlier, higher education faces barriers when attempting to use assessment evidence to fuel improvements in practice that yield gains for students. Talking about and advocating for change is one thing; realizing it in practice is quite another issue. We can look to the literature on organization development, leadership, and change for important insights about transforming ideas into practice, particularly those scholarly works that deepen our understanding about assessment practices and the AiA results.

A key element for building commitment to action is involvement. When people are engaged in deeply examining practice, asking meaningful questions, and making sense of what they learn, they are likely to be more committed to whatever actions come next because they have been part of deciding what steps to take. This type of ownership through involvement reduces the kind of buy-in and support problems that arise from top down approaches.[19] In one model for leading work teams, which was included as a reading for AiA librarian team leaders, Rees asserts that facilitative leadership produces better results for teams because power is not held by one person and decision-making is shared.[20] The work of involving others and being facilitative requires an investment of time beyond the typical model for exercising leadership, and additional energy is often necessary to hone one's skills to adopt such a stance. Olson and Eoyang describe the unique aspects of a facilitative leadership style: "True leadership toward change depends on individual and immediate connections, personal modeling, and authentic reinforcement…. Many leaders in organizations know that connectivity comes at a cost, so they shy away from making large investments in learning, communication, and iterative processes."[21] The librarians led the design and implementation of assessment that related directly to their campus's academic priorities, creating opportunities for substantive conversations with campus stakeholders about student learning and resulting in meaningful findings that informed decision-making about library programs and practices. The AiA librarians were coached and prepared to involve team members in collaborative discussions, sustain team engagement, and transform assessment results into action that enhanced student learning and success.

Factors That Support and Promote Collaborative Assessment Teams

AiA teams that were most effective with their collaborative assessment process and produced meaningful, actionable results had several factors in common:

Diversity of team members. The multiple perspectives represented by team members from different campus units and departments yielded a multifaceted view of student learning. Team members gained a fuller understanding of the unique contributions of different campus constituents to students' academic experiences. The group process is enhanced with a mix of experience and expertise.

From our AiA collaborative project we concluded that collaboration with partners outside the library who share our commitment to

FACTORS THAT SUPPORT AND PROMOTE COLLABORATIVE ASSESSMENT TEAMS

An analysis of the experience of over 200 teams of diverse campus stakeholders shows those that were most effective with their collaborative assessment process and produced meaningful, actionable results had several factors in common:

1. Diversity of team members.
2. Support from the top.
3. Alignment with institutional priorities and mission.
4. Team leader capacity.
5. Political skills and organizational knowledge.

supporting student success leads to better programs and events, increased attendance at events, and increased support for student success.[22]

Diversity is commonly noted as an important factor for effectiveness in the literature on teams. Katzenbach and Smith included developing the right mix of expertise as one of six characteristics of high-performing teams.[23] In addition, Hackman identified having the "right people" as one of six enabling conditions that are most powerful in fostering group performance effectiveness, and he included the importance of diversity on the team as part, saying, "Well-composed teams have the right number and mix of members, each of whom has both task expertise and skill in working collaboratively with others. And they are as small and diverse as possible—large size and excessive homogeneity of membership can cripple even teams that otherwise are quite well designed."[24] Furthermore, a comprehensive analysis of team diversity research proposes a model where "diversity is seen by members as an informational resource and members learn to elaborate the information diversity can offer: exchanging, processing and integrating task-relevant information. In particular, and most encouraging, leaders can increase the benefits of diversity while reducing the disadvantages by encouraging all team members to appreciate the benefits of diversity for team functioning (what are called 'diversity beliefs')."[25]

Diversity of team members, then, serves to ameliorate the likelihood of "groupthink," which can arise when people seek harmony and are reluctant to go against the consensus. As the Finnish proverb cautions, "In a group stupidity condenses." To avoid this trap, it is crucial to include diverse viewpoints and create conditions that encourage members to be critical friends who neither avoid conflict nor dominate conversation, but disagree respectfully as they give and receive feedback.

> *Our team had good collaboration and camaraderie.… [W]e all came to the project with a limited understanding about how the assessment would happen, so it allowed us all to learn together, gaining trust as we went. We also all had a shared desire to improve student services. Each of us came to the team with different skills to share.*
> —AiA librarian, reflective report

Through collaboration with their team members, the librarians gained an understanding of the priorities and functions of other campus units. One librarian commented, "My self-confidence in interacting with individuals outside the library (e.g., campus administrators, faculty members) has increased significantly." Likewise, the librarians reported that team members gained an awareness of the library, particularly in terms of its contribution to student learning and success. The collaborative discussions led to increased awareness about the multiple facets that are part of student learning, as well as common understanding of and agreement on ways that student learning could be measured and described. These discussions, which were challenging at times, were essential to the collaborative assessment work being carried out.

Support from the top. As part of the AiA application process, the lead academic administrators at the institution had to commit to supporting the collaborative assessment work that the team would conduct over a fourteen-month period. At times, the support was encouragement and acknowledgement of the value of the assessment work, and at other times the support was provided by securing access to needed resources such as institutional research expertise or finances. This commitment was critical to the success realized by the AiA teams, because the campus administration was aware of the project and team members felt they had support and upper-level commitment to their assessment work.

This project was directly part of a university-wide goal assessment program. By being so heavily involved the library has been able to get the word out about information literacy to a much larger audience than we would have on our own. The library is truly viewed now by faculty and administration as a key participant in information literacy integration and assessment across campus. —AiA team leader, reflective report

Even with this level of support, we learned that the deep, sustained collaborative approach was not for everyone. Those teams that were most successful set realistic expectations from the start about the collaborative process. They also tended to be working on campuses where a culture of assessment permeated planning and academic improvement activities. In addition, at those institutions where assessment was integrated into the library's regular practices, the AiA librarians often noted the value to the AiA project when continuous assessment was part of the library's regular practices.

The crucial role of support from the top is consistent with the literature about effective teams. Another of Katzenbach and Smith's six characteristics of high-performing teams is that they shape purpose in response to a demand or opportunity placed in their path, usually by higher-level management.[26] Similarly, Hackman highlights the importance of a supportive organizational context: "Having the material resources needed to carry out the work is of course essential. But beyond that, team performance is facilitated when (i) the reward system provides recognition and positive consequences for excellent team performance, (ii) the information system provides the team with the data and the information-processing tools members need to plan and execute their work, and (iii) the organization's educational system makes available to the team any technical or educational assistance members may require."[27]

Alignment with institutional priorities and mission. Colleges and universities establish institutional priorities to designate academic areas, concerns, and issues of particular importance to the institution and to guide campus-wide initiatives and activities. When an assessment project aligns with campus priorities, the focus is no longer isolated on the needs or issues faced by one unit or department. Everyone is working toward common goals and priorities, thereby breaking down silos and insular perspectives. As one AiA librarian noted:

The fact that we had a large project team involving a variety of campus offices means that there is a big group of people who have now experienced an assessment-based initiative that falls within and outside of their office parameters. I think that this creates a new culture of cooperation and especially assessment that I have not experienced before. I think in a large research institution it is most obvious to be rather insular in planning and implementation. This not only allowed or encouraged, it required collaboration outside of the library and I think the project's impact is broader and more significant as a result. —AiA team leader, reflective report

Hackman also identifies "compelling purpose" as one of the six enabling conditions. His description of the power of having a compelling purpose highlights the value of connecting assessment activities to campus-wide issues of importance: "A compelling purpose energizes team members, orients them toward their collective objective, and fully engages their talents."[28] The librarians led their campus teams through an assessment project that focused on a question aligned with their institution's mission and priorities and in which team members had a shared interest. The projects also integrated research with practice, which means that the design and implementation of the projects had strong connections to the ongoing work of the librarians and campus constituents. As a result, the assessment activities were situated in everyday practice, giving context and real-world relevance to the work.

Team leader capacity. The AiA team leaders had to develop their capacity of knowing how to best exercise their role in a collaborative activity. Leading a team with diverse perspectives about the institution and a wide range of experiences requires a leadership stance that is more inclusive than what is typically described in traditional, historic definitions. The leadership role most appropriate to these situations is shared leadership. In fact, there is power in shared leadership as "the best team leaders actively encourage leadership contributions from members of the teams.... Shared leadership is an extraordinarily valuable resource for accomplishing the full area of leadership functions needed for team effectiveness."[29] Preparing for this role means increasing one's level of self-awareness to capitalize on leadership strengths and invite participation from all team members, using their abilities to the project's best advantage. Rees's model for how to lead work teams asserts that facilitative leadership produces better results for teams by sharing power and decision-making.[30] She posits there is a continuum from a leader being controlling to being facilitative, with a maximum split on either side of 80/20. At times, it is appropriate to engage in a more controlling role to direct, set goals, and delegate. At other times, it is more suitable to play a facilitative role by asking questions, building consensus, and empowering others.

A benefit of a program like AiA was the structure provided through online professional development and communication, which helped the teams maintain progress from planning to implementation to action-focused results.

> *More than anything else, AiA expanded my sense of what's possible in student learning assessment. My campus team's enthusiasm for our project and for working together demonstrated to me that members of the campus community are willing (and in many cases, eager) to partner on assessment projects like this. Through AiA, I was also able to learn about and apply new assessment skills. As a result, I now feel much more capable of tackling large and small-scale assessment projects in my everyday work.*[31]

A learning community developed among the librarian team leaders in each cohort and created a means of peer sharing, advice, and feedback. The professional development facilitators were also available for input and guidance as needed. "Team-focused coaching" is one of Hackman's six enabling conditions, and he described its role in this way: "Competent and well-timed team coaching can help a team minimize its exposure to process losses and increase the chances that it will operate in ways that generate synergistic process gains."[32] Many AiA teams morphed as team members changed or participation rates varied. With these changes, group dynamics came into play. The challenges of accommodating a new team member often had more to do with the relationship aspect of group dynamics (i.e., personalities, styles of communication) than with the task aspect of group dynamics (i.e., who is doing what work), and the AiA librarians had to be proactive to manage the situation, as reflected by a librarian who commented, "I feel more confident in my ability to take a project from idea to completion and to engage with other professionals on campus to make it work."

A useful model for understanding group dynamics, developed by psychology researcher Tuckman, outlines a four-phase group development process: forming, storming, norming, and performing.[33] Understanding that these phases are common to groups is reassuring when group dynamics feel turbulent. Many AiA teams did face turbulence, especially when group members changed and there were setbacks as momentum was interrupted. This fluidity is a characteristic of contemporary collaboration and teamwork, not yet recognized and understood by many scholars who still focus on the archetypal team with well-defined and stable membership, purpose, and leadership.[34] The leadership qualities identified by the lead librarians that were strengthened through the AiA program were an awareness of the importance of inquiry and decision-making grounded in institutional context, an understanding and experience with the dynamic nature of assessment, a recognition of the personal and professional growth that emerges through collaboration with others, and an appreciation for the missions of different campus units coming together to serve institutional priorities.

Political skills and organizational knowledge. Facilitating a team through a collaborative process requires leadership from the middle and an ability to situate the project's goals within an organization's culture. Questions that the AiA lead librarians typically asked early in the project included these: Who are the right people on campus to talk to? How do I use assessment results? How should we craft a message for different constituent groups? These questions reflect the need to understand the complex, nuanced dynamics of a campus culture.

> *The main take away from our involvement with AiA has been assessing what we value, not just valuing what we assess. We understand now that context matters and librarians need to pay close attention to institutional values and how can we add value to them.* —AiA team leader, reflective report

The professional development that was part of the AiA program incorporated theory-to-practice activities, scenario building, and role-play exercises, all designed to hone the competencies needed for navigating organizational cultures. The architects of the Wabash study note the value of this competence:

> We believe the next step in developing the necessary scholarship and expertise for assessment is to create mechanisms to systematically train campus assessment leaders in the political skills and organizational knowledge they need to more fully utilize their assessment data. To effectively promote improvements in student learning, it is just as important for assessment leaders to be able to draw on the work of, for example, Kezar (2001) and Kezar and Lester (2009), on facilitating institutional change as it is for them to know the reliability of assessment measures or how to create an e-portfolio.[35]

In each of the three years of the AiA program, the librarian team leaders commented that their leadership competence increased through the professional development and assessment activities that merged research with practice. Again, harkening back to the intent of the AiA grant as a whole, one important goal was to strengthen collaborative relationships with higher education stakeholders, including campus faculty, academic administrators, and assessment officers. Since the project activities were grounded in action research, the focus was on institutional priorities and using the assessment findings to inform and improve academic initiatives in relation to these priorities. To achieve meaningful and sustainable changes, based on assessment results, the lead librarians expanded their capacity to engage their teams in collaborative inquiry and decision-making to advance shared academic goals.

Benefits of a Collaborative Approach

The reflections of AiA librarians reveal that purposefully taking a team-based, collaborative approach to assessment from the start of the project yielded significant benefits. These benefits were realized in the assessment process and the project results.

1. Generates important conversations.

Important conversations occur when assessment is collaborative. As a team, the members needed to reach a common understanding about different aspects of the project such as definitions and attributes of academic success and agree on meaningful measures of student learning. For example, What are acceptable measures of academic rapport? Or how are we defining "at-risk" students?

> By applying DCM [Dynamic Criteria Mapping], librarians and writing faculty engaged in cross-disciplinary conversations, developing consensus on what we value when we read first-year writing projects in light of research skills and information literacy and reconciling disparate disciplinary terminology. Our project assists our institution's goals of assessing components of our general education program.[36]

BENEFITS OF A COLLABORATIVE APPROACH

Reflections of leaders from over 200 diverse campus assessment teams reveal that purposefully taking a collaborative approach to assessment yields important benefits:

1. Generates important conversations.

2. Fosters an understanding of the academic contributions of different campus constituents.

3. Encourages assessment that moves beyond one project.

4. Promotes organizational change that is sustainable.

5. Reveals compelling findings with campus-wide significance about student learning and success outcomes.

Meaningful assessment required clear articulation and common agreement about the specifics of academic factors and learning attributes that would be measured.

2. Fosters an understanding of the academic contributions of different campus constituents.

Each team member brought a unique perspective on student learning and how his or her department or campus unit contributes to student learning. Team members expanded their understanding as they learned about the roles and functions of other departments. That is to say, collaborative assessment is a developmental opportunity. Development and growth occurred for team members and team leaders. The collaborative approach also led to important conversations that got to the heart (and complexity) of teaching and learning. Each team member brought experience and a unique viewpoint to the discussion of such topics and issues as (1) core learning outcomes that all undergraduate students should achieve, (2) attributes that define "academic success," (3) the connection of academic rapport to student learning, and (4) the relationship of classroom learning to career success. As one lead librarian noted, "I believe that the most valuable aspects of this project were the formal and informal conversations and discussions about student learning and assessment. We all learned something new from each other and became more aware how other departments on campus work toward similar goals and face similar challenges." These types of conversations typically had campus-wide implications because the topics discussed addressed issues and concerns applicable to more than one campus unit.

3. Encourages assessment that moves beyond one project.

Because the collaborations prompt conversations about the contributions of different campus units and their influences on students' academic experiences, assessment becomes contextualized and rich. It's quickly discovered that one project completed by one unit is not sufficient. In fact, the collaborative process tends to generate synergy around assessment. An initial project about the impact of information literacy instruction for psychology majors, for example, might prompt discussion and assessment inquiry about the information literacy competencies of history majors.

> *The project has gotten us to think critically about our instructional practices and the effectiveness of our current strategies of engaging with disciplinary faculty. It has led to more questions that we'd like to [have] answers to.* —AiA team leader, reflective report

4. Promotes organizational change that is sustainable.

Assessment produces findings, but, as noted earlier, using these findings to make changes to existing practices can be difficult. Using a collaborative approach is one means of overcoming this challenge, because the entire assessment process is iterative, building on what is learned at each stage and involving multiple stakeholders. The resulting changes that occur tend to be incremental and well-grounded.

> *[O]ur Dean of Faculty has taken a strong interest in our AiA project and wants to discuss how we might adapt the assessment methods used to evaluate information literacy skill development to evaluate the other four core liberal arts skills that make up the backbone of our college's core curriculum.* —AiA team leader, reflective report

The projects also integrated research with practice, which means that the design and implementation of the projects had strong connections to the ongoing work of the librarians and campus constituents. As a result, the assessment activities were situated in everyday practice, giving context and real-world relevance to the work. A sense of personal responsibility and ownership for the assessment process was fostered because the results led to practical knowledge that had significance and consequences for the team members.

5. Reveals compelling findings with campus-wide significance about student learning and success outcomes.

The collaborative, team-based AiA approach frequently revealed compelling findings about library contributions to student learning and success that had campus-wide significance. Deep inquiry with multiple perspectives results in findings that have implications across the campus. For example, where a library may have initially thought it would look at the impact of information literacy in first-year English classes, it found that it was often more useful and significant to consider that impact in terms of general education or a student's first-year experience. In the words of one team leader:

> *[L]ibrarians and writing faculty engaged in cross-disciplinary conversations, developing consensus on what we value when we read first-year writing projects in light of research skills and information literacy and reconciling disparate disciplinary terminology. Our project assists our institution's goals of assessing components of our general education program.* —AiA librarian

The instructional teams discovered areas of library impact in relation to issues of campus-wide concern, including the first-year experience, general education, retention, and academic rapport.

Sustainable Change through Collaborative Assessment

Much of the literature on collaboration and change within organizations resonates with the benefits discovered about the team-based approach used in the AiA program. Kee has investigated the power of deep engagement with others and sees it as stewardship: "[It] involves creating a balance of power in the organization, establishing a primary commitment to the larger community, having each person join in defining purpose, and ensuring a balanced and equitable distribution of rewards. Stewardship is designed to create a strong sense of ownership and responsibility for outcomes at all levels of the organization."[37]

Fletcher's work supports placing value on relationships, context, and connection. She writes of relational practice and identifies four key categories:

- Preserving—resolving conflict and disconnection,
- Mutual empowering—sharing information and facilitating connections,
- Self-achieving—using feeling as a source of data and responding to emotional context and others' emotional realities, and
- Creating team—listening, respecting, and responding.[38]

She writes that this work, often performed by people who are not positional leaders and often by women, is "disappeared" and marginalized in organizations.

These kinds of deep collaboration and connections require a personal investment that leaders may mistakenly avoid. Setting out with the intention to take action and to change practice means investing a personal commitment to what psychologist Edgar Schein describes as transformational learning—that is, being able to challenge deeply held assumptions about strategies and processes and, therefore, think and act in fundamentally altered ways. This type of personal and organizational learning and growth happen so rarely. Instead, most people do the same old things in superficially tweaked ways. Yet transformational learning is at the crux of authentic, sustainable change. In an interview, Schein explains that there is "an inherent paradox surrounding learning: Anxiety inhibits learning, but anxiety is also necessary if learning is going to happen at all."[39] He describes two types of anxiety associated with organizational learning: "learning anxiety" and "survival anxiety."

Schein describes how learning anxieties form the "basis for resistance to change" and can be overcome only by "survival anxiety—the horrible realization that in order to make it, you're going to have to change."[40] In Schein's view, learning happens only when survival anxiety is greater than learning anxiety. He explains that leaders can either increase survival anxiety—by threatening people with job loss or taking away rewards—or decrease learning anxiety by creating a safe environment to unlearn old ways and learn new ones. The latter approach tends to be much harder, and many organizations unfortunately prefer the easier route. Learning how to change, then, is not a happy and comfortable process. "The evidence is mounting that real change does not begin until the organization experiences some real threat of pain that in some way dashes its expectations or hopes."[41]

Our colleges and universities are indeed experiencing such real threats that dash expectations and hopes among all campus constituent groups. It is incumbent on all of us to take risks as we learn new ways to "make it" and commit to changing and improving our organizations to better meet student needs. Based on what we learned from the AiA program, we believe working collaboratively to inquire about practice and seek improvements through team-based assessment is the most effective way to move forward. The experiences of AiA teams show that the people in our organizations who are charged with taking on this work require adequate support and an investment from higher-level positional leaders in order to be effective, which resonates with the literature of organization change and leadership.

Next Steps for ACRL

As the three-year AiA program came to a close, the success of the projects motivated ACRL to identify ways to build on the AiA findings. To better inform our next steps and consistent with our commitment to a collaborative and action learning approach, in late 2015, we began seeking input beyond our own experience with AiA and what we know about the needs of the academic library community. We reached out to expert thinkers outside of libraries to clarify our own deliberations and ideas about future directions. This effort further advanced one of the primary recommendations that emerged from the Value of Academic Libraries Summits in 2011, which was a key impetus for the AiA program: Expand partnerships for assessment activities with higher education constituent groups and related stakeholder groups.[42] We identified higher education associations, organizations, and researchers of interest and invited them to have conversations; our invitations were all received enthusiastically. We scheduled twelve telephone conversations over fall and winter 2015, taking careful notes during each conversation. We had a set of prepared questions for the conversations, but we allowed the conversations to evolve organically based on the person's interests and areas of expertise.

Four broad themes and recurrent patterns emerged from our review of the notes regarding trends in higher education related to data, assessment, research, and campus leadership:

- **Astute use of evidence:** Significant effort within the higher education arena has been focused on collecting, analyzing, and interpreting data, but we now need to know if the yield in student learning improvements is proportional to the effort. Energy is now being directed toward better use of data to make improvements rather than conducting new research. This trend reinforces the value of collaborative approaches to inquiry and decision-making about academic improvements. Different constituent groups on a campus may have data, already collected, that can be merged with other sets of data to reveal findings about students learning and success. Several AiA teams, for example, were able to assess library impact by triangulating library data (e.g., circulation statistics, library use, library instruction participation) with data points related to academic achievement (e.g., GPA, assignment-level grades, persistence from one term to the next). In addition, conducting assessment through the lens of action research keeps the collaborative inquiry, conversations, and decision-making grounded in a real-world, action-oriented approach to academic improvement.

- **Leadership as advocacy**: It is essential to have broad-based leadership that has individuals at multiple institutional levels who know how to use evidence to make improvements within campus programs, departments, and units. These individuals should have the knowledge and competencies to identify and use the appropriate data in collaboration with others on campus. At its core, it's leadership that is shared, participatory, and context-based, resulting in advocacy and campus-wide investment in academic initiatives.

- **Contextual nature of the educational experience:** The emphasis is now shifting to how students are achieving general learning outcomes related to critical thinking across disciplines and through experiences in and out of the classroom. Many students need a rich array of learning experiences to complete a degree. This type of learning cannot be achieved without collaboration among campus units. As noted earlier, the diverse perspectives, expertise, and experiences brought together in the collaborative AiA projects were important to assessing and understanding the nuanced and multifaceted nature of learning and what kinds of experiences contribute to academic success.

- **Role of higher education in the quality of our national life**: With the increased scrutiny of higher education by governmental entities, the media, the business community, accrediting agencies, and taxpayer advocacy groups, to name just a few, questions are emerging about the value and contributions of higher education to the quality of our national life. David Skorton, Secretary of the Smithsonian Institution, and Glenn Altschuler, the Thomas and Dorothy Litwin Professor of American Studies at Cornell University, have contributed to a Forbes blog about leadership and are clearly strong advocates for the essential role of higher education in our national life:

   Contemporary colleges and universities, we want to emphasize, have taken on myriad functions and responsibilities in the twentieth and twenty-first centuries. In addition to their traditional roles as custodians and disseminators of knowledge, they are centers of research and discovery; gateways to the professions, providing training and technical expertise; protectors and promoters of prosperity and national security; cultural centers in towns large and small; and outposts for hard thinking about the essential components of a "good life." … We believe that robust colleges and universities are essential if the United States is to stimulate research and innovation, spur economic growth, sustain meritocratic values, and search for the defining qualities of beauty, justice, and truth.[43]

Yet this type of view is not necessarily widely held and, from the conversations we had, the higher education community needs to increase its attention on assessing and documenting the impact of colleges and universities on the education of students broadly. Without question, it's an endeavor that will require consideration of multiple perspectives and entail sustained conversation, deep thinking, and iterative knowledge building.

Conclusion

The results of our conversations with these expert thinkers outside of libraries have stimulated our thinking about future directions for professional development within the academic library community as well as how to present the findings of the AiA program to a broader higher education audience. Given all we now know from the AiA teams about collaborative assessment and campus leadership, we are disseminating AiA results to new audiences and through new channels, as with this NILOA occasional paper, and have endeavored to articulate the program's findings in such a way that they will resonate strongly with the broader higher education community and what matters most to colleges and universities.

Appendix A: Assessment in Action Program Design

The AiA program design emerged from the discussions at the national summits that ACRL hosted in 2011, funded by the US federal agency the Institute of Museum and Library Services (IMLS) through a Collaborative Planning Grant, in partnership with Institutional Research, the Association of Public and Land-grant Universities, and the Council of Independent Colleges. The summits were attended by teams from twenty-two postsecondary institutions, including senior librarians, chief academic administrators, and institutional researchers, for discussions about library impact. Fifteen representatives from higher education organizations and associations also participated in these discussions.[44] Four themes emerged about the dynamic nature of assessment in higher education from the summits:

- Accountability drives higher education discussions.
- A unified approach to institutional assessment is essential.
- Student learning and success are the primary focus of higher education assessment.
- Academic administrators and accreditors seek evidence-based reports of measurable impact.

Details about the summits and the resultant themes and recommendations are in the freely available white paper *Connect, Collaborate, and Communicate: A Report from the Value of Academic Libraries Summits*.[45]

AiA facilitators[46] worked with Etienne Wenger-Trayner and Bev Wenger-Trayner in designing the AiA program, drawing on the concept they developed of communities of practice. Wenger-Trayner and Wenger-Trayner define communities of practice as "groups of people who share a concern or a passion for something they do and learn how to do it better as they interact regularly."[47]

Unlike traditional educational models that spotlight an instructor's central role as the "sage on the stage" with primary authority and content expertise, the AiA blended-learning model emphasized the facilitative role of instructors (i.e., "guide on the side"). AiA participants worked collaboratively in face-to-face sessions, webcasts, and asynchronous online environments to create, share, and build content, processes, and products. This network supported collective learning, shared competence, sustained interaction, and a climate of mutuality and trust. In the process, a strong community of practice developed. The focus on active learning also led to a deeper understanding of what happens when knowledge and skills are applied in practice.

The design of AiA also drew on the concept of action research.[48] Action research is understood as "a participatory, democratic process concerned with developing practical knowing in the pursuit of worthwhile human purposes…. it seeks to bring together action and reflection, theory and practice, in participation with others, in the pursuit of practical solutions to issues of pressing concern to people, and more generally the flourishing of individual persons and their communities."[49] Key concepts in this definition that were emphasized in the curriculum of AiA are participatory, democratic, and practical solutions.[50]

Notes

1. Malenfant, K. J., & Brown, K. (2017, November). *Creating sustainable assessment through collaboration: A national program reveals effective practices.* (Occasional Paper No. 31) Urbana, IL: University of Illinois and Indiana University, National Institute for Learning Outcomes Assessment (NILOA). Reprinted with permission.
2. This paper incorporates material from previous reports about the ACRL program Assessment in Action, cited in note 12. This work is being released simultaneously by the National Institute for Learning Outcomes Assessment as an occasional paper in November 2017 and as a chapter in the ACRL print publication *Shaping the Campus Conversation on Student Learning and Experience: Activating the Results of Assessment in Action.*

3. Association of College and Research Libraries, *Value of Academic Libraries: A Comprehensive Research Review and Report*, researched by Megan Oakleaf (Chicago: Association of College and Research Libraries, 2010), http://www.ala.org/acrl/files/issues/value/val_report.pdf.

4. Karen Kellogg, *Collaboration: Student Affairs and Academic Affairs Working Together to Promote Student Learning*, ERIC digest ED432940 (Washington, DC: ERIC Clearinghouse on Higher Education; George Washington University Graduate School of Education and Human Development, 1999), http://www.ericdigests.org/2000-2/affairs.htm.

5. Trudy W. Banta and George D. Kuh, "A Missing Link in Assessment: Collaboration between Academic and Student Affairs Professionals," *Change* 30, no. 2 (1998): 40–46, ERIC number EJ562819.

6. George D. Kuh and Trudy W. Banta, "Faculty-Student Affairs Collaboration on Assessment: Lessons from the Field," *About Campus* 4, no. 6 (January–February 2000): 4–11, ERIC number EJ619312.

7. See Lisa Janicke Hinchliffe and Melissa Autumn Wong, eds., *Environments for Student Growth and Development: Libraries and Student Affairs in Collaboration* (Chicago: Association of College and Research Libraries, 2012), and James K. Elmborg and Sheril Hook, eds., *Centers for Learning: Writing Centers and Libraries in Collaboration* (Chicago: Association of College and Research Libraries, 2006).

8. William H. Bergquist and Kenneth Pawlak, *Engaging the Six Cultures of the Academy*, rev. ed. of *The Four Cultures of the Academy* (San Francisco: Jossey-Bass, 2008), 43.

9. These assertions augment a previous NILOA occasional paper, which argued that "librarians, both independently and in partnership with other stakeholders, are systematically and intentionally creating learning outcomes, designing curriculum, assessing student achievement of learning goals, using assessment results to identify practices that impact learning, and employing those practices to positively impact student experience." (Debra Gilchrist and Megan Oakleaf, *An Essential Partner: The Librarian's Role in Student Learning Assessment*, NILOA Occasional Paper No. 14 [Urbana, IL: University of Illinois and Indiana University, National Institute for Learning Outcomes Assessment, April 2012], 3, http://www.learningoutcomeassessment.org/occasionalpaperfourteen.htm.)

10. Charles Blaich and Kathleen Wise, *From Gathering to Using Assessment Results: Lessons from the Wabash National Study*, NILOA Occasional Paper No. 8 (Urbana, IL: University of Illinois and Indiana University, National Institute for Learning Outcomes Assessment, January 2011), 11, http://www.learningoutcomeassessment.org/documents/Wabash_001.pdf.

11. American Association of State Colleges and Universities, "2016 Academic Affairs Winter Meeting," AASCU website, accessed September 8, 2017, http://www.aascu.org/meetings/aa_winter16/.

12. Database of AiA descriptive project reports is available online at http://apply.ala.org/aia/public. In addition, a comprehensive bibliography, available online at http://www.acrl.ala.org/value/?page_id=980, captures all scholarly and practice-based literature and presentations about ACRL's AiA program and campus projects by staff, facilitators, and participants.

13. Association of College and Research Libraries, *Academic Library Impact on Student Learning and Success: Documented Practices from the Field*, prepared by Karen Brown, contributions by Kara J. Malenfant (Chicago: Association of College and Research Libraries, January 2015), http://www.ala.org/acrl/files/issues/value/contributions_report.pdf; Association of College and Research Libraries, *Documented Library Contributions to Student Learning and Success: Building Evidence with Team-Based Assessment in Action Campus Projects*, prepared by Karen Brown, contributions by Kara J. Malenfant (Chicago: Association of College and Research Libraries, April 2016), http://www.ala.org/acrl/files/issues/value/contributions_y2.pdf; Association of College and Research Libraries, *Academic Library Impact on Student Learning and Success: Findings from Assessment in Action Team Projects*, prepared by Karen Brown, contributions by Kara J. Malenfant (Chicago: Association of College and Research Libraries, April 2017), http://www.ala.org/acrl/files/issues/value/findings_y3.pdf.

14. Association of College and Research Libraries, *Academic Library Impact: Improving Practice and Essential Areas to Research*, prepared by Lynn Silipigni Connaway, William Harvey, Vanessa Kitzie, and Stephanie Mikitish of OCLC Research. (Chicago: Association of College and Research Libraries, September 2017), 62, http://www.ala.org/acrl/files/publications/whitepapers/LibraryImpact.pdf.

15. Effective practices in higher education are typically based on studies that exemplify variation in such attributes as setting, instructional design and approach, student characteristics, and institutional priorities. George Kuh, for example, identified high-impact educational saying, "The following teaching and learning practices have been widely tested and have been shown to be beneficial for college students from many backgrounds. These practices take many different forms, depending on learner characteristics and on institutional priorities and contexts." ("High-Impact Educational Practices: A Brief Overview," excerpt from George D. Kuh, *High-Impact Educational Practices: What They Are, Who Has Access to Them, and Why They Matter* [Washington, DC: Association of American Colleges and Universities, 2008], https://www.aacu.org/leap/hips). For a deeper discussion of assessment methods used by AiA teams, see Eric Ackermann, ed., *Putting Assessment into Action: Selected Projects from the First Cohort of the Assessment in Action Grant* (Chicago: Association of College and Research Libraries, 2016), which addresses methodological issues through twenty-seven cases reflecting the real-world, practical experience of librarians who participated in the first cohort of the Assessment in Action project.

16. Catherine M. Wehlburg, *Promoting Integrated and Transformative Assessment: A Deeper Focus on Student Learning* (San Francisco: Jossey-Bass, 2008), 29.

17. Association of American Colleges and Universities, "Employer Survey and Economic Trend Research," AAC&U website, accessed September 8, 2017, https://www.aacu.org/leap/public-opinion-research.

18. Lisa R. Lattuca and Elizabeth G. Creamer, "Learning as Professional Practice," New Directions for Teaching and Learning 2005, no. 102 (Summer 2005): 5, https://doi.org/10.1002/tl.192

19. James Edwin Kee and Kathryn E. Newcomer, *Transforming Public and Nonprofit Organizations: Stewardship for Leading Change* (Vienna, VA: Management Concepts, 2008).

20. Fran Rees, "From Controlling to Facilitating," chapter 4 in *How to Lead Work Teams: Facilitation Skills*, 2nd ed. (San Francisco: Jossey-Bass/Pfeiffer, 2001), 51–72.

21. Edwin E. Olson and Glenda H. Eoyang, *Facilitating Organization Change: Lessons from Complexity Science* (San Francisco: Jossey-Bass/Pfeiffer, 2001), 39–40.

22. Indiana University of Pennsylvania, "Project Description," AiA project report, Association of College and Research Libraries website, accessed September 12, 2017, https://apply.ala.org/aia/docs/project/5403.

23. Jon R. Katzenbach and Douglas K. Smith, *The Wisdom of Teams: Creating the High-Performance Organization* (Boston: Harvard Business Review Press, 1993), 116, quoted in Lee G. Bolman and Joan V. Gallos, *Reframing Academic Leadership* (San Francisco: Jossey-Bass, 2011), 98–99.

24. J. Richard Hackman, "From Causes to Conditions in Group Research," *Journal of Organizational Behavior* 33, no. 3 (April 2012): 437, https://doi.org/10.1002/job.1774.

25. Michael A. West, *Effective Teamwork: Practical Lessons from Organizational Research*, 3rd ed. (Malden, MA: John Wiley and Sons, 2012), 57–58.

26. Katzenbach and Smith, *Wisdom of Teams*, 116, quoted in Bolman and. Gallos, *Reframing Academic Leadership*, 98–99.

27. Hackman, "From Causes to Conditions," 437.

28. Hackman, "From Causes to Conditions," 437.

29. J. Richard Hackman, *Collaborative Intelligence: Using Teams to Solve Hard Problems* (San Francisco: Berrett-Koher, 2011), 165.

30. Rees, "From Controlling to Facilitating."

31. Kim Pittman, "Assessment in Action Project Reflection," ACRL Value of Academic Libraries website, September 14, 2016, http://www.acrl.ala.org/value/?p=1199.

32. Hackman, "From Causes to Conditions," 437.

33. Bruce W. Tuckman, "Developmental Sequence in Small Groups," *Psychological Bulletin* 63, no. 6 (1965): 384–99, repr. in *Group Facilitation: A Research and Applications Journal*, no. 3 (Spring 2001): 66–81, http://openvce.net/sites/default/files/Tuckman1965DevelopmentalSequence.pdf.

34. Ruth Wageman, Heidi Gardner, and Mark Mortensen "The Changing Ecology of Teams: New Directions for Teams Research," *Journal of Organizational Behavior* 33, no. 3 (April 2012): 301–315.

35. Blaich and Wise, *From Gathering to Using*, 16.

36. Elmhurst College, "Project Description," AiA project report, Association of College and Research Libraries website, accessed September 13, 2017, https://apply.ala.org/aia/docs/project/13910.

37. James Edwin Kee, "Leadership as Stewardship," unpublished manuscript, George Washington University, 2003, quoted in Kee and Newcomer, *Transforming Public and Nonprofit Organizations*, 30.

38. Joyce K. Fletcher, *Disappearing Acts: Gender, Power, and Relational Practice at Work* (Cambridge, MA: Massachusetts Institute of Technology, 1999), 85.

39. Coutu, D. L. (2002). The Anxiety of Learning," *Harvard Business Review* 80, no. 3 (March 2002): 104.

40. Schein, quoted in interview with Coutu, "Anxiety of Learning," 104–5.

41. Schein, quoted in interview with Coutu, "Anxiety of Learning," 105.

42. Association of College and Research Libraries, *Connect, Collaborate, and Communicate: A Report from the Value of Academic Libraries Summits*, prepared by Karen Brown and Kara J. Malenfant (Chicago: Association of College and Research Libraries, June 2012), 14, http://www.ala.org/acrl/sites/ala.org.acrl/files/content/issues/value/val_summit.pdf.

43. David Skorton and Glenn Altschuler, "On Higher Education: Where We Stand," *Forbes*, August 1, 2012. https://www.forbes.com/sites/collegeprose/2012/08/01/on-higher-education-where-we-stand/#347925906649.

44. Charlie Blaich, an architect of the Wabash Study, was a plenary speaker during the planning summit, and the Wabash Study experiences greatly influenced the design of AiA.

45. Association of College and Research Libraries, *Connect, Collaborate, and Communicate*.

46. AiA design/facilitation team was led by Debra Gilchrist, Vice President for Learning and Student Success, Pierce College, WA; Lisa Janicke Hinchliffe, Coordinator for Information Literacy and Professor, University of Illinois at Urbana-Champaign; and Kara Malenfant, Senior Strategist for Special Initiatives, Association of College and Research Libraries. Additional designers/facilitators participated throughout the length of the project: April Cunningham, Library Instruction Coordinator at Saddleback College in Mission Viejo, CA; Carrie Donovan, Head of Teaching and Learning for the Indiana University Libraries in Bloomington, IN; Eric Resins, Organizational Effectiveness Specialist in the Libraries at Miami University in Oxford, OH; and John Watts, Undergraduate Learning Librarian at University of Nevada Las Vegas. Libby Miles, Associate Professor of Writing and Rhetoric in the Harrington School of Communication and Media at the University of Rhode Island in Kingston, RI, was part of the facilitation team for the first eighteen months of the program. Project analyst Karen Brown, Professor at the Graduate School of Library and Information Science at Dominican University, IL, worked with the team to analyze and synthesize projects undertaken by the institutional teams.

47. Etienne Wenger-Trayner and Beverly Wenger-Trayner, "Introduction to Communities of Practice: A Brief Overview of the Concept and Its Uses," Wenger-Trayner website, 2015, http://wenger-trayner.com/introduction-to-communities-of-practice.

48. Kara J. Malenfant, Lisa Janicke Hinchliffe, and Debra Gilchrist, "Assessment as Action Research: Bridging Academic Scholarship and Everyday Practice," *College and Research Libraries* 77, no. 2 (March 2016): 140–43, https://doi.org/10.5860/crl.77.2.140.

49. Peter Reason and Hilary Bradbury, eds., *The SAGE Handbook of Action Research*, 2nd ed. (London: SAGE, 2006), 1.

50. For more detail on the AiA program design, see the print volume, *Shaping the Campus Conversation on Student Learning and Experience: Activating the Results of Assessment in Action*, which describes the entire AiA program in greater detail. The volume, to be published by ACRL in fall 2017, will include a deeper discussion of the AiA design and include a syllabus for the fourteen-month-long professional development program as an appendix.

CHAPTER 3

Academic Library Contributions to Student Success:

Documented Practices from the Field*

Association of College and Research Libraries. Prepared by Karen Brown. Contributions by Kara J. Malenfant

* Association of College and Research Libraries. *Academic Library Contributions to Student Success: Documented Practices from the Field*. Prepared by Karen Brown. Contributions by Kara J. Malenfant. Chicago: Association of College and Research Libraries, 2015. Published online at www.acrl.ala.org/value.

Association of College & Research Libraries
A division of the American Library Association

Citation:
Association of College and Research Libraries. *Academic Library Contributions to Student Success: Documented Practices from the Field.* Prepared by Karen Brown. Contributions by Kara J. Malenfant. Chicago: Association of College and Research Libraries, 2015.

Published online at www.acrl.ala.org/value.

About the Authors

Karen Brown is a professor at Dominican University (River Forest, Illinois) in the Graduate School of Library and Information Science and teaches in the areas of collection management, foundations of the profession, and literacy and learning. Prior to joining Dominican University's faculty in 2000, she developed and coordinated continuing education programs for the Chicago Library System, one of Illinois's former regional library systems. She has also held positions focusing on collection development, reference, and instruction at the University of Wisconsin, University of Maryland, Columbia University, and Bard College. She holds a PhD in media studies from New York University and master's degrees in library science and adult education from the University of Wisconsin.

Kara J. Malenfant is a senior staff member at ACRL, where she coordinates government relations advocacy and scholarly communication activities and is the lead staff member on the Value of Academic Libraries initiative and Assessment in Action program. She provides consulting services on organization development and use of ACRL's standards for libraries in higher education. Kara began her position at ACRL in fall of 2005, after working for six years at DePaul University Libraries in Chicago. She holds a PhD in leadership and change from Antioch University and an MS in library science from the University of Illinois at Urbana-Champaign.

Contents

Executive Summary[1]

Academic librarians are increasingly participating in the national dialogue about higher education effectiveness and quality. They are contributing to higher education assessment work by creating approaches, strategies, and practices that document the value of academic libraries to advancing the goals and missions of their institutions. By demonstrating the variety of ways that libraries contribute to student learning and success, academic librarians are establishing connections between different aspects of the library (e.g., instruction, reference, space and facilities, and collections) and numerous academic success factors (e.g., student retention, persistence, GPA, engagement, graduation, and career preparedness).

Assessment in Action

Over 70 higher education institutions from across North America recently completed team-based assessment projects that resulted in promising and effective approaches to demonstrating the library's value to student learning and success. Assessment in Action: Academic Libraries and Student Success (AiA) is a three-year project sponsored by the Association of College and Research Libraries (ACRL) in partnership with the Association of Institutional Research and the Association of Public Land-grant Universities, and with funding from the U.S. Institute of Museum and Library Services. When the project concludes in 2016, over 200 higher education institutions will have participated in developing assessment methods and tools.

The methods and tools designed by the teams expand the resources that higher education institutions can share and use in their campus assessment initiatives. Many of the projects are replicable at other academic libraries or contain elements that can be adapted to a college or university's unique institutional context.

Findings about Library Contributions

The findings from the assessment work of the first-year campus teams are impressive. Although these findings are not necessarily generalizable to all higher education institutions, they do point to important relationships between the library and student learning and success. Higher education institutions are encouraged to advance and refine assessment work that focuses on the academic library's contributions to an institution's mission and academic priorities. A few examples of the project findings are highlighted below.

1. Library instruction builds students' confidence with the research process.
2. Library instruction contributes to retention and persistence, particularly for students in first-year experience courses and programs.
3. Students who receive library instruction as part of their courses achieve higher grades and demonstrate better information literacy competencies than students who do not receive course-related library instruction.
4. A library's research and study space fosters social and academic community among students.
5. Library instructional games engage students, enhance information literacy skills, and increase positive attitudes toward the library and its staff.

---

[1] This executive summary is available online as a separate document, formatted to share broadly with campus stakeholders, see www.ala.org/acrl/files/issues/value/contributions_summary.pdf.

6. The library's use of social media promotes awareness of the library and builds academic community among students.
7. Multiple library instruction sessions or activities in connection with a course are more effective than one-shot instruction sessions.
8. Collaborative instructional activities and services between the library and other campus units (e.g., writing center, study skills and tutoring services) promote student learning and success.

Findings about Higher Education Assessment

The experiences of the AiA teams led to several recommendations for fostering evidence-based demonstrations of library value at higher education institutions. Six of the strategies are highlighted below. A more detailed discussion of the recommendations and strategies are available in the full report, *Academic Library Contributions to Student Success: Documented Practices from the Field*.

1. Library assessment is most effective when it aligns with institutional priorities and mission.
2. Library assessment that includes the participation of representatives from other campus departments and units (e.g., faculty, institutional research, academic administration, student services) increases the quality of the assessment design and results.
3. Libraries can contribute important data about student learning and success to an institution's accreditation self-study and review.
4. A mixed-methods approach to library assessment strengthens and enriches findings about library impact.
5. Academic librarians recognize how assessment activities advance an institution's academic mission and are poised to lead library assessment initiatives.
6. Assessment achieves sustainability and meaningful integration with the library's services and programs when it is a designated responsibility of one or more librarians.

More Information

Read the full report, *Academic Library Contributions to Student Success: Documented Practices from the Field*, for ideas and strategies that promote evidence-based demonstrations of an academic library's contributions to student learning and success. Visit, adapt, and use the assessment methods and tools developed by the AiA campus teams that are available in a searchable online collection.

About ACRL

The Association of College & Research Libraries is the higher education association for librarians. Representing more than 11,000 academic and research librarians and interested individuals, ACRL (a division of the American Library Association) is the only individual membership organization in North America that develops programs, products, and services to help academic and research librarians learn, innovate, and lead within the academic community. Founded in 1940, ACRL is committed to advancing learning and transforming scholarship.

Introduction

Academic librarians are connecting with campus partners in novel ways to examine and discover how they bring value to their institutions. To foster these partnerships, ACRL, with its partners the Association of Institutional Research and the Association of Public Land-grant Universities, and with funding from the U.S. Institute of Museum and Library Services, launched "Assessment in Action: Academic Libraries and Student Success" (AiA) to achieve three primary goals:

1) Develop academic librarians' professional competencies needed to document and communicate the value of the academic library in relation to an institution's goals for student learning and success.

2) Strengthen collaborative relationships with higher education stakeholders, including campus faculty, academic administrators, and assessment officers.

3) Contribute to higher education assessment by creating approaches, strategies, and practices that document the contribution of academic libraries.

The three-year AiA program is helping hundreds of postsecondary institutions of all types develop campus partnerships to promote the engaged library of the future. Its design is based on input from two national summits held in response to recommendations to build librarians' capacity in this area. (See APPENDIX A: ACRL and the Value of Academic Libraries Initiative for an overview.)

Each selected institution has a team with a librarian and at least two people from other campus units. Team members include teaching faculty, other librarians, and administrators from campus units such as the assessment office, institutional research, the writing center, academic technology, and student affairs. The librarians participate in a formal 14-month professional development program during which they lead their campus teams in the development and implementation of a library value project that is informed by skill-building activities and aims to contribute to assessment activities on their campus.

Throughout the project, the librarians are supported by a blended learning environment and a peer-to-peer network. This environment provides a framework for the action learning projects and is a central component of AiA. Many of the inquiry methods and processes developed during the first year of the program exemplify aspects of action research. As Shani and Pasmore explain, "Action research may be defined as an emergent inquiry process in which applied behavioral science knowledge is integrated with existing organizational knowledge and applied to solve real organizational problems."[2] Hallmark characteristics of action learning that bridges theory to practice are its grounding in the context of practice-based inquiry, the use of systematic methods of data collection and analysis to inform and influence practice, and the importance of collaboration with one's colleagues to produce meaningful results. The attention given by academic librarians to demonstrating library value is an example of a practice-based challenge that is well suited to this approach. The AiA learning community fosters a dynamic, active form

---

[2] Quoted in: Shani, A. and D. Coghlan. (2014). "Action and Collaboration Between Scholarship and Practice: Core Values of OD Research." *OD Practitioner* 46(4): 35-38, p. 36.

of learning among colleagues that combines small group engagement in problem solving through questioning, testing assumptions about practice, and reflecting on what has been learned.

Through the AiA learning and collaborative activities, the campus teams consider different aspects of the academic library (e.g., collections, space, instruction, reference, etc.) and their relationship to student learning (e.g., course, program, or degree learning outcomes) and/or success (e.g., student retention, completion, or persistence). The methods and tools that are designed and applied to practice expand the resources that academic librarians can share and use in their campus assessment initiatives. Many projects are replicable at other libraries or contain elements that are transferable to different institutional settings.

> *The project illuminated the importance of closing the assessment cycle by reporting results and making decisions based on those results.*
>
> — Webster University

The results from the first year of AiA make it clear that the contributions of academic libraries to student learning and success are gaining recognition on campuses across North America. The numerous library factors investigated and the different assessment methods used by the 75 teams selected to participate in AiA create an extensive collection of evidence-based practices that benefits the academic library and higher education communities.

This report focuses on the assessment projects conducted by those teams that participated in the first year of the program, from April 2013 to June 2014.[3] Of the 75 teams selected, 74 presented posters sessions at the 2014 ALA Annual Conference in Las Vegas, Nevada, June 27 or 28, 2014.[4] In addition, each team leader completed a final project descriptive report, which is fully searchable in an online collection, and includes images of the posters and abstracts. Each team leader was also asked to complete a reflective report and, while these individual reports are kept confidential, aggregate and anonymous comments from the reports have contributed to this synthesis. (See APPENDIX B: Final Report Template for AiA Team Leaders for reporting questions.) This publication is also informed by results from two focus groups undertaken in June 2014 with a total of 39 AiA year-one team leaders.

As the AiA team leaders prepared their posters and reports throughout spring 2014, they supported one another through a structured process that started with peer feedback within small cohort groups. After the team leaders made revisions, two additional peer reviews occurred across the cohorts. Team leaders made appropriate revisions to their posters and project reports based on this feedback. The iterative process ensured that the final posters and project reports were robust and clear. This publication highlights some of the most significant findings of these

---

[3] The second year AiA teams are already well under way, working from April 2014 to June 2015. The online application to participate in the third year of AiA (April 2015 to June 2016) was available in mid-January 2015 and due in early March 2015. Read more about applying for the third year at www.ala.org/acrl/AiAapplication.

[4] Poster abstracts are available online as a separate booklet at www.acrl.ala.org/value/wp-content/uploads/2014/06/AiA-poster-guide-ALA-AC-2014.pdf.

projects and also discusses just a few of the projects to provide a snapshot view of the rich variety of assessment methods and designs that offer effective and promising approaches for demonstrating library value. Recommendations for fostering evidence-based library advocacy and campus collaborations that emerged from the experiences of the AiA teams are also presented. In addition, this report describes a "community of practice" that is developing around academic library assessment as a result of the AiA librarians' collaborative learning experiences.

The primary audience for this report is academic librarians and library administrators. A secondary audience – higher education assessment professionals and academic administrators – will likely find the recommendations and project results useful in their assessment work on campuses.

Institutional Teams: Year One

The institutional teams for the first year of the AiA program were selected through a competitive application process designed to ensure representation from an array of geographic regions and postsecondary institutions.

Figure 1. Map of Teams Participating in First Year of AiA.

The institutions came from 29 states and 3 Canadian provinces, spanning 7 time zones, from Hawaii to Nova Scotia. Colleges included associate's (10), baccalaureate (7), master's level (31), tribal (1), special focus (1), doctoral/research universities (6), and research universities (18). FTE enrollment size ranged from under 2,000 to over 20,000 students. The institutions are also represented by a variety of different accrediting bodies, including seven U.S. regional and four Canadian, as shown in Figure 2.[5]

---

[5] For a full list of all participating institution names and locations, see www.ala.org/acrl/AiA.

The campus is seeking re-accreditation by the National Association of Schools of Art and Design (NASAD). During the re-accreditation visit process, the NASAD team highlighted the library's assessment project and recommended it as a model for other academic departments on campus.

— <u>Institute of American Indian Arts</u>

Figure 2. Accreditation Agencies.

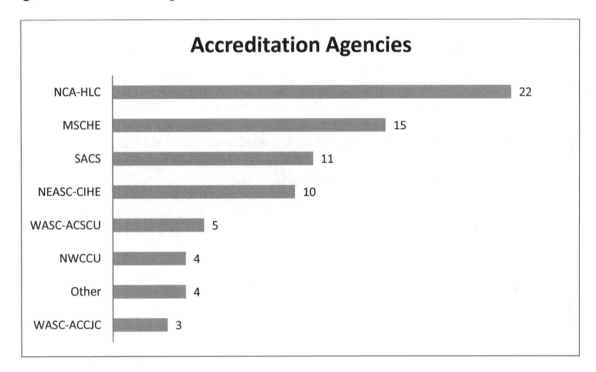

Librarians at these institutions recognized the growing importance of assessment on their campuses and saw AiA as an opportunity to position the library as a key player. While some of the AiA participants came from libraries with active assessment programs, many librarians were embarking on an assessment project for the first time. AiA provided a supportive and collaborative learning community for developing the skill sets needed to lead a campus project team as it used evidence-based approaches for demonstrating library value.

Assessment Approaches to Demonstrating Library Value

> *Even applying for this project gave us the opportunity to begin campus conversations about assessment and demonstrate the library's willingness to engage in and learn from assessment.*
>
> — AiA librarian
> (from reflective report)

As part of the AiA application process, the librarians had to indicate an initial area of focus for their assessment project and identify the members of their campus team. The librarians worked together as a cohort to learn assessment methods, project management techniques, and strategies for aligning their library with their institution's mission and academic priorities. During this initial project phase, the librarians also collaborated with their campus team members to design an assessment project that considered the library's potential contribution to student learning and success on their campus. The teams then narrowed their focus to a specific library factor and a discrete aspect of student learning and success to be assessed. A primary inquiry question was formulated that posed a possible connection between the library and student learning and/or success. Each campus team created a question that was unique to its library and its institutional context. The list of ten primary inquiry questions below exemplifies just some of the many library impact areas investigated by the campus teams.

- Is online instruction or conventional classroom training more effective in delivering information literacy instruction to General Studies Portal 188 and English 102 courses? (University of Nebraska-Kearney)

- Does exposure to primary sources through library instruction and class assignments improve students' abilities to think critically and creatively? (Appalachian State University)

- How do students in English Composition classes who are taught using the flipped classroom model of instruction compare with those in traditional one-shot classes in their ability to locate and cite information effectively? (Middlesex Community College)

- What is the most effective role a librarian can play in information literacy instruction to students of English 102: designer of online curricula, moderator in a flipped classroom, or presenter in a traditional classroom? (Northeastern Illinois University)

- How does the usage of our dedicated technology facilities contribute to the success of Miami University student scholarship and research? (Miami University)

- How do existing library services (e.g., the BIO126 information literacy program, library resources, and reference help) support the student learning outcomes designed by librarians and science faculty?
  (Greenfield Community College)

- What can we learn about the impact of the library on student success by examining use of eResources and student GPA?
  (York University)

- How effective were the library's UNIV100 games in improving student information confidence?
  (Radford University)

- Does information literacy instruction and access to library resources and services help novice Spanish-language learners meet the American Council on the Teaching of Foreign Languages (ACTFL) Standards for Foreign Language Learning?
  (Stonehill College)

- How can the library most effectively adapt its information literacy instruction program to best address the growing presence of multimedia in student research projects?
  (Mercy College)

The question posed by a campus team guided decisions about strategies for the inquiry process and the type(s) of data needed to answer the question. Depending on the question, the collection of data may have reflected direct or indirect measures of student learning and success. Direct measures typically refer to actual student work and tend to capture relatively objective data about competencies, skills, and knowledge. Indirect measures, on the other hand, represent types of data that do not measure actual abilities or competencies. A student's portfolio, for example, would be a direct measure; a survey of that student's perceptions of his or her skills would be an indirect measure of learning. Seventy-four direct measures (e.g., research papers/projects, other class assignments, or student portfolios) were used for assessment data, and 54 indirect measures (e.g., test scores, GPA, or retention rate) provided data.

Again, depending on the inquiry question, the assessment method(s) selected by the teams varied. While some teams focused on quantitative methodologies (e.g., comparison of circulation statistics with GPA), other teams used qualitative approaches (e.g., focus groups, reflection essays). Many of the teams decided to use more than one assessment method to investigate possible impact, resulting in a mixed-methods approach that could expand and enrich their findings. Changes in GPAs, for example, might be supported and augmented by student comments gathered during focus groups. All of the projects, whether using a quantitative, qualitative, or mixed-methods approach, advance higher education assessment work by creating and examining approaches, strategies, and practices that document an academic library's contribution to students' academic success. They move the profession's understanding of library value from assumptions or anecdotal observations about library impact to systematic methods for data collection and analysis. It should be noted that the teams have been careful to report their findings as relationships and correlations – not claims of causation – between library factors and academic outcomes. The assessment methods and tools that were used are summarized in the following table.

Table 1. Assessment Methods and Tools. [6]

Assessment Methods and Tools	#
Survey	41
Rubric	40
Pre/Post Test	24
Other (e.g., correlational analysis, exam, skill demonstration)	20
Interviews	13
Observation	11
Focus Group(s)	10

> *Sharing the results of this project with the liaison librarians showed them how keeping accurate statistics can help us demonstrate our own role in student success, as well as helping position them as assessment partners with their assigned colleges and departments.*
>
> – University of North Carolina-Charlotte

> *We used multimodal techniques to see student work, student perceptions, faculty/librarian perceptions, and institutional perspectives, giving us a fuller picture of student learning.*
>
> – Greenfield Community College

The projects described in the next section highlight different assessment methods and types of data collected. Keep in mind that only 9 of the 74 projects are presented and that the description of each project is brief. The full reports are posted in the searchable online collection. [7]

---

[6] The totals in this the table exceed 74 (i.e., the number of AiA teams reporting), because many teams used more than one assessment method and/or type of measure.

[7] Additional in-depth descriptions and discussions of academic library assessment methods will be included in a forthcoming book ACRL will publish with one AiA team leader as editor and other team leaders as contributors. The AiA facilitators are also working with the editors of ACRL's premier scholarly journal, *College and Research Libraries,* to consider a special 2016 issue focused exclusively on AiA projects as demonstrations of action research.

- Twenty-four institutions used a pre-test/post-test methodology to document changes in students' information literacy skills. Dakota State University, for example, focused its project on the impact of library instruction on the learning of research skills by master's degree-level students in the institution's online Educational Technology program. After completing an online library instruction tutorial as part of a research methods course, test scores increased. In Dakota State's project report, the team librarian noted the value of collaborating with the various campus units on the assessment project, "An important lesson learned from this project is the fact that when assessing the effect of the library on student learning, the library cannot do it alone. It takes the work of others within the university to truly do the work and collect meaningful data and analyze the effect."

- The development of an information literacy or similar rubric became a means for 40 libraries to gather data related to information literacy competencies. Claremont Colleges Library used a rubric to document that the information literacy competencies demonstrated in students' research papers were statistically significantly higher when a librarian was involved in first-year courses and syllabi design than with one-shot instruction. In addition, the rubric is used to assess senior theses, which provides the library with an opportunity to compile longitudinal data related to students' attainment of information literacy skills at the colleges.

- The University of Wisconsin-Eau Claire used a rubric in tandem with student reflection papers to assess the impact of the library on the development of information literacy skills by students who are enrolled in first-year composition courses. The AiA team was particularly interested in knowing if students learn when librarians collaborate with the faculty to introduce information literacy concepts. The rubric assessed students' skills related to attribution, communication of evidence, and evaluation of information. After analyzing the rubric scores from the data sample, the team concluded that greater integration of the library into writing courses will help students to apply their information literacy learning in all reading and writing experiences. End-of-semester reflection essays by the students also reinforced this conclusion. Those students who believed they achieved increased information literacy also produced research projects that received higher scores on the information literacy rubric.

- DePaul University developed a rubric to examine the reflective essays of first-generation students who participated in a self-guided library activity. The university's mission articulates a commitment to educating first-generation college students. First-generation students, however, can feel like outsiders and lack a sense of "belonging," which may contribute to academic disengagement. The library developed instructional materials for peer student leaders to deliver and grade as part of the university's First-Year Experience program. After participating in a self-guided library activity and reflecting on the process, would the students who complete the assignment be able to articulate how the library contributed to their success as learners? After using the rubric to score 97 reflective essays, the project team noted that the independent learning activities, when coupled with reflection, are an effective means for orienting students to the library and to academic life in general. Students reported an affective change towards library use, i.e., from anxiety to pride, and they were able to articulate multiple ways that the library can contribute to their academic success. As the team librarian noted, "Reflection papers may help librarians gain insight into how students navigate discovery systems and physical spaces, and students' affective relationship with libraries and research."

- Grinnell College was particularly interested in designing a student-centered approach to assessing the impact of research instruction sessions on student learning. The campus team asked students and faculty (rather than librarians) to rate student research bibliographies, and they surveyed the students about their research process. Although students were less confident in rating the timeliness and authority of the sources on their revised bibliographies, the students did revise their bibliographies following a research instruction session. Students also reported that they learned strategies for searching and evaluating sources.

- Grand Valley State University recently inaugurated its Knowledge Market, a collaborative service offered by the library, writing center, and speech lab. At the Knowledge Market, students can get help with assignments from peer consultants – other students – trained in research, writing, and speech presentation. The AiA team was interested in assessing the impact of the peer consultant program on students' attitudes, behaviors, knowledge, skills, or status. The team gathered descriptive and perceptual data from the research consultations, primarily through surveys. It was a highly collaborative method that required the various service partners to share data and methods. For example, lists of academic departments whose students used the service were shared with instruction librarians, which enabled them to provide timely and targeted instruction to high-need courses. Students reported high satisfaction with the Knowledge Market services, and the assessment findings were used to justify expansion of the services into freshman composition courses and to other campus locations. The peer consultants reported significant gains in communication skills, problem solving, flexibility, and adaptability. This collaborative assessment effort will be ongoing, and the lead team librarian reported, "The original Assessment in Action partners continue to discuss long-term assessment of the Knowledge Market and are using the independent program evaluations conducted this past year to inform that future planning."

- Prior to participating in AiA, Lasell College had focused its assessment activities on first-year students. The AiA project provided an opportunity to expand the library's assessment of students' information literacy skills by investigating the competencies of seniors. More specifically, the project team focused on seniors' critical thinking skills in relation to research. The project team implemented a mixed-methods assessment approach – focus groups, electronic surveys, and citation analysis – and found that assessment of learning is most effective when these multiple tools and data sources are used in combination. Results from the project indicate that students' information literacy skills vary, depending on requirements of their academic discipline.

- The AiA team at Murray State University aligned their assessment project with the institution's strategic priority on student retention. It used multiple library data sources (e.g., circulation, interlibrary loan, information literacy participation, lab and proxy logins, etc.) to assess the library's contribution to student retention. As the lead team librarian noted, "Prior to this project, we were making decisions about collections and instruction based on tally marks of use, and not knowing the depth or breadth of use." By triangulating the data sources, the team discovered that students who used the library in some way were nearly twice as likely to be retained from one semester to the next than students who did not use the library.

- Information literacy is one of <u>Anne Arundel Community College's</u> ten core competencies for graduating students. Given the importance of information literacy as a campus-wide core competency, the project team designed an assessment process that encompasses a combination of direct and indirect measures to investigate whether students are learning appropriate information literacy skills by the time they graduate. Numerous possible relationships were considered and will be investigated as the team continues to gather and review data: 1) evidence of student information literacy skills from student artifacts and the strength of a research assignment's directions, 2) evidence of student information literacy skills from student artifacts and student demographics, 3) frequency of faculty/librarian interactions and faculty confidence in assessing student information literacy skills, and 4) frequency of faculty/librarian interactions and course demographics (e.g., course discipline, delivery method, and duration). During the project's timeframe, only one set of measures could be gathered, but additional data will be marshalled to reach the two-semester benchmark established by the assessment design.

Library Factors and Connections to Student Learning and Success

Student learning and success encompasses a multitude of possible outcomes, and higher education institutions often define the outcomes in slightly different ways. Outcomes are typically delineated in relation to such factors as student enrollment, retention and persistence, performance and achievement, career preparedness, and graduation. Librarians are finding that they need to break apart the complex and interrelated aspects of learning to determine library impact. In addition, the various library factors that might be investigated have different types of impact on student learning and success. The primary learning outcomes and library factors considered in the AiA projects are summarized in Figures 3 and 4.[8] Thirteen projects are described in more detail to spotlight different ways that academic libraries are contributing to the academic success of students.

> *This project provided some evidence via GPA increases and student feedback, that our RA [research assistance] service is having a direct impact on academic performance and personal connections to the institution which then impact student retention.*
> — <u>Dalhousie University</u>

---

[8] Note: The totals in each figure exceed 74 (i.e., the number of AiA teams reporting), because the teams often examined more than one academic outcome and/or library factor.

Figure 3. Primary Academic Outcomes Examined.

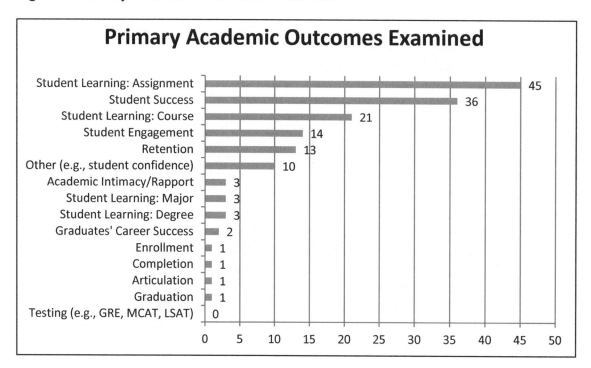

Figure 4. Primary Library Factors Examined.

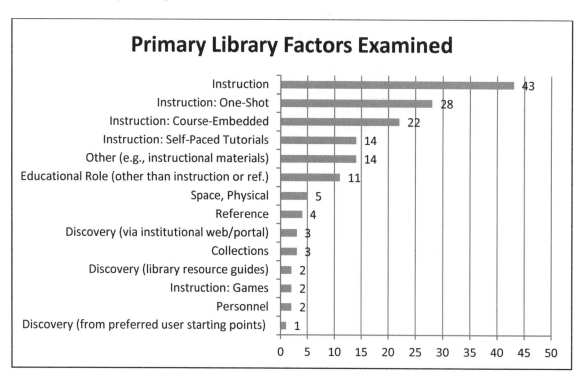

Library Instruction and General Education

> *To date, our project has significantly increased the library's role in assessment of General Education. ...This helps establish the library as an integral part of the campus culture of assessment of student learning outcomes, rather than an auxiliary unit assessing its own objectives.*
>
> – <u>University of Idaho</u>

To reach a high number of students and to establish a foundation of information literacy competencies for students as they progress through their academic careers, many academic libraries put a priority on instruction for students in general education, core curriculum, and required writing or English composition courses. Several AiA teams focused their assessment projects in this area by investigating the contribution of library instruction to the general education curriculum (31 teams) and English composition courses (18 teams), as exemplified by the two projects described below.

- The project team at <u>Kapi'olani Community College</u> was interested in aligning their assessment with the college's general education outcome goals related to critical thinking and inquiry and its strategic goal to support the success of Native Hawaiians. The team's guiding question was: How does customized library instruction for Hawaiian Studies students impact the attainment of information literacy skills? The library redesigned a library instruction learning tool called the Research Challenge and customized it for the Hawaiian Studies 270 course. The findings, collected from evaluation of student work using a <u>rubric</u> as well as student <u>survey</u> results, showed that the majority of students met or exceeded expectations for proficiency in finding sources, using these sources, and determining if the sources met their research needs. The assessment data also indicated competency areas that need improvement, and the librarians plan to review the library instruction program based on these results.

- <u>Southern Connecticut State University</u> connected its assessment project to the institution's strategic priority on student success as demonstrated by retention and graduation rates. The team investigated whether freshmen enrolled in classes that schedule library instruction sessions experience improved student success metrics (e.g., GPA, retention, engagement, iSkills score, etc.). Preliminary findings show that students in classes that have library instruction sessions are developing better library and information literacy skills than those students in classes that do not schedule a library session. The lead librarian also noted, "Getting the library involved in our campus's existing culture of assessment raises our profile and will ultimately demonstrate our value. . . . Our assessment will make it much easier to demonstrate the library's place in the university's commitment to student success."

Library Instruction and High-Impact Education Practices

The library's contribution to an institution's high-impact educational practices was considered by several AiA project teams. High-impact practices are focused, intensive instructional strategies aimed at increasing retention and student engagement, and they typically include first-year experiences, critical thinking courses, core curricula, and undergraduate research and writing intensive courses.[9] Three projects are highlighted to demonstrate this aspect of student learning and success.

- Arizona State University aims for a 90% persistence rate among its freshmen. With that goal as a framework, librarians collaborated with faculty to incorporate information literacy skills into the design of a new critical thinking course for at-risk freshmen. The project team documented that students who successfully completed the course persisted at a higher rate than those who did not take the course. More specifically, students who completed the course demonstrated increased knowledge of information literacy skills and higher levels of confidence in their information literacy skills, and these students also recognized the value of information literacy skills to their current and future academic work.

- When the Pacific Lutheran University team started their AiA experience, the librarian team leader knew that the university's First-Year Experience program had a strong assessment component, making it an ideal partner for the project. Building on this strength, the project team investigated the difference in impact on student learning of one-shot library instruction in comparison to multiple, shorter information literacy sessions. Data gathered from a citation analysis of final projects and a content analysis of student reflection surveys documented that students who received multiple information literacy sessions used library resources at a higher rate than students who participated in the one-shot sessions. The students receiving multiple sessions also reported using a greater variety of search strategies to find a broader range of sources.

- To promote persistence from semester to semester among students in developmental English courses, the AiA team at Santa Barbara City College was interested in assessing the library's impact on students' sense of belonging to the college community. They offered step-by-step customized information literacy instruction and promoted strong, positive relationships between the students and the librarians. They discovered that customized library instruction offered in multiple workshops can enhance the notion of librarian as coach and a source of support for student success, reinforce skills development, and encourage positive perceptions of library.

Library Instructional Games

As an alternative to traditional face-to-face library instruction sessions, academic libraries are increasingly creating interactive instructional games to promote information literacy competencies. As the findings from two AiA projects noted below demonstrate, library instructional games engage students, enhance information literacy competencies, and increase positive attitudes toward the library and its staff.

---

[9] Kuh, George D. *High-Impact Educational Practices: What They Are, Who Has Access to Them, and Why They Matter*. Washington, D.C.: Association of American Colleges and Universities, 2008.

- The <u>Indiana University of Pennsylvania</u> library developed a set of student-centered library outreach games, activities, and marketing materials in collaboration with the Student Affairs Division to engage students and promote the library in nonlibrary settings. Through self-reports by undergraduate students after they participated in library games or attended library events, the project team learned that students reported gains in information literacy skills, positive attitudes towards the library and its staff, and an increased likelihood of return visits to the library.

- <u>Radford University</u> developed two instructional games, the *Library Challenge Game* and the *Mobile Scavenger Game*, to address concerns about library anxiety among freshmen. The project team documented, through the use of an observational assessment <u>rubric</u> and a student <u>survey</u>, that the games did have a positive impact on the participating students' confidence related to use of the library and its resources. The project also demonstrated the library's role as an active contributor to the institution's increased attention to assessment across the campus. The team librarian found that "[t]he library games can be assessed in a way that is meaningful to the stakeholders both within and outside of the library."

Information Literacy and Multimedia Sources

Locating, evaluating, and using print resources, such as books and journal articles, have been a central focus of information literacy instruction. As students increasingly use multimedia sources in their coursework and research projects, academic librarians are considering how library instruction may need to be modified to take these additional sources and formats into account. One AiA team investigated this trend.

- <u>Mercy College</u> decided to examine how the library can most effectively adapt its information literacy instruction program to address students' increased use of multimedia sources. Their findings in a pilot assessment demonstrated results similar to their earlier assessment of information literacy instruction with print-only research projects. Most notably, students still struggle in the area of attribution. Their project reinforced the importance of expanding library instruction to include the growing repertoire of information sources that students may use.

Flipped Classroom Library Instruction

Some libraries are adapting the flipped classroom model to their instruction program by providing online information literacy tutorials that students view on their own and then using scheduled time in the library for students to work with librarians on developing research strategies and searching databases. Middlesex Community College focused its assessment project on an investigation of this instructional method.

- At <u>Middlesex Community College</u>, English Composition students have requested more hands-on time in the library, which gave the AiA team an opportunity to test the effectiveness of a flipped classroom model of instruction. Prior to participating in a class session in the library, students viewed online information literacy tutorials. The team found that students who were taught using the flipped classroom model of instruction achieved a higher level of mastery compared to students who received traditional one-shot library instruction. However, students who participated in the flipped classroom model reported a preference for the traditional lecture-style library class sessions, a finding that the library staff plans to investigate further.

Library Space and Learning

While the majority of AiA project teams investigated the impact of the library's reference, instruction, and information literacy program, 16 teams took into consideration other factors (e.g., collections, personnel, discovery) that may contribute to student academic success. Five of the 16 teams looked at the relationship of the library's physical facilities and space to student learning and success. Three sample projects are described below.

- Central Washington University investigated the impact of the Academic and Research Commons on student success for its AiA project. The Commons is a "one-stop shop" with tutoring services, reference librarians, and career services. Assessment results demonstrated that student performance in English 101 courses and the students' confidence levels regarding academic research and writing were higher when student use of the Commons' space and services was integrated into the course activities.

- Miami University's Information Commons and other dedicated technology spaces provide students with software, hardware, and staff expertise to assist with their completion of basic and complex academic projects. To move beyond simply collecting usage statistics, the AiA team documented that students who used the facilities were nearly four times more likely to score higher on a visual literacy rubric than those who did not.

- The University of Manitoba Libraries sponsors the "Long Night Against Procrastination" each semester. It is an all-night event during which the library provides its conventional services of reference, research assistance, and instruction – but during nontraditional hours. Before conducting an assessment of this event, the librarians assumed that the reference and writing services would be the most valuable factor for students. The AiA team discovered, however, that holding the event in the library produced the most significant impact, because the library space and facilities fostered social and academic support and community.

Library Use of Social Media

It is not uncommon for libraries to use social media, such as Facebook and blogs, to communicate with students and to promote library services and resources. The potential relationship of a library's social media communication to student academic success was examined by one of the AiA teams and is described below.

- Montana State University library uses social media, particularly Twitter, to engage students and to create avenues for instruction and library awareness. The AiA team decided to assess the impact of the library's social media program. Through interviews and focus groups with students, the team found that the social media program was particularly effective in building community and that this community-building contributed to student learning.

> *In terms of student learning and success, 75% or more of the students thought that the course contributed to their learning on five items measuring information literacy.*
>
> – George Mason University

Library Leadership and Evidence-Based Advocacy [10]

Leadership within the Library

At those libraries where some staff have designated assessment responsibilities, the AiA project was easily integrated into ongoing library assessment activities and evaluations of services, instructional programs, and collections. These libraries, in effect, already embraced a culture of assessment. For a significant number of the AiA librarians, however, assessment was not conducted on a continuous basis at their libraries. The AiA project put them in a new role in relation to the rest of the library staff. Several of the AiA librarians, for example, reported that their project work was somewhat isolated from other library activities. At times, the purpose of the project and the benefits to be gained from the assessment initiative were questioned by staff. As one librarian said, "[Some] library faculty are skeptical. . . . They did not want me to assess the instruction program."

The assessment projects required that the librarians increase communication and collaboration with other library staff. These interactions provided opportunities to inform the staff about the assessment process and its role in improving library services and resources. One of the team librarians commented, "Librarians have realized that talking about the value of students having a library experience as an undergraduate student is an important conversation we need to continue to have and explore." Many of the librarians reported that they are now considered the go-to person for assessment activities at their library. They also developed an awareness and understanding of the importance of continuous assessment, rather than relying on the results of individual, and often disconnected, assessment activities.

Leading the Project Teams

As noted earlier, the composition of the AiA project teams include at least two team members who are not part of the library's staff. The librarians who participated in the first year of the AiA program frequently mentioned the benefits of having different perspectives brought into the team discussions. Through their collaboration with the team members, the librarians learned about the functions and priorities of other campus units. One librarian commented, "My self confidence in interacting with individuals outside the library (e.g., campus administrators, faculty members)

---

[10] Some of the AiA project findings discussed in this section were first reported in presentations at the August 2014 Library Assessment Conference in Seattle, Wash.: Brown, Karen and Kara Malenfant. *Assessment in Action: High Impact Practices in Academic Libraries* and at the October 2014 Assessment Institute in Indianapolis, Ind.: Brown, Karen and Kara Malenfant. *Academic Libraries and Student Success: Findings and Applications from 70 Campus Teams.*

has increased significantly." Likewise, the librarians reported that team members who were not librarians gained an awareness of the library, particularly in terms of its contribution to student learning and success.

Table 2. AiA Team Members.

AiA Team Members	#
Teaching Faculty	54
Other Librarian	51
Assessment Office	28
Institutional Research	28
Library Administrator	21
Other (e.g., speech lab, teaching/learning center, doctoral student)	19
Campus Administrator	16
Student Affairs	12
Writing Center	10
Information/Academic Technology	5

Several librarians mentioned the value of having teaching faculty on the assessment team. While senior academic administrators may lend a certain cachet and leverage, the teaching faculty were particularly attuned to the potential instructional role of librarians and were helpful in designing assessment instruments that measure and document learning outcomes. As one librarian commented, "Teaching faculty believe in the value of information literacy."

During the 14-month project, several teams faced changes in membership. In a few cases, librarians moved on to new positions. More frequently, however, it was other members of the team who had to leave and be replaced. With these changes, group dynamics came into play. The challenges of accommodating a new team member often had more to do with the relationship aspect of group dynamics (i.e., personalities, styles of communication) than with the task aspect of group dynamics (i.e., who is doing what work), and the AiA librarians had to be proactive to manage the situation, as reflected by a librarian who commented, "I feel more confident in my ability to take a project from idea to completion and to engage with other professionals on campus to make it work."

Sustaining project momentum was one of the most significant challenges encountered by the librarians leading the teams. After the initial enthusiasm of launching the project, lack of time and competing priorities often took their toll. The librarians reported that when this type of disengagement started to emerge, they realized that their role as team leaders necessitated intentional and directed facilitation, including establishing a clear timeline for tasks, delegating responsibilities, and providing frequent updates. They became aware of the need not only to facilitate the group's activities but also to *lead* the collaboration.

Forging Partnerships across the Campus

> *Rockhurst's AiA project facilitated collaboration between departments and schools at the university and serves as a great example of a cross-campus assessment project.*
>
> – Rockhurst University

The librarians reported that the visibility of the library and librarians as partners on campus increased greatly as a result of the AiA projects. The word *visibility* was used again and again by the AiA librarians in their project reports. Campus administrators knew about the AiA project, because they had to sign off on the application and agree to support the assessment project (i.e., expenses, access to resources). These administrators talked with other campus administrators and faculty about the project. In addition, the team members from the different campus units talked about the project with their colleagues.

Many of the librarians also gave presentations about their project at various campus events. One librarian commented, "I was asked to speak on a panel about the progress of our project at a [workshop] last fall. This brought positive attention to the project and the library." In fact, administrators and academic staff often now mention the AiA project as a model and encourage others on campus to consult with the librarians to learn more about assessment. Institutional buy-in from campus administrators and the librarians' work with team members have expanded the library's sphere of influence on many campuses, as reflected in this statement by one of the librarians: "[AiA] signaled a change in focus for [our library], from assessment 'for internal use only' to assessment for internal and external stakeholders."

> *Our experience with this project (which will be ongoing) and knowledge of assessment principles has boosted our profile and we are now being called upon to provide assessment guidance with related projects.*
>
> – Dalhousie University

Creating a Community of Practice for Academic Library Assessment

> *Most importantly, I've identified AiA participants, both in and outside my cohort, working on assessment activities similar to ours. I feel I have a network of people I can collaborate and brainstorm with.*
>
> – AiA librarian
> (from reflective report)

In the AiA learning cohorts and within the larger AiA learning community, sharing ideas and lending general support were critical to the success of most of the projects. The librarians had shared goals and were pursuing inquiry through a collective learning experience. They reported that the face-to-face professional development sessions, in particular, enhanced collaboration.

The online learning was efficient and promoted communication but was not always the preferred mode for collaboration. As some librarians noted, participation in the online environment was occasionally uneven. While supportive communication and collaboration were certainly helpful throughout the program, critical commentary was also valued. The librarians noted the usefulness of the peer review process when designing their research questions and developing their poster presentations. Peer review seemed to be best when it integrated knowledge sharing and encouragement with structured criticism and feedback.

The AiA experience has also fostered networking among the librarians. A number of librarians reported that they are partnering with one another to prepare conference presentations and write professional journal articles. Thus, collaboration is being sustained beyond the scheduled AiA activities.

AiA was designed to foster a community of practice around assessment work in academic libraries. Etienne Wenger-Trayner, who originated the term *Communities of Practice,* defines it as "[A group] of people who share a concern or a passion for something they do and learn how to do it better as they interact regularly."[11] The review of AiA project reports indicates that a community of practice does seem to be developing. The librarians are sharing knowledge and experience as they work toward a common goal. As one librarian explained, "I know how collaborative [assessment] has to be to succeed. I know it's OK if something doesn't work the first time. I know colleagues from AiA that I can correspond with!" Another librarian also focused on the benefits of being part of an assessment community that extends beyond the AiA experience, "My AiA experiences have made me aware of how important it is to have a group of people all working towards a purpose together . . . both from AiA and my colleagues." As exemplified by these comments, the librarians are referencing the AiA learning community as a source for collaboration and building one's personal and professional capacity to lead academic library assessment activities at their institutions.

> *I think the conversations that stem from all of our projects [have] been really important . . . and the community created a forum for thinking about other projects and asking questions about other projects.*
>
> – AiA librarian
> (from reflective report)

Conclusion
The assessment findings of the 74 projects from the first year of the AiA program address numerous aspects of student learning and success on campuses across North America, and they document multiple ways that academic librarians can engage and lead campus representatives in library assessment initiatives. The projects provide methods and tools that can be replicated or adapted to a wide variety of higher education settings and context. As a result, academic

---

[11] Wenger-Trayner, Etienne. *Communities of Practice: A Brief Introduction.* www.wenger-trayner.com/theory. Etienne Wenger-Trayner, together with his business partner, Beverly Wenger-Trayner, advised the AiA facilitation team during the design process and attended the first in-person meeting of the AiA teams.

librarians can leverage and expand their role in assessment work at higher education institutions. In addition, the AiA projects advance awareness, understanding, and collaboration among higher education stakeholders around issues of library value on campuses and in the wider postsecondary education community.

APPENDIX A: ACRL and the Value of Academic Libraries Initiative

The AiA program is grounded in several ACRL initiatives, dating back to the early 1980s with the publication of *Measuring Academic Library Performance: A Practical Approach*, an assessment manual that sought to "stimulate librarians' interest in performance measures and to provide practical assistance so that librarians could conduct meaningful measurements of effectiveness with minimum expense and difficulty."[12] More recently, one of the three goal areas identified in the association's 2011 strategic plan, *The Plan for Excellence*, focuses on the value of academic libraries, and a standing committee – the Value of Academic Libraries– was established to develop and implement recommendations. In ACRL's 2012 membership survey, members were asked to select the top three issues facing academic and research librarianship today, and "Demonstrating the value of the library and librarians" was cited as a top issue facing all member segments, regardless of job title or type of library.[13]

ACRL published *Value of Academic Libraries: A Comprehensive Research Review and Report*[14] in 2010 as a review of the quantitative and qualitative literature, methodologies, and best practices currently in place for demonstrating the value of academic libraries. The report made many recommendations, and a key opportunity where ACRL has great strength was the recommendation that the association, "create a professional development program to build the profession's capacity to document, demonstrate, and communicate library value in alignment with the mission and goals of their colleges and universities." To understand how to shape such a program, ACRL convened two national summits, which were held November 29 to December 1, 2011 in Chicago, to explore and discuss strategies that prepare the library community to document and communicate the library's value in advancing the missions and goals of their colleges and universities. ACRL partnered with the Association for Institutional Research, the Association of Public and Land-grant Universities, and the Council of Independent Colleges to plan and hold these summits, with grant funding from the Institute of Museum and Library Services. The summits brought together representatives from 22 postsecondary institutions, including senior librarians, chief academic administrators, and institutional researchers, for discussions about library impact. Fifteen representatives from higher education organizations and associations also participated in the summits. A report[15] summarizes the discussions at the summits and presents recommendations based on four broad themes about the dynamic nature of higher education assessment:

- Accountability drives higher education discussions.
- A unified approach to institutional assessment is essential.

---

[12] Van House, Nancy A., Beth T. Weil, and Charles R. McClure. *Measuring Academic Library Performance: A Practical Approach*. Chicago: American Library Association, 1990.

[13] *2012 ACRL Membership Survey: Final Report*. Prepared by Mary Jane Petrowski and Avenue M Group, LLC. November 19, 2012.

[14] Association of College and Research Libraries. *Value of Academic Libraries: A Comprehensive Research Review and Report*. Researched by Megan Oakleaf. Chicago: Association of College and Research Libraries, 2010. Published online at www.acrl.ala.org/value.

[15] Association of College and Research Libraries. *Connect, Collaborate, and Communicate: A Report from the Value of Academic Libraries Summits*. Prepared by Karen Brown and Kara J. Malenfant. Chicago: Association of College and Research Libraries, 2012. Published online at www.acrl.ala.org/value.

- Student learning and success are the primary focus of higher education assessment.
- Academic administrators and accreditors seek evidenced-based reports of measureable impact.

Building on the findings of these summits, ACRL designed Assessment in Action: Academic Libraries and Student Success (AiA), a professional development program to strengthen the competencies of librarians in assessment, campus leadership, and data-informed advocacy about library value. In partnership with the Association for Institutional Research and the Association of Public and Land-grant Universities, ACRL received a second grant from IMLS to implement AiA. The Council of Independent Colleges is serving on the project's advisory board. During the three-year AiA project (2013-2016), over 200 institutions will participate in the program. As described in this report, the AiA projects are connecting academic librarians with campus partners in novel ways to examine and discover how they bring value to their institutions.

APPENDIX B: Final Report Template for AiA Team Leaders

DOCUMENT 1: Institutional and Library Profile

Note to Team Leaders: This section will be pre-populated for you with information from NCES and other existing public data sources. Team leaders will not be able to edit this section.

1. Name of institution

2. Basic classification

3. FTE enrollment

4. U.S. Regional Accrediting organization

5. Sector Affiliation

6. Fiscal Affiliation

7. Information literacy is student learning outcome for institution

8. Total librarians and other professional staff

9. Total library expenditures (salaries and wages, materials and operating)

DOCUMENT 2: AiA Project Description

*Directions to Team Leaders: Please tell us about your project. All the information in this project description section will be publicly searchable. Be sure to proofread/spell check before you submit. We will be publishing the information exactly as you enter it, without review. You can start the report, save, then come back and complete it later. You have until **June 23** to complete this section of the report.*

1. Primary outcome examined (select one or more)
   o student learning: assignment
   o student learning: course
   o student learning: major
   o student learning: degree
   o student engagement
   o student experience
   o student success
   o academic intimacy/rapport
   o enrollment
   o retention
   o completion
   o graduation

o articulation
o graduates' career success
o testing (e.g., GRE, MCAT, LSAT, CAAP, CLA, MAPP)
o Other (please describe) : _____

2. Primary library factor examined (select one or more)
   o instruction
   o instruction: games
   o instruction: one shot
   o instruction: course embedded
   o instruction: self-paced tutorials
   o reference
   o educational role (other than reference or instruction)
   o space, physical
   o discovery (library resources integrated in institutional web and other information portals)
   o discovery (library resource guides)
   o discovery (from preferred user starting points)
   o collections (quality, depth, diversity, format, or currency)
   o personnel (number and quality)
   o Other (please describe) : _____

3. Student population (select one or more)
   o undergraduate
   o graduate
   o incoming
   o graduating
   o pre-college/developmental/basic skills
   o Other (please describe) : _____

4. Discipline (select one or more)
   o Arts
   o Humanities
   o Social sciences
   o Natural sciences (i.e., space, earth, life, chemistry, or physics)
   o Formal sciences (i.e., computer sciences, logic, mathematics, statistics, or systems science)
   o Professions/applied sciences
   o English composition
   o General education
   o Information literacy credit course
   o Other (please describe) : _____

5. AiA team members (select one or more)
   o assessment office
   o institutional research
   o teaching faculty
   o writing center

o information/academic technology
o student affairs
o campus administrator
o library administrator
o other librarian
o Other (please describe) : _____

6. Methods and tools (select one or more)
    o survey
    o interviews
    o focus group(s)
    o observation
    o pre/post test
    o rubric
    o Other (please describe) : _____

7. Direct data type (artifact) (select one or more)
    o student portfolio
    o research paper/project
    o class assignment (other than research paper/project)
    o Other (please describe)

8. Indirect data type (select one or more)
    o test scores
    o GPA
    o degree completion rate
    o retention rate
    o Other (please describe) : _____

9. Executive Summary
    (150 words open)
    Prompts:
- How does the project align with your institution's priorities and needs?
- Why did you choose the outcome and library factor as areas to examine?
- What was the project's primary inquiry question?
- Why was the team composition appropriate?

10. Contribution
    (150 words open)
    Prompts:
- What are the significant contributions of your project?
- What was learned about assessing the library's impact on student learning and success?
- What was learned about creating or contributing to a culture of assessment on campus?
- What, if any, are the significant findings of your project?

11. Conclusions, Implications, and Recommendations
    (150 words open)
    Prompts:
    - What will you change as a result of what you learned (– e.g., institutional activities, library functions or practices, personal/professional practice, other)?
    - How does this project contribute to current, past, or future assessment activities on your campus?

12. PDF of poster (Permitted file types: pdf, doc, docx, rtf, xls, xlsx, csv, jpg, jpeg, png, gif, tif, tiff, ppt. Maximum file size is 5 megabytes.)
    (upload)

13. More information
    (150 words open)
    Prompts: Please list any articles published, presentations given, URL of project website, and team leader contact details.

DOCUMENT 3: Reflective Report

Directions to Team Leaders: *Please tell us about your experiences working on your project and being part of the AiA learning community. The information for this reflective section of the report remains confidential and will never be public or searchable. Karen Brown, our project analyst, will analyze this section across the entire AiA team leader group to see if there are patterns by type of institution, type of outcome examined, type of method/tool used, etc. She will synthesize and report without any identifying information. You can start the report, save, then come back and complete it later. You have **until June 23** to complete this section of the report.*

Project Experiences

1. What contributed to the success of the project?

2. What problems or delays did you encounter? How did you address or resolve these problems?

3. How has the project contributed to assessment activities on your campus?

4. Thinking about your campus assessment team, what factors contributed to a positive experience for the team members?

5. Did your campus assessment team encounter challenges during the project as a result of group dynamics, roles, assumptions, expectations, or other issues? Please explain and indicate how you or other group members addressed the challenge(s).

6. How has your campus assessment project changed administrators', faculty, and/or students' perceptions of the value of the library?

7. What have been the reactions of other library staff to your involvement in this project?

8. How will your library and institution use the results of the project?

9. How will the assessment activity created through the project be sustained on your campus?

<u>AiA Cohort and Community of Practice Experiences</u>

10. Describe 2-3 meaningful experiences within AiA that contributed in significant ways to your action learning project (e.g., your cohort, Moodle activities, in person meetings, other means). Why were they significant?

11. What specific competencies or insights have you gained as a result of the AiA experience?

12. What information or resources were particularly useful to you during the project?

13. How have your AiA experiences influenced your professional practice? What difference has it made to your performance? What has it enabled that would not have happened otherwise?

14. How prepared are you now to lead similar projects?

15. How have your learning and experiences contributed to and enriched the AiA community of practice?

16. If you were given the opportunity within AiA to focus more deeply on one more element, theory or concept, what would that have been?

CHAPTER 4

Documented Library Contributions to Student Learning and Success:

Building Evidence with Team-Based Assessment in Action Campus Projects*

Association of College and Research Libraries. Prepared by Karen Brown. Contributions by Kara J. Malenfant.

* Association of College and Research Libraries. "*Documented Library Contributions to Student Learning and Success: Building Evidence with Team-Based Assessment in Action Campus Projects.*" Prepared by Karen Brown with contributions by Kara J. Malenfant. Chicago: Association of College and Research Libraries, 2016. Published online at www.acrl.ala.org/value.

Association of College & Research Libraries
A division of the American Library Association

Citation:
Association of College and Research Libraries. "Documented Library Contributions to Student Learning and Success: Building Evidence with Team-Based Assessment in Action Campus Projects." Prepared by Karen Brown with contributions by Kara J. Malenfant. Chicago: Association of College and Research Libraries, 2016

Published online at www.acrl.ala.org/value.

About the Authors

Karen Brown is a professor at Dominican University (River Forest, Illinois) in the Graduate School of Library and Information Science and teaches in the areas of assessment, collection management, foundations of the profession, and literacy and learning. Prior to joining Dominican University's faculty in 2000, she developed and coordinated continuing education programs for the Chicago Library System, one of Illinois's former regional library systems. She has also held positions focusing on collection development, reference, and instruction at the University of Wisconsin, University of Maryland, Columbia University, and Bard College. She holds a PhD in media studies from New York University and master's degrees in library science and adult education from the University of Wisconsin.

Kara J. Malenfant is a senior staff member at ACRL, where she coordinates government relations advocacy and scholarly communication activities and is the lead staff member on the Value of Academic Libraries initiative and Assessment in Action program. She provides consulting services on organization development and use of ACRL's standards for libraries in higher education. Kara began her position at ACRL in fall of 2005, after working for six years at DePaul University Libraries in Chicago. A former Peace Corps volunteer, she holds a PhD in leadership and change from Antioch University and a master's degree in library science from the University of Illinois at Urbana-Champaign.

Contents

Executive Summary

Academic librarians from across North America continued to expand assessment practices through their participation in the Association of College and Research Libraries' (ACRL) three-year program, Assessment in Action: Academic Libraries and Student Success (AiA).[1] Launched in 2013 by ACRL, in partnership with the Association of Institutional Research and the Association of Public Land-grant Universities, and with funding from the U.S. Institute of Museum and Library Services, AiA is helping over 200 postsecondary institutions of all types investigate the library's impact on student learning and academic success. By promoting library leadership in campus-wide assessment projects, libraries are demonstrating contributions to issues of institutional significance.

Although each campus team carries out an assessment project that is unique to the institution's academic mission and priorities, the findings about different ways that libraries are contributing to students' learning benefit the higher education community as a whole by expanding the body of evidence-based assessment results related to students' academic experiences. In addition, the numerous approaches, methods, and tools that the campus teams use to assess library impact can be replicated in or adapted to a variety of different institutional settings and customized to align with specific campus academic priorities.

Compelling Evidence for Library Contributions to Student Learning and Success

The AiA project findings add support to a growing body of evidence that demonstrates positive contributions of academic libraries to student learning and success in four key areas. The findings about library impact in each of the four areas described below, which come from assessment projects conducted at different types of institutions, are particularly strong because they consistently point to the library as a positive influencing factor on students' academic success.

1. *Students benefit from library instruction in their initial coursework.*
   Information literacy instruction provided to students during their initial coursework helps them acquire a common set of competencies for their undergraduate studies. The assessment findings from numerous AiA projects that focused on information literacy initiatives for freshmen and new students underscore that students receiving this instruction perform better in their courses than students who do not.

2. *Library use increases student success.*
   Several AiA studies point to increased academic success when students use the library. The analysis of multiple data points (e.g., circulation, library instruction session attendance, online databases access, study room use, interlibrary loan) shows that students who use the library in some way achieve higher levels of academic success (e.g., GPA, course grades, retention) than students who did not use the library.

---

[1] This executive summary is available online as a separate document, formatted to share broadly with campus stakeholders. See www.ala.org/acrl/files/issues/value/y2_summary.pdf.

3. *Collaborative academic programs and services involving the library enhance student learning.*
   Academic library partnerships with other campus units, such as the writing center, academic enrichment, and speech lab, yield positive benefits for students (e.g., higher grades, academic confidence, retention).

4. *Information literacy instruction strengthens general education outcomes.*
   Several AiA projects document that libraries improve their institution's general education outcomes and demonstrate that information literacy contributes to inquiry-based and problem-solving learning, including critical thinking, ethical reasoning, global understanding, and civic engagement.

Building Evidence for Library Contributions to Students' Academic Success
Additional areas of library impact are also being investigated by AiA campus teams. While these impact areas may not have been studied as extensively as the four areas described in the previous section or the project findings may not be as consistently strong, the assessment results do build evidence for positive connections between the library's services and resources and student learning and success as noted below:
- Student retention improves with library instructional services.
- Library research consultation services boost student learning.
- Library instruction adds value to a student's long-term academic experience.
- The library promotes academic rapport and student engagement.
- Use of library space relates positively to student learning and success.

Findings about Higher Education Assessment
A team-based approach to assessment on each campus is an essential element of the AiA program design. The project reports frequently mention the value of collaboration as the campus teams investigated connections between the library and student learning. Four benefits of collaborative assessment in particular have emerged:
- The collaborative work among the team members promotes a shared understanding of an institution's academic priorities and the contributions of various campus stakeholders to these priorities.
- Collaboration leads to important discussions about student learning and academic success, which result in a clearer articulation and increased agreement about the definition, description, and measurement of student learning and success attributes.
- By leading a campus team through an assessment project, the AiA librarians build collaborative and results-oriented leadership competencies that contribute directly to improving student learning and success at the institution.
- As campus team leaders, the AiA librarians advance the mission of the library in alignment with institutional priorities.

Introduction

Academic librarians from across North America continued to expand assessment practices in the second year of the Association of College and Research Libraries' (ACRL) three-year Assessment in Action: Academic Libraries and Student Success (AiA) program. Campus teams led by librarians reported to the ACRL community, at academic conferences, and in professional and scholarly journals about their investigations of library contributions to aspects of student learning and success.[2] These assessment projects build on the findings of the 74 campus teams that completed the first year of the program.[3]

The AiA program was launched in 2013 by ACRL, in partnership with the Association of Institutional Research and the Association of Public Land-grant Universities, and with funding from the U.S. Institute of Museum and Library Services. Three primary goals frame the project's activities:

1. Develop academic librarians' professional competencies needed to document and communicate the value of the academic library in relation to an institution's goals for student learning and success.

2. Strengthen collaborative relationships with higher education stakeholders, including campus faculty, academic administrators, and assessment officers.

3. Contribute to higher education assessment by creating approaches, strategies, and practices that document the contribution of academic libraries.

The AiA program is helping over 200 postsecondary institutions of all types create partnerships at their institution to promote library leadership and engagement in campus-wide assessment. Each participating institution establishes a team with a lead librarian and at least two people from other campus units. Team members frequently include teaching faculty and administrators from such departments as the assessment office, institutional research, the writing center, academic technology, and student affairs. Over a 14-month period, the librarians lead their campus teams in the development and implementation of a project that aims to contribute to assessment activities at their institution.

The librarian team leaders are supported throughout the project by a peer-to-peer, blended learning community that combines in-person workshops and online professional development activities that emphasize skill building through collaborative problem solving and bridging theory to practice. This participatory and engaged learning approach promotes the action

---

[2] Individual teams' descriptive project reports are available at https://apply.ala.org/aia/public. Additionally, a comprehensive bibliography at http://www.acrl.ala.org/value/?page_id=980 lists dozens of journal articles, conference presentations, and other public reports. It aims to capture all scholarly and practice-based literature and presentations about AiA and campus projects conducted as part of the AiA program by campus team members, facilitators, and ACRL staff.

[3] Read more about the first-year participating institutions in the January 2015 report synthesizing results, "Academic Library Contributions to Student Success: Documented Practices from the Field," available at http://www.ala.org/acrl/files/issues/value/contributions_report.pdf

research focus of AiA. As each campus team identifies important questions related to institutional priorities and addresses them through a collaborative assessment process, the findings promote meaningful action around student learning and inform future library practice. Through these projects, the AiA librarians take a leadership role that has resulted in increasing the visibility of the library and its contributions to academic initiatives on the campuses.

> *Overall, [the project] contributes to the increasingly high-profile role the library is playing in college-wide assessment efforts, with administrators now consistently appointing librarians to key assessment committees and assessment-focused search committees.*
>
> —AiA librarian, reflective report

This report focuses on the assessment projects conducted by those teams that participated in the second year of the program, from April 2014 to June 2015, and presented poster sessions at the 2015 American Library Association Annual Conference in San Francisco, California, June 26 and June 27. In addition, each team leader completed a final project descriptive report, which includes abstracts and images of the posters. These reports are fully searchable in an online collection. Each team leader was also asked to complete a reflective report and, while these second reports are kept confidential, aggregate and anonymous comments from the reflective reports have contributed to this synthesis. This publication is also informed by results from two focus groups undertaken in June 2015 with a total of 21 AiA second-year team leaders. The projects described in this report highlight only a few of the projects; the full reports of 64 projects are posted in the searchable database.

Institutional Teams Represent a Variety of Higher Education Settings

The 64 higher education institutions that completed and reported on their participation in the second year of the AiA program included a variety of types of colleges and universities and came from 34 states in the United States as well as from Canada (see table 1 and figure 1).

Table 1. Types of Institutions for AiA Teams

Institution Type	Year 1	Year 2	Total
Associate's Colleges	10	11	21
Baccalaureate Colleges	7	15	22
Master's Colleges and Universities	31	10	41
Doctoral/Research Universities	6	3	9
Research Universities	18	22	40
Tribal University	1	0	1
Special Focus Institutions	1	3	4

Figure 1. Map of Institutions Selected to Participate in the Second Year of AiA.

The work of the campus teams is contributing to their institution's ongoing assessment activities, and the lead librarians have noted that their findings are often spotlighted in accreditation reports. The institutions are represented by a variety of different accrediting bodies, including seven U.S. regional and one Canadian (see table 2).

> *Reviewers' comments spoken during recent site-visits by . . . accreditation agencies, made it evident to my community of scholars and administrators that our library services and learning outcomes of our information literacy instruction associated with the Assessment in Action project were innovative and aligned with best practices in higher education.*
>
> —AiA librarian, reflective report

Table 2. The Accreditation Agencies of AiA Institutions

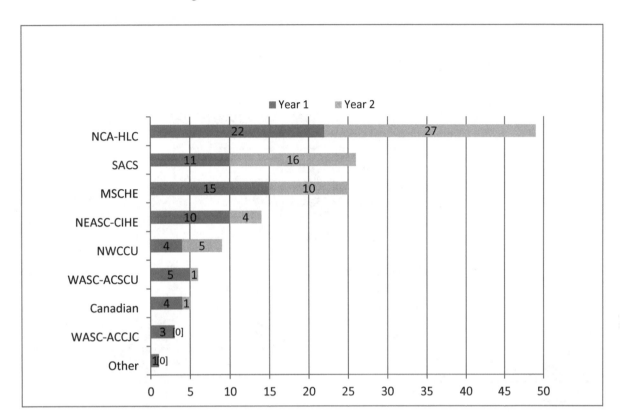

Connections between Library Factors and Academic Outcomes Investigated

The campus teams considered different library factors (e.g., collections, space, instruction, reference, etc.) and their possible connection to aspects of student learning and success (e.g., course or program learning outcomes, student confidence, retention, persistence) in relation to the institution's mission and academic priorities. Each team formulated an inquiry question that provided a framework for its assessment project by positing a relationship between the library and student learning or success. The questions also indicated the type of data needed to measure the library factors and academic outcome attributes and the method(s) most appropriate for collecting the data. Connections between 14 different academic outcomes and 14 distinct library factors have been assessed during the two years of the program (see tables 3 and 4).

Table 3. The Number of AiA Projects that Assessed Academic Outcome

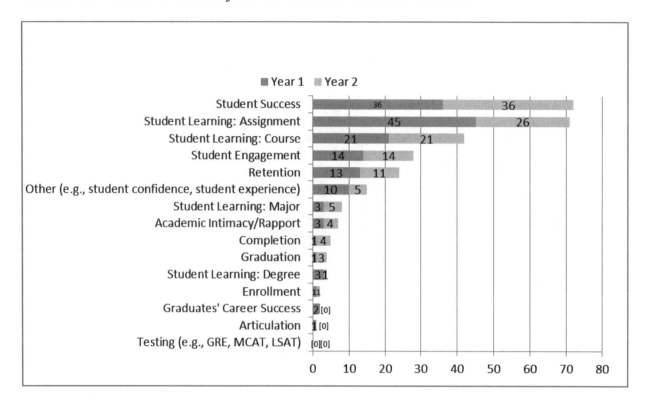

Table 4. The Number of AiA Projects that Assessed a Library Factor

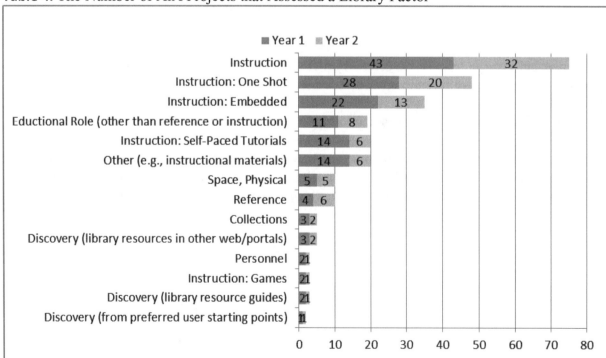

The following ten sample inquiry questions from the second year of the program reflect the variety of student learning and success factors investigated.

- Will an evidence-based medicine instruction session improve students' accuracy and source quality in answering clinical questions? (A.T. Still University)
- How does information literacy contribute to critical thinking in undergraduate students? (Arkansas Tech University)

- What understanding do students have of the concepts of "web" and "database"? (Des Moines Area Community College)

- What is the influence of instructional collaboration between global learning faculty and library faculty on students' information literacy? (Florida International University)

- Does one-shot information competency library instruction in courses prior to English 103, a freshman/sophomore-level research and writing course, contribute to students' success in English 103? (Pierce College at Fort Steilacoom)

- Does student use of library resources, spaces, and services correlate with greater self-efficacy in student-defined measures of success? (Wake Forest University)

- What impact does the number of library instruction sessions and access to a course LibGuide have on the quality of sources students enrolled in developmental reading use for a course project? (Joliet Junior College)

- Does a residentially embedded peer reference service positively impact students' academic success and retention? (Michigan State University)

- How do the library's facility and physical spaces impact the student success of undergraduate transfer students and STEM majors? (University of North Carolina Wilmington)

- Is there a relationship between the use of personalized library services by at-risk students and academic success? (Fulton-Montgomery Community College)

An Expanded Array of Replicable Assessment Approaches for Demonstrating Contributions

The increasing variety of methods and tools that the AiA teams have used to assess library impact are expanding and creating new approaches and practices that academic librarians can share and incorporate into their campus assessment initiatives. Many of the assessment approaches can be replicated or adapted for use in a variety of different institutional settings and customized to align with specific campus academic priorities.[4]

---

[4] For more on assessment techniques, see the recently released casebook showcasing 27 reflections by first-year AiA team leaders on the inquiry methods they used in their assessment projects, *Putting Assessment into Action: Selected Projects from the First Cohort of the Assessment in Action Grant*, ed. Eric Ackermann (Chicago: Association of College and Research Libraries, 2016).

> *My biggest insight from this project was the realization that it is possible to measure the impact of attitudes and confidence in a meaningful way in relation to library instruction. This insight, I believe, will be the beginning of a new way to approach assessment that I will apply in future projects.*
>
> —AiA librarian, reflective report

The approaches are developed to guide the collection of the data needed to answer the inquiry question formulated by the campus team. Surveys, rubrics, and pre- and posttests were the most common methods employed by teams in Year 2, which parallels the types of assessment methods most frequently used by AiA teams in the previous year. Fifty percent of the campus teams in Year 2 combined two or more assessment methods for their studies. This mixed-methods approach typically brought together quantitative and qualitative data for analysis, leading to a robust, contextualized assessment of the factors being investigated. The two projects described below highlight this approach.

- At <u>Montclair State University</u>, the assessment project focused on government documents and data information literacy in the e-sciences, specifically as it relates to the university's new master's in public health program. A multimodal assessment process was implemented that included pre- and posttest measurements of one-session information literacy class outcomes, use of embedded online research guides, student reports of the influence on their learning of one-on-one research appointments with librarians, and faculty perceptions of the library's impact on students' success in two public health courses. The team found that these multiple assessment methods captured both quantitative and qualitative measures of student learning and also took into account the different learning styles of students.

- The <u>Utah State University</u> campus team investigated the relationship between course grades and library instruction provided to psychology students at strategic points during their degree-specific coursework. Although the team began with one assessment method, an analysis of grade transcripts, it soon incorporated two additional tools to supplement the initial data and inform future directions: (1) student surveys of confidence with research skills and proficiency, and (2) a faculty focus group to determine skills that instructors want their students to have to be successful. The team found correlations between library instruction and higher grades. The lead librarian noted the benefits of collecting quantitative and qualitative data, "While some of the correlations are slight, we believe the feedback we received from students and faculty in the qualitative portion will increase those connections."

The following table presents a summary of assessment methods and tools used in Year 1 and Year 2 projects.

Table 5. Summary of Assessment Methods and Tools

Assessment Methods and Tools	Year 1	Year 2	Total[5]
Survey	41	31	72
Rubric	40	26	66
Pre- and Posttest	24	23	47
Other (e.g., correlational analysis, content analysis)	20	15	35
Observation	11	9	20
Interviews	13	7	20
Focus Group(s)	10	6	16

Mining Data with Embedded Technology Applications

Some assessment tools and methods introduced AiA campus teams to new approaches for documenting connections between the library and the academic success of students. The use of technology applications embedded in library systems and e-learning platforms, for example, provided a means for the campus teams to mine library data and assess academic outcomes. The three projects described below focused on this approach.

- To assess the contribution of the library's Ask-a-Librarian service to student retention, the campus team at Colorado Mesa University used LibAnalytics data and SPSS to determine connections with student reenrollment or graduation. The assessment project also collected qualitative feedback from students using a LibAnalytics form and with a follow-up survey administered to a subset of students.

> *In the past, the library had only "we think" and "we feel" anecdotal student success contributions—we could be qualitative about ourselves, reflectively, but had little data to support these statements. Now we have some and will continue growing that pool of data from our various services, so that we can analyze and contribute further to assessment activities.*
>
> —Colorado Mesa University

- Since 2007, the CUNY Borough of Manhattan Community College has provided 24/7 chat reference using OCLC's QuestionPoint service. To understand better how the service was being used, the campus team analyzed the chat reference transcripts generated during 2013, which document approximately 810 transactions. By using both quantitative and qualitative measures, the library learned that the service's users are persistent (i.e., logging in more than once), but English fluency issues and technology barriers are challenges to the service's effectiveness for some students. These findings have prompted expanded discussion about library best practices and ways to address issues that may detract from the academic success of community college students.

---

[5] The totals on the table columns do not add up to 74, 64, or 138 (i.e., the number of AiA teams reporting on Year 1, Year 2 and Years 1–2, respectively) because many teams used more than one assessment method and/or type of measure.

- The <u>City University of Seattle's</u> project investigated how librarian-created modules and library-hosted discussion forums embedded in the university's learning management system, Blackboard, are used by students. The primary goal was to develop processes and methods for assessing the library's instruction program and to collect baseline data. The institution's information technology director created a report that showed, in real time, the number of times students clicked in librarians' modules and forums. This data set was correlated with students' scores on the university's information literacy rubric. With this baseline data, the library staff has been able to identify potential gaps in its provision of instruction to the university's students and plans to initiate conversations with faculty about ways to ensure adequate and equal levels of library support across the university.

Using the Framework for Information Literacy for Assessment

During the second year of the AiA program, the draft *Framework for Information Literacy for Higher Education* (developed by ACRL) was introduced, discussed within the academic library profession, revised, and eventually accepted by the ACRL Board of Directors. Draft versions of the *Framework* were used by two campus teams to assess and redesign their library instruction.

- The <u>Florida International University</u> campus team focused on a university priority, Global Learning for Global Citizenship. Through this university initiative, the library reaches every student, which provided an opportunity to study instructional collaboration between discipline faculty and library faculty. The team began by creating a global learning information framework of 40 indicators based on the *Framework for Information Literacy* (June 17, 2014, draft version) and then aligned it with the Association of American Colleges & Universities Information Literacy VALUE Rubric. Although 100% of the discipline faculty and librarians who participated in the assessment agreed that "information literacy is an important student competency" and 93% of these faculty agreed that information literacy "should be taught collaboratively," the AiA team found that there is confusion among discipline faculty about the definition of information literacy, and the discipline faculty and librarians perceive students' information literacy competency performance differently. In general, discipline faculty tended to define information literacy in terms of skill-based and process-based concepts, rather than essential concepts about information, research, and scholarship. Librarians perceived student performance significantly lower than the global learning faculty on 16 of the 40 Global Learning Information Literacy Framework indicators. The four areas with the most significant difference in perceptions of students' information literacy performance were (1) research as inquiry, (2) authority is contextual and constructed, (3) format as process, and (4) information has value. As a result of these findings, the library will expand its collaboration with the global learning faculty, including discussions to clarify information literacy concepts.

- When a new curriculum was implemented at <u>Luther Seminary</u> in 2014, courses in which students typically received information literacy instruction were eliminated. The *Framework for Information Literacy* provided a means for the library to restructure its approach to instruction. The librarians worked with five faculty over two semesters and used the *Framework* to match information literacy skills with course assignments; develop rubrics; survey students; gather data; and look for ways to improve library services, instruction, and support. As an initial piece of the university's move towards more intentional assessment of student learning, the library gained valuable information for collaborating with faculty to develop assignments that incorporate information literacy, creating rubrics, and using a combined quantitative and qualitative learning assessment approach.

Compelling Evidence for Library Contributions to Student Learning and Success

In addition to creating and using methods and tools for conducting assessment in new ways, the AiA projects are yielding impressive findings about student learning. These findings benefit the higher education community by expanding the body of evidence-based assessment results related to students' academic experiences. Four findings about library impact stand out. These findings, which come from assessment projects conducted at different types of institutions, are particularly strong because they consistently point to the library as a positive influencing factor on students' academic success.

1. ***Students Benefit from Library Instruction in Their Initial Coursework***
   Academic libraries typically place a high priority on information literacy instruction for freshmen and new students to provide these students with a common set of competencies for their undergraduate studies. It's not uncommon for the information literacy instruction to occur in courses required of most or all new students, including general education, first-year experience, and English or composition courses. The assessment results from several second-year AiA projects that focused on information literacy initiatives in these types of courses document that students benefit from the instruction as highlighted by the two projects described below.

   - A 50-minute information literacy session is part of the Freshmen Experience 101 course at West Virginia State University. The AiA campus team analyzed students' perceptions of their ability to locate information by comparing pre- and post-session responses to a survey. The 371 self-reported responses indicated that the instruction enhanced students' overall learning experience and their perception of their ability to locate information improved significantly.

     > [T]he students' perceived learning revealed that information literacy instruction could improve their locating of information ability, demonstrated by the statistically significant difference between students' pre- and post-instruction perceptions of their ability to locate information.
     >
     > —West Virginia State University

   - In the first-year English composition courses at Our Lady of the Lake University, library instruction includes multiple in-person library sessions and required online video tutorials. Pre- and posttest data from 16 course sessions documented a positive relationship between students who completed the online tutorials and their course grades.

In addition, the students reported increased confidence in finding and using quality sources, and 88% of the students found the video tutorials to be informative and helpful.

Several projects from the first year of the AiA program also documented positive contributions of library instruction to students' learning during their initial coursework, including studies by <u>Claremont Colleges</u>, <u>Pacific Lutheran University</u>, the <u>University of Wisconsin-Eau Claire</u>, and <u>DePaul University</u>.

2. *Library Use Increases Student Success*
The results of several AiA library impact studies document that students who used the library in some way achieved higher levels of academic success than students who did not use the library. Two of the second year AiA projects that examined connections between library use and academic success are highlighted below.

- The campus assessment team at <u>Eastern Kentucky University</u> was interested in looking specifically at undergraduate use of online library resources. The results of its study present evidence that documents strong, positive connections between student use of the library and impact on student learning and success. On average, undergraduate students who logged in to access the libraries online resources had a .20 higher GPA (on a 4.0-point scale) than students who did not access online resources. Additionally, 69% of the study's students who attained high grades (3.0–4.0 GPA) had accessed online resources at least once compared to 58% of students who attained low grades (0–1.0 GPA) and had not accessed any online resources.

- The impact of library use on student success and persistence was the focus of the AiA assessment project at the <u>Illinois Institute of Technology</u>. The team, consisting of the university's retention task force chair, the director of housing, the director of assessment, and the library's coordinator of research and instruction, identified 644 library users (out of a total data set of 2,413 students) who entered the library building, received instruction, visited the Research Help Office, checked out laptops, utilized study rooms, and accessed online resources. These library users had a higher GPA than students who did not have the same level of library usage. The average GPA of the identified group of library users was 3.29, compared to an average GPA of 3.09 of the 2,413 students.

These projects add support to investigations in the first year of the AiA program that point to the benefits gained when students use the library. The campus assessment teams at <u>Murray State University</u> and <u>York University</u>, for example, triangulated multiple data points to document that library use contributed to students' academic success.

3. *Collaborative Academic Programs and Services Involving the Library Enhance Student Learning*
To provide more comprehensive and integrated approaches to academic support for students, libraries are finding that partnerships with other campus units are yielding promising benefits. Although campuses vary widely in the types of academic support they provide, libraries are realizing numerous opportunities for collaboration to expand and enhance these academic efforts. The benefits of a collaborative approach to academic programs and

services that involves the library were documented by projects in the AiA program's second year at Eastern Mennonite University and the University of Nebraska at Omaha.

- The Hartzler Library at Eastern Mennonite University partnered with the Academic Support Center to provide drop-in tutoring services on the main floor of the library during evening hours in the Fall 2014 semester. The AiA assessment team measured the impact of the collaborative services on students' assignment and course grades and on retention rates from the fall to the spring semesters. A high percentage of students, 88%, reported they that their assignment and course grades improved as a result of tutoring. In addition, the retention rate was slightly higher for students who attended drop-in tutoring services, as documented by a 94.8% return rate in the Spring 2015 semester, compared to a 93.6% average retention rate for the university overall.

- Prior to the AiA project at the University of Nebraska at Omaha, the library had not been a direct partner with university initiatives designed to aid student populations that needed extra academic support. The campus assessment team investigated the impact of having a roving librarian at the Project Achieve office, an academic office that serves students with disabilities, first-generation students, and limited-income students. Based on pre- and post-assessment surveys distributed to Project Achieve students during the Fall 2014 and Spring 2015 semesters, students reported higher confidence in finding and using resources for course assignment after a librarian was embedded in the student services office.

During AiA's first year, similar partnerships between the library and other campus units were investigated. The campus team at Grand Valley State University, for example, documented a high level of student satisfaction with Knowledge Market, a collaborative academic service offered by the writing center, speech lab, and library.

4. *Information Literacy Instruction Strengthens General Education Outcomes*
   The library's role in a college's or university's general education curriculum varies widely from campus to campus. The general education curriculum at most colleges and universities is designed to reach all undergraduate students with a broad liberal arts and sciences learning experience that revolves around a core set of institutionally defined proficiencies and academic outcomes. A focus on inquiry and problem solving for students' personal and professional lives and attention to significant social questions typically frame the courses and learning activities. At some institutions, such as Pierce College at Fort Steilacoom, Temple University, and Western Michigan University, information literacy is identified as a core general education proficiency or competency. On other campuses, the library provides instruction and resources to further and complement the institution's general education curriculum. In AiA's second year, some participants investigated the library's impact on their institution's general education outcomes. These projects are advancing our knowledge of library instruction in relation to aspects of inquiry-based and problem-solving learning, including critical thinking, ethical reasoning, global understanding, and civic engagement.

- Arkansas Tech University identifies critical thinking as a student success indicator, and it is a specific goal of the general education program. The library offers a one-credit hour elective course, Introduction to Library Resources, which is designed to promote higher-order thinking in students. The AiA team at the university investigated whether critical thinking skills were indeed being used in the course. The assessment was based on the TRAILS (Tool for Real-time Assessment of Information Literacy Skills) pre- and posttest rubric for 12th grade. Although the results were inconclusive in connection with many attributes of critical thinking, the rubric did measure and show a positive association between students' ability to use information literacy skills to apply higher-level thinking toward creating a viable thesis statement and supporting the statement with authoritative and relevant resources.

> *The most significant contribution of the project was that it brought information literacy (IL) awareness to stakeholders within the university. The project opened a conversation about the benefits of library instruction throughout the curriculum. We were able to show the correlation between information literacy and critical thinking and the importance of students' abilities to seek, evaluate, and use information.*
>
> —Arkansas Tech University

- At Temple University, the library reaches a large number of students in general education courses. One of those courses, Philadelphia Arts and Culture, enrolls students from all majors at all levels. In the course, students complete the same research assignment three times during the semester and have tended to display improvement between the first and second assignments, but hit a plateau between the second and third assignments. The AiA campus team examined the second and third set of student papers from the course to determine students' achievement of information literacy outcomes as demonstrated in the research papers after participating in a brief library workshop. The team used a three-point rubric that assessed (1) selection of sources, (2) attribution of sources, and (3) integration of sources in the research papers. Thirty sets of papers were assessed before and after the workshops. Overall, students who had library instruction achieved a higher rubric score than those who did not have library instruction.

These results add to the findings from teams in the first year of the AiA program that document positive connections between library instruction and general education outcomes, as exemplified by the projects at Illinois Central College, Michigan Technological College, Southern Connecticut State University, the University of Idaho, and the University of Redlands.

Building Evidence for Library Impact

The AiA projects are building evidence for library impact in other areas as well. The results of some of these investigations are described below. While these impact areas may not have been studied as extensively as the four areas discussed in the previous section or the project findings may not be as consistently strong, the assessment results do build evidence for positive connections between the library and students' academic success.

Student Retention Improves with Library Instructional Services

At most higher education institutions, student retention is designated as a high priority, and the campus library's contributions to this priority are receiving attention and recognition as a result of assessment studies that investigate the connection. Determining retention rates can include different measures, but the focus is typically on a student's continued progress from one semester to the next or a student's persistence toward degree completion. One of the eleven AiA projects in Year 2 that investigated retention in relation to library factors is highlighted below.

- The guiding inquiry question for the NorthWest Arkansas Community College (NWACC) campus team was, "Do the NWACC library's information literacy instruction sessions for English Composition I have a measurable effect on student success and retention?" The team tracked students' attendance in all of the information literacy sessions that are part of the English composition course to assess the impact on performance in the course and retention from the Fall 2014 semester to the Spring 2015 semester. The project's findings revealed that a significant percentage of the students who attended the information literacy sessions in the fall term (83.7%) enrolled in the spring term, compared with only 62.5% of the students who did not attend all of the sessions. Final course grades were also significantly higher for those students who attended the information literacy sessions.

> *This project is one of the first that the library has undertaken to track the impact of our information literacy instruction services. In that regard, the simple acts of collecting, studying, and reporting data to our colleagues throughout the college is a huge step for us—it's a way of communicating to other stakeholders that we take student learning seriously and want to be active participants in facilitating student success and retention.*
>
> —NorthWest Arkansas Community College

This study documents the benefits of library instruction for improving an institution's student retention and corroborates the findings about retention and persistence of AiA projects from the program's first year. Arizona State University, for example, found that at-risk freshmen students who successfully complete a critical thinking course with an integrated information literacy component persist at a higher rate than those who do not take the course.

Library Research Consultation Services Boost Student Learning
Several campus teams in AiA program's Year 2 were interested in assessing the impact of library research consultation services that provide one-on-one assistance to students. At some institutions, consultation services provide opportunities for customized, focused instruction, which is highlighted in the overview of Wayne State University's assessment of its research consultation services. At other institutions, such as Michigan State University, research consultation services are offered off-site from the library and may use a new service design.

- At Wayne State University, the campus team formulated its inquiry question, "How do students describe the experience of the research consultation and its value to them?" and conducted semi-structured interviews with four undergraduate and six graduate students who completed an in-person research consultation session with a librarian. The two most prominent themes to emerge from an analysis of the interview data were "learning" and "confidence." All ten students reported learning about a resource, service, and searching technique and having more confidence in doing research as a result of the consultation session.

- The Michigan State University libraries are one of a network of five student services that form a hub adjacent to the undergraduate student dorms. When the libraries changed the staffing of this research assistance service from librarians to trained students, there was a significant increase in activity. The AiA project team was interested in exploring the impact of the peer research assistants (PRA) on aspects of student success as demonstrated by student GPA and retention. Although the team discovered the complexity of factors that likely affect retention issues, particularly among first-year students, a positive association between those students who used the PRAs and retention was documented. In addition, the GPAs of students at all degree levels who met with the PRAs were higher than students who did not use the service.

In the first year of the AiA program, the impact of library research consultation services was also studied. Dalhousie University, for example, documented a positive connection between the library's one-on-one Research Assistance initiative and improved student GPAs, and Dakota State University found that the personal assistance of librarians with online graduate education students was a contributing factor to improved grades on research papers.

Library Instruction Adds Value to a Student's Long-Term Academic Experience
First-year courses that all freshmen take provide excellent opportunities for the library to reach a majority of students and present core information literacy instruction that serves as a foundation for their subsequent coursework. Many academic libraries are increasingly looking at the impact of this instruction as students move through their academic studies. In addition, the development and assessment of library instruction provided after the first year is receiving attention, particularly when information literacy competency is designated as one of the college's or university's core proficiency. As students progress in their studies, library instruction usually needs to use a scaffolded approach to teach more specialized research strategies or discipline-specific content. Two AiA projects highlighted below address issues related to the assessment of library instruction beyond the first year.

- The Briggs Library staff at the University of Minnesota, Morris collaborated with instructors of the freshman writing course by providing a two-class library instruction program. The librarians were interested in assessing the program's long-term efficacy and formed an AiA campus team to design and test a four-year panel study. The inquiry question that guided the team's development of a survey-based assessment method was, "What information literacy skills are retained after course completion, and how does additional library instruction in upper-level classes allow further skill development?" Survey results of two freshman writing classes in Spring 2015 showed improvement in student information literacy skills as a result of the library instruction sessions. Additionally, seniors who participated in the assessment also demonstrated information literacy improvement; however, the limited number of seniors who participated in the assessment was low and other potential influencing factors make the project's results about seniors less definitive. Findings from the assessment of freshmen and seniors' information literacy competence are being used to implement a full four-year panel study beginning in Fall 2015.

- At Champlain College, all undergraduate students receive information literacy instruction seven times throughout their undergraduate studies, regardless of their major. The information literacy is fully course-embedded, sequential, and scaffolded. The AiA program provided an opportunity to design and test a developmental rubric with a primary goal to build a longitudinal model of information literacy assessment. For the project, the team sampled a set of 57 annotated bibliographies prepared by freshmen, which represented 10% of the Class of 2017. Each artifact was assigned a key code prior to assessment, which will allow for tracking in future assessment activities throughout a student's undergraduate studies. The findings from the first year of assessment revealed that students performed better than expected in two areas: (1) selecting appropriate strategies and tools to access information, and (2) attribution. However, there was lower performance related to identifying questions for investigation and synthesizing information located in sources. These initial findings provide the librarians with useful information for revising freshmen-level information literacy in areas that students find challenging. As a result of the AiA project, the library now has a rubric and assessment process that it plans to use with common assignments that students complete in their junior and senior years.

The value of information literacy competencies as students complete upper-level courses and capstone projects was also investigated during AiA program's first year, including a project at Lasell College that assessed information literacy skills of graduating seniors.

The Library Promotes Academic Rapport and Student Engagement

Academic libraries can play a unique role in contributing to students' sense of academic rapport with the college or university. Academic rapport can influence student motivation, academic engagement, and enjoyment of courses and learning in general. Faculty and staff availability, responsiveness, interacting and showing an interest in students, and understanding that students encounter personal problems that may affect their academic work are all attributes that foster academic rapport. Some academic libraries are investigating ways that they might create conditions that promote academic rapport as exemplified by the University of Alberta's AiA project.

- To enhance the library experience of Aboriginal (native) students at the <u>University of Alberta</u>, the library initiated PLAS: Personal Librarian for Aboriginal Students. Incoming students were partnered with a librarian, who maintained contact with the student and provided research strategies in face-to-face meetings or by email. Students and librarians who participated in the program were surveyed at the end of the academic or project year. Preliminary survey results indicate that the program encouraged students to visit the library and to use the services and collections more effectively. As the lead team librarian noted, "[The program] created a positive environment for their learning and research, and helped demystify the library and lessened their anxiety toward it."

> *We are pleased to announce that the library administration has approved the continuance and even growth in the initiative! In the coming academic year it will serve the same audience (Aboriginal students); however, during this year relationships will be built with campus partners who serve international students and "academic-at-risk" students.*
>
> —University of Alberta

Projects in the first year of the AiA project also looked at library factors in relation to promoting academic rapport. The campus team at <u>Montana State University</u>, for example, found that the library's social media activities had a positive impact. As the lead librarian noted, "[Social media] create community, and that community contributes to student success. Our research suggests that community building is a new value for the library and a new role libraries can play with regards to student success."

Use of Library Space Relates Positively to Student Learning and Success
Several AiA campus teams have investigated the role of library space and its potential impact on students' academic experience. Five institutions in AiA program's second year studied this relationship, and the projects at <u>Knox College</u> and <u>Wake Forest University</u> highlight the numerous factors that can be assessed.

- At <u>Knox College</u>, the AiA team studied the academic preferences of students enrolled in STEM courses, particularly in relation to their use of the campus libraries. Using a mixed methods approach that collected data through a focus group, a survey, interviews, and observation, the team examined how and why students used the science library and what factors might increase use. The assessment results indicated preferences for a variety of study spaces that accommodate quiet, communal, and collaborative study for individuals and groups.

- Future programs and services at the Z. Smith Reynolds Library at <u>Wake Forest University</u> will be informed by the work of the AiA campus team, which focused on the key question, "Does student use of library resources, spaces, and services correlate with greater self-efficacy in student-defined measures of success?" The team learned that the library frequently serves as an important space for studying and academic connection with other students, particularly during students' freshman year. The library staff is now considering ways to expand the library's role in promoting student academic engagement.

In the first year of the AiA program, Central Washington University, the University of Massachusetts Dartmouth, the University of Manitoba, and the University of Northern Colorado also investigated ways that library space contributes to student learning and success.

Collaborative Assessment Fosters Library Leadership

The importance of assessment as a means for the library to expand and strengthen its role as a partner in advancing the academic success of students on a campus has been an important outcome of the AiA projects in both the first and second years of the program. A collaborative, team-based approach to these assessment activities has been particularly important. The project reports frequently note ways that collaboration furthers understanding among diverse campus constituents and advances library leadership.

Collaborating for Understanding

The design of the AiA program requires the creation of an assessment team consisting of members who represent campus units or departments beyond the library, which means that a team-based approach to assessment is established from the start. The AiA librarians have reported that the collaboration among team members promoted a shared understanding of an institution's academic priorities and the contributions of various campus stakeholders to these priorities. As a result, AiA participation fostered engaged communities of inquiry among campus teams and served as a developmental opportunity for all team members, not just the librarian leaders.

> *Our team had good collaboration and camaraderie. . . . [W]e all came to the project with a limited understanding about how the assessment would happen, so it allowed us all to learn together, gaining trust as we went. We also all had a shared desire to improve student services. Each of us came to the team with different skills to share.*
>
> —AiA librarian, reflective report

Diverse expertise and experience are again reflected by the campus teams' compositions in Year 2, as indicated in the following table.

Table 6. The Compositions of AiA Teams

AiA Team Members	Year 1	Year 2	Total
Teaching Faculty	54	47	101
Other Librarian	51	47	98
Library Administrator	21	32	53
Institutional Research	28	31	59
Assessment Office	28	28	56
Other (e.g., speech lab, teaching/learning center, doctoral student)	19	15	34
Writing Center	10	11	21
Information/Academic Technology	5	7	12
Campus Administrator	16	8	24
Student Affairs	12	8	20

Establishing partnerships across the campus for assessment work prompts consideration of the unique roles and functions of different campus units in relation to students' academic success. Several librarian team leaders reported that discussions about the primary focus of the project, the type of data needed to answer the inquiry question, and the most appropriate method(s) for gathering the data led to increased awareness among the team members about different perspectives on student learning and institutional priorities among the various campus units and departments. Identification of multiple types of data and sources for generating data, particularly beyond what the library might produce on its own, also expanded and enriched the teams' understanding of how student learning could be measured and described.

> We learned about data collection, data cleanup, collaboration, teamwork, and the importance of buy-in from all parties. We learned to go beyond simple counts and to search for relationships to larger issues.
>
> —AiA librarian, reflective report

The collaborative approach also led to important conversations that got to the heart (and complexity) of teaching and learning. Each team member brought experience and a unique viewpoint to the discussion of such topics and issues as (1) core learning outcomes that all undergraduate students should achieve, (2) attributes that define "academic success," (3) the connection of academic rapport to student learning, and (4) the relationship of classroom learning to career success. As one lead librarian noted, "I believe that the most valuable aspects of this project were the formal and informal conversations and discussions about student learning and assessment. We all learned something new from each other and became more aware how other departments on campus work toward similar goals and face similar challenges." These kinds of discussions also occurred in the libraries among the staff as a project progressed. The potential contributions of library instruction within the broader context of students' learning and academic experiences on the campus, for example, were considered. Meaningful assessment required clear articulation and common agreement about the specifics of academic factors and learning attributes that would be measured. These discussions, which were challenging at times, were essential to the collaborative assessment work being carried out.

Collaborating for Results
Collaboration with other campus units was also a means for the libraries to broaden their contribution to academic services and initiatives on the campus. The AiA program was the framework for several libraries to initiate a new program, service, or library practice and assess its impact.

- At the University of Pittsburgh-Pittsburgh Campus, for example, a new outreach effort was developed for referring students to the library who visited or contacted non-subject academic units. As the lead librarian explained, "[T]he project was successful in opening communication and building partnerships with campus departments including the Office of Student Affairs and ultimately led to mutual opportunities that were previously unexplored."

- At <u>Wake Technical Community College</u>, the library collaborated with the English faculty and discovered new ways to expand its contributions to campus-wide assessment. The campus team investigated the impact of the library's information literacy instruction on student success. In addition to documenting a positive impact, the library increased its relationship with the English faculty and also noted that other departments on the campus recognized the library as more than a facility for books.

In these two examples, the librarians took a leadership role that was collaborative and results oriented, and that initiative contributed directly to improving student learning and success at the institution.

Collaborating to Increase Library Advocacy

By leading a campus team through an assessment project, the AiA librarians advanced the mission of the library in alignment with institutional priorities. The library's contributions to enhancing student learning and increasing academic success and the critical role of librarians in documenting these efforts were noticed. On many campuses, the library is now recognized for its ability to plan and carry out assessment in ways that produce meaningful evidence about student learning. In more than one instance, AiA librarians saw the fruits of their efforts realized when the other team members or faculty and administrators outside the library advocated on behalf of the library. As one lead librarian explained, "The two non-librarians [on the team] are enthusiastic supporters who found the whole experience meaningful."

> *After the project, the campus community (including administrators) is becoming more aware of the value of the library space in the students' academic experience. Faculty have told me their students were very pleased with the service and they began advertising drop-in tutoring in their classes the second semester of the service because it was so successful with students the first semester.*
>
> —AiA librarian, reflective report

The AiA librarians reported that the team-based assessment project expanded and strengthened their leadership and advocacy skills as they led the campus team and, in the process, put theory into practice. While it is relatively easy to acknowledge the importance of effective project management, the actual experience of negotiating group dynamics and keeping a team on track is more difficult. For many of the librarians, the AiA professional development fostered professional and personal growth by integrating action with reflection. As members of a learning community during the 14-month program, the librarians were able to problem solve and test ideas in a collaborative, supportive environment. In their project and reflective reports, the librarians frequently mentioned building competencies in the following areas: (1) initiating partnerships with individuals and departments across campus, (2) feeling confident with leading team-based activities, (3) managing the process and practice of assessment, and (4) communicating the library contributions to students' academic success based on the project findings. This learning changed the librarians at an individual, personal level, which was then realized through their increased presence and involvement within the library and on the campus.

> *I think this project has granted me some authority on campus and among our library staff that I didn't have previously—I feel more comfortable being able to approach faculty with ideas and be an advocate and representative of the library now that I've led a project that involved professionals from all over campus.*
>
> —AiA librarian, reflective report

Conclusion

As the AiA campus teams investigate and report on the impact of different library factors on student learning and success, the evidence-based assessment findings about the positive contributions of the library to students' academic success grow. The project activities are grounded in action research, which means that the focus is on institutional priorities and using the assessment findings to inform and improve academic initiatives in ways that are meaningful and sustainable. As a result, the library is increasingly recognized as integral to advancing the academic success of students at higher education institutions.

CHAPTER 5

Academic Library Impact on Student Learning and Success:

Findings from Assessment in Action Team Projects[*]

Association of College and Research Libraries. Prepared by Karen Brown. Contributions by Kara J. Malenfant.

[*] Association of College and Research Libraries. *Academic Library Impact on Student Learning and Success: Findings from Assessment in Action Team Projects*. Prepared by Karen Brown with contributions by Kara J. Malenfant. Chicago: Association of College and Research Libraries, 2017. Published online at www.acrl.ala.org/value.

Association of College & Research Libraries
A division of the American Library Association

Citation:
Association of College and Research Libraries. *Academic Library Impact on Student Learning and Success: Findings from Assessment in Action Team Projects*. Prepared by Karen Brown with contributions by Kara J. Malenfant. Chicago: Association of College and Research Libraries, 2017.

Published online at www.acrl.ala.org/value.

About the Authors
Karen Brown is a professor at Dominican University (River Forest, Illinois) in the School of Information Studies and teaches in the areas of assessment, collection management, foundations of the profession, and literacy and learning. Prior to joining Dominican University's faculty in 2000, she developed and coordinated continuing education programs for the Chicago Library System, one of Illinois's former regional library systems. She has also held positions focusing on collection development, reference, and instruction at the University of Wisconsin, University of Maryland, Columbia University, and Bard College. She holds a PhD in media studies from New York University and master's degrees in library science and adult education from the University of Wisconsin.

Kara J. Malenfant is a senior staff member at ACRL, where she coordinates government relations advocacy and scholarly communication activities and is the lead staff member on the Value of Academic Libraries initiative and Assessment in Action program. She provides consulting services on organization development and use of ACRL's standards for libraries in higher education. Kara began her position at ACRL in fall of 2005 after working for six years at DePaul University Libraries in Chicago. A former Peace Corps volunteer, she holds a PhD in leadership and change from Antioch University and a master's degree in library science from the University of Illinois at Urbana-Champaign.

Contents

Executive Summary

Since 2013, over 200 postsecondary institutions of all types have participated in the Association of College and Research Libraries' (ACRL) Assessment in Action program (AiA) that created campus-wide partnerships at institutions to promote collaborative assessment and library leadership.[1] The AiA program was launched by ACRL, in partnership with the Association of Institutional Research and the Association of Public Land-grant Universities, and with funding from the US Institute of Museum and Library Services.

At each participating institution, an AiA team, consisting of a librarian and at least two representatives from other campus departments or units, planned and implemented a project that aligned with institutional priorities and contributed to campus assessment activities. The extensive collection of assessment methods and tools used by the campus teams during the three-year AiA program point to multiple types of library factors and their potential impacts on students' academic outcomes. Higher education institutions are encouraged to replicate or adapt these approaches to expand understanding of student learning and to assess library contributions to academic outcomes at their institutions.

Compelling Evidence for Academic Library Contributions to Student Learning and Success

The higher education community now has compelling assessment findings that tell a strong story about the multiple ways that academic libraries are contributing to student learning and success. While each institutional context is unique and the AiA project findings about library impact are not generalizable to all academic settings, the demonstrations of positive connections between the library and aspects of student learning and success in five areas are particularly noteworthy.

1. ***Students benefit from library instruction in their initial coursework.***
   Information literacy instruction provided to students during their initial coursework helps them acquire a common set of competencies for their undergraduate studies. The assessment findings from numerous AiA projects that focused on information literacy initiatives for freshmen and new students underscore that students receiving this instruction perform better in their courses than students who do not.

2. ***Library use increases student success.***
   Several AiA studies point to increased academic success when students use the library. The analysis of multiple data points (e.g., circulation, library instruction session attendance, online database access, study room use, interlibrary loan) shows that students who used the library in some way achieved higher levels of academic success (e.g., GPA, course grades, retention) than students who did not use the library.

---

[1] This executive summary is available online as a separate document, formatted to share broadly with campus stakeholders. See www.ala.org/acrl/files/issues/value/y3_summary.pdf.

3. ***Collaborative academic programs and services involving the library enhance student learning.***
   Academic library partnerships with other campus units, such as the writing center, academic enrichment, and speech lab, yield positive benefits for students (e.g., higher grades, academic confidence, retention).

4. ***Information literacy instruction strengthens general education outcomes.***
   Several AiA projects document that library instruction improves students' achievement of institutional core competencies and general education outcomes. The project findings demonstrate different ways that information literacy contributes to inquiry-based and problem-solving learning, including effective identification and use of information, critical thinking, ethical reasoning, and civic engagement.

5. ***Library research consultations boost student learning.***
   One-on-one or small-group reference and research assistance with a librarian enhances academic success, as documented by such factors as student confidence, GPAs, and improved achievement on course assignments.

Having overall consistent assessment findings of library impact in these five areas—across a body of over 200 projects—is strong in part because of the variation. Each setting is unique; each library program and service differed in its design and implementation (as appropriate for that unique local context); students had many difference characteristics and backgrounds; there was a multiplicity of methods for investigating the library impact on students.

Because the assessment findings are derived from action research, which situates the investigations in authentic institutional contexts, the results reflect "on the ground" practices in terms of resources available and campus priorities. While libraries should routinely assess for internal improvement, findings from the AiA projects lessen the need to question whether investments of time, resources, and energy in these areas will bring about a positive impact.

Promising Evidence of Library Impact

The AiA projects continue to build evidence of library impact in other areas as well. Investigations in four areas point to evidence of promise. The assessment of library impact in these areas, however, tends not to have been investigated as extensively as those noted above or the findings may not be as consistently strong. Even so, the growing number of studies in these four areas have yielded promising results about positive connections between the library and students' academic success.

- *The library contributes to improved student retention.*
- *Library instruction adds value to a student's long-term academic experience.*
- *The library promotes academic rapport and student engagement.*
- *Use of library space relates positively to student learning and success.*

Advancing Library Leadership through Action Research

The action research framework, which emphasized improving practice through systematic investigation of a question grounded in institutional context, engaged the librarians in an immersive process of ongoing interaction with one another and collaboration with their campus team members. The librarians led the design and implementation of assessment that related directly to their campus's academic priorities, creating opportunities for substantive conversations with campus stakeholders about student learning and resulting in meaningful findings that informed decision making about library programs and practices. The leadership qualities that were strengthened through this process include an awareness of the importance of inquiry and decision making grounded in institutional context, understanding and experience with the dynamic nature of assessment, and a recognition of the personal and professional growth that emerges through collaboration with others.

Introduction

Since 2013, over 200 postsecondary institutions of all types have participated in the Association of College and Research Libraries' (ACRL) Assessment in Action program (AiA) that created campus-wide partnerships at institutions to promote collaborative assessment and library leadership. This report focuses on the third year of the program and synthesizes results from the team-based projects led by librarians at fifty-five higher education institutions primarily from across North America. These assessment projects contribute additional findings to the evidence of library impact generated by the 148 campus teams that participated the first two years of the program.[2]

The AiA program was launched by ACRL, in partnership with the Association of Institutional Research and the Association of Public Land-grant Universities, and with funding from the US Institute of Museum and Library Services. Three primary goals framed the project's activities:

1. Develop academic librarians' professional competencies needed to document and communicate the value of the academic library in relation to an institution's goals for student learning and success.

2. Strengthen collaborative relationships with higher education stakeholders, including campus faculty, academic administrators, and assessment officers.

3. Contribute to higher education assessment by creating approaches, strategies, and practices that document the contribution of academic libraries.

At each participating institution, an AiA team, consisting of a librarian and at least two people from other departments or units, planned and implemented a project that aligned with institutional priorities and contributed to campus assessment activities. The teams were led by the librarian, and other team members typically included teaching faculty and administrators from such departments as the assessment office, institutional research, the writing center, academic technology, and student affairs. Over a fourteen-month period, the librarians worked with their campus teams to investigate connections between library factors and aspects of student learning and success.

The lead librarians were supported throughout the project by a peer-to-peer learning community that combined in-person workshops and sequenced online professional development activities designed to advance an action research approach to assessment. This approach emphasizes an assessment process that merges theory with practice to yield results that inform and improve practice. Skill building through collaborative and reflective problem solving was the centerpiece of the professional development. The AiA librarians increased their assessment and leadership competence as they guided their campus team through a process of identifying an inquiry

---

[2] Read more about the first-year and second-year participating institutions in reports synthesizing the projects results each year: *Academic Library Contributions to Student Success: Documented Practices from the Field* (January 2015), available at www.ala.org/acrl/files/issues/value/contributions_report.pdf, and *Documented Library Contributions to Student Learning and Success: Building Evidence with Team-Based Assessment in Action Campus Projects* (April 2016), available at www.ala.org/acrl/sites/ala.org.acrl/files/content/issues/value/contributions_y2.pdf.

question related to institutional priorities, determining appropriate assessment methods, interpreting the data, and communicating the project results. This team-based approach has produced assessment results that connect directly to practice and promote sustainable change around library services and programs that contribute to student learning and success. The library also increases its visibility and gains recognition among campus constituent groups for its advancement of academic initiatives at the institution.

> *[Tulsa Community College] librarians learned through this project that a more college-wide and coordinated effort toward curriculum development and assessment was needed to achieve success in [library] instruction. An information literacy steering committee was formed as a result of this project and librarians now serve as embedded liaisons to each academic division.*
>
> • <u>Tulsa Community College</u>

The third year of the AiA program ran from April 2015 to June 2016, and results of the assessment projects were presented in poster sessions at the 2016 American Library Association Annual Conference in Orlando, Florida, June 24 and 25. Each team leader completed a final project descriptive report, which includes an abstract and image of the poster, and these reports are fully searchable in an <u>online collection</u>.[3] In addition, the team leaders completed a reflective report and, while these second reports are kept confidential, aggregate and anonymous comments from the reflective reports have contributed to this synthesis. This publication is also informed by results from two focus groups conducted in June 2016 with a total of twenty-one AiA third-year librarians. The projects described in this report highlight only a few of the third-year projects; full reports on the projects are posted in the searchable database.

Participation by a Variety of Higher Education Institutions

The fifty-five AiA campus teams that participated in the third year of the AiA program represented a variety of types of colleges and universities and came from twenty-four states, the District of Columbia, and Australia (see table 1 and figure 1).

---

[3] Assessment in Action respondent search page, accessed April 10, 2017, <u>https://apply.ala.org/aia/public</u>.

Table 1. Types of institutions for teams selected into the AiA program, Years 1–3.

Institution Type	Year 1	Year 2	Year 3	Total
Associate's Colleges	10	13	3	26
Baccalaureate Colleges	7	15	10	32
Master's Colleges and Universities	32	11	18	61
Doctoral/Research Universities	6	4	2	12
Research Universities (High/Very High Research Activity)	18	23	21	62
Tribal Colleges	1	1	0	2
Special Focus Institutions (medical, culinary, theological seminary)	1	6	1	8
TOTAL	75	73	55	203

Figure 1. Map of institutions selected to participate in the third year of AiA.

The institutions are represented by a variety of different accrediting bodies, including seven US regional, one specialized, and one Australian (see table 2).

Table 2. The accreditation agencies of institutions selected into the AiA program, Years 1–3.

At some institutions, an accreditation self-study was underway during the AiA program period, and the campus project was an important contribution to the final report.

> *Our Director of Assessment is pleased that we did this project; it became one of our Action Projects for accreditation, using actual assessment of student learning to demonstrate the value of the library. It has also demonstrated ways to assess student learning that go beyond satisfaction surveys. (Our accrediting agency made a specific request that we find ways to assess learning as opposed to satisfaction.)*
>
> - <u>Northern Michigan University</u>

Investigating Connections between Library Factors and Academic Outcomes

Each campus team generated an assessment inquiry question that took into consideration the institution's mission and academic priorities and focused on the relationship between a library factor (e.g., collections, space, instruction, reference, etc.) and an aspect of student learning and success (e.g., course or program learning outcomes, student confidence, retention, persistence). In the third year of the AiA program, campus teams investigated eleven attributes of student learning and success and thirteen library factors (see tables 3 and 4).

Table 3. The number of AiA projects that investigated the listed academic outcome.

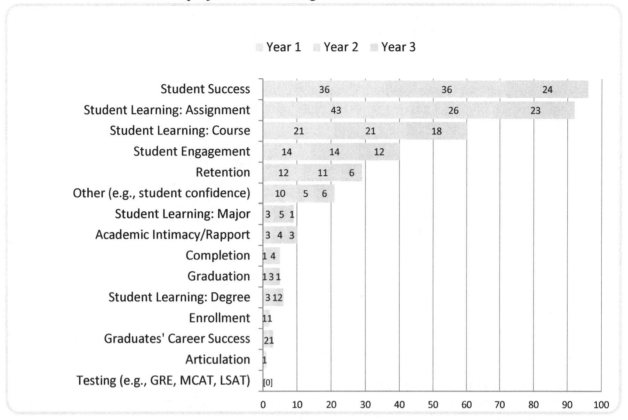

Table 4. The number of AiA projects that assessed the listed library factor.

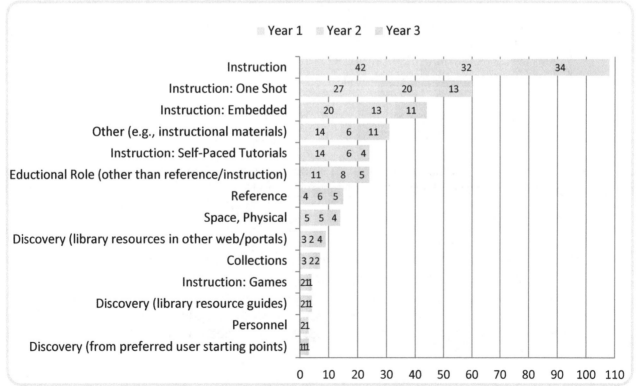

The following ten sample inquiry questions from the third year of the program highlight the various types of library impact examined. For some campuses, the inquiry question focused on determining whether or not the library had an impact on students' academic outcomes. Other institutions investigated how the library might be contributing to student learning and success.

- What impact can expanded library engagement based on the ACRL *Framework* have on information literacy knowledge, skills, and habits of mind in a university writing program? (Boston University)

- Does embedding a librarian and library resources into an online-only class improve quality of students' research skills? (California State University, Fullerton)

- How important are information literacy skills to achieving success as a medical student? (Edward Via College of Osteopathic Medicine)

- What is the impact of integrating information literacy learning outcomes in a first-year general education course? (State University of New York at Fredonia)

- Do students select space in the Learning Studio that best suits their needs? (University of Kansas)

- Do students at [the University of Pittsburgh-] Greensburg demonstrate a progressive increase in their information literacy skills as they move through their coursework toward degree completion? (University of Pittsburgh-Greensburg)

- How does library engagement affect the grade point averages (GPAs) of sophomores and juniors at the University of Southern California? (University of Southern California)

- Does faculty-librarian collaboration benefit student disciplinary research and writing practices? (University of St. Thomas)

- What type of library instruction is most effective for students in upper-level communication courses? (University of Wyoming)

- How does research instruction impact students' ability to transfer research skills from one project to the next? (University of Massachusetts Boston)

Assessment Methods and Approaches

The inquiry question also informed a team's decisions about the most appropriate data needed to answer the question and the means for generating the data. Both quantitative and qualitative assessment approaches were used by the campus teams, with a large percentage incorporating a mixed-methods approach. As in the previous two years of the program, surveys, rubrics, and pre- and posttest methods were the most common assessment methods employed to generate data (see table 5).

Table 5. Summary of assessment methods and tools.

Assessment Methods and Tools[a]	Year 1	Year 2	Year 3
Survey	41	31	28
Rubric	40	26	19
Pre- and Posttest	23	23	14
Other (e.g., correlational analysis, content analysis)	20	15	13
Interviews	13	7	4
Observation	10	9	4
Focus Group(s)	10	6	4

a. The totals on the table columns do not equal 74, 64, 52, or 190 (i.e., the number of AiA teams completing the program and reporting in Year 1, Year 2, and Year 3, respectively) because many teams used more than one assessment method and/or type of measure.

The numerous methods and tools that the AiA teams have used to investigate library impact over the past three years are providing the academic library profession with a wide array of approaches to consider for assessment initiatives. These approaches expand and enrich the profession's knowledge of different ways to assess student learning and success in relation to library services, resources, and practices. In Year 3, for example, the use of ethnographic methods at the University of Iowa and Dynamic Criteria Mapping at Elmhurst College introduced new AiA approaches to generate data that helps us better understand the complexities of students' academic experiences.

- At the University of Iowa, the campus team investigated the libraries' outreach and informal learning activities in relation to students' critical and creative inquiry and their knowledge creation. These activities are part of the libraries' new engagement program and include, for example, Break from Busyness (BFB), which provides opportunities for short breaks from studying to participate in such activities as redacted poetry and zine making. While the team found that assessing student learning and engagement with interviews and surveys after the events was difficult, the use of ethnographic and autoethnographic methods during the events resulted in rich, multilayered data about library engagement. The assessment methods captured student perspectives on the college experience and their perceptions of the library. This information provides insights into students' needs and suggests ways that the library can plan programming that addresses those needs.

- Dynamic Criteria Mapping (DCM), a qualitative, constructivist method of writing assessment, was used at Elmhurst College to investigate the impact of information literacy instruction in freshman composition classes. After reading student papers from first-year English composition courses, librarians and writing faculty participated in a workshop consisting of a series of generative small-group and large-group discussions to explore connections between information literacy and student writing. DCM is designed to engage academic communities in consensus-building discussions, which was the result of the assessment activities at Elmhurst College. The library plans to expand its use of this methodology to include more student artifacts and involve more workshop participants.

> By applying DCM [Dynamic Criteria Mapping], librarians and writing faculty engaged in cross-disciplinary conversations, developing consensus on what we value when we read first-year writing projects in light of research skills and information literacy and reconciling disparate disciplinary terminology. Our project assists our institution's goals of assessing components of our general education program.
>
> • Elmhurst College

The third year of AiA saw several campus teams include the ACRL *Framework for Information Literacy in Higher Education*[4] in their projects and use elements of the *Framework* to assess student learning (i.e., Arcadia University, Augusta University, Boston University, DeSales University, University of New Mexico, and University of Minnesota Duluth). Arcadia University, for example, applied the ACRL *Framework* in its library instruction and gained insights into how students learn the integration of research and writing processes, and the University of New Mexico used the Information Creation as a Process frame as a lens to understand better how students perceive different information formats in their research. Both projects are briefly described below.

- Arcadia University assessed reflective writing as a means to help students think about research as an iterative process and the connection of research to the writing process. After modifying and expanding the reflective assignments in the first-year writing course, the AiA campus team developed a rubric to assess students' reflective assignments and their final argument papers. The complex and time-intensive scoring of these student products limited the study to an evaluation of the work of ten students. The findings, however, showed that students had only minimally conceptualized research as a part of the writing process. In addition to expanding assessment in this area, one recommendation that the campus team made was to provide students with clearer assignment prompts and to improve the scaffolding of reflective activities to help students learn how to reflect more deeply.

- The University of New Mexico campus team considered the Information Creation as a Process frame to study how students perceive and understand different information formats. In the Spring 2016 semester, 668 students enrolled in a Freshman English course participated in flipped library instruction, which included using an online tutorial about

---

[4] Association of College and Research Libraries, *Framework for Information Literacy for Higher Education* (Chicago: Association of College and Research Libraries, 2016), www.ala.org/acrl/standards/ilframework.

information formats, evaluating different formats, and choosing appropriate sources to support their writing. The assessment results indicate that students' understanding of formats, in general, tends to be rudimentary and often mistaken. The lead librarian noted, "We need to talk with students about the communicative purpose of formats and how that purpose is reflected in both the product and process."

Taken together, the results of studies that investigated aspects of the *Framework* reveal new findings about the complexities of student learning and the potential impact of information literacy instruction on students' academic success.

The extensive collection of assessment methods and tools used by the campus teams during the three-year AiA program point to multiple types of library factors and their potential impacts on students' academic experiences. Higher education institutions are encouraged to replicate or adapt these approaches to expand understanding of student learning and to assess library impact on students' academic success at their institutions.

Strengthening and Expanding Compelling Findings

Four compelling findings about library contributions to student learning and success were highlighted in last year's AiA summary report:[5]

1. Students benefit from library instruction in their initial coursework.
2. Library use increases student success.
3. Collaborative academic programs and services involving the library enhance student learning.
4. Information literacy instruction strengthens general education outcomes.

The results of the third-year assessment projects, which are discussed in this report, strengthen these findings with additional evidence. The findings of projects that assessed library research consultation services in the previous two years, and now in Year 3, indicate a strong association between research consultations and improved student learning. These results support adding a **fifth** area of compelling library impact:

5. Library research consultations boost student learning.

While each institutional context is unique and the AiA project findings about library impact are not generalizable to all academic settings, the demonstrations of positive connections between the library and aspects of student learning and success in these five areas are particularly noteworthy. Having overall consistent assessment findings of library impact in these five areas— across a body of over 200 projects—is strong in part because of the variation.[6] Each setting is

---

[5] Association of College and Research Libraries, *Documented Library Contributions to Student Learning and Success: Building Evidence with Team-Based Assessment in Action Campus Projects*, prepared by Karen Brown with contributions by Kara J. Malenfant (Chicago: Association of College and Research Libraries, 2016), www.ala.org/acrl/sites/ala.org.acrl/files/content/issues/value/contributions_y2.pdf.

[6] A forthcoming ACRL action-oriented research agenda, by OCLC Research, is expected to be released in summer 2017. It will augment the findings of this report by considering a wider array of evidence. It will consider the AiA projects and take a deep look at over 500 documents, including scholarly and practice-based literature from the LIS

unique; each library program and service differed in its design and implementation (as appropriate for that unique local context); students had many difference characteristics and backgrounds; there was a multiplicity of methods for investigating the library impact on students.

We now have compelling assessment findings that tell a strong story about the multiple ways that libraries are contributing to student learning and success. We know much more about effective library practice; libraries that engage in these five practices can anticipate positive contributions to students' academic experiences. While these project findings may not be generalizable, as you would expect of social science research from a positivist perspective, they can be adapted to other settings with care and consideration to local context. Because the findings are derived from action research, which is situated in authentic institutional contexts, the results reflect "on the ground" practices in terms of resources available and campus priorities. Therefore, we urge academic libraries to grow and strengthen high-quality programs and services in these areas of effective practice. While libraries should routinely assess for internal improvement, findings such as these from the AiA projects lessen the need to question whether investments of time and energy in these areas will bring about a positive impact.[7]

Specific projects by Year 3 AiA teams that support findings of effective practice in these five areas are described below.

1. Students benefit from library instruction in their initial coursework.

Seventeen campus teams in Year 3 investigated the impact of library instruction on first-year students' academic experience, adding assessment findings to a growing body of literature about the contributions of this instruction to students' learning in their initial coursework. Multiple aspects of library instruction were assessed, which adds richness to our understanding of student learning and success. Three projects, each of which investigated a different type of library instruction impact, are highlighted below.

- The University of Texas at San Antonio focused on the information literacy competence of incoming freshmen to determine how library-created instruction and online content might be used to target specific needs early in a student's academic career. A mixed-methods approach that included pretests (354 students) and posttests (226 students) and a rubric-based evaluation of 210 bibliographies showed that students improved their ability

---

field and higher education. It will address two primary questions—(1) What are the ways that library services align with and have impact on student learning and success? and (2) How can librarians communicate their alignment with and impact on student learning and success in a way that resonates with higher education stakeholders?—and recommend priority areas for action and for future research.

[7] Effective practices in higher education are typically based on studies that exemplify variation in such attributes as setting, instructional design and approach, student characteristics, and institutional priorities. George Kuh, for example, identified high-impact educational practices, and, as the Association of American Colleges and Universities notes in its description of them, "The following teaching and learning practices have been widely tested and have been shown to be beneficial for college students from many backgrounds. These practices take many different forms, depending on learner characteristics and on institutional priorities and contexts."("High-Impact Educational Practices: A Brief Overview," excerpt from George D. Kuh, *High-Impact Educational Practices: What They Are, Who Has Access to Them, and Why They Matter* [Washington, DC: Association of American Colleges and Universities, 2008], https://www.aacu.org/leap/hips).

to recognize information literacy terms and criteria. Their level of competence with applying criteria correctly, however, revealed patterns of confusion. The librarians and course instructors are now collaborating on curriculum approaches and content that address the deficiencies identified by the assessment.

- At St. Catherine University, the campus team investigated how the timing, frequency, and methods of information literacy instruction had an impact on the information literacy skills of first-term students. A pilot group of sixty-eight students had three sessions of library instruction at different points in the semester, and a control group of sixty-nine students participated in a one-shot instruction session. A pretest and posttest administered to all students and a rubric-based evaluation of a random sample of sixty-four student papers indicate that information literacy skills did increase. The instructional variables, however, did not significantly impact students' information literacy competence. The campus team attributed the lower-than-expected results to the possible influence of several uncontrolled external variables, including different student populations and variations in librarian and faculty teaching styles and levels of experience. The findings also suggest that students are still developing their information literacy competencies at the end of their first semester and library instruction should be provided beyond the first semester of coursework for students to adequately gain the proficiency necessary for academic success.

- At the University of Massachusetts Boston, librarians taught over 580 library research instruction classes in the 2015–2016 academic year, making this time-intensive, but high priority, library effort an ideal area for inquiry by the AiA campus team. The team narrowed its focus to a study of the university's ENGL 102 course, which is designed to help students connect research to the writing process and to address skills needed to satisfy the institution's Writing Proficiency Requirement. To measure the impact of library research instruction on student learning, a pretest was administered to 281 students, 222 booklets that students completed in the class were evaluated using a rubric, and a posttest was administered to 250 students at the end of the semester. One of the key results of the study revealed that students understood and appreciated ways that they could use library resources to research topics and find credible sources. Based on these findings, which support the value of this library instruction, the library is expanding its focus to all English courses and piloting a new model that embeds research instruction throughout the course by breaking it into smaller chunks and encouraging faculty to assume greater responsibility for teaching more of the components themselves. As a result, more students enrolled in English courses benefit from library instruction and librarians' time in the classroom is reduced.

Some of the other factors considered by Year 3 campus teams that studied library instruction provided during students' first year of coursework include library use (Brandeis University), teaching methods (Catawba College; Hunter College, City University of New York; and Northeastern Illinois University), specific student populations (Northern Michigan University and the University of Illinois at Urbana-Champaign), student dispositions (University of Minnesota Duluth), and collaboration with discipline faculty (Elmhurst College). The results of these projects further reinforce and strengthen project findings about this library impact area from Year 1 (e.g., <u>Fairfield University</u>, <u>Towson University</u>, and <u>Virginia Polytechnic Institute and State University</u>) and Year 2 (e.g., <u>Joliet Junior College</u>, <u>Our Lady of the Lake University</u>, and <u>West Virginia State University</u>).

2. Library use increases student success.

AiA projects in the first and second years of the program documented connections between library use and student academic success (e.g., <u>Eastern Kentucky University</u>, <u>Illinois Institute of Technology</u>, <u>Murray State University</u>, and <u>York University</u>). These projects investigated multiple library factors (e.g., database access, circulation, library instruction session participation, interlibrary loan, library visits, use of study rooms) in relation to student success as documented by such academic outcomes as GPAs, course grades, and persistence. A positive association between library use and student academic outcomes emerged from these projects. Assessment of library use was also the focus of some investigations in Year 3, as exemplified by the project at <u>California State University, East Bay</u>.

- The AiA project at <u>California State University, East Bay</u> found that library use contributed to student success. The campus team aligned its project with university initiatives to increase the academic success of transfer students. The team's assessment work was guided by its inquiry question, "Do course-integrated information literacy sessions positively affect a transfer student's use of library resources and their California State University East Bay GPA?" The assessment findings indicate that library instruction did impact transfer students' library use. Students who participated in course-integrated library instruction were much more likely to use library resources and were also more likely to have a higher GPA than students who did not receive the instruction. The findings also revealed that the library reaches only 10 percent of transfer students through course-integrated library instruction during their first year. To increase this percentage, the library will expand its instructional efforts with upper-division courses and develop additional resources for transfer students.

> *Using Library EZProxy, Circulation, and Institutional GPA data, the study found that new transfer students who received information literacy instruction were significantly more likely to use library resources and have a higher GPA.*
>
> • <u>California State University-East Bay</u>

Additional studies in the third year about library use were conducted at <u>Brandeis University</u>, <u>Nevada State College</u>, and the <u>University of Southern California</u>. The AiA studies in this impact area have considered multiple library use factors to provide insights about different ways that library use may contribute to student academic success.

3. Collaborative academic programs and services involving the library enhance student learning.

As libraries increasingly partner with other academic units on their campuses, assessment findings about the impact of collaborative approaches designed to increase student learning and success are emerging. One of the four campus projects in Year 3 that investigated this area of library impact is highlighted below.

- To inform the University of Miami's planning of its new Learning Commons, which will provide services to support students transitioning into the university environment, the AiA campus team decided to investigate lab sessions provided by the Intensive English Program through a pilot collaborative initiative between the campus libraries and the Writing Center. The team analyzed the bibliographies of student research papers and conducted interviews with students about their experiences with research and writing. Although the overall pool of students included in the study was small, some initial data about the pilot bridge programming was generated. In general, students reported that they felt supported through the program, and they used more library resources. More attention and instruction, however, need to address the skills of selecting and using appropriate sources in research writing. The AiA project was particularly useful in that the academic units identified successful collaborative practices for advancing the goals of the Learning Commons.

The results of these projects expand findings about collaborative initiatives from other Year 3 campus teams (i.e., Drexel University, Lincoln University, and Seattle University) and from AiA projects in previous years, including Central Washington University, Eastern Mennonite University, Grand Valley State University, Indiana University of Pennsylvania, and the University of Nebraska at Omaha.

4. Information literacy instruction strengthens general education outcomes.

Several projects in the first two years of the AiA program studied the impact of information literacy instruction on students' achievement of institutional core competencies and general education outcomes. In Year 2, for example, the Arkansas Tech University AiA team documented positive associations between library instruction and students' critical thinking, and the campus team at Temple University found that students enrolled in one of the university's general education courses scored higher on the research paper rubric evaluation if they received library instruction than students who did not have library instruction. Projects completed in Year 1 also demonstrated positive connections between library instruction and general education outcomes, including investigations at Illinois Central College, Michigan Technological College, Southern Connecticut State University, the University of Idaho, and the University of Redlands.

This area of investigation continued in Year 3, as exemplified by campus team projects completed at Boston University and the University of Minnesota-Duluth, which are described below.

At Boston University, a long-standing goal of the College of Arts and Sciences' Writing Program is the development of foundational skills and habits of mind of undergraduate students, which include research and information literacy. The AiA campus team saw possible connections between the comprehensive approach of ACRL's *Framework for Information Literacy in Higher Education* and the goals of the Writing Program. The team's guiding inquiry question was, "What impact can enhanced library engagement based on the ACRL *Framework* have on information literacy knowledge, skills, and habits of mind in a university writing program?" The assessment focused on two frames from the ACRL *Framework*: (1) Research as Inquiry, and (2) Searching as Strategic Exploration. Using a rubric-based assessment and student reflections, the project findings documented that enhanced, expanded librarian engagement with students can increase students' understanding and incorporation of the threshold concepts reflected in the two frames. In addition to these encouraging findings, the project led to further librarian/faculty collaboration, including creation of a co-led seminar for librarians and writing instructors on threshold concepts, information literacy, and collaboration.

> *[T]he project showed: 1) how librarian/faculty collaboration in the development of assignments and activities can inculcate information literacy habits of mind in students, and 2) how student portfolios and reflective essays can be used to assess the success of those efforts.*
>
> • Boston University

- The first-year writing course at the University of Minnesota-Duluth is designed to fulfill the institution's information literacy learning outcome. Based on the librarians' experiences working with students who frequently abandon their research efforts after a cursory search, the AiA campus team decided to focus on students' ability to persist when conducting research in the course. By analyzing students' dispositional changes throughout the research process and focusing on learners who persist, the project documented that library instruction is associated with an increase in behaviors and attitudes related to persistence and help-seeking. The library plans to build on the project's findings to include a larger sample size and to expand collaboration with first-year writing instruction to develop student persistence in the research process.

The College of DuPage, Hawaii Pacific University, John Carroll University, and the State University of New York at Fredonia also focused on institutional core competencies and general education in Year 3. Over the three years of the AiA program, the campus teams that studied library contributions to this academic priority have generated important findings about library impact on aspects of student learning and success.

5. Library research consultations boost student learning.

> *Research consultations are social encounters. They are ideal for encouraging the teaching and counseling roles of librarians. While librarians recognize that we often act as counselors at the desk or in a research consultation, it was surprising to discover that some students also see librarians in that role. When [students were] asked, "What did you find valuable in your one-on-one or group consultation with the reference librarian?" replies were not just about the discovery of library resources, or the newfound confidence in using them, but students also remarked on how useful librarians were in helping to motivate them.*
>
> • Bentley University

Building on the results of previous AiA projects that demonstrated a positive connection between library research consultations and students' academic achievement (e.g., Dalhousie University, Dakota State University, Michigan State University, and Wayne State University), six institutions in Year 3 conducted assessment projects that studied this type of library service, with five institutions documenting a positive impact (Boston University, College of the Holy Cross, Lincoln University, Queensland University, and the University of St. Thomas) and the sixth institution establishing a methodology for collecting and analyzing data about the impact (Southern Illinois University). Overviews of two projects highlight approaches for assessing the impact of library research consultations, each focusing on a different student population.

- The College of the Holy Cross's year-long Montserrat seminar is required of all first-year students and is designed to develop foundational competencies that include critical thinking, writing, and communication. Given the emphasis placed on writing in the seminar and its continued importance throughout a student's academic experience at the college, the AiA project team crafted an inquiry question to address this priority: "Do Freshmen who engage in Personal Research Sessions (PRS) and library instruction sessions select more appropriate sources for their research?" Using a rubric to evaluate and score students' research papers, the assessment documented that PRS contributed to students' ability to identify and evaluate sources for relevancy. The team also learned that PRS did not seem to correspond to differences in students' understanding of when and how to cite sources properly. The library plans to contribute its findings to the current campus-wide assessment of the Montserrat program and to expand its investigation of other research and instruction with upper-class programs.

- To align with Queensland University of Technology's institutional priority on student success and retention, the AiA campus team investigated the contributions of the library's Academic Skills Adviser (ASA) consultation services to this institutional effort. The team analyzed the GPAs of students who were experiencing significant academic challenges and were referred to the ASA services. The study's findings indicate that those students who attended an ASA consultation achieved higher academic success than students who were referred to the ASA services but did not attend a consultation.

> *This project enabled us to set up a process that combines data from disparate systems to create meaningful reports that will allow us to monitor and measure the impact of our services and investigate opportunities for program improvement.*
>
> - Queensland University of Technology

The growing evidence from AiA projects about positive connections between library research consultations and student academic success demonstrates an area of effective library practice.

Promising Evidence of Library Impact

The AiA projects continue to build evidence of library impact in other areas as well. Assessment of library impact in these areas, however, tends not to have been investigated as extensively as in those noted in the previous section, or the findings may not be as consistently strong. The previous five areas are based on evidence of effectiveness, as demonstrated by effective practices, and all academic libraries should strive to grow and strengthen programs, services, and resources in those areas. The four areas discussed in this section point to evidence of promise. The growing number of studies in these four areas in particular contribute to investigations that yield promising results about positive connections between the library and students' academic success.

1. The library contributes to improved student retention.

The priority given to retention and persistence on most higher education campuses has resulted in several AiA projects that focused on library contributions to this academic outcome. In Year 3, for example, six AiA institutions investigated retention and persistence in relation to library instructional services and student use of library collections. Campus teams considered multiple factors, including library use (Nevada State College), information literacy instruction (Northern Michigan University) and library research consultations (Queensland University of Technology and Southern Illinois University). Students' online library use and its impact on academic success was the focus of the Nevada State College's AiA team's assessment project, as described below.

- As Nevada State College increasingly emphasizes the importance of using evidence to inform academic decision making, the AiA campus team saw an opportunity to investigate the connection between online library use and student success as demonstrated by semester GPAs, one-term retention, and good academic standing. Various data points (e.g., student demographics, student success data, and library use measured by EZProxy sessions) were analyzed for possible relationships. The project data documented a positive connection to all three types of academic outcomes. To generate data that refines and adds to the institution's understanding of this connection, plans are underway to investigate the relationship between the use of library services and assignment-level success measures.

Twelve projects in Year 1 and eleven projects in Year 2 also examined this academic outcome. Even though the complexity of factors and influences that may affect students' progress from one semester to the next or their persistence toward degree completion is considerable and determining reliable methods for assessing such progress is challenging, the results of several AiA projects show promising associations of the library to retention and persistence, including Year 1 projects at Arizona State University, Dalhousie University, and Murray State University, and Year 2 projects at Eastern Mennonite University, Michigan State University, NorthWest Arkansas Community College, and the University of Mississippi Medical Center.

2. Library instruction adds value to a student's long-term academic experience.

At most higher education institutions, a significant portion of library instruction time, effort, and resources is directed toward freshmen students, largely because required first-year courses are important opportunities to teach a common, foundational set of information literacy competencies that these students will use throughout their academic studies. The high number of AiA projects that consider the impact of library instruction on freshman academic achievement reflects this interest and importance. A growing number of libraries are considering the information literacy competencies of students beyond the freshman year. Some AiA studies have examined the impact of first-year instruction as students move through their coursework, while others have studied the contributions of library instruction to the sophomore, junior, or senior academic experience. Two assessment studies conducted during the third year of the AiA program, which are described below, also investigated the impact of library instruction offered after the first year of college or university study. The project at <u>Bentley University</u> focused on business degree students, and <u>Georgetown University</u>'s study considered graduate students. Both institutions saw positive contributions of the library.

- Students enrolled in <u>Bentley University</u>'s Integrated Business Project (IBP) course apply research methods in their study of real-world business problems. The AiA team investigated the impact of library research consultations on students' learning in one section of the course (7.5 percent of students enrolled in IBP course sections). Survey results of students' experiences indicate a 36 percent increase in students' level of confidence when applying research methods after consulting with reference librarians.

- <u>Georgetown University</u> studied the connection between library-instructional interventions (e.g., research instruction, web-based tutorials, and research consultations) provided to graduate students and the applicability and transferability of the skills to workplace situations. These skills include the ability to identify, synthesize, and communicate information from relevant sources and to propose solutions to industry and work-based problems. Students who participated in library intervention reported a positive impact of the instruction on their research skills confidence (87 percent) and indicated that the skills taught were "very" applicable (55 percent) or "quite a bit" applicable (27 percent) to current or future workplace settings.

> *The study's findings suggest that research libraries are a critical partner and tool for students to advance their workplace information fluency.*
>
> - <u>Georgetown University</u>

Studies in Year 3 at <u>Drexel University</u>, the <u>University of North Carolina-Greensboro</u>, and the <u>University of Wyoming</u> also add to this multifaceted area of assessment activity and build on the work of Year 1 projects (e.g., <u>Anne Arundel Community College</u> and <u>Lasell College</u>) and Year 2 projects (e.g., <u>Champlain College</u>, the <u>University of Minnesota-Morris</u>, and the <u>University of South Dakota</u>).

3. The library promotes academic rapport and student engagement.

When students feel a sense of belonging and connectedness to a campus, learning is enhanced and academic success is more likely. Their academic engagement, motivation, and general enjoyment of courses and learning typically increase with academic rapport. In each of the three years of the AiA program, campus teams considered the unique role that the library may play in a student's sense of academic rapport. At the University of Alberta, for example, the library initiated PLAS: Personal Librarian for Aboriginal Students, and an assessment of its effectiveness by the campus team in Year 2 found that in addition to encouraging students to visit the library, use its services, and make better use of the services and programs, PLAS "created a positive environment for their learning and research, and helped demystify the library and lessened their anxiety toward it" (University of Alberta team). In the first year of the AiA program, Montana State University documented a positive connection between the library's social media initiatives and students' sense of community.

In Year 3, Seattle University's AiA team focused on this academic outcome in its study of transfer students.

- Early in the university's first quarter, the Library and Learning Commons staff members e-mail transfer students to introduce themselves and describe various services. To increase a sense of personalization and engagement, the e-mails also include a short video introduction and information about two welcome events. The AiA campus team assessed impact of this communication on students' academic experience. The survey findings indicate that students (57 percent) found the video helpful, and those students who attended the welcome event indicated that the event made them "more likely to use one or more of the library and learning commons services." In fact, the student respondents recommended increasing the social, interactive, and personalized aspects of the library program and to include more information about the library and its staff during the Transfer Orientation activities.

Academic rapport and intimacy encompass multiple attributes, and the AiA projects exemplify different ways that these various factors can be investigated to assess the library's contribution to students' sense of connection with their institution.

4. Use of library space relates positively to student learning and success.

Several AiA campus teams have investigated students' use of library space and its connection to their learning and success. Numerous aspects of this impact area were studied in the first two years of the AiA program, including the location of service points in relation to student learning (e.g., Eastern Mennonite University), the role of space in fostering academic and social community (e.g., University of Manitoba, University of Mississippi Medical Center, and Wake Forest University), and students' use of library space and its connection to student success (e.g., University of Northern Colorado). An assessment project conducted during Year 3 at Davidson College studied how reconfiguring library space might improve students' academic experience.

- Co-curricular experiences that extend learning beyond the classroom and include leadership, service-learning, community-engagement, and entrepreneurship activities are given a high priority at Davidson College. The AiA project team used surveys and focus groups to generate data that compared the library's impact on students involved in co-curricular programs with their peers. Co-curricular students ranked aspects of the library, such as space/comfort, services, and collections, as more important than their peers. However, they were less satisfied with space than were their peers. The AiA librarian at Davidson College explains how the findings inform decision making about library space and services: "By focusing on themes that emerged in the project's focus groups, the Davidson College Library will create an agenda for agile development of the library space and service—subsequent improvements will be assessed, revised, and reassessed. These recursive changes should maximize Library impact on co-curricular students, and may also be relevant to the student body as a whole."

Additional projects in the third year of the AiA program that investigated library space as an impact factor considered student engagement (University of Iowa), student use of space (University of Kansas), and the library as a place for research and scholarly collaboration (Lincoln University).

Advancing Library Leadership through Action Research

In each of the three years of the AiA program, the librarians commented in their project and reflective reports that their leadership competence increased through the professional development and assessment activities that merged research with practice. The action research framework, which emphasized improving practice through systematic investigation of a question grounded in institution context, engaged the librarians in an immersive process of ongoing interaction with one another and collaboration with their team members. The librarians led the design and implementation of assessment that related directly to their campus's academic priorities, creating opportunities for substantive conversations with campus stakeholders about student learning and resulting in meaningful findings that informed decision making about library programs and practices. The leadership qualities that were strengthened through this process include an awareness of the importance of inquiry and decision making grounded in institutional context, understanding and experience with the dynamic nature of assessment, and a recognition of the personal and professional growth that emerges through collaboration with others. These qualities also reflect key elements of an action research approach.

Understanding of Institutional Context

The librarians led their campus team through an assessment project that focused on a question aligned with their institution's mission and priorities and that had shared interest among the team members. The projects also integrated research with practice, which means that the design and implementation of the projects had strong connections to the ongoing work of the librarians and campus constituents. As a result, the assessment activities were situated in everyday practice, giving context and real-world relevance to the work. A sense of personal responsibility and ownership for the assessment process was fostered because the results led to practical knowledge that had significance and consequences for the librarians and their professional practice.

Through their work on the AiA projects, the librarians frequently expanded their participation in institutional assessment activities. Because the team-based approach to assessment prompted discussion about how different campus units interact and influence student learning, one project completed by one unit wasn't enough. The collaborative process often generated campus-wide synergy around assessment.

> *The main take away from our involvement with AiA has been assessing what we value, not just valuing what we assess. We understand now that the context matters and librarians need to pay close attention to institutional values and how can we add value to them.*
>
> • AiA librarian, reflective report

Facilitating the Dynamic Nature of Assessment

The librarians developed leadership skills that anticipated and were responsive to the dynamic nature of organizational cultures and practices. The team-based approach required collaboration throughout the assessment design, implementation, and analysis phases, a process that was iterative and generative as discussions took place. Important conversations occurred as team members shared their perspectives on student learning and considered how different departments and campus units contribute to enhancing a student's experience at the institution. Critical dialogue was needed to reach common understanding about different aspects of the project, including agreed-upon definitions of learning characteristics and attributes of academic success, and consensus about meaningful measures of these attributes. For example, what are acceptable measures of academic rapport? Or how are we defining "at risk" students? It's a dynamic, developmental process.

> *The discussions regarding exactly what information literacy is and how it relates to a student's skill set were particularly revealing....Conversations about how to increase critical thinking and information literacy brought to light the challenge of creating useful surveys.*
>
> • AiA librarian, reflective report

An action research framework also anticipates the dynamic nature of assessment and acknowledges the likelihood that adjustments to the process will occur as it unfolds. For many librarians, leadership was required to navigate multiple tasks and dimensions of the project as it changed over the fourteen-month process. Even mistakes provided opportunities to learn and improve.

Having gone through the process of the AiA project, I am better versed at planning out assessment projects. I have a stronger base of experience to refer to when creating a research question and gathering meaningful data. I also feel that the process of failure and reaching dead-ends in my AiA project helped me become more creative in using failure to create knowledge. I realize that data cannot tell the whole story, which helps me understand the type of questions I can ask that could reasonably answered in a data project.

- *AiA librarian, reflective report*

Since the projects were designed to inform decision making and to improve programs and practices, the likelihood of change was built into the process. Change by its very nature is dynamic and fluid. Through the professional development and project activities, the librarians learned to negotiate and navigate this evolving and often ambiguous process.

Embracing Professional and Personal Growth

As the librarians led their campus teams, they honed their leadership skills and recognized significant growth at a personal and professional level. The librarians positioned themselves as contributing members of the broader campus environment, and they saw their influence on the academic work of the institution. Their knowledge of and experience with assessment led to recognition by others, and, in the process, the library's value on campus was enhanced. At several institutions, the AiA librarians moved into new leadership roles in the library and on campus that required a broader set of leadership competencies.

Leading a team-based assessment project also increased the librarians' competence with proposing action steps based on evidence and implementing changes in library services and practices. As they made decisions based on project findings, they expanded their capacity to lead and initiate change.

One of the most important things I learned was that people on campus really do want to work with librarians. Honestly, I was a bit cynical about faculty perceptions of librarians, and worried that folks on campus might not be willing to take on a project of this scale with me. Everyone I invited to the campus team was excited to be part of the project, and excited to work with me. This gave me a lot of confidence, and makes me excited to form more partnerships in the future…. I'm also much more comfortable with assessment work, and in fact advocated for assessment to be a larger part of my role. It's now part of my job title!

- *AiA librarian, reflective report*

Communication skills as demonstrated by facilitation, collaboration, and presentations were also strengthened through the project activities. Over the fourteen months, the librarians facilitated a group process that required communication of a shared vision and delegation of a procedure for carrying out the assessment. The facilitation also necessitated an understanding of interpersonal communication and collaboration to move the project forward. Once the project findings were completed, the librarians considered the various campus constituent groups that would benefit from learning about the results, and they initiated conversations and delivered presentations to communicate the project outcomes and propose evidence-based actions.

Conclusion

A strong community of practice around academic library assessment has emerged through the AiA program and continues to develop. During each year of the program, the librarians were involved in a collective learning experience that encouraged sharing ideas and providing critical feedback about their assessment work. The process also fostered networking among the librarians, which has been sustained beyond the AiA activities. Many of the librarians have presented about their assessment experience and ongoing work at conferences, written journal articles, or prepared book chapters, as documented by the growing Assessment in Action Bibliography.[8]

> *I felt a part of a community of practice, thrust into a unique experience, all trying to find our way and learning from one another.*
>
> • AiA librarian, reflective report

The results of over 200 AiA campus team projects document positive library impact in several important areas related to students' academic experiences. The projects also demonstrate how academic librarians can engage institutional constituent groups and lead assessment initiatives. In the process, they have increased awareness about library contributions to student learning and success on their campuses and within the wider postsecondary education community.

---

[8] "Assessment in Action Bibliography," ACRL Value of Academic Libraries website, accessed April 10, 2017, http://www.acrl.ala.org/value/?page_id=980.

CHAPTER 6

Value of Academic Libraries Statement

The Value of Academic Libraries Statement, below, articulates the various ways academic libraries provide direct and indirect value to institutions of higher education.

Librarians can use this to develop their own talking points and "elevator speeches" highlighting the essential role that academic libraries play as "one of the few units in a modern institution of higher education that can provide an impact on all realms of institutional importance, from student enrollment to faculty productivity to institutional reputation, while balancing services and resources for all constituency groups and stakeholders in higher education."

Approved by the ACRL Board of Directors on June 25, 2016, the Value of Academic Libraries Statement was authored by Adam Murray (James Madison University) and Lorelei Tanji (University of California, Irvine), members of the ACRL Value of Academic Libraries Committee, on behalf of the Committee.

Association of College & Research Libraries
50 E. Huron St. Chicago, IL 60611
800-545-2433, ext. 2523
acrl@ala.org, http://www.acrl.org

VALUE OF ACADEMIC LIBRARIES STATEMENT

EXECUTIVE SUMMARY:

Academic libraries provide critical direct and indirect value to institutions of higher education in the following areas:

I. SUPPORT RECRUITMENT, RETENTION, & MATRICULATION

- Academic libraries provide services and facilities that attract students and help increase the likelihood of persistence and graduation.

II. ENHANCE STUDENT LEARNING

- Academic libraries provide opportunities for students to learn marketable skills or to apply what they have learned in their courses in a real-world environment.

- Several studies show correlations between students' use of academic libraries and positive changes in GPA.

- Academic libraries support student learning in areas that employers increasingly seek, such as: critical and creative thinking, written and oral communication, and integrative- and lifelong-learning.

- Academic libraries provide an environment that fosters student engagement across all elements of the curriculum and student population.

III. SUPPORT FACULTY RESEARCH & TEACHING

- Academic librarians assist faculty with the research process and help faculty navigate the shifting landscape of scholarly communication.

- Academic libraries provide an infrastructure for open data management and open access publishing required by a growing number of granting agencies and foundations.

- Increased access to faculty research through institutional repositories and university presses enhances institutional standing and positively impacts economic development.

- Academic librarians support faculty teaching by highlighting new electronic and alternative resources, and provide faculty support in the transition to online course delivery.

IV. RAISE INSTITUTIONAL VISIBILITY & CONTRIBUTE TO THE COMMUNITY

- Academic libraries serve as a driver of innovation by facilitating the implications of new technology on pedagogy, course delivery, and research productivity.

- Academic library facilities foster collaboration, and serve as a unique area on campus that promotes interaction between people of many different cultures, ethnicities, gender identities, and backgrounds.

- Library services and resources contribute to the welfare of the communities in which institutions of higher education operate.

- Special collections and archives help preserve the history of the institution or region for future generations.

Association of College & Research Libraries
50 E. Huron St. Chicago, IL 60611
800-545-2433, ext. 2523
acrl@ala.org, http://www.acrl.org

VALUE OF ACADEMIC LIBRARIES STATEMENT

While academic libraries have long held a rhetorical position as the "heart of the university," the multiplicity of roles which academic libraries and librarians can fulfill, in part because of advances in technology, transforms this rhetorical phrase into a description of reality. Academic libraries are one of the few units in a modern institution of higher education that can provide an impact on all realms of institutional importance, from student enrollment to faculty productivity to institutional reputation, while balancing services and resources for all constituency groups and stakeholders in higher education.

Academic libraries provide critical direct and indirect value to institutions of higher education in the following areas:

I.   SUPPORT RECRUITMENT, RETENTION, & MATRICULATION

Contributions to student enrollment.

Institutions of Higher Education compete for a limited population of traditional college students, with drives for recruiting the best and brightest students.[1] **Academic libraries provide resources, services, and facilities that appeal to the best students and can help attract them to an institution**. The resources and services provided by academic libraries provide access for low-income students, assisting with affordability of higher education. The collections and support provided to graduate, professional, and doctoral students helps attract students into these programs. Non-traditional, transfer, and international students are able to receive assistance from academic libraries, often assisting them with the transition to a different educational environment than what they had previously experienced.

Contributions to student retention & graduation rates.

Numerous studies have demonstrated correlations between use of academic library resources, collections, services, and facilities with student retention.[2] Academic libraries provide services and facilities that **nurture students' academic and social integration** with institutions of higher education, faculty, and fellow students, **helping increase the likelihood of graduation. This has a positive effect on institutional funding in the face of performance-based funding models**.

II.   ENHANCE STUDENT LEARNING

Supporting student success.

Academic libraries employ student workers in varying levels of employment, serving as a host for internships, graduate assistantships, and service-learning or volunteer experiences. These experiences can provide opportunities for students to **learn marketable skills or to apply what they have learned in their courses in a real-world environment**. Positive experiences with academic libraries can help confirm students' interests in pursuing further study in a field, leading to graduate or professional school placements.[3]

Promoting student achievement.

As with student retention and graduation rates, numerous studies have demonstrated **significant correlations between students' use of academic libraries and positive changes in GPA**.[4] Students with higher GPAs are also likely to do well on professional or educational tests such as the GRE or the CAAP.

Fostering student learning.

In a global, knowledge-based economy, academic libraries play a significant role in contributing to student learning in the area of information literacy. This contribution may take the form of credit-bearing courses, on-request instruction sessions, mentoring undergraduate or graduate research projects or internships, and providing "traditional" one-on-one research assistance in a variety of settings. In addition to information literacy, academic libraries provide services and resources that support student learning in areas of increasing importance for employers, such as **critical and creative thinking, written and oral communication, and integrative- and lifelong-learning**.

Improving the student experience.

Academic libraries are unique within institutions of higher education in that they provide an informal academic environment that is **deliberately managed to foster student engagement across all elements of the curriculum and student population**.[5] This ranges from organizing the library facility as a service which promotes collaboration, experience with diversity, and time spent writing and studying to aligning liaison services with learning communities, writing-intensive courses, undergraduate research, and other high-impact educational practices.[6] Academic libraries are ideally situated to provide both academic and social engagement opportunities, which help keep students focused, nurture feelings of integration, and tend to lead to positive learning experiences and graduation.

III. SUPPORT FACULTY RESEARCH & TEACHING

Contributing to faculty research productivity.

Academic librarians play an evolving role in assisting faculty with the research process, **helping faculty navigate the shifting landscape of scholarly communication**. Academic librarians provide assistance to faculty, administrators, and tenure/promotion committees in evaluating faculty research and creative activities, including open access publications, impact factors, and altmetrics. Librarians help connect faculty who may be working on related research, and provide counseling on authors' rights issues.

Participating in faculty grant proposals and funding.

Academic libraries **provide an infrastructure for open data management and open access publishing** required by an increasing number of granting agencies and foundations. Many academic libraries provide funding for defraying the cost of publishing in an open access format. Successful grant proposals are predicated on the provision of adequate research collections and materials, which academic libraries facilitate.

Improving faculty teaching.

Many academic libraries employ instructional developers, designers, or liaisons to **assist faculty with updating assignments to reflect electronic and alternative resources, and to support faculty in the transition to online course delivery**.

IV. RAISE INSTITUTIONAL VISIBILITY & CONTRIBUTE TO THE COMMUNITY

Enhancing institutional reputation or prestige.

Special collections and archives serve as a direct means of attracting external attention, through engaging experts seeking to use these resources, along with regional/national/global media consideration for unique holdings.   The distribution of faculty research through institutional repositories and university presses **enhances institutional standing as a generator of new knowledge, which in turn has economic development implications**. Academic libraries are often active participants in institutional fundraising, either directly linking philanthropic activities to library technology, spaces for students, or collections or by indirectly acting as an "upsell" feature for donor proposals in other areas of the university. Academic libraries are also able to be the recipient of national or international awards, generating further prestige for the institution.

Acting as drivers of innovation and technology.

Rapid changes in technology have large-scale implications for academic libraries; as a result, many academic libraries serve as an early experimenter with new technology. This allows academic librarians the opportunity to help drive innovation at institutions of higher education by **facilitating the implications of new technology on pedagogy, course delivery, and research productivity**.

Promoting diversity and global awareness.

Academic library facilities are deliberately designed to foster collaboration, and **serve as a unique area on campus that promotes interaction between people of many different cultures, ethnicities, gender identities, and backgrounds**.

By being of value to the community.

Institutions of higher education actively **contribute to the welfare of their surrounding communities**. Academic libraries can play a key role in this, by providing means for cultural engagement through the promotion of literacy, digital literacy, history, and broadband infrastructure. Many academic libraries provide borrowing privileges for community members, supporting lifelong learning within their communities, and can develop innovative partnerships with such entities as Chambers of Commerce, hospitals, and small business development units.

Preserving institutional and regional history.

Academic libraries serve as a repository for archives of the institution as well as the region, **preserving the history of the institution or region for future generations**.

About

This statement was authored by Adam Murray (James Madison University) and Lorelei Tanji (University of California, Irvine), members of the ACRL Value of Academic Libraries Committee. It was influenced in its basic concept by the United Kingdom's Society of College, National and University Libraries statement on the value of academic libraries *and was modeled on the areas of research outlined in ACRL's 2010 publication* Value of Academic Libraries: A Comprehensive Research Review and Report. *The ACRL Value of Academic Libraries committee proposed the statement and it was approved by the ACRL Board of Directors on June 25, 2016.*

Endnotes

1. Jon McGee, *Breakpoint: The Changing Marketplace for Higher Education* (Baltimore: Johns Hopkins University Press, 2015).
2. Gaby Haddow and Jayanthi Joseph, "Loans, Logins, and Lasting the Course: Academic Library Use and Student Retention," *Australian Academic & Research Libraries 41,* 4 (2010): 233-244. Gaby Haddow, "Academic Library Use and Student Retention: A Quantitative Analysis," *Library & Information Science Research 35,* 2 (2013): 127-136. Krista Soria, Jan Fransen, and Shane Nackerud, "Library Use and Undergraduate Student Outcomes: New Evidence for Students' Retention and Academic Success," *Portal: Libraries and the Academy 13,* 2 (2013): 33-45. Krista Soria, Jan Fransen, and Shane Nackerud, "Stacks, Serials, Search Engines, and Students' Success: First-year Undergraduate Students' Library Use, Academic Achievement, and Retention," *The Journal of Academic Librarianship 40,* 1 (2014): 84-91. Adam Murray, Ashley Ireland, and Jana Hackathorn, "The Value of Academic Libraries: Library Services as a Predictor of Student Retention," *College & Research Libraries* (2016: forthcoming). Angie Thorpe, Ria Lukes, Diane Bever, and He Yan, "The Impact of the Academic Library on Student Success: Connecting the Dots," *portal: Libraries & the Academy 16,* 2 (2016): 373-392. John Stemmer and David Mahan, "Investigating the Relationship of Library Usage to Student Outcomes," *College & Research Libraries 77,* 3 (2016): 359-375.
3. Kayo Denda and Jennifer Hunter, "Building 21st Century Skills and Creating Communities: A Team-based Engagement Framework for Student Employment in Academic Libraries," *Journal of Library Administration 56,* 3 (2016): 251-265.
4. John Stemmer and David Mahan, "Investigating the Relationship of Library Usage to Student Outcomes," *College & Research Libraries 77,* 3 (2016): 359-375. Sue Samson, "Usage of E-resources: Virtual Value of Demographics," *Journal of Academic Librarianship 40,* 6 (2014): 620-625. Shun Han Rebekah Wong and Diane Cmor, "Measuring Association between Library Instruction and Graduation GPA," *College & Research Libraries 72,* 5 (2011): 464-473. Krista Soria, Jan Fransen, and Shane Nackerud, "Library Use and Undergraduate Student Outcomes: New Evidence for Students' Retention and Academic Success," *Portal: Libraries and the Academy 13,* 2 (2013): 33-45.
5. George Kuh and Robert Gonyea, "The role of the academic library in promoting student engagement in learning," *College & Research Libraries 4,* 4 (2003): 256-282.
6. Adam Murray, "Academic Libraries and High-impact Practices for Student Retention: Library Deans' Perspectives," *portal: Libraries & the Academy 15,* 3 (2015): 471-487.

Reflections

The following nine reflections demonstrate the ongoing effectiveness of the Assessment in Action (AiA) program and the impact of team-based assessment pertaining to student learning and success. While these essays represent only a fraction of the 203 librarian-led teams, they reflect on a broad range of institutions, projects, viewpoints, and data collection methods. Although varied in context, these reflections share the themes of communication, flexibility, and diversity.

Collaboration was a cornerstone of the AiA program. Strong communication between faculty and institutional stakeholders was key to building these important partnerships on campus, and to laying the groundwork for project success and ongoing impact. While the value of communication skills is not a new concept, implementation is often easier said than done. When assessing library impact for transfer students, Grigg remarks that "often librarians design research studies in a vacuum and how important it is to connect with other campus stakeholders." In Baugess and Martin's reflection on their assessment of a library internship program, they state, "Regular communication with stakeholders during a large project is one of the most valuable lessons from completing the AiA program." With repeated communication coming from multiple staff from before implementation to after the project completion, Bush reflects that "the continued collaborative communication and programming was one of the most fruitful outcomes of the project."

Flexibility and scalability continue to be important components of success for librarians who often must do more with less. Librarians reflected on the scalability of their projects, and how their projects could be modeled for future assessment needs. Haldeman and Brennan state that due to the AiA program, "the library was able to adapt to change rapidly, and we found ourselves in a position to better focus on the benefits of assessment to support evidence-based decision making and change." In addition, Jahng reports that her AiA project was "scalable, enabling the embedding of information literacy instruction throughout ENGL courses and the major." At Grand Valley State University, O'Kelly found that even with limited resources, the library had "methodically built a replicable process for measuring and analyzing the relationship between library instruction and student retention." Liss also reflects on the scalability of his project, noting it "has paid and continues to pay dividends at BU while also contributing to the broader goals of the AiA program."

Two of these nine reflections address the importance of serving a diverse student body. Bishop's project focuses on students qualifying as first generation, limited income, or disabled—and resulted in support from the library dean to create a new accessible entrance. Bush reflects that it was key that "our new library administrator understood our growing focus on students and our culture of inclusivity, creativity, and openness." Goebel found success in expanding by fivefold a personal librarian program for Aboriginal and International Students, and was pleased to find that as a result of the AiA program, "the library was perceived as providing leadership in a collaborative effort of direct support for Aboriginal students."

Additional public AiA reflections can be found online, including blog entries from Hope J. Houston, Associate Director & Manager of Reference Services, Bentley University; kYmberly Keeton, Academic Librarian/Assistant Professor of Library Science, Lincoln University; and Kim Pittman, Information Literacy & Assessment Librarian, University of Minnesota Duluth. Each team leader completed a final project descriptive report and these reports are fully searchable in an online collection. The team leaders also completed a reflective report at the end of their participation, and while these second reports are kept confidential, aggregate and anonymous comments from the reflective reports contributed to reports synthesizing each year of the AiA program. They can be found in the first section of this book and on the ACRL Value of Academic Libraries website.

A Stone Soup Approach to Building Large-Scale Library Assessments

Mary O'Kelly, Grand Valley State University

AN OLD FOLK TALE[1] tells about a traveler who has nothing to eat and comes upon a town whose residents have no food to share. The traveler begins boiling an old stone, claiming that he can make a delicious stone soup that is plain but nutritious and would be even better with just a bit of herbs, and a little vegetable, and maybe a small piece of meat. Little by little the community contributes what they have to the soup and, after the stone is cast aside, they all share in the hearty meal. Similarly, library assessment can be built from small, even failed or rock-bottom attempts, into large-scale, culture-enhancing projects that result in the library having good stories of its impact to tell.

Assessment in Action Cohort 2013–14

When we started our Assessment in Action (AiA) project, we intended to measure the effectiveness of our library's Knowledge Market, a collaborative program that combines three peer-learning services in one location: library research, writing, and oral presentations. Each of the three is administered and funded through a separate unit on campus, though the library is the physical and technological host. We wanted to see if the three services worked and brought more to student experience with a shared location.

In hindsight, there are several red flags in that brief description: "effectiveness," "separate units," and "worked" stand out as poorly defined and nearly prohibitively complicated to facilitate in just one year. However, we saw the value in deliberately measuring a key academic support that offers students an opportunity to engage in peer learning. The service also offers the library an opening to solidify ongoing, meaningful, and productive partnerships with other educational support services.

The idea of the Knowledge Market was developed by the libraries' former dean, Lee Van Orsdel, with significant operational and strategic input from former associate dean Julie Garrison and former director and assistant director of the writing center, Ellen Schendel and Patrick Johnson.[2] As we were designing our new library building in 2008–09, Dean Van Orsdel heard from local employers that they actively sought to hire graduates with solid written and oral communication skills and the ability to find and discern high-quality information. Writing centers and libraries have coexisted for years, and we wanted to take this opportunity to fully integrate and philosophically align ours. Through careful planning and a deliberate invitation for the School of Communication to develop a speech lab, the three initial employer-desired skills—research, writing, and speech—were captured in a collaborative peer-learning service. The services operate in the same space at the same time, with no walls or doors to separate the peer consultants from the students seeking assistance.

After the first pilot year, and as our 2013–14 AiA project, we set out to measure the effectiveness of the program. To get started we chose grade point average (GPA) and retention as proxy measures of student success. As the project progressed, the writing center and speech lab found themselves on a different reporting timeline than what was required by AiA. The library downshifted its expectations and instead focused on students using only the research segment of the service. We collected evaluation surveys from students, asking if they found the service helpful, if it was comfortable, and if they felt more confident completing their assignment. We measured student perceptions of the services—which they found very helpful—general characteristics of students who used the services, and some of the perceptions of the peer consultants working in the Knowledge Market. We also worked with Institutional Analysis (institutional research on most campuses) to look for differences between GPA the semester prior to library instruction and after library instruction, and fall-to-fall retention between students who used the service compared to those who did not. In short, students found the service helpful and comfortable, but there was no significant difference in GPA or retention.[3]

Tying the Library to Critical Education Practices and Retention

At several points during the project I felt stuck. The assessment project as proposed had a timeline and deliverable expectations that matched neither our academic calendar nor the reporting expectations of various committees, administrators, and accreditors. The way we proposed to work and the way we actually worked did not match. The library project was understandably a lower priority for non-library collaborators, and within the library we did not yet have a strong culture of assessment and data sharing. My collaborators and I were collecting our data, but the synthesis of all three services on the AiA project was not happening—the library's relationship with Institutional Analysis strengthened while the writing center and speech lab found themselves bound by their own programs' priorities.

Yet something lit a spark. Given that student engagement with academic support services appears to positively influence retention, could student engagement with the library as an academic support service also influence retention? It certainly supports the strategic mission of the university; retention has been an explicit goal in our strategic plan going back to at least 2010. In a state with declining high school enrollments, economic challenges, and unstable state funding, keeping students engaged and successful through to graduation is something on which our institution is willing to expend considerable effort.

Our library also enjoys institutional support for information literacy. It is an explicit learning outcome of our general education program[4] and, as of early 2017, is a campus-wide learning outcome. The institution has adapted the Association of American Colleges and Universities' (AAC&U) LEAP VALUE rubrics and George Kuh's high-impact educational practices,[5] each of which have direct ties to library services and resources. Making those connections clear, visible, and repeatable—especially as they relate to student success—not only reinforces the library's position as a strategic academic partner but also helps keep enhanced library programming top-of-mind both inside and outside the library.

Some literature supports—if lightly—the potential for librarians to positively influence student achievement. In their book devoted to identifying and advocating for factors that directly contribute to student success, Kuh, Kinzie, Schuh, and Whitt write, "many librarians know a good deal about how students spend their time, what they think and talk about, and how they feel, yet they are an underused educational resource."[6] Taken from another angle, the theories and concepts presented in Seidman's *College Student Retention: Formula for Student Success* and Braxton and colleagues' *Rethinking College Student Retention* can readily be mapped to common library activities;[7] for example, library faculty regularly engage with student research projects, peer research consultants provide meaningful peer learning opportunities, thoughtfully designed library environments encourage social interaction, and so on, yet that explicit library connection is not mentioned in any significant way. This gap highlights a need for more intensive, rigorous examination of library activities as critical educational practices that, along with other complex factors, positively contribute to the overall college learning experience.

New Projects Inspired by Assessment in Action

Prior to Assessment in Action, I had outlined a plan to improve our library instruction data collection so that we had reliable, usable numbers. In the five previous years, instruction data had been collected with six different tools, and during one unfortunate upgrade we lost two years' worth of data. With help from the liaison librarians, who do nearly all of our library instruction, I created a simple yet stable form using LibAnalytics to collect basic instruction information: librarian, course code, course number, section number, professor name, time in class, subjects covered, methods used, and so on. By the 2013–14 academic year, the year we participated in AiA, we were consistently collecting usable data on every single instruction session—but were not collecting any student-level data.

During AiA training I learned new approaches to planning a large-scale assessment project and was inspired by stories shared in my cohort. My previous attempts to measure and evaluate library activities had been more haphazard, less methodical. Even though the project I started in AiA ended up with more perceptual and demographic data than advanced measures of student success, I found I was able to transfer skills and concepts to this newly sparked plan for large-scale assessment of library instruction. With Institutional Analysis and three groups of liaison librarians, I initiated a multiyear exploration of the relationship between library instruction overall and student retention, in addition to exploring over two dozen additional questions about the reach and impact of our library instructional services.

To start analysis and interpretation of the instruction data, we needed advanced analytical skills. The associate dean and I met with the director of Institutional Analysis, explained our goals, and asked for his expertise. Our request was clear and specific: we would send information about library instruction sessions once or twice a year to the analyst, who would match student data with instruction sessions and then return the results in aggregate (depersonalized) to the library.

I wrote a list of twenty-seven questions, such as number of students reached, grade level, major program, and so on, that I hoped to have data analyzed to inform. Every year since then, we have added a question or two; last year's list had thirty-two questions. That list is sent to the analyst along with the data. One of those questions was substantive: Is there a correlation between in-person library instruction and student re-enrollment the following fall? (We define retention as year-to-year re-enrollment to differentiate retention from persistence to graduation.) The answer was yes, and it was statistically significant. Not wanting to rely on one year, I repeated the question the following year and met again with the analyst to discuss some of the details. By the third year of replication, with sample sizes over 18,000 annually, I determined it was time to share the results. I've been presenting and writing about it ever since[8] and now have about fourteen other institutions interested in replicating our approach.

Building a Community of Practice in the Library

Assessment can feel overwhelming, especially in the face of institutional and accreditation pressures, but many hands make light work. I was pleasantly surprised by how friendly and accommodating our Institutional Analysis staff were. It is all too easy—and understandable—to get bogged down in the more negative perceptions of large-scale library assessment: "I don't have the staff to do a big study like that," "The stats people on my campus won't help at all," or "My library doesn't have the budget for an assessment librarian so we'll never be able to do it." However, with one knowledgeable and skilled statistician willing to provide only two or three work days a year and instruction librarians willing to report on the course, code, and section for each session they teach, we have methodically built a replicable process for measuring and analyzing the relationship between library instruction and student retention.

The work has also been enriched by the community of librarians who do assessment (with or without the title) and share their work through AiA and other venues, such as the ARL Library Assessment Conference, the Southeastern Library Assessment Conference, the ARL-ASSESS email list, and the AALHE ASSESS list. I have attended, presented at, and communicated through each of these venues, and my work is better for it.

Most significantly, our library culture has embraced regular data collection and sharing, not simply for the sake of having data but in order to make informed decisions and advocate for our programs and services. There is power in being confident about offering reliable, replicable evidence. It demonstrates to campus stakeholders, especially university administrators, that the library is committed to regular evaluation and communication about its work. By taking this approach, we no longer assume others see the value in libraries: We make it plain. We give those stakeholders clear language and understandable data that they, in turn, can use to tell success stories to donors, legislators, and the community. At our institution, library data has been used in grant applications, assessment reports, budget rationales, new staffing requests, new program proposals, and accreditation self-studies.

All this advocacy and communication work takes ongoing commitment, so in 2016 we formalized a University Libraries Data and Assessment Committee that helps gather and report on the abundant data collected at all library locations. Instruction librarians continue to collect, analyze, and present on data, and nearly all library departments—from user experience and circulation to web services and archives—openly share assessment results.

Community Status

In early 2017 I learned that the Dean of Students/Vice Provost for Student Affairs was working on a campus-wide audit of practices that directly or indirectly support student retention. I immediately responded with three specific activities conducted by the library, including information about our instruction-retention connection and about the Knowledge Market—our original Assessment in Action project:

- *Library instruction:* Faculty librarians teach between 9,000 and 10,000 students per year and work closely with classroom faculty to integrate information literacy into the curriculum. With assistance from Institutional Analysis, a correlation has been found between library instruction and student re-enrollment the following fall.
- *Knowledge Market:* Research consultants, who are high-achieving and well-trained student employees, offer one-to-one peer research assistance to fellow students in the library's

Knowledge Market. Research consultants apply best practices in peer learning to encourage increased confidence and self-efficacy.

- *Librarian consultations:* Faculty librarians meet with individual students or small groups to help students develop advanced information literacy skills. The consultations also provide an opportunity for students to develop a research mentoring relationship with a library faculty member, and, as a result, several library faculty have served as thesis, scholarship, and independent study mentors.

That retention audit resulted in a final internal report, which included the contributions from University Libraries. I also was invited to participate in a provost-led retention initiative, which kicked off with an open brainstorming meeting. Faculty at the meeting were very curious about the study and interested in helping design a secondary study to start unraveling causation, or at least begin to explore the role of faculty in encouraging student use of the library. After participating in that meeting, I overheard comments in two unrelated campus meetings that "the library is doing really interesting work on retention." After receiving the final retention report, I noticed that our three activities were not the only mentions of library services. The graduate school cited the library as a critical support service for students; the Office of Undergraduate Research mentioned a new library scholars program that its office supports through summer grant for high-achieving students; the Women, Gender, and Sexuality Studies department described a new initiative that pairs upper-division students with first-year students in the major to learn advanced library research and information literacy skills; and the College of Nursing touted the liaison librarian's involvement in their burgeoning online and hybrid courses.

This external recognition of our commitment to assessing the library's impact on student success has elevated the visibility and status of library assessment activities. Publicly promoting library activities such as instruction (as it relates to student retention), librarian consultations (as student-engagement practices), and peer-tutoring services (originating in the library and not student affairs), and having ready evidence of how well those activities support student achievement, has resulted in increased visibility on campus and new opportunities for librarian involvement in retention programs, assessment committees, collaborative partnerships with institutional research staff, exploratory conversations with faculty on potential research partnerships, invitations to speak, contributions to campus newsletters and magazines, increasingly detailed library instruction plans, and a stabilizing culture of data collection, analysis, and storytelling.

Biography

Mary O'Kelly was the head of instructional services at Grand Valley State University Libraries throughout the Assessment in Action project. In that role she was responsible for strategic planning and assessment of library educational activities, including classroom instruction, online library learning, and student-to-student peer research consultation services. Mary received a Bachelor of Arts degree from the University of Michigan and a Master of Library and Information Science degree from the University of Wisconsin at Milwaukee. Mary currently serves as the associate dean for education and user services at Western Michigan University Libraries. Reach her at mary.okelly@wmich.edu.

Notes

1. One version of the story is available in Marcia Brown's Caldecott Honor book, *Stone Soup: An Old Tale*, published by Charles Scribner & Sons in 1947. It also appears in numerous other collections of folk tales and legends from around the world.

2. Ellen Schendel, Julie Garrison, Patrick Johnson, and Lee Van Orsdel, "Making Noise in the Library: Designing a Student Learning Environment to Support Liberal Education," in *Cases on Higher Education Spaces: Innovation, Collaboration, and Technology*, ed. Russell G. Carpenter (Hershey, PA: IGI Global, 2013), 290–312.

3. A summary of the project and downloadable PDF of the final poster presentation are available on the Assessment in Action project description page: Grand Valley State University, "Project Description," AiA project report, Association of College and Research Libraries website, accessed November 17, 2017, https://apply.ala.org/aia/docs/project/5400.

4. Grand Valley State University, "Student Learning Outcomes of the General Education Program," accessed November 17, 2017, http://www.gvsu.edu/gened/student-learning-outcomes-79.htm.

5. Association of American Colleges and Universities, "VALUE," accessed November 17, 2017, https://www.aacu.org/value; "High-Impact Educational Practices: A Brief Overview," excerpt from George D. Kuh, *High-Impact Educational Practices: What They Are, Who Has Access to Them, and Why They Matter* (Washington, DC: Association of American Colleges and Universities, 2008), https://www.aacu.org/leap/hips.

6. George D. Kuh, Jillian Kinzie, John H. Schuh, and Elizabeth J. Whitt, *Student Success in College: Creating Conditions That Matter* (San Francisco: Jossey-Bass, 2010), 312.

7. Alan Seidman, ed., *College Student Retention: Formula for Student Success*, 2nd ed. (Plymouth, UK: Rowman & Littlefield, 2012); John M. Braxton, William R. Doyle, Harold V. Hartley III, Amy S. Hirschy, Willis A. Jones, and Michael K. McLendon, *Rethinking College Student Retention* (San Francisco: Jossey-Bass, 2013).

8. Most slides and publications are available through the Grand Valley State University institutional repository: ScholarWorks@GVSU, accessed November 17, 2017, http://scholarworks.gvsu.edu.

CHAPTER 8

Filling In the Potholes

Providing Smooth Pathways for Successful Library
Instruction for First-Year Students

Adam Brennan, Tulsa Community College

Lisa Haldeman, Tulsa Community College

PARTICIPATING IN THE ASSOCIATION of College and Research Libraries' (ACRL) Assessment in Action (AiA) program has led to significant change in instruction and assessment for
the Tulsa Community College (TCC) Library. Closer work with the TCC Institutional Research
and Development department has helped TCC librarians to understand effective assessment strategies and common mistakes in assessing students' information literacy skills. The library's information literacy steering committee has made great progress in coordinating instruction efforts across
four campuses and setting expected information literacy learning outcomes. Also, the library has
recently partnered with course design leaders in the redesign of our First Year Experience (FYE)
course, which will include significant library instruction and assessment integrated into the FYE
curriculum. Finally, we have built new relationships with more faculty in an effort to increase our
library instruction and expand the number of students using the library's services.

Introduction and Background

TCC, located in Tulsa County, Oklahoma, is a two-year institution with 129 associate degree programs and forty workforce certificate programs. Annual enrollment for 2015–16 was 25,039 students, making TCC one of the largest educational institutions in the state.[1] TCC has four main
campuses throughout the city of Tulsa, with a physical library at each of these campus locations.

In the fall of 2015, the TCC Library and the Academic Strategies curriculum team, through the
AiA grant, began a college-wide assessment project to evaluate the impact of librarian-led information literacy instruction on students enrolled in Academic Strategies, a student success and study
skills course required for much of the incoming student population. Our primary focus was to
assess students' ability to critically evaluate information online after librarian-led instruction. The
lesson used the CRAAP test, a way to evaluate information using five criteria: currency, relevance,
authority, accuracy, and purpose. After attending a one-hour-and-twenty-minute lesson, students
were assessed through a multiple-choice quiz. The quiz required students to review live websites
and answer questions about their currency, relevance, accuracy, authority, and purpose. TCC librarians taught 112 Academic Strategies classes in fall 2015 and spring 2016 attended by 1,762
students. Out of 974 students who took the assessment quiz, 471 passed with a score of 70 percent
or higher on the first attempt after instruction.

We gleaned two noteworthy insights from our participation in this project. First, librarians
concluded that flaws in the quiz design led to inconsistent results. After examining initial student

assessment scores in September 2015, we realized that three of the questions were unclear in their wording. While we were concerned that editing the quiz questions would skew our data, we also understood that if we did not clarify these three questions, we would have to discard all of the data resulting from these questions. In the future, the library plans to work more closely with the institution's research and development department to ensure that library assessment tools are created to be valid and reliable. Secondly, the librarians learned that preconceived notions of our first-year students' ability to navigate web resources as digital natives were overestimated, and future assessment should begin without such assumptions.

The experience librarians gained in putting together a course-wide assessment tool proved to have practical applications during a period when college leadership and administration prioritized a shift in institutional thinking toward assessment. TCC faculty were asked to align their classroom teaching with a new reflective portfolio process adopted by the college. The college licensed WEAVE, a software platform used to track faculty performance portfolios college-wide. WEAVE was just beginning to be implemented at TCC at the same time TCC librarians were participating in AiA. AiA was, for us, a head start on the kinds of processes, thinking strategies, and interdepartmental partnerships with faculty that leadership positions in the college would later use in portfolio planning through WEAVE. This positioned the library at the vanguard of institutional change.

While other areas of the college were still coping with the college-wide restructuring that comes with a large institutional move, the library was able to adapt to change rapidly, and we found ourselves in a position to better focus on the benefits of assessment to support evidence-based decision-making and change. The library had already moved from the buy-in stages of accepting change to implementation. As a result, we formed stronger partnerships with divisions outside of the library, such as our institutional research and assessment department. Our work in the AiA grant also changed the way some of these entities perceived the library and librarians and, as a result, increased library usage. Work toward assessing our college survival skills course would later influence our information literacy instruction design in classroom teaching environments and shape the library's method of tying concepts in the ACRL *Framework for Information Literacy for Higher Education* into information literacy instruction.

Curricular Impacts of AiA

In November 2015, TCC was selected as one of thirty community colleges nationwide to join the Pathways Project, a national initiative funded by the Bill and Melinda Gates Foundation and led by the American Association of Community Colleges (AACC).[2] The Pathways Project is a multiyear commitment to raise college graduation rates through clearer student academic pathways and a strong focus on the entire student experience.[3] Pathways guides TCC's goal setting and decision-making in order to reverse low graduation, retention, and transfer rates for students by restructuring core college functions. Since Academic Strategies was an established course that was recommended for all incoming students, the college felt that a redesign of the course curriculum was absolutely critical to the Pathways Project transition. Academic Strategies would change from a three-credit-hour course to a two-credit-hour course titled First Year Experience Seminar and would emphasize the integration of advising, financial aid, and other core student services, including the library, into the curriculum.

Through our close and successful collaboration during the AiA project with Academic Strategies leaders and instructors, TCC Library was invited to participate in the Academic Strategies course redesign. Because of the impact of library instruction during and after the AiA project, Academic Strategies leadership felt that library instruction for all Academic Strategies students was vital to the success of the course. During the AiA project, all Academic Strategies course sections were required to have a one-hour library instruction session in order to collect as much data for the project as possible and allow librarians to have an initial point of contact with new TCC students. After the AiA project ended, our librarians continued to encourage library instruction with all Academic Strategies instructors, although library instruction was not a mandatory part of the Academic Strategies course. This encouragement from our librarians made a strong impression on the Academic Strategies leadership team, cementing the library as one of the fundamental components of the course.

In January 2017, three members of the AiA library team (Lisa Haldeman, Adam Brennan, and Jamie Holmes) were asked by the Academic Strategies course leadership to create a library module for the new First Year Experience Seminar course curriculum, which would replace Academic Strategies in fall of 2017. First Year Experience Seminar, per the guidelines set up by the Pathways Project, would be a required course for all incoming students beginning in the fall of 2017. This module, now one of eight foundational components of First Year Experience Seminar, would allow the library the opportunity to reach all incoming first-year students.

Approaching the design phase of First Year Experience Seminar required a careful and thorough evaluation of our data from the AiA project. First, it was imperative that we considered the instruction data collected both during the project and after the AiA cohort ended. While 112 Academic Strategies classes were taught during the AiA study of 2015–16, only 75 classes were taught in 2016–17, resulting in a 33 percent reduction in library instruction. Of the 75 classes that were taught from fall 2016 to spring 2017, 46 classes had a careers-focused library lesson. The remaining 29 classes were either a repeat of the AiA lesson and assessment or a general library overview lesson and library tour. Through this analysis, we recognized that many instructors were using the library in their careers assignment rather than repeating the lesson and assessment created for the AiA project. This realization was key in creating a library lesson and activity that incorporated careers for the First Year Experience Seminar course.

Reflecting on the data collected during the project, we discovered that our Academic Strategies students lacked many of the basic skills needed for college research. We assumed that our students would have a better understanding of basic website evaluation since many of our students were born and raised in the era of digital technology and the internet. Our data showed that only 48 percent of students evaluated during our AiA cohort year passed the quiz with a score of 70 percent or higher on the first attempt after instruction, which was below our predictions for student performance. The First Year Experience Seminar course content would then need to include the data from the AiA project as well as what our librarians were teaching in the year after. Thus, both pieces became focal points of the library curriculum for the First Year Experience Seminar course redesign.

Using the data and information gained through the AiA grant, we created a library module that included a lesson, activity, and assessment that presented library concepts at a basic level. Our goal was to design a lesson and activity that would introduce students to our library resources so that they could use that information in future research projects for other courses. A lesson centered on a careers research assignment with a focus on basic library skills was created for the First Year Experience Seminar library module along with an activity and vocabulary assessment.

The First Year Experience Seminar course curriculum offers the library an opportunity to continue the work started in AiA, and we plan to collect data from this course to guide our collaboration and design of library instruction in other courses. We also plan, in the future, to complete a longitudinal study on the long-term effects of library exposure on student success using information collected from the First Year Experience Seminar course data.

Perception of Library after AiA

AiA changed the perception of the library and library instruction within the college, resulting in a shift in thinking among students and faculty with respect to library services. During the initial planning of the lesson and assessment for the AiA project, the AiA library team members stressed to the other TCC librarians that it was vital to the integrity of the data that all librarians teach the same prescribed lesson and assessment in order to have consistent data for the AiA project. Some of our librarians felt that this would conflict with the creativity of their library instruction lesson planning and affect their existing collaboration with faculty. After the AiA project was complete, the AiA library team realized that it was vital to have input from all of our librarians in order to allow for dynamic and responsive faculty collaboration and student instruction. During the First Year Experience Seminar planning in the spring of 2017, the First Year Experience Seminar library course planners asked the other librarians for their input on the design of the library module. As a result, the other librarians were eager to assist with the First Year Experience Seminar lesson design and felt more positively about instruction simply because they were included in the overall decision-making for the course module creation.

Likewise, instructor promotion of library services to their students has increased exposure of the library. Before AiA, Academic Strategies instructors brought their classes to the library for a brief library tour and visit with a librarian. During AiA, however, instructors were required to bring their classes to the library for a full library instruction session. Because of the successful interaction our librarians had with instructors during the AiA project year and afterward, many of our instructors continued to bring their classes in for library instruction. This increased usage was due directly to the fact that our instructors felt that our quality of instruction had benefitted from the addition of the assessment process.

Furthermore, many of our English Composition I and II instructors also teach Academic Strategies/First Year Experience Seminar sections at TCC. Collaborative relationships built between faculty and librarians during and after the AiA project have led those instructors to promote the library to their Composition I and II students as a valuable college resource. Our goal is for students to feel comfortable enough with the library and librarians to return for assistance with other classes, and instructors who promote the library and library services in their courses have added to the overall positive perception of the library with students.

Influence of AiA on Library Instruction

A library-wide movement toward assessment had a ripple effect on how instruction was delivered beyond information literacy instruction in the college first-year experience courses. The meeting notes, lesson plans, and committee work created for assessment in Academic Strategies formed the basis for standardizing library instruction in other courses. The assessment project created an opening for incorporating the ACRL *Framework* into TCC library instruction. We used knowledge practices within the *Framework* to form the baseline for our assessment of students' abilities to discern information from a reputable website. Without TCC's involvement in the assessment project, we would not have begun the work necessary to transition away from the *Information Literacy*

Competency Standards for Higher Education to the *Framework* so early or embarked on the creation of tools designed to help us incorporate elements of the *Framework* into our assessment. The most significant of these projects at TCC was the creation of the information literacy toolbox,[4] a research guide housed on the TCC Library website that catalogs lesson plans, activities, and learning objectives that tie library activities to the ACRL *Framework*.

Information literacy instruction at TCC before the ACRL *Framework* that used the ACRL *Information Literacy Competency Standards for Higher Education* had become fairly homogenous from course to course. The TCC library taught 485 one-shot instruction sessions during the 2015–16 school year, reaching 8,279 students.[5] Most classes that came in to receive direction on the use of library services and resources were English composition courses researching a contemporary issue that required the student to make a persuasive argument for or against a position on that issue. As library orientations at TCC are voluntary, students from these composition courses had varying amounts of exposure to library services. As a result, most instruction across Composition I and II courses (by far the majority of our library's overall instruction) was done in the one-shot model and tended to repeat the same set of technical skills and research strategies. Which research strategies a particular class would focus on in instruction, such as generating keywords or a research thesis, were at the discretion of the individual librarian teaching the one-shot session.

The *Framework* toolbox was designed to tie concepts from the ACRL *Framework* to our lessons and skills being taught in the classroom and act as a baseline of objectives to be covered across instruction as a whole. The lesson plan designed for Academic Strategies during the assessment project would become the template for lesson plans and also form the template for how we tied these plans back to the *Framework* for our courses. These lesson plan templates allowed us to deconstruct the elements of our one-shot instruction and see where duplication of instruction was happening from course to course. This further allowed us to add a tiered structure to our composition courses in which the instruction in the Composition II lesson plan built on concepts introduced in the Composition I lesson plan. Working with assessment in mind helped to focus work on what sorts of standard objectives needed to be included in courses across the college. Each section of the lesson plan template started with performance indicators that we wanted a student to exhibit. The performance indicators were all paired with an assessment technique that was developed under our work with the AiA assessment project and a learning outcome. For example, as part of the Academic Strategies lesson plan used in the AiA assessment project, we wanted students to recognize the significance of information formats and modes of delivery: a learning outcome with ties to the "Information Creation as a Process" frame. The performance indicator we tied this to was the ability to use the CRAAP test to evaluate the website. We assessed this performance indicator with a quiz on comparing websites. Because of the AiA project, assessment techniques influenced how we built these pairings of outcomes and performance indicators. We had to think very carefully about how the three were interrelated.

Work in the AiA assessment project also saw a shift in library instruction from being instructor-driven to being a collaborative instructor/librarian process. A major challenge to standardizing instruction at TCC during the time that we were developing a *Framework* toolbox was that our library instruction was heavily tailored by faculty input. We used an à la carte menu in which instructors would choose library services from a list and custom build their instruction session. What we found was that faculty tended to make very broad or very narrow selections based on their familiarity with library services. Faculty also tended to select the same services regardless of their course. As a result, entry-level courses were receiving virtually the same instruction as advanced courses. As we began to tie library services to parts of the *Framework* and develop our own objectives using templates developed under AiA, we recognized the issues with the à la carte menu and redesigned our instruction customization to be driven by librarian recommendations working in concert with faculty.

Experiences from the AiA project would also trickle over into instruction and assessment design in the library's current work in designing an activity that could be evaluated and graded for Tulsa Community College's new First Year Experience Seminar. The collaborative relationship formed between librarians and Academic Strategies leadership led to an invitation to participate in designing a library module in the new First Year Experience course. Librarians on the First Year Experience task force incorporated lessons and skills from the AiA project to build a vocabulary activity focusing on basic research skills and library services in the new library module. We learned to design simple lessons for students who have minimal research experience. Librarians also plan to use institutional resources to check the vocabulary activity for reliability and validity.

Reflections from Experiences in AiA

Assessment in Action was an exercise in meeting unforeseen challenges with creativity and flexibility. We had to be able to change to meet the needs not only of our assessment project, but of our partners around the college as well. For example, our original assessment model included an essay and a grading rubric that we had intended to use in concert with a website evaluation activity. While we had early buy-in from faculty with this assessment method, faculty leadership in Academic Strategies reversed their support on using a rubric as the assessment project expanded to include a larger student population. Within less than a week, librarians had to redesign the assessment tool as an online quiz automatically graded through the Blackboard course management system. We had very little time to discuss the impact of this decision among the librarians, and it led to a hastily designed and untested assessment piece. Changing the assessment caused considerable doubt on our collection methods. In conversations since the quiz assessment, librarians have discussed reviving the unused rubric for future assessment projects.

As the library moves forward from assessment reflection and faculty at TCC continue to use WEAVE to track their professional portfolios and adjust their instruction, the TCC Library has been able to use its experiences in AiA to maneuver in ways to best support faculty curriculum by building on relationships from the project. As part of the Pathways Project, TCC librarians have been assigned to academic departments to act as liaisons and keep the library informed of changes in curriculum and instruction that would affect research and library services. Liaison efforts are creating stronger partnerships with faculty across all disciplines. AiA made the transition to library liaisons easier by offering a collaborative model between faculty and librarians. Future assessments of library instruction, specifically in English Composition I and English Composition II sessions, will benefit from lessons learned in instructional design from the library's work in the First Year Experience Seminar and will exist within the greater framework of institution-wide assessment.

The Assessment in Action project gave the library multiple opportunities for college-wide collaboration with faculty, unified our outcomes and priorities with the library toolbox, and reframed our perspective on student learning needs. We had the opportunity to work with dozens of faculty in the classroom as we assessed the project. We were able to take an active hand in the design of the college's First Year Experience course with a module on the library. Assessment from the project reset our teaching outcomes for first-year students to begin with a more basic introduction to the library and research concepts. Our work helped facilitate a change in our library that moved us toward a "one college" philosophy in which our services and assessment became more heavily integrated with those of the college's through the library's interdepartmental partnerships. We look forward to building on the momentum of the AiA program through current and future endeavors with the college.

Biographies

Adam Brennan is a Reference and Instruction Librarian at Tulsa Community College, as well as a TCC and University of Oklahoma graduate. He has been a peer reviewer for the *Journal of Academic Librarianship*, has presented at national conferences over using library resources to create free textbooks, and has been published nationally for his contributions to assessment in research instruction. Reach him at adam.brennan@tulsacc.edu.

Lisa Haldeman is the Library Director at Tulsa Community College's Northeast Campus. Lisa is a 2014 graduate of the University of Oklahoma's School of Library and Information Studies, and her library career has included both school and academic librarianship. She has presented at numerous state and national conferences and is currently serving as library liaison to the TCC School of Engaged Learning and the OpenStax/Open Educational Resources Initiative. Lisa has also been appointed to the ACRL/CJCLS OER Task Force for 2017–18. Reach her at lisa.haldeman@tulsacc.edu.

Notes

1. "Institutional Data," Institutional Research and Assessment, Tulsa Community College, accessed July 17, 2017, http://ira.tulsacc.edu/content/institutional-data.
2. "TCC Selected for National Pathways Initiative," News and Events, Tulsa Community College, November 2, 2015, http://www.tulsacc.edu/about-us/news-and-events/publications/week/tcc-selected-national-pathways-initiative.
3. "Guided Pathways Council to Oversee Implementation of New Strategies," News and Events, Tulsa Community College, April 18, 2016, http://www.tulsacc.edu/about-us/news-and-events/publications/week/guided-pathways-council.
4. "Librarian Framework and Instruction Toolbox: Home," LibGuides, Tulsa Community College, May 31, 2017, http://guides.library.tulsacc.edu/frameworktoolbox.
5. *TCC Library Annual Report 2015–2016*, Library, Tulsa Community College, 5, accessed July 17, 2017, http://library.tulsacc.edu/ld.php?content_id=13831284.

CHAPTER 9

Building Campus Partnerships and Improving Student Success Through a Collaborative Drop-in Tutoring Service

Stephanie Bush, Eastern Mennonite University

EASTERN MENNONITE UNIVERSITY is a small liberal arts university located in the scenic Shenandoah Valley of Virginia. EMU's size has allowed for building many relationships that cross the boundaries typically found in higher education; for example, it is not uncommon for students and faculty to share lunch together in the campus dining hall. But despite this closeness, the Hartzler Library, like many other academic libraries, has struggled to connect with departments on campus and has grappled with finding ways to develop meaningful working relationships with other academic services. When the opportunity to participate in the second year of the Assessment in Action (AiA) grant arose, the library quickly recognized that AiA's combination of training and action research could help forge new working relationships with academic departments and administrators across campus.

Background

To understand how the AiA program impacted the library's ability to develop relationships with key campus stakeholders, it is important to identify the factors and events that led up to the development of the project. Library users have frequently criticized the library in the annual survey for outdated interior spaces that are not conducive to building relationships with the campus community and make it difficult for students to work individually or in groups. The issue was concerning enough that the provost created a Library Design Committee in 2012 charged with redesigning the library. The committee included faculty and administrators from departments across campus and gathered data strategically from both students and faculty. Two main concerns emerged:

- The physical space of the library needed renovations to become both more appealing and functional to library users.
- The current layout underutilized the opportunity for relationship building with the departments housed in the library, particularly with the Academic Success Center (ASC).

Committee members recognized the synchronous ways in which the ASC and the library support students' academic needs and proposed that the ASC be moved from the third floor of the library to the more central main floor. Committee members stated that this physical change could lead to integrated services at the reference desk so students might have one-stop shopping for academic services in the library. A local architectural firm designed the renovation plans, but the university repeatedly denied funding for the renovation, leaving the project stalled.

With the announcement that applications were being accepted for the second year of the AiA project, I met with the director of the Hartzler Library and discussed potential projects that could build upon the previous work of the library committee and potentially assist in securing funding for the renovation. From my work with the undergraduate student population, I knew that students were hesitant to use the tutoring services provided by the ASC because of the extra step of scheduling an appointment in advance. I had also noticed that students did not know that the ASC was located on the third floor of the library, as many students asked for directions at the reference desk. The library director and I concluded that our AiA project should be to develop and assess an ASC sponsored drop-in tutoring service centrally located on the main floor of the library. The drop-in tutoring project would align with the institutional climate of assessment and retention as well as help the library investigate the practicality of the Library Design Committee's recommendation to relocate the ASC to the main floor of the library.

Forming the Team

The first step in preparing our application for the AiA program was forming our team. One goal of the AiA program was to develop relationships with campus stakeholders therefore I wanted to capitalize on recent campus trends at EMU in choosing team members who would be eager to participate in the project as a way to support campus initiatives. Eastern Mennonite University had steadily developed a culture of assessment in the years preceding the AiA project. The university hired its first Director of Institutional Research and Effectiveness in 2007 and launched various assessment initiatives across campus. I previously established a working relationship with the director through collaborating on the development of a number of information literacy assessment tools and was eager to build on our existing relationship and incorporate the director's expertise into the AiA project.

In conjunction with developing a culture of assessment, the university had recently adopted a strategic plan with a goal of increasing retention rates and created a new position, the Director of Retention. The director was tasked with uncovering why students leave EMU and providing support services to students before they become at risk for withdrawing from the university. The hiring of the Director of Retention afforded the library an uncommon opportunity for relationship building with a new employee who would also benefit from the program as a means of advocating for his new role.

In addition to the Director of Institutional Research and Effectiveness and the Director of Retention, I invited the Director of the ASC, a key player in the partnership, to join the team. The Writing Program director was also invited to join the AiA team as writing was one of the most in-demand subject areas for tutoring. Lastly, I approached the Dean of Student Success. The Dean of Student Success works with students who struggle academically to identify interventions that will help them overcome their challenges before they are dismissed from the university. The dean had little interaction with the library before the AiA project, however, as the project developed, it became clear that the proposed program would closely align with the objectives of her position. I invited each team member via email and included information about the proposed project, highlighted how it aligned with institutional priorities, and suggested how the proposal might help them fulfill their current work objectives. I also offered to meet in person to discuss any concerns the potential team member had about agreeing to participate.

Every potential team member accepted the invitation. A few were hesitant about the time commitment and clearly stated the extent to which they felt they could contribute, but no one declined to participate. As well as the project aligning with their current work objectives and institutional priorities, offering to meet in person to discuss the project may have persuaded team members to accept, particularly those members with whom the library had no previous relationship. Our final team was set and included myself (the Instructional Services Librarian) as team leader, and the Director of Institutional Research and Effectiveness, Director of the Academic Success Center, Director of Retention, Director of the Writing Program, and the Dean of Student Success as team members.

Once the team was in place, the project concept identified, and acceptance into AiA secured, I held two in-person planning meetings with the team before our project launched in the fall of 2014. Every member of the team attended these meetings, and our conversations were informal nevertheless productive. We spent time at the beginning of each meeting in casual conversation and shared light snacks. The team members worked well together and discussed their goals around student success. During these meetings, I gave updates on the progress of the project and solicited feedback from the team. They readily gave suggestions for improving the project, signaling that each member was invested in its success. The planning meetings were critical to building lasting relationships between the library and the team. The impact of developing team camaraderie early in the project carried through the implementation as well as through the years since the project ended, and the collaborative environment that developed during the AiA program facilitated and influenced programs and initiatives that have launched in partnership with the library since.

Implementation

Our AiA project launched in the fall of 2014 and was driven by this inquiry question: What is the effect of drop-in tutoring services on students' grades and retention rates? Drop-in tutoring services were provided by the Academic Success Center on the main floor of the library during weekday evenings in the areas of writing, nursing, mathematics, science, and history. Students who came for tutoring were asked to register on WC Online (ASC's tutoring scheduling software) or on sign-in sheets at the time of tutoring, allowing their student identification numbers to be captured. At the end of the fall semester, an electronic survey was distributed via email to students who used the service. Students were asked to self-report the impact the tutoring had on their grades and their satisfaction with the service. We used the students' identification numbers to gather demographic and retention information about students who used the tutoring services.

Results

The data supported our belief that a drop-in tutoring program would provide an easily accessible means of improving students' grades and retention rates. When asked if drop-in tutoring helped them earn a better grade in a course, 65 percent of students responded yes, and 88 percent reported that drop-in tutoring helped them get a better grade on a specific assignment or exam. Overall, students reported a positive experience with drop-in tutoring, as 56 percent reported the service to be moderately to very helpful and 88 percent stated they would return for drop-in tutoring services. In addition to improved grades and positive perceptions, the drop-in tutoring service had a small impact on retention rates of students who attended tutoring. Of undergraduates who attended drop-in tutoring in the fall semester, 94.8 percent returned to EMU for the spring, compared to the university-wide rate of 93.6 percent.

At the end of the AiA project, I discussed the results of the drop-in tutoring service with the director of the ASC. We decided to continue the service the following semester since it had been beneficial to both our departments. The drop-in program was a relatively easy add-on to the tutoring services already provided by the ASC and was very popular. At one point, the drop-in tutors were busier than the traditionally scheduled tutors. The continued collaborative communication and programming were one of the most fruitful outcomes of the project. Before the AiA program, there was very little interaction between the library and the ASC, even though the ASC was housed in the library. Synchronistic goals were identified only a few years earlier during the space planning work of the Library Design Committee. The AiA project facilitated the development of a service that met the academic needs of students and the goals of the university while developing a relationship between library and ASC staff. Presently, at the beginning of each semester, staff from the ASC and the library communicate to plan the details of the semester's upcoming drop-in tutoring service. So while this project did not (yet) result in a renovation and permanent move of the ASC to the main floor—the goal that inspired the project—it created a bifurcated plan that offers tutoring in two ways.

Beyond the increase in communication and collaborative planning, the campus community now views the library and the ASC as partners in providing academic services to students. At the beginning of the semester, the director of the ASC sends an email to all faculty informing them of the subject areas in which tutoring services are offered. This email includes general information about drop-in tutoring and encourages faculty to direct students to access the evening tutoring on the main floor of the library. The director of the ASC assumed the responsibility for communicating this library-based service to faculty, demonstrating the new collaborative relationship between the ASC and the library to faculty members. Subsequently, this has improved the library's relationship with faculty from across campus, as they regularly refer students to the drop-in tutoring service. I have observed faculty recommending the service to students during library instruction sessions and have heard faculty comment to students that it is a convenient and less intimidating way to get tutoring help. Faculty workload is high at EMU, and it can be difficult for faculty members to incorporate new programs into their teaching plans. One of the advantages of continuing the program beyond the end of AiA is that it has given faculty time to incorporate the service into their workflow and teaching.

One of the most compelling ways the drop-in tutoring program impacted the library is through the forming of new relationships between the library and students, particularly first-year students and conditionally admitted students. Data revealed that the largest group of undergraduates who used the tutoring service (44.4 percent) were first-year students. Of those who used the service, 13.8 percent were both first-year and conditionally admitted students who needed to maintain an acceptable grade point average to remain enrolled. First-year students and conditionally admitted students could feel intimidated by the process of scheduling a tutoring appointment using online scheduling software; the drop-in tutoring could have been appealing because of its accessibility.

The ease with which students could access tutoring services may have also contributed to students returning. On the end-of-semester survey, 88 percent of students responded they would return for tutoring services, and some students have continued to use the drop-in tutoring services every year. These students develop positive working relationships with tutors and feel comfortable returning to the same tutor for help. Students benefit academically from establishing a relationship with a tutor as they can choose to receive academic support not just for the assignment, but for the duration of the course. Students now view the library as a place to find academic support; this new perception encourages them to return to the library as they recognize the library can help them as they progress through their academic careers.

In addition to helping form meaningful academic relationships with students, the AiA project was conducive to establishing relationships with a variety of campus administrators. Some relationships, like those with the Director of Institutional Research and Effectiveness and the Director of Retention, were ripe for development, as we all had similar goals. There were particular challenges to serving as the team leader to administrators with whom I had not worked before; many of them hold doctoral degrees and leadership positions on campus. I worked to avoid the pitfalls of the imposter syndrome by reminding myself that each administrator had agreed to serve as a team member. I focused on being a collaborative leader, telling them how grateful I was for their participation and that I respected their time constraints. I emailed agendas in advance of our meetings with notes to clarify any confusing items so that each of us could arrive prepared and made an effort to start and end meetings at the designated times to keep from encroaching on their other job responsibilities.

Conclusion

The relationships formed between the library and team members during the AiA project have remained strong since the end of the project, with many of them resulting in new collaborations. The library's partnership with the ASC highlighted the concept that the library is indeed a partner in supporting the academic success of students. In particular, in the years since the end of the project, the Dean of Student Success has on more than one occasion referred a student to a librarian for help. For instance, the dean sent a student to meet with me when she learned that he had received a low grade in a writing course because he struggled finding sources for a paper. Similarly, when the campus transitioned to using a new student information system in the 2016–17 academic year, the dean approached the library staff with an offer for librarians to use the software as well. The ASC had already begun using the software for scheduling and tracking purposes, and the dean suggested that librarians could use the software in the same manner. We began using the software in the spring of 2017 and hope it will lead to an increase in the number of students requesting an appointment with a librarian.

Our ability to form new working relationships with administrators and stakeholders during the formal AiA program and in the years following has positively and permanently changed how the library is perceived across campus. Efforts to respect each team member's time constraints throughout the program along with a focus on collaboration helped the library build the necessary new connections with team members. Notably, both faculty and students have incorporated the drop-in tutoring program into their workflows and study habits. No longer is the library just a place to study; the campus community now sees it as a partner to academic departments with similar objectives of improving student learning and success. The benefits of the new relationships and positive perceptions are only beginning to come to fruition, and undoubtedly the impact of the AiA project will continue to increase the library's value on campus in unexpected ways for the coming years.

Biography

Stephanie Bush is the Instructional Services Librarian at Eastern Mennonite University in Harrisonburg, Virginia. She completed her Master of Science in Library and Information Science from Florida State University and her Bachelor of Arts in English from the University of California, Davis. Stephanie enjoys the challenge of helping students navigate through the information fog to help them find resources that are both appropriate and interesting for their research work. Reach her at stephanie.bush@emu.edu.

Becoming Part of the Conversation through Assessment of Undergraduate Library Internships

Clinton K. Baugess, Gettysburg College

Kathryn S. Martin, Gettysburg College

Introduction

Any recent attendee at an academic library conference would likely note the large number of panels, posters, presentations, and roundtables that focus on libraries partnering and collaborating with other campus stakeholders, such as admissions, international student services, the writing center, and so on. Our library is no different.

Gettysburg College is a four-year liberal arts institution located in Gettysburg, Pennsylvania, with an enrollment of 2,600 students.[1] Musselman Library serves its campus population with thirteen librarians and nineteen staff members. In a small college environment, collaborating with other campus stakeholders is not only desirable, it is essential if the library wants to move forward with any service or initiative.

After decades of carefully developing relationships, cross-department and cross-division collaboration is an expectation and the norm, and the library has a reputation of being a strong partner. Colleagues across campus are open and receptive to new ideas that mean better serving students. Indeed, forming partnerships with stakeholders is part of the library's current strategic plan.[2] It is only through strategic partnerships with faculty and other administrators on campus that the library will be able to gain traction on its own goals around information literacy, diversity and inclusion, and communicating the library's value with assessment data.

The library's participation in the third cohort (2015–16) of the Association of College and Research Libraries' (ACRL) Assessment in Action (AiA) program enabled the library to partner with colleagues in our Office of Institutional Analysis and the Center for Career Development in order to assess the library's long-standing, but never formally assessed, undergraduate library internship program. Through this distinctive program, the library has provided internships since 1998 for over 100 participants who have gone on to careers in libraries, archives, museums, and related fields.

Through this partnership, we not only obtained much-needed assessment data about the program's impact, but also learned what makes for a successful partnership, gained new insight into how the library's mission overlaps with the goals that drive our campus colleagues' work, and developed a model for cross-division assessment projects that could be implemented across our campus.

Institutional and Library Priorities

Gettysburg College has long placed a value on the high-impact educational practices (HIPs) outlined in George Kuh's 2008 report.[3] The Gettysburg curriculum is centered around completing a senior capstone; conducting undergraduate research; studying abroad; having common intellectual experiences, such as taking a first-year seminar; service learning; and participating in other experiences, including internships.

Supported by our Center for Career Development, 80 percent of 2017 graduates completed an internship, a percentage that has steadily increased since 2013 when 67 percent participated.[4] Hoping to further increase students' participation in this area, Gettysburg's 2017 strategic plan includes a goal of providing all of our graduating students with the foundational skills to launch into graduate or professional school or careers, as well as access to mentors and a professional network.[5]

Musselman Library actively contributes to this part of Gettysburg's strategic plan. Over the course of nineteen years, the library's internship program has grown from a single, year-long internship for a recent graduate to several endowed, semester- and summer-long internships within the library, ranging across reference, special collections and archives, and music librarianship.

At the time of our assessment, the library provided internship opportunities for three to four Gettysburg students and recent graduates each academic year. Our original internship opportunity, the Barbara Holley '54 Internship, is a one-year, paid internship with benefits allowing a recent college graduate from any institution who is interested in librarianship to gain experience working in all library departments. Providing a shorter experience, the Robert '44 and Esther Kenyon Fortenbaugh '46 Internship is a semester-long, paid internship for a current Gettysburg student with the opportunity to work in a specific library department, such as special collection and archives, research and instruction, or technical services. Supporting a student who may be unable to complete an internship during the academic year, the Diane Werley Smith '73 Internship is a summer-long, paid internship allowing a current Gettysburg student to work in special collections and archives.

Given the history, scale, and success of our program, we consider it to be a key part of how we serve our campus community. However, before the AiA program, we had never conducted a formal assessment of the program's impact on student learning, career and professional goals, and early professional employment and success. Similarly, we had not communicated to our campus community about how the library's internship program, as a high-impact practice, supports student learning and success.

Working with a Campus Team

We assembled a four-member team to carry out our AiA assessment project. Given the focus on the library's internship program, the team included two librarians from different library departments who regularly work with interns. Drawing upon local campus expertise with student learning assessment and Gettysburg College students' career preparation, the team also included administrators from Career Development and Institutional Analysis.[6]

At the outset of the AiA project, the library worked under the direction of our 2013–16 strategic plan, which included an objective of cultivating relationships with other campus departments on the topic of assessment and effectively communicating the library's value using assessment data.[7] The library's acceptance in the third cohort of the AiA program provided credibility to our assessment efforts, gave weight to our conversations with campus partners about shared areas of assessment interest, and enabled the library to assert itself as part of assessment efforts on campus. With the full commitment of administrators from Career Development and Institutional Analysis to serve on the campus AiA team, we established cross-divisional support for our internship assessment.

This project also aligned closely with the mission of Career Development to help students develop a career plan and build their professional network and Institutional Analysis's mission to assess student learning. Additionally, participation in this assessment project was beneficial to the Center for Career Development since the department had previously collected more quantitative than qualitative data regarding student internships. The project was one way to develop skills for collecting qualitative data in that area. For Institutional Analysis, it provided a way for staff to learn about the assessment needs of the library and Career Development and to explore how other research methods, such as interviews, could be used to assess student learning. This assessment also provided a good model that Career Development and Institutional Analysis, as well as other departments on campus that provide internships, could use and build upon.

A number of factors helped establish the groundwork to make this fourteen-month project a success for all those involved. From the beginning, it was important to have open conversation and agreement as a team about our shared goals, how the AiA program's structure would inform our collective work, and a timeline that made sense within our campus context and individual schedules. Even though Gettysburg is a small campus and working collaboratively is a norm, it was important for the team leader to ensure that all team members were able to articulate what they felt they could contribute realistically and what they wanted to learn through the project in order to establish a commitment to a collective mission.

The team developed its own timeline based on the assessment cycle for the project to stay on track to meet project milestones. Meetings were scheduled every two weeks for continual check-ins on progress, and flexibility was incorporated to allow for other commitments, such as conference attendance and busy times of the academic year. Individual areas of interest were matched with assigned responsibilities and evenly distributed across all team members. The team agreed upon the best way to communicate throughout the process (email), and a network drive was set up to allow team members to share documents easily.

Being a small college presented both benefits and challenges as the project progressed. The shared commitment to the institutional goals of career preparation and assessment of student learning was an important factor contributing to the project's success. It allowed for a natural partnership with our colleagues in Career Development and Institutional Analysis, and the directors of both departments provided support for the project by allowing a significant time commitment by all members.

However, it is important to note that a time commitment, such as fourteen months, can be a burden to members of a small department staff with many other ongoing projects to attend to. Early in the planning process, we acknowledged as a team that there would be times in the semester when we would need to pause our work because of other commitments or would be unable to meet as a full group. We were able to easily accommodate updated project deadlines to adapt to busy schedules along the way since our project timeline had built-in flexibility, and the team leader facilitated regular communication across the team, such as check-in emails to individual members or collective update emails about our overall progress and next steps.

To sustain momentum, we needed to acknowledge the limitations of what we would be able to get done realistically at different points in the academic year and, just as important, to celebrate when we reached certain project milestones, like completing our survey design or receiving institutional review board (IRB) approval. We celebrated small successes through informal lunches (paid for by the library) where we could be together but not doing project work. To celebrate the completion of the project, the team gathered for a lunch and received small thank-you gifts from the library. Additionally, the team leader wrote individual thank-you letters to the various team members and their division heads.

Establishing the Research Question and Method

After the team was established and the timeline was in place, we agreed that the assessment would focus on a three-part research question:

> What impact (if any) does completing an undergraduate library internship have on preparation and success in graduate or other advanced training; career and professional goals; and early professional employment and success?

To explore our research question, the team relied upon two research methods—an online survey and a semi-structured interview, which we conducted by telephone. We identified the online survey as a method that would enable us to reach former interns who were spread geographically across the United States and internationally. After looking at a number of tools for administering an online survey, we decided upon SurveyMonkey, which was easy to learn, fit within our budget, and supported our data needs.

In order to administer the survey and conduct interviews, the team needed to submit all relevant materials to Gettysburg's IRB before moving forward, which was a new process for the majority of the team. As part of the application process, all team members needed to complete an online training program that required a significant time commitment. Once that was completed, our team member from Institutional Analysis was extremely helpful with the IRB application process, assuring that the research and survey process was transparent, the results were kept anonymous, and plans were in place for storing our data.

We designed our online survey with twenty-nine items. Combining existing data collected by the library and our colleagues in the Development, Alumni, and Parent Relations division, we were able to identify ninety-six interns from 1998 to 2015. Of those ninety-six, we were able to gather an email address, a physical mailing address, or both for eighty-three. Of the eighty-three possible participants, we received forty-five complete responses, a response rate of 54.2 percent. To receive greater detail for some questions beyond what a survey would make possible, we used the survey to identify participants for a series of follow-up semi-structured phone interviews.

Overall, respondents were extremely pleased with their internship experience, and a majority indicated that it had positively impacted their careers. A majority of respondents also indicated that their internship positively influenced their acceptance to a graduate program. Additionally, survey results showed that the internship positively impacted students' decisions to pursue a career in libraries, archives, museums, or related fields and helped them to identify possible areas of specialization that matched their work-related interests.

At a programmatic level, we sought to learn what participants valued from their overall experience in order to inform the program's design. Figure 10.1 provides a listing of major themes that previous interns said they valued the most from their experience.

Treated as a colleague/ member of staff	Mentorship	Acquisition of practical skills	Seeing the "big picture" of how an academic library functions
Confirmed or clarified career choice	Personalized experience	Breadth of experience	Good preparation for graduate school

FIGURE 10.1
Themes for "most valued" part of library internship.

While we will not go into depth here, the final report containing the survey, interview questions asked, and the complete findings is available on Gettysburg College's institutional repository.[8]

Becoming Part of the Conversation

Regular communication with stakeholders during a large project is one of the most valuable lessons from completing the AiA program. We felt a strong need for accountability to our upper administrators in the library, Career Development, and Institutional Analysis, who had given their support and staff time to work on this project. For the librarians on the team, we needed to acknowledge and value the great amount of personal investment our library colleagues have in the internship program. To make internships successful experiences, they require a significant amount of time to plan, organize, and implement. Given this sense of accountability, we made sure to communicate regularly to library staff throughout the AiA program and afterward.

For librarians and library staff, that meant meeting at various points with internship supervisors, our colleagues who most directly work with interns. These conversations were essential to identifying outcomes, interpreting results, and identifying next steps. At various points in the process, we also gave short updates on our progress at library-wide staff meetings, during monthly librarian meetings, and individually with the library dean. Our colleagues were supportive and eager to hear what we were doing and our findings. It was also important for our library dean to be up-to-date in order to report on our work during meetings with our associate provost and provost.

For the other members of our team, we relied upon them to share our progress in their respective meetings with their upper administrators. From our librarian perspective, we felt that our partners knew best how to frame our common talking points into a form that matched what their administrators wanted to know and how frequently they wanted to be updated.

As we reflect on the project, we see areas for improvement. If we had been able to get everything accomplished within the fourteen months of the AiA program, it would have been ideal. However, the ideal rarely matches with reality, especially in a project like this in which all team members juggle a number of other responsibilities. As a result, we had to be flexible. For example, by the end of the project, we had not fully completed the analysis of our results and did not have a formal report to share on campus. We needed to acknowledge how much we had been able to get done and accept that some unfinished work would extend into the next few months.

From the library side, we felt concern about asking our campus partners to do a lot of work after the agreed-upon fourteen months. We wanted to respect their time and work commitments. As a result, much of the final analysis and communication about the findings have happened through the two librarians on the team. However, we have made sure to keep our campus partners updated.

Keeping the Conversation Going—Immediate Impact

Even with these challenges, the project results have impacted library and institutional practice in a number of ways. For all of the team members, going through the assessment cycle itself has been enormously valuable. Our partners have been able to see how that cycle was applicable within a library and how it would work in their own organizations.

It was also the first time that the assessment cycle was part of an ongoing conversation across the entire library. It clarified the value and need for articulated formal outcomes, developed local expertise (particularly for the two library team members), and increased assessment capacity within the library. We are now seeing the same assessment cycle being applied across different library departments. We have been able to facilitate this process by sharing what we have learned with our colleagues, being open and available to answer questions and provide feedback about assessment projects, and applying what we now know in our regular work responsibilities.

For the internship program, there have been several areas of immediate impact. A final report was written by the team and shared with the entire library staff, and a meeting was held to go over the findings and identify and discuss possible next steps—both immediate and into the future. Because everyone was included in this process, the project progressed to something in which the entire library staff had ownership. As a result of these conversations, we changed how we plan to recruit applicants in order to increase diversity, redesigned elements of the internships in different library departments, implemented a standard exit interview as an assessment for all interns to provide more standardization, and laid the groundwork for future assessments by identifying what data we will need and how it should be recorded.

Keeping the Conversation Going—Long-Term Goals for Impact

While we have been able to make immediate changes as a result of our assessment, many areas will continue to require attention. We have taken time to think strategically about our next steps with our project partners and others on campus. However, our current findings allow us to articulate a clear and compelling narrative, supported by data, about the impact our internship program has on students. Moreover, we can communicate how the library's internship program aligns with strategic institutional goals to support student learning and career preparation.

One of the most valuable aspects of this assessment has been the establishment of individual partnerships with Institutional Analysis and Career Development. Those offices are now aware of what the library internship program provides to students, and we have evidence of how these internships prepare students for graduate school and their professional careers, which can be communicated to students seeking internships on campus. We plan to develop our connection with Career Development going forward. For example, we are exploring ways to supplement our internship program by developing additional externship opportunities in other archives, libraries, and museums.

With Institutional Analysis, we are keen to explore other ways in which we may work together to assess the library's contribution to student learning, particularly with our library instruction program. As a result of our conversations on assessment, a librarian is now serving on our campus's committee on learning assessment, alongside colleagues from Institutional Analysis, which is an excellent start.

Outside of our team members, we are sharing our findings with colleagues in other divisions, such as Admissions and Development, Alumni, and Parent Relations. The library has not always effectively shared information about our program beyond the academic division. Because we have provided admissions with language about the program and its impact, that office will be able to share this opportunity with prospective students.

Our colleagues in development have a long-standing relationship with our library dean. As a result of the work they have done together, the library has secured endowments for our internship programs. We are keen to build upon those endowments, and the findings of our assessment project provide a compelling narrative for development officers to share with potential donors who are interested in supporting students' career exploration.

Elsewhere on campus, there are a number of programs that have a similar interest in demonstrating their impact, such as our campus centers for public service and leadership. We hope that by sharing the story of our partnership, the model for our assessment project, our findings, and how we have been able to use them, we will serve as a model for these and other programs on campus.

This assessment has also clarified the need to develop new partnerships on campus. For example, through library-wide conversations about our existing program, we identified a strong need to diversify the profile of our interns in order to feel that we were embodying our library's diversity statement.[9] Historically, our applicants have been white, female, and from particular academic departments, such as history and English. We plan to share our assessment results with the Office of International Student Services as well as the Office of Multicultural Engagement and work with them to attract and recruit a more diverse applicant pool.

Conclusion

Through the partnership with our colleagues in Career Development and Institutional Analysis, we have started a conversation about how the library supports student learning and success, as well as career preparation. This is a conversation that could have taken place with enough drive and determination, but the AiA program itself has provided a way to spend time developing relationships with campus partners, exploring a central question together, and developing our own professional understanding of how library assessment can be used to demonstrate library value.

During the program itself and well beyond, we have gathered data that has informed our professional practice—both immediately and in the future—in ways that help not only the library, but our partners and campus colleagues as well. We experienced successes and challenges, but by starting the conversation itself, we gained momentum that will continue to inform how the library conducts assessment and partners with others. Indeed, with the library's embrace of the assessment cycle, we have much to do.

Biographies

Clinton K. Baugess is a Research & Instruction Librarian and instruction coordinator at Gettysburg College's Musselman Library. He served as Team Lead for Gettysburg's participation in Cohort 3 (2015–2016) of *Assessment in Action*. He has supervised and mentored numerous library interns as part of the library's undergraduate internship program and continues to explore ways to assess and demonstrate the library's contribution to student learning and success. Reach him at cbaugess@gettysburg.edu.

Kathryn S. Martin is the Cataloging & Collections Librarian at Gettysburg College's Musselman Library. She was a team member for Gettysburg's participation in Cohort 3 (2015–2016) of *Assessment in Action*. Her main duties include monograph and ebook cataloging as well as collection assessment. She has worked closely with library interns in Technical Services since 2012. Reach her at ksmartin@gettysburg.edu.

Notes

1. Office of Institutional Analysis, *Gettysburg College, Gettysburg College Fact Book: 2016–2017* (Gettysburg, PA: Gettysburg College, 2017), A-3, https://www.gettysburg.edu/about/offices/ees/institutional_analysis/college_fact_book.dot (requires Gettysburg College login).

2. Musselman Library, Gettysburg College, *Musselman Library Updated Strategic Priorities: 2016–2018* (Gettysburg, PA: Musselman Library, 2017), 3–4, 6, http://cupola.gettysburg.edu/librarypubs/62/.

3. George Kuh, *High-Impact Educational Practices: What They Are, Who Has Access to Them, and Why They Matter* (Washington, DC: Association of American Colleges and Universities, 2008), 17.

4. "Participation in High-Impact Learning Experiences," Gettysburg College Facts and Figures, under "High-Impact Practices," accessed May 21, 2017, http://www.gettysburg.edu/facts_figures/.

5. Gettysburg College, *The Unfinished Work: A Strategic Direction for Gettysburg College 2016–2021* (Gettysburg, PA: Gettysburg College, 2016), 9, http://www.gettysburg.edu/plan/.

6. The team was comprised of Clinton Baugess, Research and Instruction Librarian (and team leader); Kathryn Martin, Cataloging and Collections Librarian; Katherine Mattson, Associate Director of Career Planning; and Qin Zhang, Assistant Director of Institutional Analysis.

7. Musselman Library, Gettysburg College, *Musselman Library Strategic Plan 2013–2016* (Gettysburg, PA: Musselman Library, 2013), 7, 8, http://cupola.gettysburg.edu/librarypubs/24/.

8. Clinton K. Baugess, Kathryn S. Martin, Qin Zhang, and Katherine Mattson, *Undergraduate Library Internships at Musselman Library, Gettysburg College* (Gettysburg, PA: Musselman Library, Gettysburg College, 2017), http://cupola.gettysburg.edu/librarypubs/65/. See also our AiA project report and poster in the AiA collection: Gettysburg College, "Project Description," AiA project report, Association of College and Research Libraries website, accessed November 17, 2017, https://apply.ala.org/aia/docs/project/13988.

9. Musselman Library, Gettysburg College, "Musselman Library Diversity and Inclusion Statement," Musselman Library, accessed May 29, 2017, https://www.gettysburg.edu/library/information/general/diversity.dot.

CHAPTER 11

Positively Impacting the Library Experience of Aboriginal and International Students

Nancy Goebel, University of Alberta

In the Beginning

The announcement of the Assessment in Action (AiA) initiative by the Association of College and Research Libraries (ACRL) provided a catalyst for the creation of a Personal Librarian program and associated assessment within the University of Alberta Libraries (UAL). The timing was perfect because the university had established goals related to Aboriginal and international students that the libraries had not yet directly and strategically targeted. During the 2014–15 AiA year, the UAL AiA librarian project lead focused on the creation of a Personal Librarian program for first-year Aboriginal (Native/Indigenous) students. In this 2014–15 pilot and the 2015–16 year, the program was referred to as the "Personal Librarian for Aboriginal Students Program." In the 2016–17 academic year, the program expanded to include first-year undergraduate international students, so it became more generally named the "Personal Librarian Program."

FIGURE 11.1
The Personal Librarian Program logo.

In the Personal Librarian Program, students were partnered with a Personal Librarian based on the discipline of the student's major. For example, a biology major would be partnered with a Personal Librarian in the Science Library. During the academic year, these students would receive about twenty emails (using mailout.com) with research tips from the Personal Librarian program. Students also received a few emails with positive messages such as "Happy Holidays" or "Welcome to the Winter Term." Each email provided students with their Personal Librarian's phone number, office location, and email address, and students were encouraged to contact their Personal Librarian with any questions they might have about their undergraduate research. Table 11.1 shows how the students were distributed (based on their major and the subject area of the library) among six University of Alberta Libraries.

169

PERSONAL LIBRARIANS BY LIBRARY					
	2014–15	2015–16	2016–17		
LIBRARY	Aboriginal Students	Aboriginal Students	Aboriginal Students	International Students	Total Students
Humanities/Social Science	86	93	92	315	407
Science	40	58	52	486	538
Campus St. Jean	5	2	2	4	6
Education	24	25	27	16	43
Health Science	4	17	14	9	23
Augustana	20	22	18	43	61
Total	179	217	205	873	1,078

TABLE 11.1
Personal librarians by library

In the AiA year 2014–15, 179 Aboriginal students participated in the program. In year two, 2015–16, 217 Aboriginal students participated. When the program expanded in 2016–17, there were 205 Aboriginal students and 873 international students, for a total of 1,078 students matched with Personal Librarians. In the expansion year, it was anticipated by unit library managers and the Personal Librarian program librarian that the increase in the number of students using the service in the Humanities/Social Sciences and Science Libraries (to a total of 407 and 538 students respectively) might necessitate more than one Personal Librarian in each of these libraries. However, Personal Librarians have been able to manage the increased workloads as this work is essentially a component of their public services work.

An exciting and insightful aspect of the AiA program was the requirement to work with campus entities beyond the library walls. It is rather eye-opening, in fact, that it takes the intentionality of a program such as AiA to develop a library service not by simply collaborating with partners outside the library but by fully engaging them in the planning and implementation stages of the program. The AiA program created excellent opportunities for conversation and collaboration with persons and departments whose roles involve the direct support of Aboriginal students. A number of these collaborative partners served on the AiA committee through the entire pilot year and provided excellent insights and feedback regarding what, when, and how to communicate with students. Where the library could have made reasonable guesses, these partners offered informed opinions based on working directly with this population of students for many years. One teaching faculty member on the committee was able to provide excellent experience-based advice related to the action research components of AiA. In the long term, perhaps most importantly, campus partners served as informed advocates of the program; they directed students to the relevant Personal Librarian when and if the student communicated any uncertainties or anxiety about using the library's services or facilities. Further, these individuals explained to students the role of librarians (and other library staff) in the student's undergraduate experience and, likely, enhanced their engagement, success, and decision to return for another academic year. This group of collaborators was pivotal in terms of creating a model that would strategically support the needs of first-year Aboriginal students.

Due to participation in AiA, there were a number of assessment initiatives connected with the Personal Librarian program. These include the following:

- *Email open rate:* Because the students receive an email most weeks during the fall and winter academic terms from the Personal Librarian program, we are able to assess the rate at which students open the email using the built-in analytics at mailout.com (now owned and assumed by http://campaigner.com). In addition, we were able to retrieve information such as when and which emails bounced and what URLs students clicked on within the emails. The software provided students with a mechanism to unsubscribe if they wished, and, if they did unsubscribe, that information was then available for administrative purposes. The availability of these components for assessment and reflection was integral to the assessment considerations.
- *Student survey:* At the end of each academic year, students were asked to complete an online survey. They were asked questions about their knowledge of, or participation in, the Personal Librarian program and their perception of its impact on their use of services, facilities, and collections. In addition, they were asked to respond to questions regarding how and if the Personal Librarian program impacted their stress related to library-based research.
- *Librarian survey:* At the end of the academic year, Personal Librarians were surveyed in order to ascertain their perspectives on the program, in terms of both operations and impact on Aboriginal students.
- *Record of interaction with Personal Librarians:* Lastly, when students communicated with their Personal Librarians, the Personal Librarians were asked to keep records on each interaction and to file some basic information in an online form. This process did not provide a full picture of all interactions, as it required the Personal Librarian to remember to record the interaction and it required students to identify themselves as participants in the Personal Librarian program.

An Expanding Program

The AiA year ultimately served as the foundation for a program that strategically established the possibility of additional and significant growth over time. The AiA year quickly became known as the pilot year of the Personal Librarian program, and assessments of the AiA pilot year clearly indicated that the program had value and impact. Responses from students were very positive, with many indicating that the program contributed to their decision to return to campus for another academic year and decreased their anxiety related to library-based research.

One significant unknown on the library side of things prior to the program was the volume of inquiries to expect from the students; as is often the case, it was imagined that the Personal Librarians would feel a significant increase in workload because of their role in the program. While the participation rate of students in all measures deemed the program to be a success and worthy of expansion, UAL Personal Librarians felt the workload impact was acceptable, even negligible. It is to their credit that the public service librarians felt this to be a part of, not even an extension of, their public service work.

Following the submission of a final AiA report to UAL's senior administration in year two of the program, the leadership decided not only to continue with the program, but also to expand it to include first-year international students. Feedback from students, Personal Librarians, and partners from Aboriginal offices was also positive and strongly endorsed the value and expansion of the program. In terms of numbers, the first-year international student population was four to five times the size of the first-year Aboriginal student population, but sufficient evidence existed that the program was scalable, so it was expanded the following academic year. In fact, in the pilot year, we made intentional efforts to recognize and document stages that would be easily scalable and those that would require broader conversation or additional resources. When the administrative directive came to increase the Personal Librarian program fivefold, the program was ready to accommodate such an increase.

As the program was expanded to include international students, we needed to consider which pieces of the initial AiA Personal Librarian program would continue and if anything should be added, removed, or changed in any way. The pilot year structure had been built intentionally with the potential of expansion embedded into the design; this provided a strong foundation and made the transition run smoothly. For example, we were sure to document the process of managing student records so that we were consistent in how this information was managed. The biggest change was quite pragmatic. In the pilot year, we had partners from Aboriginal offices involved in the planning and execution of all parts of the initiative. When the program expanded, persons and departments that directly support international students were informed of the initiative through a one-time face-to-face meeting with the lead librarian. The AiA team decided that there were simply too many potential collaborators in the International offices for them to have the same level of direct involvement with the program that partners from the Aboriginal offices had in the pilot year so they were not directly involved in the implementation of the program. Instead, partners were asked for input and informed about the kind of information updates regarding the program that they could expect to receive. These individuals still needed to play the advocate role for the initiative with students, so it was important that they understood the purpose of the Personal Librarian program. This was a significant departure from the model established in working with the partners in the Aboriginal support offices, as they were heavily involved in the development of the initiative and the overall direction. However, in terms of keeping the program sustainable, it was important to differentiate between the partners we had in the Aboriginal support offices and the advocates we had in the international support offices. The Aboriginal partners were fully engaged in the development of the program (development of email content, selection of software, development of assessment methods), and staff in the international offices were involved as advocates only. In any case, the AiA model of extending beyond the borders of the library for the program still served as the model for the expansion of the initiative.

Working with campus partners on the administration as well as the assessment of the Personal Librarian project provided a unique opportunity to consider assessment outside of the parameters of the library. The AiA project committee engaged in the process to develop the assessment tools for the Personal Librarian program, and their conversations served to further both the collaborative nature of the initiative and a culture of assessment involving campus entities. It was uncommon to experience this kind of cooperative planning and collaboration and a new opportunity to create assessment strategies and opportunities through collaboration. Through the assessment process, the library was perceived as providing leadership in a collaborative effort of direct support for Aboriginal students. Remarkably, the partners in the various Aboriginal support offices grew to know each other more because the library brought them together more frequently so the program served to strengthen their working relationships as well. As we move further into the combined Aboriginal/international student program, the commitment to assessment and collaboration with external partners remains, though it changes as the program evolves. While is not practical to directly involve all partners and advocates in the program operations, but we do share results of assessment with them after each academic year.

The Impact

The Personal Librarian program's multifaceted assessment components as outlined above provided the positive evidence necessary to grow the program. The assessment also provided insight into the impact of the program—impact on the library and the university is one consideration; impact on the involved student populations is a second consideration.

Impact on the Library and the University

When the AiA year began, there were a number of institutional priorities in place that aimed to further support and engage Aboriginal students. Decreasing library anxiety for these students by increasing their awareness of library services, collections, and facilities became a clear focus of the Personal Librarian program. Providing support to their undergraduate research increased engagement and, as reported in their survey responses, retention of the students. As the program expanded to include international students, there were, again, obvious links to university strategic documents that point to supporting and engaging international students. On the broader scale in Canada, institutions were responding to the Truth and Reconciliation Commission process and report,[1] which outlined and provided recommendations to address the injustices done to countless Aboriginal youth through the residential school system. More recently, the Canadian Federation of Library Associations created a Truth and Reconciliation Committee "to promote initiatives in all types of libraries to advance reconciliation by supporting the Truth and Reconciliation Commission Calls to Action and to promote collaboration on these issues across the Canadian library communities."[2] These two initiatives provide an important framework for university libraries in terms of direction for the support and engagement of Aboriginal students.

Impact on Students

Regarding Aboriginal students, there is considerable programmatic data related to the impact of UAL's Personal Librarian program.[3] In the year-end surveys, Aboriginal students offered affirmative comments such as:

- "It helped me fell ok about asking for help."
- "This was a wonderful program, it made my first year at U of A easier. I had someone I could ask questions at all times, and the responses were extremely fast. This was one of the most positive experiences I had had this year."
- "It's kinda neat getting the emails and reading through them. I'm in a program where I haven't ever needed to do research but now I'm sorta more comfortable with the idea of getting a book from the library. It seems less overwhelming."

In addition, reports from international students (after the expansion of the program) provide valuable insight into how the program positively impacted their student experience:

- "I never asked questions at a library at home before. It was new to me but so helpful. I thought I knew more than I do and it helped."
- "Thank you for the help and information. I can really appreciate it."

Figure 11.2 shows the summary of the three years of the program to date, when students were asked if they feel more comfortable asking library staff for help.

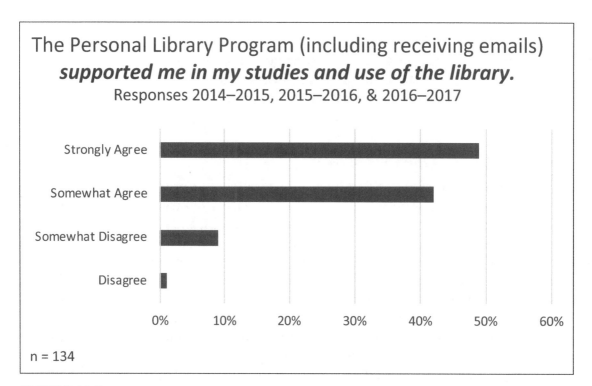

FIGURE 11.2
Students feel more comfortable asking library staff for help

Students were also asked if their participation in the Personal Librarian program supported them in their studies and use of the library. Responses strongly affirmed this (see figure 11.3).

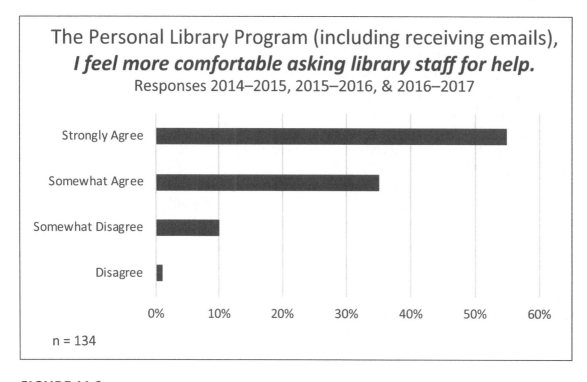

FIGURE 11.3
Students feel the Personal Librarian program supported their studies

Why Does the Impact Matter?

As time has passed and the program has expanded, what is most exciting to consider is not just that there was measurable impact, but also why that impact matters. It matters, in terms of reduced student anxiety, that students make comments such as this at the end of the year: "It makes the library less scary." In a general sense, there is a growing awareness of student stress on college and university campuses. When the library can play a role in creating a more positive and stable environment for students and, ultimately, improve their academic experience, many broader institutional goals are also being met. The climate at the University of Alberta is one that acknowledges the importance of retention of Aboriginal and international students and recognizes and celebrates the enriched culture of diversity. In addition, it matters that students simply have a more positive college and university experience and more positive engagement with the library.

It is hard to know, beyond anecdotally, the impact that AiA or the Personal Librarian program (in its AiA infancy or its more current form) has had on how the library is perceived externally. The Native Studies liaison librarian participated in the AiA teams in an advisory capacity, and the services she offers to the Aboriginal Student Support Office increased as a result of this participation. Most notably, she now schedules in-center office hours for students. This is something that the librarian considered previously, but not enacted until the AiA program provided the impetus. The library and university administration have appreciated the evidence we have been able to share regarding the development and impact of the Personal Librarian program and its support of and engagement with Aboriginal and international students. While the formal AiA team has disbanded, the Personal Librarian lead consults former members as necessary. And, of course, the lead communicates with former members several times each academic year regarding the status and growth of the program. The faculty member who was on the AiA team offered these summary comments regarding his participation on the team and his observation of the impact of the Personal Librarian program:

> As a professor, I had the chance to better understand how students relate to the library and its resources once they take on a research project I have designed. In this particular case, I learned that inequities and barriers exist for Indigenous students at every step of the assignment, from my design and my objectives, to the research that takes place in a material and virtual environment and in relation to library staff, and to the writing and presentation of the finished work. While I was hoping to help improve students' experience of the library and its collections and resources and improve the library's capacity to meet its own goals, I ended up also improving my own assignment and course design so as to better meet my goals as an instructor and those of my program and department. I also strengthened the already good relationship I had with the staff at the library and especially with the librarians. This relationship goes a long way to foster information literacy and research skills in our students, since goals can be discussed and common ones established.
>
> The further research I undertook in collaboration with the librarian in charge of the Personal Librarian program opened my eyes to the emotional aspects of library use. It also led me to draft an additional article in my own field, through which I have begun to understand that most of my students experience libraries very differently than I ever did as a bookworm and early researcher. Developing an awareness of the prevalence of library anxiety among students—and especially where cultural and class differences are present—would be highly beneficial for all

instructors and, of course, to the students who must take their courses and complete their assignments and sometimes fail to do so because of barriers rather than because of what instructors can perceive as negligence.

Since I led my faculty's efforts to include and engage with Indigenous students on the institutional level throughout this project, I can also attest (although anecdotally) that Indigenous students' image of the entire faculty was positively affected. Indeed, simply showing interest in students and contacting them showed that they are seen as important and that they will be cared for—even if they decide not to take part in the program.

I also had the chance to work with individuals in service-providing positions, with whom I would normally have no contact. These conversations and relationships can also change the ways in which instructors function. I have found them most helpful in my informal interactions with students. Being aware of what activities take place but also what challenges students face and how they view and use services allow me to adjust my own calendar and expectations and see other sides of the academic year cycles and to understand how students relate to the university through other means than their courses.

Jérôme Melançon, Political Studies, Augustana Campus, University of Alberta
(Effective July 2016: Lecturer, University of Regina)

The AiA program provided the incentive and infrastructure for a new and exciting initiative that was led by the libraries and engaged many campus offices in the support of Aboriginal and international students. ACRL and the AiA leadership should be commended for having the foresight and providing the vision to create a program that provided external engagement, leadership, and assessment opportunities for librarians as never before. The result has been a fascinating and broad development of initiatives across North America's college and university libraries that engage librarians outside of library walls and improve the experience of students on their campuses.

Biography

Nancy Goebel is Head Librarian of the Augustana Campus Library of the University of Alberta (Canada). Nancy's strong interest in information literacy has led her to spearhead: fifteen annual *Augustana Information Literacy in Academic Libraries* workshops featuring high-profile international speakers; the creation of information literacy awards for students and faculty; the production of the DVD *It Changed the Way I Do Research Period: Augustana Talks Information Literacy*; the open source information literacy assessment software WASSAIL; the Information Literacy Assessment and Advocacy Project (ILAAP); the University of Alberta's Personal Librarian program; and the augustana human library. Reach her at nancy.goebel@ualberta.ca.

Notes

1. "TRC Findings," Truth and Reconciliation Commission of Canada, accessed July 10, 2017, http://www.trc.ca/websites/trcinstitution/index.php?p=890.
2. "Truth and Reconciliation," Canadian Federation of Library Associations/Fédération canadienne des associations de bibliothèques, 10 July 10, 2017, http://cfla-fcab.ca/en/programs/truth-and-reconciliation.
3. Jérôme Melançon and Nancy Goebel, "Personal Librarian for Aboriginal Students: A Programmatic Assessment," *College and Research Libraries* 77, no. 2 (2016): 184–96.

You Spin Me Right Round (Like a Record)

—Or, Does the Assessment Loop Ever Truly "Close"?

Iris Jahng, University of Massachusetts Boston

DEPARTMENTAL LEARNING GOALS are part of the University of Massachusetts Boston's (UMass Boston) strategic plan to examine student progress and assess student learning. Many academic departments, including English and sociology, have explicitly incorporated information literacy into their student learning goals. English (ENGL) 102 is an integral part of the freshman writing curriculum and addresses skills needed to satisfy the institution's Writing Proficiency Requirement, which undergraduate students must pass in order to graduate. Students learn to write research-based essays and connect research to the writing process in ENGL 102, making it an ideal candidate for a course-embedded assessment of the impact of information literacy instruction on student learning. This work has already been impactful at many levels: within the library, on campus, and between UMass Boston and other institutions.

Project: Everything Is Cool When You're Part of Team (UMass Boston and Team AiA)

Librarians, English faculty, an institutional researcher, and a sociologist (Team AiA) partnered to participate in Assessment in Action's (AiA) 2015–16 cohort and embark on a collaborative assessment of student learning in the second composition course, ENGL 102, for first-year students. Our primary inquiry question was this: How does research instruction impact students' ability to transfer research skills from one project to the next? Our secondary exploratory query was this: Is there an interest in co-taught or librarian-supported, faculty-led research instruction classes? While this was always a question we were interested in exploring, we saw that we could pursue this second aspect when we realized that we had a mix of participating faculty who wanted entirely librarian-led instruction, faculty who wanted to handle the instruction themselves, and faculty who preferred a "hybrid" model where both librarians and faculty handled different pieces of the instruction.

We were interested in assessing whether undergraduate students enrolled in participating ENGL 102 sections

- understood the difference between looking up information online and conducting sustained, in-depth research on a topic
- used keywords, subject language, and controlled vocabulary to search for and access information on their paper topics
- understood how to handle conflicts between what they found and what they wanted to research, or avoiding "cherry-picking"

We were able to look into our additional query because participating faculty teaching ENGL 102 agreed to the following instructional models:

- seven professors (fourteen sections): librarian-led instruction
- one professor (four sections): solo faculty-led instruction
- two professors (six sections): hybrid (both faculty- and librarian-led) instruction

Team AiA's project demonstrated some of the benefits of integrating writing and research (information literacy) instruction while showing that librarians and English faculty are natural partners in accomplishing this. It also highlighted the library instruction program's contributions to student learning and established librarians as potential collaborators in future student learning assessment efforts. Through this project, we gained a clearer picture of the impact of information literacy instruction on student success. This finding is important because UMass Boston has over 16,000 students and five instruction librarians as of spring 2017, and the scalability of our instruction program is a very real concern. Instruction librarians taught 562 classes in 2016 and 447 classes in 2017; given this immense workload, it is important to measure our impact on student learning and success so that we can improve our instruction program and our individual efforts.

Our findings included but were not limited to the following:

- Students understood and appreciated the ways they could use library resources to research their paper topics and access credible sources.
- The value in collaborating to assess student learning outcomes extends beyond one project and one department.
- Information literacy instruction doesn't necessarily require a librarian in the classroom.

Because of AiA, we are now more confident in designing information literacy instruction sessions with built-in assessments. We continue to collaborate with the English department by expanding our focus to all ENGL courses and by piloting a new instructional model that breaks information literacy instruction into smaller chunks and encourages faculty to assume responsibility for teaching more components themselves. That way more students enrolled in ENGL courses benefit from information literacy instruction, and the reduced amount of time a librarian spends in the classroom makes the project scalable, enabling the embedding of information literacy instruction throughout ENGL courses and the major.

Our project is built on work that librarians have been doing with the sociology department and serves as a successful model for future collaborative assessment efforts. Since the sociology department has a learning goal dedicated to information literacy (students will know "how to access and evaluate scholarly sources"), librarians have been working with sociology faculty to assess whether students can identify, access, cite, and evaluate scholarly sources. We invited a sociology faculty member to join Team AiA because we wanted her to serve as a bridge between our first collaborative assessment of student learning and the one that Team AiA was attempting, sharing valuable insights and lessons learned. The English department also has a learning goal addressing information literacy ("Build students' inquiry and research abilities by encouraging them to work with both primary and secondary source material, develop research methods using library and database resources, connect research to the writing process, and practice the skills of organizing, developing, and supporting research-based arguments"), so AiA seemed like a natural opportunity to bring faculty from different departments together to work on a shared interest. Librarians will continue this work with the English department and the Composition Program, exploring and assessing different ways we can work together to further facilitate student learning and success.

Post-project: Here Comes the Sun (Team AiA Debrief)

After the spring semester ended in May 2016, Team AiA met in the library to discuss our findings, explore next steps and future possibilities, and just share problems and issues and workshop ideas and solutions for assessing student learning with other like-minded campus colleagues. What was originally slated to be a one-hour meeting stretched into nearly three hours of nonstop discussion about student learning assessment. The exciting thing about this debrief was that the library was responsible for bringing faculty across departments together to talk about their shared interest in assessing student learning. They talked about their experiences with different classes and sets of students and asked for advice on how to do things better next time. I would have ended the meeting earlier if the conversation hadn't taken on a life of its own, and if the attendees weren't so clearly engaged in what they were talking about and so excited to be talking to others who were similarly enthusiastic about assessment.

In addition to bringing together a team of people with shared interests, our AiA project has given faculty a greater appreciation for what librarians offer as educators and as partners, impacted the way we think about our instructional program within the library, and opened up potential new avenues for further librarian-faculty collaboration.

One benefit of working so closely with teaching faculty in the design and execution of a collaborative assessment project was that the faculty gained a better understanding of what librarians do and how we approach our work. We were fortunate that the English department chair was a member of Team AiA, and that the newly hired director of the Composition Program volunteered her ENGL 102 students to participate in our project. Our efforts in creating a lesson plan and materials that represented the interests, values, and goals of both teaching faculty and librarians paid off almost immediately, when the program director flipped through the booklet all students in participating ENGL 102 sections completed during their scheduled library instruction sessions and exclaimed excitedly, "I love how much reflection and transfer are emphasized!"

Reflection was consciously built into the entire lesson plan. It was there in the very first minutes of class, when students reflected on their assignment and research topic, what they were hoping to discover about their topic, and the questions they were hoping to answer through the research process. Research was presented not as a tedious activity that students had to do in order to write their final paper, but as an opportunity to really explore their topics and find what about the topics they found truly fascinating. After students had time to explore two databases and find some interesting articles and books, they were asked to identify the *best* source they found, briefly summarize it, describe how they were thinking about using it in their paper, and provide a representative quote. This set of questions was borrowed from an English faculty member on Team AiA, as it is something he regularly asks his ENGL 102 students to work through to help them evaluate the sources they find. Since it directly addresses source evaluation, we dedicated time toward the end of class for students to do this important work. This easy, seamless integration of instructional materials provided by librarians and by faculty further demonstrated that we are natural partners when it comes to promoting student learning and success. Finally, at the end of class, students reflected on the most interesting thing they discovered about their research topics, their understanding of the differences among the databases they used to explore their topics, and how their initial thoughts about their research topics had changed. While very few students were able to address the last batch of reflective questions at the end of class, the answers we received revealed that these students were able to see that databases largely differed in terms of subject coverage and interface design and that their preferences for one database over another often boiled down to things like aesthetic preferences or previous experience with one over the other.

Within the library, we had staff discussion about shifting to an instructional model where librarians spend less time in the classroom and instead focus their efforts toward "training the trainers": instead of instructing students, librarians would instruct teaching faculty and empower them to handle information literacy instruction. Fortunately, Team AiA's efforts paid off, as the English department chair saw not only the dedication of the instruction librarians at UMass Boston, but also how few of us there are to accomplish this type of embedded work. On top of our AiA instruction sessions, all instruction librarians taught additional instruction sessions, which resulted in a heavy teaching load during the spring 2016 semester.

It quickly became clear to the English department chair that having librarians meet with individual English classes was an unsustainable approach to ensuring that more students enrolled in English courses would benefit from information literacy instruction; one possible solution we approached was having librarians work with teaching faculty behind the scenes to prepare lesson plans, instructional materials, and handouts and help build up faculty members' confidence that this was something they were capable of doing themselves. Bolstering this idea was the fact that I had discovered (via personal communication with several ENGL 102 instructors) that they were already teaching their students research skills without librarian assistance. One faculty member actually used our AiA instructional materials as a benchmark to evaluate how well he was teaching his students—and when he told me this, I was excited by this discovery. This seemed to indicate that it wouldn't be too terribly difficult to identify more faculty that were either doing something similar already or could be persuaded to try it out themselves.

Post-post-project: Ch-ch-ch-ch-changes (in the Classroom Directly Influenced by AiA)

One idea that English faculty introduced early and often throughout the course of our team's work was that of knowledge transfer. They wanted students to realize that the research skills they developed and sharpened as a result of research instruction were not only applicable to their research paper assignment in ENGL 102, but were also relevant to their assignments and projects in other classes and contexts. This emphasis on knowledge transfer has already transformed one aspect of my own teaching (and some of my colleagues', as well): in the classes I now teach, students are directly told that if they're comfortable using or searching one database, then they are capable of successfully using ANY database; while interfaces change, the way you search does not. Knowledge transfer can occur at many different levels, that is, between classes, assignments, and even tools.

Students are now explicitly encouraged to try using their search terms in several databases to see for themselves that the way they brainstorm keywords, connect them with Boolean operators, and use limiters to filter and refine their search results are not database-specific; rather, they are things they should be doing everywhere they go. All databases were designed as research tools, and because of this, all of their features are there because they will help you do your work more efficiently and effectively. While we look forward to formal assessment, it appears that students are now more comfortable exploring multiple different databases without having to be introduced to them by their professor or a librarian. For example, a demonstration of how search results are changed by adding additional keywords in a database such as Academic Search Complete might now be followed by trying that precise combination of keywords in a second database such as ProQuest Central, JSTOR, or ScienceDirect. After seeing a librarian do this, students seem more willing to try searching multiple databases using their own sets of keywords.

This past academic year, we have observed more students having multiple databases open in different tabs and their apparently growing comfort at exploring new databases and unfamiliar interfaces. While this change is small, it is a real change directly resulting from our involvement and close collaboration with the English faculty on Team AiA. Professors frequently nod along approvingly when students learn that interfaces change but the way they search does not, and more students appear to attempt to search more databases. This is but one small example of how AiA has led to increased understanding for both faculty and librarians: faculty have a clearer view of how their students benefit from library instruction and a deeper appreciation for the expertise of librarians, and librarians are discovering new facets of the impact they have on the student learning that occurs in ENGL 102.

Post-post-project: With a Little Help from My Friends (Relationship Building)

Additional opportunities for librarian-faculty collaboration point to the impact of AiA at UMass Boston. Composition Program faculty met on January 19, 2017, to plan for the upcoming spring semester; I was invited by the program director to attend the meeting and introduce myself and the library's information literacy instruction program, discuss what we learned as a result of our departments' AiA collaboration, and introduce the library's assessment projects and recruit interested faculty to participate. This was an ideal opening to build on the work we began with AiA and further strengthen the library's already-strong relationships with the English department and the Composition Program. Even though this was the first faculty meeting I had been invited to at UMass Boston, I wasn't as nervous as I thought I would be. Team AiA's findings were still fresh in my mind, and I was excited to talk to our composition faculty about our shared successes and to discuss the various ways we could continue working together.

After consulting with my fellow librarians, we decided to promote the following initiatives: our growing collection of asynchronous instructional materials that faculty could incorporate into their own teaching (and offer up librarians as information literacy consultants); our development of lesson plans and an information literacy curriculum specifically geared toward the needs of ESL, ELL, and international students; and a cross-institutional collaboration between UMass Boston and some of our biggest feeder community colleges to measure students' information literacy and identify gaps that instruction librarians could then address both at the community college level and also when the students transfer into UMass Boston. This last initiative began as a discussion at ACRL New England's AiA Symposium on September 13, 2016, at Assumption College between Cecilia Sirigos, Team AiA's research design and resident statistics expert librarian, and a librarian from Massasoit Community College, which happens to be one of UMass Boston's biggest feeder schools. In my opinion, this growing collaboration is the most exciting thing to come as a result of AiA, as it has the potential to empower the library to contribute to ongoing student retention efforts here at UMass Boston, since many of the participating community colleges are our feeder schools.

Just as we expected, composition faculty were excited to hear about our assessment initiatives, and there was great enthusiasm and willingness to participate. After the meeting, librarians contacted interested faculty members to let them know more about our ongoing projects and what their involvement in them would entail. I contacted fifteen faculty members about our attempt to shift our instructional program away from heavy reliance on librarian presence in the classroom and toward librarians acting more as instructional consultants. I knew that this would go over well with our composition faculty because we discovered through our work for AiA that there are a number of faculty who don't schedule instruction sessions with a librarian, but are instead handling this themselves (with varying levels of confidence in their ability to do this successfully). Thus, we knew that an opportunity exists to offer our instructional expertise in a new form to teaching faculty and that this would very likely be well-received since it was compatible with what they were already doing.

While the library would like to shift our instructional program toward a model where librarians act as information literacy consultants to teaching faculty, and there already exists space for us to do so, I didn't want to push the idea onto our faculty too hard. Although a sizable number of faculty are already assuming responsibility for teaching this material to their students, many faculty members also truly value what librarians bring into their classrooms, our expertise, and the effect of our instruction on their students. Therefore, while I truly believe that this model is the future of the library's instruction program, I didn't want faculty to feel as if they were being pushed toward teaching it themselves before they were necessarily ready to do so. Instead, it was presented as just one of several options and a show of the library's flexibility in how we can partner with faculty toward our shared goal of student success. This desired shift in our instructional program is a significant impact of AiA and constitutes one way we're using our findings to inform librarians' future instructional collaborations, and faculty buy-in is an essential ingredient for a successful transformation of library instruction at UMass Boston.

My gentle "Hey, I know you are doing this already and we'd love to help you in whatever ways you'll find most beneficial" approach to introducing the library's information literacy instruction program and the various models we have for partnering with faculty has generated some initial movement. Of the fifteen faculty members I contacted to discuss our asynchronous instructional materials addressing many different aspects of information literacy, I heard back from four: two faculty members who did not schedule library instruction sessions, one faculty member teaching four ENGL 102 sections that my colleague Cecilia (from Team AiA) and I worked with in fall 2016, and one faculty member with whom I regularly work each semester. I don't know how the first three faculty members incorporated our asynchronous materials into their teaching, but I do know that the fourth faculty member used our lessons on citing sources and plagiarism to facilitate in-class discussions with her students about the importance of acknowledging where their information comes from and why citations are taken so seriously in the academic community.

A steady, patient approach seems most likely to yield enduring changes to the library's information literacy instruction program and our faculty's receptiveness to assuming greater responsibility for the teaching and development of their students' information literacy—with librarians available to them as consultants, rather than as a physical presence in the classroom. During our work on AiA, librarians encountered multiple faculty members who had taken it upon themselves to instruct their students in research techniques and library resources, but lacked confidence in the strength of their instruction. By sharing instructional materials like lesson plans and handouts, talking about instructional methods and learning activities, and even teaching instruction sessions ourselves, we discovered that our composition faculty were on point with their own instructional efforts, and we were able to affirm and confirm that they were successfully instructing their students. This approval carried quite a bit of weight with faculty, as they regard librarians as the true experts in this domain. In fact, maybe the AiA hybrid instruction sessions can be regarded as a sort of "training wheels" for priming faculty to take the wheel, so to speak, and tackle information literacy instruction themselves.

In email communications after the composition faculty meeting, the program director was thankful for my making library-based research and information literacy instruction seem less daunting to faculty and for letting them know of the various ways we can work together. I also learned that she is aware of the publications drawing parallels between writing studies threshold concepts and information literacy threshold concepts; this seems like another potentially fruitful avenue for continued conversations and future collaborations.

Conclusion: Wanna Be Startin' Somethin' (Wait, Isn't Assessment a Loop?)

Working on AiA was enormously beneficial in myriad ways: we learned about the impact of information literacy instruction on student learning; we strengthened the library's already-strong relationships with the English department and the Composition Program; we brought together people from various campus units over a shared interest in and commitment to assessment; and we established the library as a viable partner in future assessment efforts and as an active participant in creating a campus-wide "culture of assessment." I admit that while I am proud of my team's work and the outcomes of our efforts, it doesn't quite feel like we've truly "closed" any assessment loop that may have been initiated by our participation in AiA. This hands-on introduction to the world of assessment has me questioning whether a loop is the best metaphor for the assessment cycle, and if it ever truly comes full circle. Given my experiences, I now wonder if it makes more sense to think of assessment as more like a spiral, or if we should dispense with assessment metaphors and just focus on not losing momentum after we report out the results of an assessment project. Or, if we insist on keeping metaphors that address the circular motion, yet also incorporate the additional project offshoots and varying options for continuation, maybe …an assessment hurricane?

What I am certain of, however, is that I can't wait to see what happens next. It'll be exciting to see what the future holds for the library's partnerships with the English department and the Composition Program, our cross-institutional collaborative assessment of students' information literacy, and our efforts to shift our information literacy instruction program to a "librarians as consultants" model.

Biography

Iris Jahng is a Pedagogy and Learning Design Librarian at the University of Massachusetts Boston. She received an MLIS from San Jose State University, a MA in philosophy from San Diego State University, and a BA in philosophy from the University of California San Diego. Her interests include open educational resources, critical information literacy, and applied ethics. She may be contacted at iris.jahng@umb.edu.

Don't Wait for Them to Come to You
Partnering with Student Support Services

Katie Bishop, University of Nebraska at Omaha

AT ANY INSTITUTION a positive culture is a critical element in overall organizational effectiveness. In my four years at the University of Nebraska at Omaha (UNO) Libraries I have seen the transition of a dean, an associate dean, two directors, and multiple faculty and staff. Notwithstanding this turnover, the library staff members have successfully come together to create a new student-centered, inclusive, and engaged library culture. Many factors went into this change, and the leadership turnover actually served to strengthen our library organizational model into one that is more open and communicative. However, the culture changes in my unit, Research and Instruction Services (RIS), launched with my Assessment in Action (AiA) project.

Initial Collaboration Project

While RIS was doing many things right, with a robust information literacy instruction program, an established liaison network to academic departments, and a strong collections strategy, I believed we could do more to help underserved populations on campus. At UNO the number of first-generation, ethnically diverse, or military-affiliated students increases each year. Student support services assist these populations considered at risk for attrition. Partnering with one of these established programs offered an opportunity for providing information literacy and other library services specifically to underrepresented or vulnerable student populations. However, I not only wanted to develop a solid partnership, I also wanted to have evidence of the value of this type of outreach and support. Because we already had a roving research assistance program for academic departments, suggesting roving to a student support services office made sense both to library administration and to program staff. In addition, this project addressed UNO's strategic plan to be student-centered and would potentially address a perceived unmet campus need, an important factor when planning any new initiative.[1] After looking at a few programs, Project Achieve (our federal TRIO Student Support Services Program) seemed like the most optimal fit.

As a TRIO program, Project Achieve supports between 180 and 200 students qualifying as first-generation, limited-income, or disabled. The staff there serve as advisors, review essays, provide tutors, and develop programming. This high level of staff involvement from the partnering office is ideal because it primes students to take advantage of additional services (such as help from a librarian).[2] Furthermore, students in the program often spend several hours a week studying or socializing in the Project Achieve office, so bringing library services to them made sense. Ultimately I wanted to answer this question: What is the effect of having a librarian embedded in a student support services office on student confidence when conducting research and on their use of and attitudes toward library resources and staff?

To answer this question I roved to the Project Achieve office three hours per week. Prior to starting my roving hours, I sent out a pre-assessment survey asking students to self-assess their use of the library, feelings toward library staff, and perceived research abilities. I followed this up with a post-assessment survey of the same questions toward the end of the first academic year of roving. Fifty-five surveys were collected for the pre-assessment and thirty-six for the post-assessment. I found that high satisfaction with research services staff is correlated with an increase in student confidence when conducting research, and that students in the Project Achieve program reported higher confidence in finding and using resources after a librarian was embedded in the PA office. In addition, the count of roving reference transactions at Project Achieve demonstrated an unmet need. These transactions accounted for 27 percent of the total numbers. In other words, this small group of students accounted for nearly a third of the total roving statistics compared to roving reference at colleges such as Education, Public Administration, and the College of Business.[3] Roving reference may be more successful when partnered closely with other campus staff. Even though this case study was quite small, finding that familiarity and satisfaction with library staff correlate to student confidence when conducting research was key to expanding outreach efforts at the library going forward.

Furthermore, the relationships I developed with the students in Project Achieve felt stronger and more meaningful than the relationships I have with the students who come to my office hours or email me for consultations. Project Achieve students seek me out at the library even though I am not the specific librarian for their major. When they need help from a subject specialist, they ask me to make the introduction for them. I've been invited to their research presentations and college graduations. After breaks I get warm greetings and even hugs from these students when I first see them. By working with Project Achieve I've been able to attend their awards luncheon and see students interact with deans and the chancellor. I've volunteered with the campus Habitat for Humanity group, which is run through Project Achieve. Students seemed to appreciate the informal time spent sharing a meal or in activities such as hauling garbage and huddling together on a rickety porch during a thunderstorm. Having roving hours in an office where students come to hang out, take a break, and chat with their friends allows for bonding moments where I can fully share in successes and provide support through challenges. The relationships students form with peers, staff, and faculty on campus help students become more engaged and help improve retention. By closely partnering with a student support services program, librarians may be able to develop deeper, more meaningful relationships with students, providing social or emotional support in addition to educating; these relationships are associated with greater rates of engagement, which leads to higher persistence.[4]

I had always suspected that outreach to student support services and other student groups could be beneficial to both the program offices and the library.[5] However, we didn't have a structure in place for creating and maintaining these additional partnerships. Creating a small project gave me data that demonstrated an association between librarian involvement and student success. Armed with my data from my partnership with Project Achieve, I worked with my then-director on outreach to other student support services programs, again looking at programs working with underserved students. With offices right down the hall from Project Achieve, the Thompson Learning Community (TLC) was the next logical partner. Students enter this program after being awarded a scholarship for students with a demonstrated financial need. Unfortunately, roving turned out to not be the best intervention because in TLC, advising and tutoring are stronger at the peer level than at the staff level. This did not deter me, though. I knew there was a way to make outreach work at the different programs once I understood the need of each student population.

Creating an Outreach and Instruction Librarian Position

In the meantime, about a year into my initial project, my director retired and I was hired to assume that role. Because of the positive relationships I developed through outreach to student support services, I wanted the replacement for my position to prioritize outreach. The library dean had retired a semester prior, and the associate dean was also transitioning. With an interim dean coming in, I knew I had to convince my unit and the other unit directors of the benefits of aligning my open faculty line away from traditional liaison work and toward outreach and instruction. The conclusions from my AiA project provided me with a positive case study, but I needed to also demonstrate that this move is the logical next step for liaison librarians.

Reviewing job descriptions, academic literature, and conference presentations provided me with solid evidence supporting the creation of this type of position. Outreach positions have been advertised in a variety of forms for decades, but traditional reference positions are shifting more toward outreach to specific student populations.[6] Liaison roles have been adjusting over the past five to ten years, with some moving away from the traditional collections, reference, and instruction to more functional, skill-based models.[7] In addition librarians are using more user-focused techniques to understand the skill level and needs of student researchers.[8] Reaching out and engaging library users is considered a key part of many of these new and realigned positions.[9] In a study of academic library strategic planning, 71.4 percent of the plans examined contained some form of outreach, marketing, or public relations as a goal.[10] By presenting the current trends in liaison librarianship to my unit and current library leadership, I was able to get support and approval to realign each subject specialist position as it opens. The new Outreach and Instruction Librarian is now responsible for coordinating outreach to dual enrollment and other school groups; participating in student involvement events; collaborating with Student Affairs, Student Government, the UNO Book Store, and other partners on student-centered outreach efforts; and developing programs to engage student learning communities.

Expanding Partnerships with Student Support Services

When the new Outreach and Instruction Librarian arrived, we worked together to develop an outreach plan for the upcoming year. Past outreach efforts had been conducted by different library staff working with a variety of groups across campus, so we needed to coordinate those efforts. In addition, there were several opportunities for new partnerships, but we had to be strategic about the next steps to ensure success. The outreach plan involved reviewing current efforts, identifying key areas of expansion based on campus and library priorities, and developing a set of best practices for implementing new partnerships and programing.

As part of the AiA program I learned to value both qualitative and quantitative data. Therefore our best practices involve a multimodal assessment effort including interviews with support services staff, exit slip surveys, attendance counts, usage statistics, and roving reference counts. While numbers give a snapshot of use, the qualitative data from student support services staff and students tells a richer story of the impact of our outreach. The outreach plan and assessments are further outlined below.

The first step to any new partnership is a needs assessment. This initial interview helps keep the expectations of both program staff and librarians in line with the type of help we can provide.[11] In addition, understanding the mission and outcomes, student population, and current programming offered helps us tailor interventions to match student expectations. Programming and interventions developed based on the needs assessment are evaluated by looking at the quantitative statistics and by a follow-up interview with the program staff at least once every academic year.

With an outreach plan in place, I directed the Outreach and Instruction Librarian to maintain the close partnership with Project Achieve, look into ways to improve collaboration with TLC, and reach out to the Office of Military and Veteran Services (OMVS). These programs were the best starting places because they already had working relationships with the library to various degrees. I had partnered with Project Achieve and TLC, and OMVS staff had met with the directors to explore collaboration opportunities. UNO prides itself as being one of the country's top military-friendly institutions as recognized by rankings from the *Military Times* and *U.S. News and World Report*, so OMVS is a key strategic partnership for the library. In addition, TLC and OMVS followed the Project Achieve model of being high-touch programs working with students needing an extra level of help. Whether because of a financial need in the case of TLC or because of other unique concerns as active military or veterans, these more vulnerable students benefit from additional support; we wanted the library to be a vital partner in helping provide it.[12]

During the needs assessment with TLC we learned that the students meet with peer advisors, complete regular study hours, and participate in a Passport events program that requires second-year TLC students to attend a specific number of campus events. In response to this information, RIS staff developed a series of undergraduate workshops that were listed as TLC Passport events. To help with peer advising and study hours, we reserved library tables for TLC advisors and students.

Through a separate assessment of Composition II final papers, we knew that undergraduate students seemed to generally need more information literacy instruction, particularly on evaluating sources. With this need in mind, the workshops were open to any undergraduate student who needed help with research. However, we marketed the workshops heavily both through the Passport program and to Comp II instructors. Ultimately, the workshops were well attended both by TLC students and by Comp II students whose instructors had assigned them to attend for extra credit. We learned that while historically it had been difficult to get students to attend workshops, piggybacking on other programs and courses has a significant impact on attendance. We had five workshops during the fall 2016 semester with sixty-five students attending, mostly TLC students (roughly 28 percent of the students participating in the second-year program). Encouraged by this success we streamlined the series down to three for spring 2017 and had fifty-seven attendees, mostly Comp II students.

Alongside our partnership with TLC, we were also developing strategies for working with the Office of Military and Veteran Services. After the needs assessment interview, the Outreach and Instruction Librarian worked to develop programming that would best meet the needs of this particular student population. She created a LibGuide and offered roving at the OMVS office. Roving was less successful based on transaction counts, so after the follow-up interview with OMVS staff, her current intervention is a research checklist presented at OMVS student orientations, along with a training plan for OMVS staff on library research skills so they will be more equipped to help their students at the point of need. The follow-up conversations also helped OMVS realize that their student population was underachieving in composition courses, so they will be adding students enrolled in composition to their advising check-ins.

In addition OMVS staff came to the library and offered training on how to best serve military and veteran students and their families. We've incorporated this type of training from other offices on campus as well. We've hosted two Safe Space Workshops provided by the Gender and Sexuality

Resource Center and will soon be hosting a workshop from the Accessibility Services Center. All members of the library staff are encouraged and invited to attend. These train-the-trainer events both help make the library a more inclusive space and also remind all library staff that we are committed to supporting our students in every way possible.

Expanding Outreach Initiatives

Along with specific interventions to various student support services programs, we've developed a more coordinated outreach effort across the library. Hiring an Outreach and Instruction Librarian has vastly increased our broader outreach efforts. With this new priority, three of the RIS associates now report directly to the Outreach and Instruction Librarian, creating a focused team. Prior to hiring this position and restructuring, we had a few pockets of general student outreach, but developing new outreach programming was haphazard at best. It was difficult to maintain our display cases, and outreach projects were often abandoned. With this new team in place, outreach initiatives are not only completed, but are also assessed for their success and viability. For each event we record how many library staff participated, time spent, partnering organization, audience, and attendance. Projects are tweaked, rethought, or sustained based on results.

Our largest broad outreach initiative is participating in De-Stress Fest, events held during Prep and Finals weeks developed by Student Involvement. In the past we had held a few events at the library, but these events were not well advertised so attendance was often low. By creating a partnership with Student Involvement, we were able to tap into their budget and marketing. We were supplied with games, bubble wrap, and other crafting supplies. This left us with funds available for additional events. All of our programming made it on the De-Stress Fest calendar, and our events were well attended. De-Stress Fest events have library-wide participation, with staff and faculty from every unit participating in some way including hosting game nights, helping out during a crafternoon (an afternoon of crafting activities), or finding new programming for our interactive video wall.

As part of the AiA project I gained an appreciation for assessing and evaluating programs to make sure they are not only successful, but also sustainable. After our first semester partnering on De-Stress Fest events, we realized that events that take a lot of prep and staff time may not be viable even if they are well attended. For example, when we had multiple crafting nights, students did attend and enjoy these events, but we had to staff each station for hours over the course of several days. By scaling these events down to one or two afternoons or evenings, we are still accomplishing a fun outreach activity, but aren't placing an undue burden on staff. To make up for the loss of a few active events we increased our passive events, handing out pages of coloring sheet, squares of bubble wrap, pipe cleaner "Fidget sticks," stuffed animals for students to cuddle, and mini Zen gardens created using our makerspace. Over the past academic year we've had forty-two general outreach events for UNO students with nearly 3,000 students attending the events. This doesn't count students engaging our interactive displays or our informal whiteboard assessments. By expanding outreach to include fun events, we hope to increase students' social engagement with the library. Because my AiA study found a small correlation between student satisfaction with library staff and overall confidence when conducting research, we wanted students to view the library as a welcoming environment with friendly staff who care about students. Positive student engagement, including cultivating a supportive environment, is associated with higher retention rates for first-year students and with six-year graduation rates.[13]

Campus Recognition

Our new dean started on the same day as our new Outreach and Instruction Librarian. Throughout the search we wanted to make sure the new library administrator understood our growing focus on students and our culture of inclusivity, creativity, and openness. Over the past eighteen months the dean has embraced this culture, agreeing to open and staff a more accessible lower-level entrance and extending library hours to 24/7 during parts of Prep and Finals weeks. Furthermore, promoting and strengthening partnerships and collaborations has become a priority on the UNO libraries' new strategic plan.

This spring the UNO Student Government recognized the library's newly energized focus on outreach to students. Representatives partnered with our Outreach and Instruction Librarian on an event for National Library Week. Student Government supplied coffee and doughnuts, and we held a social media contest with library selfies to win a study space over finals stocked with goodies. During its awards ceremony, the Student Government presented a letter of commendation to our dean and also gave him the 2016–17 John Christensen Student Service Award recognizing faculty who go above and beyond for students outside of regular instruction. This acknowledgement of the library's student-centered culture further validates our outreach efforts and encourages us to form new partnerships and explore new services.

Biography

Katie Bishop is the Director of Research and Instruction Services and Humanities Librarian at University of Nebraska at Omaha. She holds an MA in American Studies from the University of Iowa, and an MS in Library and Information Science from the University of Illinois. Her research interests include assessment, change management, and instruction. Reach her at kbishop@unomaha.edu.

Notes

1. Candice Dahl, "Library Liaison with Non-academic Units: A New Application for a Traditional Model," *Partnership: The Canadian Journal of Library and Information Practice and Research* 2, no. 1 (January 2007): 5.

2. Emily Love, "A Simple Step: Integrating Library Reference and Instruction into Previously Established Academic Programs for Minority Students," *Reference Librarian* 50, no. 1 (March 1, 2009): 10, https://doi.org/10.1080/02763870802546357.

3. Katie Bishop, Connie Sorensen-Birk, and Derek Boeckner, "Don't Wait for Them to Come to You: Partnering with Student Support Services" (poster presentation, American Library Association Annual Conference, San Francisco, CA, July 26, 2015), Criss Library Faculty Proceedings and Presentations 52, http://digitalcommons.unomaha.edu/crisslibfacproc/52.

4. George Kuh, "Why Integration and Engagement Are Essential to Effective Educational Practice in the Twenty-First Century," *Peer Review* 10, no. 4 (2008): 27; Mandy Savitz-Romer, Joie Jager-Hyman, and Ann Coles, *Removing Roadblocks to Rigor: Linking Academic and Social Supports to Ensure College Readiness and Success* (Washington, D.C.: Institute for Higher Education Policy, 2009), 17–18.

5. Pauline S. Swartz, Brian A. Carlisle, and E. Chisato Uyeki, "Libraries and Student Affairs: Partners for Student Success," *Reference Services Review* 35, no. 1 (February 20, 2007): 112–13, https://doi.org/10.1108/00907320710729409.

6. Colleen Boff, Carol Singer, and Beverly Stearns, "Reaching Out to the Underserved: More Than Thirty Years of Outreach Job Ads," *Journal of Academic Librarianship* 32, no. 2 (March 2006): 137–47, https://doi.org/10.1016/j.acalib.2005.12.007; Therese F. Triumph and Penny M. Beile, "The Trending Academic Library Job Market: An

Analysis of Library Position Announcements from 2011 with Comparisons to 1996 and 1988," *College and Research Libraries* 76, no. 6 (September 2015): 736, https://doi.org/10.5860/crl.76.6.716.

7.   Steve Cramer, Margaret Burri, Jutta Seibert, and Lynda Kellam, "New Models for New Roles: Creating Liaison Organizational Structures That Support Modern Priorities" (panel, ACRL 2015, Portland, OR, March 28, 2015); Janice M. Jaguszewski and Karen Williams, *New Roles for New Times: Transforming Liaison Roles in Research Libraries* (Washington, DC: Association of Research Libraries, 2013), 7, http://www.arl.org/component/content/article/6/2893.

8.   Jaguszewski and Williams, *New Roles for New Times*, 12.

9.   Jaguszewski and Williams, *New Roles for New Times*; Cramer et al., "New Models for New Roles."

10. Laura Saunders, "Academic Libraries' Strategic Plans: Top Trends and Under-recognized Areas," *Journal of Academic Librarianship* 41, no. 3 (2015): 289, https://doi.org/10.1016/j.acalib.2015.03.011.

11. Ronald Martin Solorzano, "Adding Value at the Desk: How Technology and User Expectations Are Changing Reference Work," *Reference Librarian* 54, no. 2 (April 1, 2013): 89–102, https://doi.org/10.1080/02763877.2013.755398.

12. Savitz-Romer, Jager-Hyman, and Coles, *Removing Roadblocks to Rigor*; Patricia A. Brown and Charles Gross, "Serving Those Who Have Served—Managing Veteran and Military Student Best Practices," *Journal of Continuing Higher Education* 59, no. 1 (February 18, 2011): 45–49, https://doi.org/10.1080/07377363.2011.544982.

13. National Survey of Student Engagement, *Engagement Insights: Survey Findings on the Quality of Undergraduate Education* (Bloomington: Indiana University Center for Postsecondary Research, 2016), 12, http://nsse.indiana.edu/html/annual_results.cfm.

Assessing Information Literacy for Transfer Student Success

Karen Stanley Grigg, University of North Carolina at Greensboro

WHILE UNIVERSITY OF NORTH CAROLINA at Greensboro (UNCG) Libraries has an extensive first-year library instruction program, our significant population of transfer students have not taken part in this initiative. Librarians often teach 300- and 400-level courses to students who have a diverse range of educational experiences, and it became clear that this meant students came to UNCG with just as diverse a variety of information literacy skills. We were unable to identify how much information literacy instruction transfer students have had or how skilled they are with library research when they arrive on campus. A literature search on transfer students and information literacy skills yielded scant results at that time that we could use as a basis for our understanding of this population. Since we wanted to serve this population in a more focused manner, three librarians in the Research, Outreach, and Instruction department formed a research team and surveyed all incoming transfer students in the fall of 2014. The goal of the research study was to identify the information literacy skills and needs of our incoming transfer students to find opportunities to provide needed outreach and instruction to help these students succeed. We asked basic demographic questions, gave several "test" questions related to information literacy, and asked the students what skills they believed they needed help obtaining.

Results showed that the transfer students over age twenty-nine and transfer students from community colleges scored the least knowledgeable on basic information literacy skills and that students who reported having previous information literacy instruction scored the most knowledgeable. The team planned to engage in further studies and saw the Assessment in Action (AiA) program as an excellent opportunity to learn more about assessment and to connect with other campus entities that work with transfer students. UNCG has made adult learners a priority, and, as research tends to support that library engagement correlates with student retention and success, this project aligned with the goals of the university.[1]

Collaboration across Campus

One early goal of our AiA project was to discover natural allies on campus outside of the library. Some of the external relationships I formed were crucial to the ongoing research in which I am engaged with transfer students and adult learners; I realized that prior to AiA, I had been operating in a silo, unaware of how many entities on our campus were also providing services and resources to our transfer students. Most notably, I made connections with our New Student Transitions and First Year Experience Director, and the main coordinator for transfer student orientations and programming, and also with the Associate Director for Programs, Campus Activities and Programs in the Campus Activities & Programs office, who is also heavily involved with assessment. We also connected with the director of the Office of Assessment, Evaluation, and Research Services (OAERS), who provided us with graduate student statisticians to help us with analyzing our data. The library eventually employed one of the student statisticians post-AiA to help us with all of our statistical needs. Without AiA, I doubt we would have made all of these connections, and now we are continuing to partner with those with whom we worked on the project, both on transfer student issues and on other library issues.

In our initial team meetings, I became keenly aware that collaborating with campus entities outside the library provided information and opportunities we would not have had otherwise. The team member heavily involved with transfer students made us aware of several opportunities for the library to be involved with outreach, such as involvement in the Transfer Student Expo, the Transfer Student Orientation, and meetings with staff in the Transfer Student Center on campus. Another team member made some creative suggestions for designing our survey study that expanded my perspective. One such suggestion was that, rather than always generating new data, we might want to leverage data that already exists, such as pulling student information from the registrar for classes that have had library instruction and comparing the GPA of these students to the general student population. Another suggestion was that, rather than asking students to answer demographic questions, we use their unique ID number and pull this information directly from the registrar. Ultimately, all agreed these techniques required more time and staff hours than available in this context, but these are approaches I will try in future studies, and I might not have realized that we had the ability to access this data without our partners' knowledge base. I realized how often librarians design research studies in a vacuum and how important it is to connect with other campus stakeholders.

The team weighed two different projects and opted to implement both. The first study was pretest-intervention-posttest information literacy sessions in a class specifically for incoming transfer students, FFL 250 (Enhancing the Transfer and Adult Student Experience). The second study was a follow-up survey to our initial incoming transfer student cohort to see if their information literacy skills had improved, and if so, if those students who had interacted with librarians had greater improvement. The addition of the pretest-intervention-posttest study arose when we were asked to provide library instruction for this group of incoming transfer students, and since we often use pretest and posttest assessment, it seemed logical to capture and use this data in addition to our original study.

Once we gathered our data, we connected with the director of the Office of Assessment, Evaluation, and Research Services (OAERS), a division of the Department of Educational Research Methodology (ERM), who provided us with graduate student statisticians to help us with analyzing our data using SPSS statistical software. This office allows ERM graduate students to gain valuable experience designing and analyzing assessments, both internal, to UNCG, and external, to the community. Prior to AiA, I was not aware that we had an entire department that would provide these services to faculty researchers. One graduate student was assigned to each project, and these students analyzed our data, met with us several times, and presented final reports, results, and graphs and tables we could use for publications and presentations. Their excellent work during this project led to one of the student statisticians becoming employed part-time for the library, as library administration had many assessment projects ongoing and had employed statisticians in the past. She spent twenty hours a week here analyzing data for other research projects and advising any of us who wanted help designing assessment projects. After AiA, this graduate student met with me to assist in planning future focus groups and shared her expertise on qualitative research. My one regret is that we did not know this service was available prior to designing our assessment instruments. Though this student has graduated and is now working full-time elsewhere, I plan to meet with OAERS again in the fall semester of 2017 and ask if we can partner with one or two ERM students to help plan, implement, and assess our focus groups.

The process of learning to use the AiA Assessment Cycle has been very useful for me as a researcher. I had conducted previous research projects, but did not have an effective method for planning outcomes and criteria, nor did I consider collaborating with entities outside the library. Most MLS programs offer at most one research methods class, though many do not require it, and many academic libraries expect incoming hires to already have well-honed research skills. The AiA structure of regular Moodle interactions provided an opportunity to seek and give guidance to other AiA cohort members, and the periodic streaming sessions on the research process and types of research helped to supplement the concepts we learned during our in-person meetings at ALA conferences. While I participated in a focus group at ALA for AiA participants, I have not stayed in touch with my cohort members. I am considering capitalizing on those relationships to see who might have been involved in qualitative research to talk to them about focus groups and ask about their experiences with their projects.

I encountered some challenges during the AiA process. While the webinars and information provided by facilitators and the cohort structure of support through the offering and receiving of guidance were supposed to provide a community of practice, some of the cohort members seemed to disappear over the year, and some groups were more active than others. My sense was that some participants either left their supporting organizations, or changes in strategic directions or job duties made it difficult to complete the project. Another struggle I had was that the initial timeline I identified was overly optimistic, and we were constrained near the end of the year to complete our data analysis in time. OAERS did, in fact, provide two excellent student statisticians, but it took more time than we expected for our project to pass through the pipeline on our end. Additionally, several of my AiA team members whom I invited to the project had high-level positions with many obligations, and multiple in-person meetings were impractical. However, we are a Google institution, so we did much of our work by email and Google Docs and managed to collaborate with minimal in-person meetings. Both of these challenges, while stressful for me as a team leader, helped me develop strategies for managing project expectations, building contingency plans, and creating timelines that allow for unexpected delays, especially when working with external entities. One of AiA's objectives was to build participants' skills in finding natural collaborators across the campus. One reason we often work in silos is because collaborating outside our usual circle requires comfort with some level of uncertainty and ambiguity. The alliances and relationships we build across campus are well worth working outside of our comfort and control zone, but in order to ensure the success of our projects, we must be flexible with how we collaborate and with our timeline, as well as developing contingency plans.

Findings

I was disappointed that the data in both studies did not reflect what I hoped to find, most likely due to the challenges we faced. Our pretest was not sent out before the class as we were expecting, so we had to reallocate instruction time, and, for a variety of reasons, one session's data had to be removed, making our sample size small. There were not statistically significant improvements in skills in the posttest, but we did find a significant increase in student comfort doing basic library tasks. Both tests were useful in recording which tasks incoming students found the most challenging. The survey also suffered from a smaller sample size. Almost half of our survey emails bounced back, speaking to retention issues!

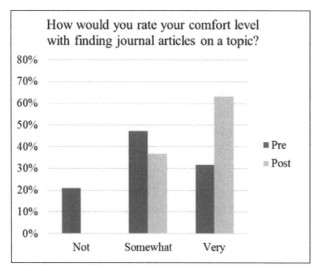

FIGURE 14.1

Figure 14.1 compares student comfort with finding journal articles on a topic prior to library instruction session with comfort post-instruction.

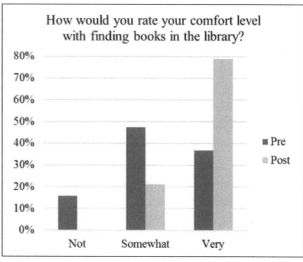

FIGURE 14.2

Figure 14.2 compares student comfort with finding books on a topic prior to library instruction session with comfort post-instruction.

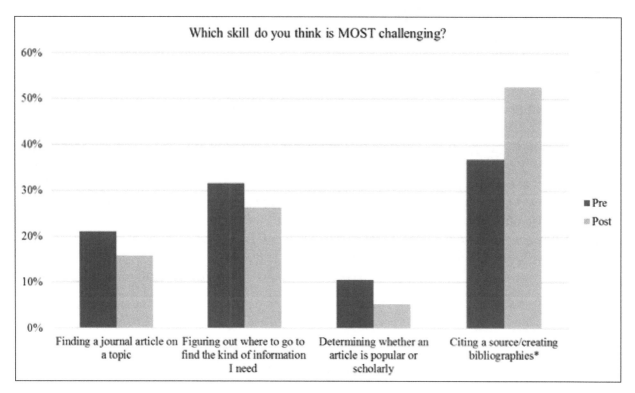

FIGURE 14.3

Figure 14.3 compares the research skill considered most challenging prior to library instruction session with that identified post-instruction.

We did not find the statistically significant variations in populations that we found in our initial study, but this fact could be a result of the students having completed a year of instruction. The most significant finding from this study was that students who reported having library instruction the previous year were four times as likely to have sought out a consultation from their liaison. This again suggests that library instruction increases comfort with library research and librarians.

As the team leader, I gave a report to all the liaisons about our findings and made our data available to all so that each liaison could use our findings when developing information literacy instruction. Survey data broke down results by department, so liaisons were able to see how well their students performed on the information literacy tasks and what skills the students indicated they needed most. Our transfer students have specific student orientation days in the summer, and, as the team leader for this project, I now lead these tours so that I can provide targeted information about the libraries' services and collections likely to interest transfer students. For example, transfer students are likely to be commuters and more likely to have to balance their coursework with work, family duties, or both. I address remote access and extended library hours in depth with our transfer students, and I also discuss liaison consultations, since the students who made a connection with their liaisons were far more likely to seek out these consultations. We are teaching the same course this fall and will be adjusting our approach to instruction and topics based on the feedback we received from students in our AiA study. Additionally, we are meeting this summer with some of our community college feeder school cohorts to discuss potential handoff instruction and other ways we can collaborate.

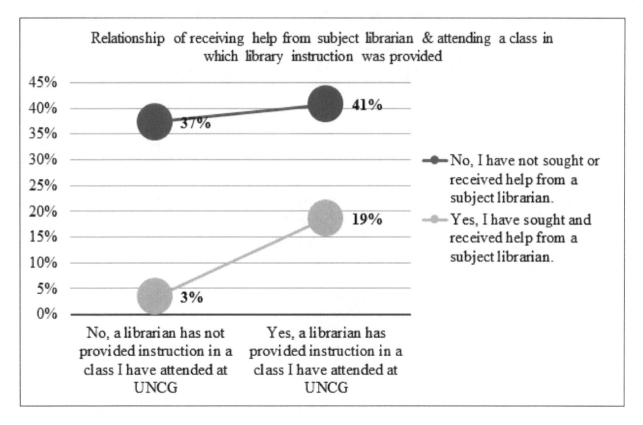

FIGURE 14.4

Figure 14.4 shows the positive correlation between receiving library instruction and seeking help from a subject librarian.

Through this project and participation in AiA, we have set the stage for other campus entities to see us as a partner in research and in student success. Librarians at UNCG are all tenured and tenure-track, but not all UNCG faculty realize that we also engage in original research. When we coordinate with other units on campus, especially in research, we gain visibility and credibility. Institutional acknowledgement also comes with our continuing focus on transfer students, which connects with the university initiative on adult students. Though our AiA project was primarily quantitative, the exposure to qualitative research throughout this project has given me the confidence and basic skills to plan several focus groups as we plan to repeat the project in the upcoming fall semester. The student statistician hired by the library had worked closely with us to begin planning for our fall focus groups. Her departure introduces some ambiguity, in that we will need to contact OEARS again directly and work with new students, but I am confident that the groundwork we laid with this department will allow us to continue partnering with this useful service. In addition, our former dean retired, and both she and the acting dean strongly supported our participation in AiA and assessment in general. In fact, the acting dean was an AiA team member. She is still the Associate Dean of Public Services, but our newly hired dean has not arrived, so it is yet unknown whether library outreach to transfer students will be a priority in the future. However, we expect that the relationships we have built and the skills we have obtained will help with future projects of any type.

One challenge will be nurturing these new relationships. In a large, bureaucratic organization, it is not always reflexive to reach outside of one's own unit to scan for natural partnerships across the university. AiA required us to make those important connections, but it will take time and practice to sustain them; I hope repeating this project will help us in that effort. I plan to lead larger conversations within the library about how we can build in an exercise of identifying natural partners outside the library when we take on new assessment projects. I find that I am asked to be involved with assessment efforts more often now that I have completed AiA, and I am asked for my feedback by other librarians. I would like to offer a workshop to any interested librarians about the AiA program and the cycle of assessment.

I have also presented and published about my experiences with AiA and my research projects. I made a presentation at the Library Assessment Conference, and, in November 2016, was invited to join a panel of speakers on the topic of transfer students and the library at the 2016 National Institute for the Study of Transfer Students Conference, making contacts with librarians and other university staff across the country who work closely with transfer students. This is evidence that AiA provided the tools I needed to continue expanding my community of practice.

Conclusion

Over the past two years, I have continued focusing my research and outreach activities with transfer students. Though one campus team member has moved on to another position, and another has not been active in participating with the library efforts, I found a champion in the Transfer Student Office who has been actively recruiting the library's involvement with transfer student relations. The library had already given optional tours during all orientations for incoming students, but I now am staffing a table at the Spartan Expo fair for potential and enrolled transfer students, presenting at the incoming transfer student orientation, and planning further outreach opportunities at the Transfer Student Center. I have collaborated with several of our largest feeder community college librarians, and am working on co-delivering library instruction both on the community college campuses and virtually. Based on our AiA assessment measures, I have adjusted instruction sessions to address those skills most needed by our incoming transfer students. And I am going to be presenting for the second year running at the National Institute for the Study of Transfer Students (NISTS) conference in Atlanta, where I am making national contacts with people across the campus who work with transfer students. We will be conducting focus groups in Spring of 2018 to examine some of the broader issues and challenges faced by transfer students, rather than focusing solely on library skills and needs. Additionally, we will be working on additional quantitative research focusing on existing data, perhaps analyzing student attendance at library instruction sessions and identifying through enrollment how many transfer students have attended, and then tracking and comparing their overall GPA to those transfer students who have not attended library instruction sessions. Additionally, I am continuing to share our research results and knowledge of transfer students to other librarians who work with these students.

Biography

Karen Stanley Grigg has been the Science Liaison Librarian at the University of North Carolina at Greensboro (UNCG) Libraries and Archives since 2013. Prior to taking this position, she was the Collection Development Services Librarian at Duke University Medical Center Library for eight years, and began her career in academic librarianship in 1999 as the Agricultural and Life Sciences Librarian, and later the Textiles and Engineering Services Librarian, at North Carolina State University (NCSU) Libraries. She received her master of library science from the University of North Carolina at Chapel Hill in 1998, and has a BA in English literature and some additional undergraduate studies in wildlife biology and mathematics. Her hobbies include backpacking, bicycling, and geocaching. Reach her at ksgrigg@uncg.edu.

Notes

1.   Soria, Krista M., Jan Fransen, and Shane Nackerud. "Library Use and Undergraduate Student Outcomes: New Evidence for Students' Retention and Academic Success." *Portal: Libraries and the Academy* 13, no. 2 (2013): 147–64.

Opening Doors for Libraries on Campus and Beyond

Ken Liss, Boston University

THE BOSTON UNIVERSITY LIBRARIES were a latecomer to Assessment in Action (AiA), not even beginning our application to the third year of the program until after the original deadline had been extended by an extra three weeks. The suggestion to apply came from the Associate University Librarian for Graduate and Research Services, who is also head of the libraries' assessment committee. She was aware of my involvement in a small-scale project experimenting with new approaches to information literacy instruction in the first-year writing classroom of the university's College of Arts and Sciences. She knew, as well, of conversations about IL learning outcomes that the Associate University Librarian (AUL) for Undergraduate and Distance Learning and I had begun with the head of the university's new Office of Program Learning Outcomes Assessment. The two AULs and I saw AiA as an opportunity to expand the libraries' knowledge and skills around assessment and learning outcomes, to broaden the focus of our assessment activities into information literacy instruction, and to enhance the libraries' standing as a partner with faculty and others in promoting and assessing student success.

Even with the extended deadline, time was tight. We had to develop a proposal, build a team, and get sign-off from the provost's office in four weeks. Our application was not finalized and submitted until three hours before the deadline. But despite that Johnny-come-lately beginning, Boston University's involvement in AiA has paid and continues to pay dividends at BU while also contributing to the broader goals of the AiA program.

AiA team members from the libraries, the College of Arts and Sciences Writing Program, and the Program Learning Outcomes Assessment office have built on the relationships that developed through AiA. They have continued to collaborate with each other and other partners on projects both on campus and beyond. At BU, those collaborations have included joint leadership of a seminar on threshold concepts for librarians and writing instructors, expanded experimentation with instruction based on the ACRL *Framework for Information Literacy for Higher Education* (the focus of our AiA project), and active participation in the development of an information literacy component in the university's new general education program.

Beyond BU, AiA team members, along with others from the university, have been accepted into multi-institution programs run by the Association of American Colleges and Universities and the Dartmouth College Institute for Writing and Rhetoric. These activities are opportunities for us to learn from others and to share our own success with collaboration and with library contributions to institutional goals and assessment with colleagues at other institutions.

Boston University's Assessment in Action Project

Undergraduates in the College of Arts and Sciences (CAS), the largest of BU's many schools, take a two-semester sequence of topic-based writing seminars. These seminars are managed by the CAS

Writing Program[1] and taught by a combination of full-time and part-time lecturers and graduate teaching fellows. Undergraduates in other BU schools (Engineering, Business, Communication, Education, Fine Arts, Hospitality Administration, Health and Rehabilitation Sciences) also enroll in one or both of these courses to fulfill their writing requirement. That makes the writing program and its seminars a "high-touch" element engaging with a high percentage of undergraduate students early in their time at the university.

The second course in the writing sequence, WR150, is designated a writing and research seminar, with information literacy or "learning to conduct college-level research" as one of its stated goals. Under the leadership of the AUL for Undergraduate and Distance Learning, the libraries have in place a long-standing practice of assigning a librarian to every section of WR150. There are as many as 160 sections each year, with the bulk of them taught in the spring semester.

The nature and degree of librarian involvement in WR150 have been left up to the individual writing instructors and their assigned librarians. For most, this has consisted of traditional library "one-shot sessions" focused on tours, search techniques, introductions to the library website and its discovery system and databases, and so on. Some sections have done more, while some instructors have chosen to handle the information literacy component on their own.

Neither the writing program nor the libraries had developed a consistent understanding of or pedagogical approach to information literacy. The writing program conducted assessments of student learning (alternating quantitative and qualitative assessment year to year), but information literacy received only cursory attention (e.g. "How many sources did the student cite in their paper?"). The libraries did not conduct any assessment of their work with students in the writing program.

I joined the BU Libraries staff in March 2014 as Head of Liaison and Instruction Services and was put in charge of our support for the CAS Writing Program. I also took on the librarian assignment for several of the classes myself.

Two of the WR150 instructors I worked with had leadership roles in the CAS Writing Program: one as the writing program's curriculum coordinator, and the other as chair of an initiative called WRX, designed to provide writing program faculty "a structured opportunity to experiment with innovative writing pedagogies and course models."[2] These two instructors were already experimenting with a curriculum that asked students to develop a semester-long independent research project related to a broad course theme and to present their research in several genres for several audiences. During the 2014–15 academic year, we further experimented in their classes with a new approach to information literacy based on the ACRL *Framework for Information Literacy for Higher Education*, then in draft form.

That work formed the basis for our application and ultimate acceptance into AiA. Our team consisted of myself and the AU for Undergraduate and Distance Learning from the libraries, the two instructors from the writing program, and the Director of Learning Assessment in the Office of the Provost.

Our AiA project involved two sections, one control and one experimental, of each of the instructors' WR150 classes during the fall 2015 semester. The control group sections were provided a one-shot instruction session, an optional meeting with the librarian for each student, and an online guide to research resources tailored to the topic and assignments of the course. The experimental sections were provided with an instruction session, flipped classroom videos, required individual meetings with the librarian, a librarian presence in Blackboard, and a course research guide (same guide for both sections of each class). The focus of these efforts was on two frames from the ACRL *Framework*: Research as Inquiry and Searching as Strategic Exploration.

Changes in students' understanding of research as inquiry were assessed using a rubric developed by the team to measure improvement in their topic or question from the initial question they posed near the beginning of the course to the topic or question reflected in their final paper. Students' understanding of searching as strategic exploration was assessed via analysis of two different reflective essays they completed during the semester. The results of the assessment showed a greater understanding of both frames among the students in the classes that had enhanced librarian engagement.

The project also led to greater understanding of assessment methods and how to apply them to the new approach to information literacy embodied in the ACRL *Framework*. Those understandings and the relationships developed or strengthened during the course of the project began to bear additional fruit, on campus and beyond, even before the conclusion of our involvement in AiA.

Extending Library/Writing Program Collaboration and Assessment

With the analysis of our AiA results underway in the spring of 2016, our team began to lay the groundwork for an expanded assessment project to be conducted the following academic year. We saw a shared understanding of the ACRL *Framework* and *Framework*-based learning outcomes, as had developed among our team, as the key. We developed a plan to bring those ideas to a wider group of librarians and writing instructors as preparation for more extensive assessment the following spring.

One writing instructor on the team and I developed and co-led a seminar series for librarians and faculty members from the CAS Writing Program. There were three sessions, with assigned readings and discussions, designed to explore how threshold concepts were shaping pedagogy in both writing and library studies and to examine the ACRL *Framework* and librarian/writing instructor collaboration, as we had experienced it, among a wider group.

Topics of the seminar were threshold concepts and their use in writing programs; threshold concepts and the new ACRL *Framework*; and librarians and writing instructors collaborating. Some two dozen librarians and instructors took part in some or all of the sessions. For many, this was the first opportunity they had had to discuss information literacy learning objectives together and to engage in a big-picture view of library/writing program collaboration.

The spring 2016 seminar for librarians and writing instructors was followed in fall 2016 with another three-part seminar for all instruction librarians at BU, again with readings and discussions about the ACRL *Framework* and information literacy learning outcomes. The aims of these sessions were (*a*) to begin to develop broad, assessable goals for our instruction program; (*b*) to develop ways to share ideas and techniques; and (*c*) to foster creativity and experimentation in pursuit of our goals.

In spring 2017, when the next large wave of WR150 classes was scheduled, the writing instructors and I created a research pedagogy initiative to encourage librarians and writing instructors (including many of those who had participated in the seminars) to develop their own assignments and lesson plans based on one or more of the ACRL frames. More than twenty sections took part. Students in these sections were asked to complete an expanded set of reflection questions about research and information literacy for further assessment and analysis of student learning and pedagogical approaches to information literacy. We also collected, with IRB approval, student portfolios from these sections, as well as faculty syllabi, assignments, and exercises.

We submitted an application to participate in the 2017 Dartmouth Summer Seminar for Composition Research offered by Dartmouth College's Institute for Writing and Rhetoric in collaboration with the Council of Writing Program Administrators.[3] The program, now in its seventh year, focuses on "Data-Driven Inquiry: Process, Methods, Results."[4]

Our application, based on our new initiative and building directly on the work we had done in AiA, proposed scaling this research up within our own program with three purposes in mind:

1. to take a more rigorous approach by setting up experimental and control groups to test our curricular experiments and further educate ourselves about analyzing data;
2. to involve more faculty and librarians in our program, thereby fostering more opportunities for innovation around teaching research in our program; and
3. to publish our results, bringing both our collaborative approach and the value of academic libraries to a wider audience.

We also saw our participation in the seminar as an opportunity to share our experience with assessment and collaboration around information literacy with a national and international group of writing program faculty and administrators.

Our application was accepted, and one of the instructors and I spent two weeks at Dartmouth with some three dozen writing instructors, writing program administrators, and composition scholars from across the United States as well as from Jamaica, Kuwait, and Qatar. (I was the only librarian and the first one to participate in the seminar since it began in 2011.) The program consisted of lectures, workshops, practice sessions, and individual and group consultations. The syllabus covered a range of research methods, including quantitative and qualitative analysis, carrying out critical analysis with (and of) statistics and statistical software, and preparing for publication. There were extensive readings and assignments to complete each evening.

We came away from the seminar with a scheme for coding and analyzing two types of data we had collected during our expanded research pedagogy initiative: faculty assignments and student reflections—and with a lot more work to do in the months to follow.

Equally important, we were able share and spread our ideas, sending other participants back to their home institutions with new ways of thinking about information literacy and librarian/faculty collaboration in the writing classroom. The impact was evident in some of the reactions to our twenty-five-minute presentation—"'New Possibilities and Mind-Boggling Questions': Research Dispositions in the Writing Classroom"—on the last day of the seminar.

The cochair of the Student Success in Writing Conference (a writing instructor at a university in Georgia) suggested we present at the conference in April and also at the International Conference on Information Literacy in September 2018. The Director of Writing and Rhetoric at a college in Maine invited us to do a workshop for librarians and writing instructors at her institution. Several people asked for suggestions for the kind of assignments that lead to learning about information literacy in ways that go beyond the mechanics and techniques of research. Others said they would change their approach to working with the librarians on their campuses. "Just with talking informally with you two over the seminar I've gained a much deeper understanding of the information literacy field—and how it can change so quickly!" said one. "Very helpful. I will no longer just plunk a 'library day' into my FYW course."

Information Literacy, the Writing Program, and General Education at BU

The CAS Writing Program, with its broad reach across much of the undergraduate student body, has long been a central focus of the libraries' information literacy efforts at BU. Our involvement with the writing program in AiA and the expanded activity that has grown out of that collaboration have presented an opportunity to better assess and improve those efforts.

The skills and relationships we developed through AiA and the increased attention it brought to the libraries have also led to opportunities to work with the writing program and others in broader university initiatives. Chief among these is an ambitious new general education program called the BU Hub. The Hub, announced in the spring of 2016, is BU's first-ever attempt to develop a university-wide general education program that applies across all schools and programs and all four years of an undergraduate student's time at BU.

A task force report released that spring—*The BU Hub: A Vision for University-wide Undergraduate General Education at Boston University*— focused on "the knowledge, skills, and habits of mind that all BU undergraduates need to thrive in their professional, personal and civic lives."[5] It identified six core capacities, one of which (the Intellectual Toolkit) included Research and Information Literacy as one of several "how to's for thinking and living that, exercised often, become enduring habits."[6]

The roadmap for the BU Hub is a complex one.[7] It includes piloting new and revised courses, proposed by faculty, in the 2017–18 academic year, with full launch for all incoming freshman in the fall of 2018, followed by a process to assess, revise, and improve the program. Guiding that effort will be an implementation task force and the relatively new Center for Teaching and Learning (CTL).

In spring 2017, CTL put together a team to participate in the Institute on High-Impact Practices and Student Success of the Association of American Colleges and Universities (AAC&U). Among the aims of the institute were "to help campus- and system-based teams devise equitable, integrative, learning-centered pathways that deeply connect with the assets students bring to college" and "to integrate and transform curricular and cocurricular practices to support higher levels of student success."[8]

The BU team put together for the institute was focused on support for the Hub, including three major areas: information literacy, writing-intensive courses, and multimodal composition. The team included three members of our AiA group: the AUL and me from the libraries and the Director of Learning Assessment. (She had suggested including the library, based on the work we had done in AiA.) Also participating were the interim director of the CAS Writing Program, the interim assistant director for Writing across the Disciplines, and three members of the CTL staff.

(In addition, the writing instructors and I, all members of our AiA team, were named coleaders of a group revising the curriculum for WR150, which is seen as one of the main pathways through which students will meet the information literacy requirement of the Hub.)

At the AAC&U Institute, held at BU in June, we worked with facilitators and with teams from other academic institutions to discuss and refine our plans and effective ways of implementing and evaluating them. We were also able to share the new approaches being taken at BU, including how the libraries and information literacy are contributing to institutional goals and initiatives, with a broader audience of higher education professionals. Perhaps most importantly, we strengthened our working relationship as a team, paving the way for further collaboration as important players in the evolution of the BU Hub.

Conclusion

At the outset, the BU Libraries' participation in Assessment in Action appeared to offer an opportunity to bring more formal assessment practices to bear on an experimental collaboration with writing program faculty. Indeed, that proved to be the case. In-person workshops at the ALA Annual and Midwinter conferences, together with virtual meetings and communication with other members of my cohort, were very helpful in developing effective assessment techniques. We have continued to put the new knowledge and skills learned at AiA to good use with the writing program and in other areas.

More surprising has been a potentially longer-lasting impact related to the broader goals of AiA. As those goals make clear, assessment is not just about understanding how we're doing and how to do it better. It's about communicating the value of what we do.

The collaboration and demonstration of library value that came out of our project have helped the libraries secure a more central place in new and emerging institutional goals and efforts to address them. We are being included, in formal and informal ways, in learning initiatives on campus and in engagements around student learning with faculty and administrators in other colleges and universities.

That is helping to ensure that we—libraries in general and the BU Libraries in particular—are seen as partners, not just as auxiliaries or support, in efforts to create an experience that, in the words of the BU General Education report, "embraces and exploits the social, institutional, and intellectual richness of residential higher education."[9]

Assessment in Action was developed as part of the ACRL Value of Academic Libraries initiative, which aimed to help academic librarians participate in "the national conversation on assessment, accountability, and value."[10] The BU Libraries' participation in AiA and the relationships that emerged have brought us into that conversation, on campus and beyond, in ways that we had not anticipated.

Biography

Ken Liss has been Head of Liaison & Instruction Services at the Boston University Libraries since 2014. He has been a librarian since 1992 and has worked at Boston College, the Harvard Business School, and the Boston Public Library as well as at a nonprofit organization and a library software company. Prior to becoming a librarian, Liss was a journalist and a public relations specialist. Reach him at kliss@bu.edu.

Note

1. Boston University Arts and Sciences Writing Program homepage, accessed December 3, 2017, http://www.bu.edu/writingprogram/.
2. Boston University College of Arts & Sciences Writing Program. The WRX Initiative. Boston: Boston University, 2015).
3. Dartmouth Institute for Writing & Rhetoric Summer Institutes & Seminars webpage, accessed December 14, 2017, http://writing-speech.dartmouth.edu/research/summer-institutes-seminars.
4. Dartmouth Institute for Writing & Rhetoric Summer Institutes & Seminars webpage, accessed December 14, 2017, http://writing-speech.dartmouth.edu/research/summer-institutes-seminars.
5. Boston University Task Force on General Education, *The BU Hub: A Vision for University-wide Undergraduate General Education at Boston University* (Boston: Boston University, 2016), 1.
6. Boston University Task Force on General Education, *The BU Hub: A Vision for University-wide Undergraduate General Education at Boston University* (Boston: Boston University, 2016), 6.
7. "Roadmap: Developing a University-wide General Education Program," Boston University, accessed December 3, 2017, http://www.bu.edu/gened/roadmap/.
8. "About the Institute," 2017 Institute on High-Impact Practices and Student Success, Association of American Colleges and Universities, accessed December 3, 2017, https://www.aacu.org/summerinstitutes/hips/2017.
9. Boston University Task Force on General Education, *The BU Hub*, 1.
10. Oakleaf, Megan. *Value of Academic Libraries: A Comprehensive Research Review and Report* (Chicago: American Library Association, 2010), 6.

CHAPTER 16

Professional Development for Assessment:

Lessons from Reflective Practice*

Lisa Janicke Hinchliffe

---

* Reprinted from *The Journal of Academic Librarianship*, Volume 41/Issue 6, Lisa Janicke Hinchliffe. "Professional Development for Assessment: Lessons from Reflective Practice," pages 850–852, copyright 2015, with permission from Elsevier. https://doi.org/10.1016/j.acalib.2015.10.004.

The Journal of Academic Librarianship 41 (2015) 850–852

Contents lists available at ScienceDirect

The Journal of Academic Librarianship

METRICS

Professional Development for Assessment: Lessons from Reflective Practice

Lisa Janicke Hinchliffe

University of Illinois at Urbana-Champaign, USA

It is a bit of a cliché to say "you never really know something until you teach it to someone else" but at the heart of that saying is something that we have all experienced. It is that "ah-ha" moment of insight that comes from puzzling through how to best present a topic to novices, or even to other experts, or while coaching someone through the struggle to understand how to design and implement a program.

For this column, I have invited my five co-facilitators of the ACRL *Assessment in Action* (http://www.ala.org/acrl/aia) program to reflect on their experiences teaching librarians about assessment in order to draw out the lessons they have learned. Collectively we have more than 60 years of experience as teachers to our librarian colleagues, doing this work that inspires us, challenges us, and helps us grow in our own assessment work. Each facilitator has focused their reflections on a particular topic related to assessment and their observations of librarian learning. We still have much to learn and look forward to continuing these conversations for years to come.

"OUTCOMES" BY DEBRA GILCHRIST, VICE PRESIDENT FOR LEARNING AND STUDENT SUCCESS, PIERCE COLLEGE, LAKEWOOD, WASHINGTON

Outcomes have become an increasingly important part of higher education since we seriously shifted our framework and mindset from teaching to learning. Learning outcomes, program outcomes, degree outcomes, course outcomes, class session outcomes, etc., have helped us to describe the student experience at many levels and what we want them to be able to do and consider while in the academy and beyond.

In teaching librarians how to construct and assess outcomes, I have learned that our natural inclination is to think about content ("what do I want to teach them?") before we think about the student and their actions ("what do I want the student to be able to do as a result of my teaching or of this library program?"). Focusing on the later question facilitates development of the best student-centered outcomes. Describing the students' actions and thinking sets the stage for effective instruction, programming, and assessment.

Since strong outcomes begin with strong verbs, I have learned to coach librarians to think deeply about the student experience and select the verb that best describes the true depth of knowledge/ability they wish for their students. For example, an outcome "to describe *xyz*" is very different than "to analyze *xyz*." My advice is continue to hone the outcome and not settle for the first thoughts as continuing

to ask "why do I want the student to do this?" will help achieve the right depth.

Outcomes are an important first step in an overall instructional design strategy, so it's important to provide opportunities to "test" the alignment of the learning outcome, the assessment, and the pedagogy/program experiences. The outcome is the foundation; once it is set then we can determine the best way to see that outcome revealed in the student work (i.e., in the assessment — how will the student demonstrate it), program or instructional activities (i.e., what will the program activities consist of or what pedagogy will we design), and finally when we are evaluating the assessment (i.e., what criteria will tell us that the student has done this well?). Re-drafting as a natural part of the workshop process also reinforces the most critical reason we engage in this work — change and continuous improvement. Because outcomes assessment is often portrayed as data gathering, I have also discovered the importance of using coaching approaches that reinforce philosophies of outcomes assessment practice. I emphasize that it is not only about satisfying a need for data or evidence, but also about determining for ourselves what is effective and then consciously and continuously working to improve that experience for students. The more we know, the more we engage in critical and reflective practice as individuals and as a library. And, the more we engage in critical and reflective practice, the more our students succeed.

"ALIGNMENT" BY APRIL CUNNINGHAM, INSTRUCTION/INFORMATION LITERACY LIBRARIAN, PALOMAR COLLEGE, SAN MARCOS, CALIFORNIA

When I am teaching about assessment, one of my goals is to help librarians make their assessment projects relevant. In her book on action research, Mary MacAteer recommends that we ask the following question, which I have used to focus my own assessment efforts and which has shaped the way I teach librarians to understand the purpose of their assessment: "Do the consequences of my actions measure up to the educational principles and values that motivate my work?" (2013).

When I return to this quote during the planning and analysis phases of assessment projects, I find that I center my assessment choices on the most essential elements of my work. When I share it with librarians during assessment workshops, however, I am often met with resistance to the idea that assessment can be so personal and so potentially idiosyncratic, depending on which principles and values we each choose to prioritize. So I also teach about the need to look outside our

http://dx.doi.org/10.1016/j.acalib.2015.10.004

immediate surroundings to find resonance between our assessment goals and the educational principles and values that motivate campus leaders.

Through this work, I have learned that many librarians have a clear sense of how their work fits with their institutions' goals, but that others struggle to find connections. Connecting our efforts to our community's key concerns is necessary for meaningful assessment, but we should also try to find these connections from the very start of planning, changing, or discontinuing any library action that is related to student outcomes (Association of College and Research Libraries, 2010). One approach for making these connections from the ground up is to use a logic model that guides librarians to articulate their otherwise unstated expectations and assumptions. Creating a model that identifies the planned work, intended results, and required resources can be helpful for recognizing gaps between actions, short-term outcomes, and long-term learning goals like the ones that are most valued by our communities. The Kellogg Foundation has created a "Logic Model Development Guide" (2014) that explains how to use this approach.

Logic models help us clarify the purpose of our actions and assessments, but I balance their potential over-simplification by encouraging librarians to also look at the variety of theories and models of how college affects students (Long, 2012). This helps us to maintain perspective when we find that our assessment efforts are not answering all of the questions we have about student learning and the role of our libraries in students' success. Reflecting on the complexity helps us to remember that the effect of education on students is too multidimensional to understand if we allow assessment to become detached from our values. We have to stay focused on our educational principles so that we recognize when our inferences about the consequences of our actions have meaning and utility for ourselves and for our institutions.

"LEADERSHIP" BY CARRIE DONOVAN, ASSISTANT DEAN, RESEARCH & INSTRUCTION SERVICES FERRIS STATE UNIVERSITY, BIG RAPIDS, MICHIGAN

As creative and curious professionals, librarians ask questions about the world, our work, and the effect of what we do. From my perspective, the application of this curiosity toward measuring our impact is becoming a bigger part of daily professional practice for librarians. For this to be more than navel-gazing focused solely on ourselves, we look to professional partners, broad contexts, and campus priorities with which to engage. Such engagement offers the opportunity for librarians to influence and lead, if we are willing to embrace it. Through my experience as a facilitator for the Assessment in Action program, especially, I've learned that librarians leading assessment initiatives can create a powerful force for change and I strongly believe that we are uniquely situated to do so.

If applying assessment principles to our everyday work can result in the ability to make informed decisions, allocate staff and resources effectively, and identify areas needing improvement, what does it mean when we take these approaches into an institution-wide context? From observing the impressive work of the 200 + librarians who have participated in Assessment in Action over the past three years, I have developed a clearer idea of what it looks like when librarians lead institutional assessment initiatives, including:

- Identifying shared goals and philosophies to unite a campus team
- Developing strategic partnerships that extend beyond any single project
- Facilitating connections with campus colleagues across departments and roles
- Aligning departmental priorities with campus mission
- Communicating evidence in order to show impact and bring about change.

Assessment initiatives benefit from librarians' understanding and awareness of the academic experience beyond disciplinary boundaries, in and outside of classrooms, and across a continuum of learning.

In addition to measuring the impact of library resources or services on teaching, learning, and research, librarians who lead assessment initiatives cultivate knowledge of campus culture, leverage the expertise of colleagues, and seek out strategic collaborations. While the impetus for an assessment project may begin within the library, librarians' inclusive and encompassing perspectives are a solid foundation for leadership of institutional teams addressing campus-wide outcomes. Leadership of this nature often situates librarians in positions that are high-profile in that we are addressing questions of critical importance to higher education and to our institutions. While introducing a certain intimidation factor, the high-stakes nature of leading assessment initiatives is precisely what makes them so worthwhile for librarians who are seeking to demonstrate value and create change.

"RESULTS" BY ERIC RESNIS, ASSESSMENT COORDINATOR (CENTER FOR TEACHING EXCELLENCE) AND ORGANIZATIONAL EFFECTIVENESS SPECIALIST (LIBRARIES), MIAMI UNIVERSITY, OXFORD, OHIO

Sampling has occurred. Data has been collected. What now? While reporting results may seem like an easy and straightforward process, it can easily become daunting and overwhelming. There are many considerations to take into account, and I offer this advice when reporting and following up on results from my experience teaching and coaching others about assessment.

First, don't forget the overall purpose of assessment: improvement. Provide a clear picture of your results and their meaning, and resist the temptation to only focus on the highly-positive results from your analysis. Even if your results are not what you aimed for, they will provide a baseline for improvement. We cannot be perfect all of the time (or even most of the time)!

If results aren't anything as you anticipated, there is no reason to feel defeated. Remember that assessment is a cycle, and that you are allowed (and encouraged) to revisit other tenets of the cycle when the unexpected occurs. That said, do take a close look at the results that you did obtain. Sometimes "poor" results include nuggets of unexpected information that are in fact positive, and may spark a new line of inquiry.

Try not to focus solely on percentages whenever possible. We love percentages; they are easy to calculate, and they are easy to discuss. However, they often misrepresent the story we are trying to tell. Percentages don't indicate significance of a difference in figures, nor do they prove correlation. Yes, you may need to refresh yourself on some basic statistical methods. Someone in your library, or on your campus, would be happy to help refresh you on analyses of variance, regressions, and other methods of interest. When sharing the results with others, be sure to clearly indicate what the method does and how it relates to your research question.

One last note about presenting results: clarity and context are of key importance. Have you explained everything clearly to an audience that may not have your knowledge of the project, your institution, or the methods you utilized? Is the information presented appropriate for your audience? What you present to your dean or director may be very different than what you present to a general audience of librarians.

And finally, it's not over simply because you have compiled and reported the results. How will you act? Create an action plan that includes how you will either revisit the assessment cycle, or how you will make changes to the services at the heart of your analysis. If appropriate, make a commitment to follow-up so you can determine if your changes are making a difference.

"PERSEVERANCE" BY JOHN WATTS, UNDERGRADUATE LEARNING LIBRARIAN, UNIVERSITY OF NEVADA, LAS VEGAS

As I have consulted with librarians about their assessment projects, one of the bottlenecks I observe them facing is seeing the project through to completion. Because of the collaborative nature of our work, library assessment can require a great deal of juggling. In the whirlwind of a semester, it is possible that details will be lost, communication will be dropped, and what you thought you would learn from your assessment doesn't surface. This is where perseverance and a little assessment moxie arrive on the scene.

Perseverance in an assessment project is the endurance to see your way through the project despite difficulty. One touchstone that can alleviate the pressure of the false assessment finish line is to consider the following principles of assessment:

1. Assessment is a multi-step cycle that begins with developing outcomes and ends with planning change based on what you learned.

2. This cycle is not linear, which is to say that you often don't move seamlessly from one step to the next uninterrupted. Rather, it's a recursive process that requires constant reflection and re-configuration throughout in order to make meaningful connections between your project outcomes and what you learned.

Sometimes when we near the end of the cycle we find a gap between what we set out to learn and the data that we actually collected. Or, halfway through, we realize that the instrument we chose was not tightly aligned with our outcomes and didn't provide enough validity.

Perseverance is what allows us to see this not as a setback, but as an opportunity to revisit an earlier step of the assessment cycle with informed eyes and make changes to the project that will provide more meaningful and shareable results. Rather than considering a visit to previous steps a failure, I consider it a natural part of the process. Simply having a framework like the assessment cycle in mind, can offer us enough structure to regroup, make improvements, and move forward.

Beyond challenges with the design of the assessment project, librarians can face stumbling blocks in the form of scheduling conflicts, lack of buy-in from campus partners, and many of life's disruptions. The inherently collaborative nature of assessment is what makes it a rich and powerful process. However, with the involvement of multiple individuals, the potential for complications increases. This is nothing new for librarians, who have a professional legacy of building partnerships and affecting change despite adversity.

As with any long-term process in which most aspects are beyond your control, assessment will cause you to question your expertise, to reframe your thinking, and to doubt what you thought you knew. But – if you persevere – it can also bring a new depth of understanding, breakthroughs in awareness, and a rejuvenation of your professional practice.

REFERENCES

Association of College and Research Libraries (2010). *Value of academic libraries: A comprehensive research review and report.* researched by megan oakleaf Chicago: Association of College and Research Libraries.

Kellogg Foundation (2014). Logic model development guide. Retrieved from http://www.smartgivers.org/uploads/logicmodelguidepdf.pdf

Long, D. (2012). Theories and models of student development. In L. J. Hinchliffe, & M. A. Wong (Eds.), *Environments for student growth and development: Librarians and student affairs in collaboration* (pp. 41–55). Chicago: Association of College & Research Libraries.

McAteer, M. (2013). *Action research in education.* London: Sage.

Advancing Assessment to the Future

Though the Assessment in Action program in its original format has come to an end, its achievements lay a foundation for future work. The reflections in Section 2 demonstrate how the intentional model of collaboration and reflection influenced individuals at their own institutions. They encountered challenges, but the rewards suggest the real value gained from undertaking these projects.

Taking a broader view, Chapter 17 comes from the OCLC Research team who authored the ACRL report, *Academic Library Impact: Improving Practice and Essential Areas to Research*. They conducted an extensive literature review on the impact of library resources on student learning and success, which included a synthesis of findings from 178 AiA projects. The report identifies six priority areas for future research. This chapter shows that the methods and results of the AiA program are significant in three of those areas: communication, collaboration, and institutional mission and alignment. The authors recommend effective practices in each of these to further advance research in the field.

In the final chapter, a long-standing member leader in ACRL, Lisa Janicke Hinchliffe, reflects on her involvement in the Value of Academic Libraries initiative and the Assessment in Action program. She focuses on evidence of academic library impact on student success, collaborative approaches to assessment, and library leadership on campus. In all these areas, the AiA teams advanced strategic and sustainable assessment work within the higher education landscape.

ACRL aims to continue the momentum from Assessment in Action and put the program's valuable lessons to good use. A one-day traveling workshop, "Assessment in Action: Demonstrating and Communicating Library Contributions to Student Learning and Success," delivers key elements of the AiA curriculum and collaborative model to new institutions. Two new programs provide funding to create and share work that demonstrates the impact of academic libraries on student learning and success. The first, the Value of Academic Libraries Travel Scholarships (announced in October 2017), supports librarians and information professionals presenting at non-library conferences in order to communicate the important role of the library to higher education stakeholders. The second program offers research grants for new work in the priority areas identified in the *Academic Library Impact* report. Through these avenues and those still to come, ACRL offers opportunities for growth and advocacy within the profession into the future.

Assessing for Alignment

How to Win Collaborators and Influence Stakeholders

Stephanie Mikitish, Rutgers University

Vanessa Kitzie, University of South Carolina

Lynn Silipigni Connaway, OCLC Research

MORE THAN EVER, academic library administrators and staff must demonstrate and communicate their library's value to institutional stakeholders, funders, and governance boards. An essential area for library administrators and staff to explore is how the library advances its institution's mission and goals, particularly those related to student learning and success.[1] This chapter reports on findings from an action-oriented research agenda project that examined how academic libraries can contribute to student learning and success and demonstrate these contributions.[2] The Association of College and Research Libraries (ACRL) commissioned the project, entitled *Academic Library Impact: Improving Practice and Essential Areas to Research*, and awarded it to OCLC Research.

The three data sources that informed findings from the report included a substantive review of literature published from 2010 to 2016 on this topic, including all projects from the ACRL program Assessment in Action: Academic Libraries and Student Success (AiA);[3] focus group interviews with academic library administrators from diverse colleges and universities; and semi-structured, individual interviews with provosts[4] from these same institutions.

This chapter identifies how researchers and professionals can leverage the AiA approach to advance three key priority areas: communication, collaboration, and institutional mission and alignment. The chapter summarizes these priority areas, discusses the major differences between AiA and non-AiA projects, and suggests ways the AiA approach can contribute to effective practices and investigate selected research questions from the report. The team has based these recommendations on analysis of provost interviews. These interviews provide researchers and professionals with the needed perspective of higher education administration, which often is missing in current work.

Methods

The report employed a mixed-methods approach; the use of both qualitative and quantitative data collection and analysis methods strengthened the research design, results, and findings. The literature review included documents published between 2010 and 2016 and retrieved from library and information science (LIS) and higher education databases that addressed the impact of library resources on student learning and success.[5] The project team retrieved a total of 535 documents.

Of these documents, 166 (31%) were theoretical (i.e., literature reviews, discussions of a theoretical model or framework, thought pieces), and 369 (69%) were research (i.e., empirical studies), including 178 AiA projects.

To supplement the literature, the project team recruited an advisory group of library administrators from fourteen institutions for an online focus group and in-person brainstorming sessions. Library administrators represented community colleges ($n = 2$, 14%), four-year colleges ($n = 2$, 14%), and research universities ($n = 10$, 71%) from secular ($n = 11$, 79%), nonsecular ($n = 3$, 21%), public ($n = 9$, 64%), and private ($n = 5$, 36%) institutions representing the four geographical regions of the US. Focus group questions elicited how the members of the advisory group supported their institutions' mission and goals and communicated both this support and their library's value to high-level stakeholders. The advisory group then participated in two follow-up brainstorming sessions to provide feedback on the preliminary results of data analysis. Each advisory group member also connected the project team with a provost from each of their institutions for individual, semi-structured interviews by telephone. Focus group responses informed the questions for these interviews. Specifically, advisory group members wanted to know how the library's communication of value compared to those of other departments or units within each institution, as well as elements of a successful, modest funding request. The data related to the interviews and sessions include recordings, transcriptions, and detailed recorder notes.

The project team imported the data from the literature review and interviews into NVivo and coded, or categorized them by relevant themes.[6] These themes consisted of outcomes (e.g., student learning, success); library resources (i.e., collections, spaces, services); and, when applicable, research document characteristics (e.g., data analysis methods, institution types, etc.). Once the project team coded the data by themes, they calculated descriptive statistics to compare how often each data source discussed the themes. Post hoc analysis techniques identified trends and patterns within the data sources.[7]

Based on results from coding and statistical analyses, the report identified six priority areas that represent the codes, or themes, most identified by the data sources. These priority areas are interrelated; addressing one priority area often effects change in other areas. The report also provided effective practices for library implementation and research questions requiring further study.[8]

This chapter addresses three of these priority areas: communication, collaboration, and institutional mission and alignment. The authors chose these areas because there were statistically significant differences[9] between how AiA and non-AiA studies approached these themes. The differences suggest that future studies targeting these priority areas could benefit from using the AiA approach of team-based collaborative assessment. Key differences between AiA and non-AiA approaches were in how researchers conducted the assessments; how administrators, faculty, and staff outside the library were involved in the assessment; and how researchers reported the assessment results to stakeholders.

Priority Area: Communicate the Library's Contributions

The library administrators and provosts interviewed identified the library's ability to effectively communicate its contributions to student learning and success to institutional stakeholders as a central priority. The project team coded the communication theme most often in the data as compared to the other themes. Despite its importance and prevalence, the highly contextual nature of communication eludes reduction to a series of best practices. For this reason, library administrators and staff experience difficulty getting the attention of potential stakeholders, such as faculty.

Provosts recognized this difficulty and identified a gap between stakeholder perceptions and how the library contributes to student learning and success, adding value to the institution.[10] This gap results in a series of "myths" about the library if stakeholders recognize only certain resources the library provides, such as collections. The following provost discusses one myth about the library that many of her colleagues adopt:

> The big myth …is that, that many faculty don't engage with the library, because they feel that, "Well, the library is online." Right? Students can access everything from a distance. (Provost PP04)

Another gap in perception regards the language used to communicate library value. A key finding from the report was that library administrators and staff use the word *service* as a catch-all term to describe the library's resources, whereas provosts prefer more specified terms, such as *teaching and learning, customer service,* or *space.* A recent large-scale study of how teaching faculty and librarians view the library suggests that better communication can decrease these gaps.[11]

The literature reviewed addressed communication less frequently than library administrators and provosts. This theme ranked fourth among the themes identified in this data source, and its frequency was not significant, defined as being one or less than one standard deviation from the mean of all theme frequencies. However, the communication theme was more prevalent in AiA projects than any other theme. The difference between the frequency of the theme in AiA projects versus non-AiA projects was also statistically significant.

One of the reasons AiA projects focused more on communication as compared to non-AiA projects was that the AiA program required the applicants to form teams of "senior librarians, chief academic administrators, and institutional researchers,"[12] with at least two members working outside the library. This partnership guaranteed communication started from the earliest stage and continued throughout the life of each project, with team leaders raising awareness over time about the library's resources and programs with these outside stakeholders. In addition, library administrators and staff could learn what terms stakeholders used when describing library value and adopt these terms to better communicate with them. Partnerships with outside stakeholders also fostered collaboration, an interrelated priority area discussed in the next section.

The action research design of AiA projects also may have contributed to their focus on communication. Since different types of data and different approaches will appeal to different stakeholders, using a variety of methods can facilitate communication with more audiences. AiA projects used a greater variety of methods (i.e., more quantitative methods, including correlation) and were twice as likely to use mixed methods as non-AiA projects. These differences were statistically significant. Having more options to communicate research findings is crucial, given the highly contextualized nature of how individuals in different areas and levels of an institution communicate value. The following provost account exemplifies the importance of context for library administrators and staff when communicating with others:

> There is not one specific thing a library can do because the environments are so different. Thinking of how these new learning environments work, and how the library would enhance students' and faculty's ability to access and process knowledge, data, [and] information in those particular kinds of environment[s] …that is what libraries need to do to be successful. (Provost PP02)

Changes at the administrative level in an institution signify that the type of data one administrator prefers to receive may differ from a replacement's preferences.[13] For this reason, library administrators and staff should embrace the use of varied and mixed methods to increase the ability of their research findings to communicate value regardless of context.

Communicating with various institutional stakeholders also addresses an effective practice identified in the report: Librarians should "explore ways to effectively communicate both up and out, regarding both message and the method" of how the library affects student learning and success.[14] Studies that adopt the AiA approach of involving collaborators and audiences from areas outside the library (e.g., presenting findings at a higher education conference) have a greater likelihood of being noticed and read by administrators.

Findings from the report denoted additional communication-related effective practices to implement at the library that complement the team-based component of the AiA approach. These practices are

- "Communicate with those outside of the library and high in the institution's administration because they can offer a bird's-eye view of what the library should be doing and can be advocates …and supporters …if they feel invested in and a part of the library."
- "Determine the terminology used by provosts to communicate the library's value and adopt this terminology in subsequent communications."[15]

Research questions for the communication priority area that would benefit most from leveraging the AiA approach are

- RQ1: "How do faculty envision the integration of library services, collections, and spaces for teaching and learning?"
- RQ2: "What are the main barriers to communication between library administrators and staff and educational stakeholders (e.g., students, faculty, administrators)?"
- RQ3: "How are other units effectively communicating with stakeholders?"[16]

Using the AiA approach, future studies exploring how the library contributes to student-centered outcomes should continue to involve project team members from outside the library. These members can provide the context critical for developing, executing, and reporting study findings in ways that resonate with institutional stakeholders. Possible team members include faculty and teaching assistants (RQ1); students, faculty, and administrators (RQ2); and administrators and staff in instructional support units, such as writing and tutoring centers (RQ3).

Team members also can suggest ways that other researchers outside LIS have framed topics or problems in non-LIS literature. LIS researchers can utilize these suggestions to identify important areas and methods addressed within non-LIS studies to better demonstrate the library's contribution to student learning and success. Library administrators and staff then will be able to showcase these new forms of data collection and analysis in outside venues, such as higher education outlets, directed toward provosts and higher education administrators. Outside literature applicable to the identified research questions include pedagogical research, which also may appear in the literature for specific disciplinary areas (RQ1); white papers, reports, and journals; and daily or weekly digests, such as Inside Higher Ed, which provide timely discussions and perspectives on student learning and success topics (RQs 2 and 3). Finally, the research designs addressing these research questions should continue to vary in their application to capture diverse institutional contexts, informed by the three communication-related effective practices outlined above.

Priority Area: Collaborate with Educational Stakeholders

Collaboration between library and non-library stakeholders represents another theme that the project team frequently identified in all three data sources. Both the literature reviewed and the interviews with library administrators identified this theme second-most, and both frequencies were significant (i.e., more than one standard deviation from the mean of all theme frequencies). Collaboration also became more popular over time within the literature reviewed; the proportion of documents including the collaboration theme doubled from 2010 to 2016.[17]

The project team identified collaboration less often in the provost interviews; further, the frequency of the collaboration theme in the provost interviews was not significant. Collaboration ranked fourth among the other themes, following communication, mission alignment and strategy, and teaching and learning. However, this finding does not suggest provosts do not envision collaboration as important. Instead, they view collaboration as facilitated by mission alignment and strategy. Therefore, when contemplating how to communicate value, library administrators and staff should consider how collaboration integrates into the goals and missions of their respective institutions. One area where provosts want library administrators and staff to collaborate is in using space. Library stakeholders can achieve such collaboration by offering meeting space to both institutional stakeholders and outside community members or by hosting writing and tutoring centers. This type of collaboration also provides provosts with a visual indication of the library's value. Per the following provost account

> I think [space] is one of the most effective ways to get the message out. That… might involve, as an example, making meeting rooms in the library more generally available for people to come and do projects. Creating …the library as this sort of center of intellectual activity. (Provost PP09)

This provost's account also highlights the interrelationship between the communication and collaboration priority areas. For library administrators and staff to effectively communicate their value, they must collaborate. Such collaboration fosters a mutual investment in creating and communicating library value that strengthens the library's position within the community.

There are several factors that library administrators and staff must consider when collaborating. These factors include whom to collaborate with (e.g., inter-institutional or intra-institutional collaborators) and at what level (e.g., individual, course, departmental, and program levels; sharing space versus coordinating services).[18] Like communication, the types of collaboration library administrators and staff adopt are highly contextual and vary based on institutional priorities.

There were a few statistically significant differences between AiA and non-AiA projects related to collaboration. Thematically, AiA projects focused on collaboration more than non-AiA projects. However, only one AiA project involved collaboration between institutions, while nearly a quarter of non-AiA projects involved such collaboration. The AiA approach has demonstrated that a variety of institutional stakeholders will work with library administrators and staff on grants. Now, library stakeholders should extend this approach to similar stakeholders outside the institution. For instance, library administrators and staff could work with researchers on joint grant applications or publications.[19] Such collaboration invests outside stakeholders in the project's premise, execution, and results, while also augmenting the project with different disciplinary perspectives.

More specific collaboration-related effective practices to implement the collaborative aspect of the AiA approach are

- "Understand that there are different types and levels of collaboration and consider looking at literature from other related fields to see what is said about libraries and" similar issues that libraries are facing or may face.
- "[Partner] with academic …administrators, academic services staff, faculty, students, alumni, and other members of [the regional and] local communities" to reach shared institutional goals.
- "Partner with institutions outside the university or college, such as government and commercial institutions."[20]

Research questions for the collaboration priority area that would benefit most by strategically employing the AiA approach are

- RQ1: "How can library administrators and staff collaborate with [other educational stakeholders] to increase student learning and success?"
- RQ2: "What can library administrators and staff learn from institutional units that have [positively] increased student learning and success?"
- RQ3: "How can library administrators and staff contribute to areas that demonstrate the most promise for benefiting from library collaboration to increase positive student learning outcomes?"[21]

One way for library administrators and staff to approach RQs 1 and 2 is to collaborate with outside stakeholders to develop research questions and methods that resonate with the populations these stakeholders represent. Perhaps the most significant benefit of this collaboration is that these stakeholders, particularly teaching faculty and administrative staff, can connect library administrators and staff to *potential* library users normally not included in library studies. Projects investigating RQ3 might begin with a collaborative literature review discussing significant areas of interest to both library and non-library stakeholders and conclude by reporting study results in library and non-library venues.

Priority Area: Match Library Assessment to the Institution's Mission

A final priority area that aligns with the AiA approach is matching libraries' assessments to their institution's mission of promoting "institutionally identified student outcomes."[22] Unlike the other themes, the project team found only provosts to consider mission alignment and strategy a significant theme. The provosts focused on this theme slightly less than communication. The lack of focus on this theme in the other data sources suggests that it represents a gap between how provosts and library administrators and staff envision the library's contribution to student-centered outcomes. Namely, the latter conceive library value by effective collaboration and communication, whereas provosts envision collaboration and communication *in service of* mission alignment and strategy. If library administrators and staff align their spaces, collections, and services with the intuition's mission, they will engage in effective collaboration and communication.

In the literature reviewed, there was a significant difference between the proportion of research and theoretical documents focusing on this theme. Theoretical documents addressed this theme more than research documents, indicating that library administrators and staff say this theme is important, but do not actually study it.[23] Further, the proportion of all literature reviewed examining this theme decreased from 2010 to 2016. A recent study echoed this finding by reporting that most of the 722 library directors surveyed felt less strategically aligned and valued by their supervisors and their administration than those responding in 2013 to the same survey.[24]

One benefit of the AiA approach as related to mission alignment and strategy is that it attracted project teams from diverse institutions. AiA projects had more proportional participation from the four areas of the US and more representation of community colleges and colleges than non-AiA projects. The grant-funded nature of the program may have facilitated the ability of the AiA approach to foster a more diverse set of project teams and may have been of greater benefit to less resourced and smaller institutions, such as community colleges. Since the AiA approach encouraged research on library value across various institutions, findings from AiA projects offer broader approaches for aligning the value of academic libraries with their institutional missions. Future researchers should maintain this diversity of approaches. Not all libraries have the resources to perform wide-scale studies, and for this reason, it is crucial that libraries collaborate intra-institutionally to capture the various contexts in which libraries must demonstrate their value.

While the team-based and collaborative aspects of the AiA approach can take many different forms (e.g., configurations of teams, levels of collaboration), the assessment aspect of the AiA approach must closely attend to the structures of mission strategy and alignment. In an example provided by Provost PP09, if library administrators and staff wish to develop buy-in for an open access policy, they must consider how this policy aligns with their institution's mission. Stakeholders, such as faculty, may not be interested to hear that open access provides a moral good. Instead, what might incentivize them is hearing that posting an early version of their study in the university's repository is likely to get them increased citations, which they need to meet institutional promotion and tenure policies.

Effective practices related to mission alignment and strategy facilitated by the AiA approach are
- "Work with teaching and learning support services and directly with faculty and students to build a culture of assessment using both qualitative and quantitative data for collection, analysis, and reporting."
- "Be open to adopting less traditional roles for services, collections, spaces, and staff to fulfill the strategic mission of the university."
- "Be aware of student and faculty demographics and respond to their needs and characteristics."[25]

Research questions for the mission alignment and strategy priority area that would most benefit from employing the AiA approach are
- RQ1: "In what ways have the support by library administrators and staff of the institution's mission and [specific] goals affected student learning and success outcomes?"
- RQ2: "How do libraries compare to other support units in demonstrating their impact on the institutional mission and goals?"
- RQ3: "How do library administrators and staff support accreditation efforts, and are these efforts recognized by the institution?"[26]

RQ1 directly addresses the need to frame findings using institution-specific goals that affect its mission. RQ2 emphasizes the importance of other contextual layers, such as comparing the impacts of library resources on student-centered outcomes to those of other institutional units. The collaborative assessment aspect of the AiA approach can ensure that the research questions, methodology, and discussion of the study facilitate comparison among these units. For instance, a project that partners libraries with writing centers may collect and analyze the same students' essays to compare the effects of their interventions on grades. RQ3 offers an example of one institutional goal—accreditation. Other student support services, such as information technology, want to demonstrate how their resources support this goal, but the administration and other higher education stakeholders may not view these services as supporting accreditation. The AiA's team-based collaboration aspects can benefit libraries and these other units by identifying assessments that align with institutional priorities in a more comprehensive manner through the consideration of multiple inter- and intra-departmental contexts.

Conclusion

The AiA program contributed a diverse set of library impact studies that inform current and future work. These studies address three themes considered crucial to provosts in articulating library value: communication, collaboration, and institutional mission alignment and strategy. Researchers can harness the advantages of this approach in order to address several priority areas identified in the *Academic Library Impact* report as essential for library administrators and staff to explore. A key way the AiA approach can further research in the communication priority area is by using a wide variety of methods to appeal to different areas and levels of senior leadership. By using a variety of methods, researchers will be able to ensure they can communicate their empirical research in outside venues, such as higher education outlets. Another way that library administrators and staff can incorporate the AiA approach to communication is by establishing partnerships with stakeholders outside the library. Library stakeholders should recruit other stakeholders at a variety of levels and areas, both inter- and intra-institutionally. These partnerships allow library administrators and staff to solicit the input of these stakeholders when developing, executing, and reporting study findings.

Partnering with outside stakeholders also links to the collaboration priority area, illustrating how these areas are interrelated. This area can benefit from an AiA approach by emphasizing inter-institutional collaboration to foster a mutual investment in creating and communicating library value. Intra-institutional collaboration is also important to increase the diversity of perspectives and resources libraries can bring to bear and represents an area for improvement within the AiA approach. Library administrators and staff should collaborate with stakeholders from a variety of institutions to fully capture the various contexts in which libraries must assess and demonstrate their value. Such collaboration also augments the research projects with various disciplinary perspectives.

Finally, the AiA approach can strengthen research and practice in the mission alignment and strategy priority area. By adopting this approach, library administrators and staff can clarify library value and how it contributes to the institution's mission. Such clarification is important since provosts place a high value on this alignment. Further, library administrators and staff should communicate assessment and value in a way that resonates with this mission (e.g., by using terms included in the institution's mission statement and other institutional documentation). A final benefit of an AiA approach is that it engenders inter-institutional comparison of how library resources impact student-centered outcomes to other departmental units. Such comparison also facilitates collaboration, since library staff must work with these units, and communication, in order for libraries to demonstrate mission strategy and alignment in a comprehensive manner that embraces inter- and intra- institutional contexts.

Acknowledgement: The authors would like to thank Erin Hood and Brittany Brannon, both of OCLC, for their help with this chapter.

Biographies

Stephanie Mikitish, PhD, is the user engagement and assessment librarian at the John Cotton Dana Library at Rutgers University–Newark. Her work guides the development and improvement of spaces, services, workflows, and resources that support the instruction and research endeavors of the Rutgers–Newark community. Reach her at mikitish@libraries.rutgers.edu.

Vanessa Kitzie, PhD, is an Assistant Professor at the School of Information and Communications, University of South Carolina. Her research interests center on how to improve information agencies and systems in meeting people's needs, particularly marginalized groups. She is the current Chair of the American Library Association (ALA) Gay, Lesbian, Bisexual, and Transgender Round Table (GLBTRT) Advocacy Committee. Reach her at kitzie@mailbox.sc.edu.

Lynn Silipigni Connaway, PhD, is a Senior Research Scientist and Director of User Research at OCLC Research. She is the Past President of the Association of Information Science & Technology (ASIS&T) and was the Chair of the American Library Association (ALA) Association of College and Research Libraries (ACRL) Value of Academic Libraries Committee. Dr. Connaway is the co-author of the 4th and 5th editions of *Basic Research Methods for Librarians* and of the 6th edition, titled *Research Methods in Library and Information Science*. She has authored numerous other publications and frequently is an international and national speaker on how individuals get their information and engage with technology and the assessment and development of user-centered library services. To find out more about Dr. Connaway, visit http://www.oclc.org/research/people/connaway.html. Reach her at connawal@oclc.org.

Notes

1. Lynn Silipigni Connaway, William Harvey, Vanessa Kitzie, and Stephanie Mikitish, *Action-Oriented Research Agenda on Library Contributions to Student Learning and Success* (Dublin, OH: OCLC Research, January 10, 2017), http://www.oclc.org/content/dam/research/themes/acrl-research-agenda-jan-2017.pdf.
2. Association of College and Research Libraries, *Academic Library Impact: Improving Practice and Essential Areas to Research*, prepared by Lynn Silipigni Connaway, William Harvey, Vanessa Kitzie, and Stephanie Mikitish of OCLC Research (Chicago: Association of College and Research Libraries, 2017).The report is available as a free PDF at http://www.ala.org/acrl/sites/ala.org.acrl/files/content/publications/whitepapers/academiclib.pdf for download, and in print for purchase through the ALA store website.
3. AiA was undertaken by ACRL in partnership with the Association for Institutional Research (AIR) and the Association of Public and Land-grant Universities (APLU). The program, a cornerstone of ACRL's Value of Academic Libraries initiative, was made possible by a three-year National Leadership Demonstration Grant from the Institute of Museum and Library Services.
4. Throughout this chapter, the term *provost* is used as a catch-all to indicate all senior academic officers. See Appendix C of the main report, Association of College and Research Libraries, *Academic Library Impact,* for more details.
5. Association of College and Research Libraries, "Assessment in Action: Academic Libraries and Student Success," accessed January 4, 2017, http://www.ala.org/acrl/AiA.
6. For further instruction about how NVivo can be used for coding of data, see Lynn Silipigni Connaway and Marie L. Radford, *Research Methods in Library and Information Science*, 6th ed. (Santa Barbara, CA: Libraries Unlimited, 2017), 290–96.
7. For more information about the data collection and analysis methods, as well as for the full codebook, see the report Association of College and Research Libraries, *Academic Library Impact.*
8. For additional explication of these areas, as well as exemplary studies and proposed research designs, see the report Association of College and Research Libraries, *Academic Library Impact.*

9.   Statistical significance is defined as *p* < 0.05 for Association of College and Research Libraries, *Academic Library Impact*.

10. McGraw-Hill Education, *The Changing Role of Libraries*, white paper (New York: McGraw-Hill Education, 2016), https://learn.mheducation.com/rs/303-FKF-702/images/Whitepaper_AccessEducation_RoleofLibraries_10-2016_v4%20%283%29.pdf.

11. McGraw-Hill Education, *The Changing Role of Libraries*.

12. Association of College and Research Libraries, "Assessment in Action: Academic Libraries and Student Success."

13. Susan Resneck Pierce, "Producing Academic Leaders," *Inside Higher Ed*, January 26, 2011, https://www.insidehighered.com/advice/2011/01/26/producing-academic-leaders; American Council on Education, "Chief Academic Officer Survey: The CAO Job," infographic, accessed August 3, 2017, http://www.acenet.edu/news-room/Documents/Chief-Academic-Officer-Survey-the-CAO-Job.pdf.

14. Association of College and Research Libraries, *Academic Library Impact*, 46.

15. Association of College and Research Libraries, *Academic Library Impact*, 46.

16. Association of College and Research Libraries, *Academic Library Impact*, 3.

17. Association of College and Research Libraries, *Academic Library Impact*.

18. Association of College and Research Libraries, *Academic Library Impact*.

19. Amanda Nichols Hess, Katie Greer, Shawn V. Lombardo, and Adriene Lim, "Books, Bytes, and Buildings: The Academic Library's Unique Role in Improving Student Success," *Journal of Library Administration* 55, no. 8 (2015): 622–38, https://doi.org/10.1080/01930826.2015.1085241; Kate S. Wolfe, "Emerging Information Literacy and Research-Method Competencies in Urban Community College Psychology Students," *Community College Enterprise* 21, no. 2 (2015): 93–99.

20. Association of College and Research Libraries, *Academic Library Impact*, 8, 63.

21. Association of College and Research Libraries, *Academic Library Impact*, 9.

22. Association of College and Research Libraries, *Academic Library Impact*, 50.

23. Association of College and Research Libraries, *Academic Library Impact*.

24. Christine Wolff-Eisenberg, *US Library Survey 2016* (New York: Ithaka S+R, 2017), http://www.sr.ithaka.org/publications/us-library-survey-2016.

25. Association of College and Research Libraries, *Academic Library Impact*, 51.

26. Association of College and Research Libraries, *Academic Library Impact*, 4.

CHAPTER 18

Conclusion

Reflecting on the Past, Looking to the Future

Lisa Janicke Hinchliffe, University of Illinois

AS THIS BOOK DEMONSTRATES, the impact of the Assessment in Action program has been wide-ranging, from individual growth and development to institutional transformation. Along the way, the Association of College and Research Libraries (ACRL) has fulfilled its strategic goal that academic libraries demonstrate alignment with and impact on institutional outcomes. As ACRL President in 2010–11, I had the honor of leading the board of directors in establishing the Value of Academic Libraries Initiative, developing the Plan for Excellence that provided strategic guidance and budgetary alignment with its priorities, and then chairing the first Value of Academic Libraries Committee. The initiative has been flourishing since its inception, and the IMLS grant-supported Assessment in Action program has been a cornerstone of that success. As AiA enters its next phase of development, ACRL will continue to focus on developing a broad and inclusive community of practice that enables academic and research librarians to develop their skills and abilities to impact student learning and success and transform their institutions.

The Design of Assessment in Action

The Assessment in Action (AiA) program design emerged from the discussions at two national summits that ACRL hosted in 2011, funded by an IMLS Collaborative Planning Grant, in partnership with the Association for Institutional Research, the Association of Public and Land-grant Universities, and the Council of Independent Colleges. The summits were convened in response to the recommendations in *The Value of Academic Libraries: A Comprehensive Research Review and Report*[1] that ACRL create a professional development program to build the profession's capacity to document, demonstrate, and communicate library value in alignment with the mission and goals of their colleges and universities with the goal of determining what such a program should be.

The summits were attended by teams from twenty-two postsecondary institutions, including senior librarians, chief academic administrators, and institutional researchers, for discussions about documenting and communicating library impact. Fifteen representatives from higher education organizations and associations participated in the discussions as well. Details about the summits and the resultant themes and recommendations are in the freely available white paper, appendix B, *Connect, Collaborate, and Communicate: A Report from the Value of Academic Libraries Summits.*[2]

Four themes emerged about the dynamic nature of assessment in higher education from the summits:

- Accountability drives higher education discussions.
- A unified approach to institutional assessment is essential.
- Student learning and success are the primary focus of higher education assessment.
- Academic administrators and accreditors seek evidence-based reports of measurable impact.

223

In addition, summit participants communicated clearly that any program that ACRL developed needed to

- increase librarians' understanding of library value and impact in relation to various dimensions of student learning and success
- articulate and promote the importance of assessment competencies necessary for documenting and communicating library impact on student learning and success
- create professional development opportunities for librarians to learn how to initiate and design assessment that demonstrates the library's contributions to advancing institutional mission and strategic goals
- expand partnerships for assessment activities with higher education constituent groups and related stakeholders
- integrate the use of existing ACRL resources with library value initiatives

This guidance served as the touchpoints for developing the AiA program and the related IMLS National Leadership Demonstration Grant application, undertaken in partnership with the Association for Institutional Research (AIR) and the Association of Public and Land-grant Universities (APLU). The grant supported the design, implementation, and evaluation of AiA in order to strengthen the competencies of librarians in campus leadership and data-informed advocacy, to foster collaborative campus relationships around assessment, and to build an evidence base about the impact of academic libraries on student learning and success as well as to document effective assessment practices and strategies.

Specifically, AiA was designed to serve three broad goals:

- Goal 1: Develop the professional competencies of librarians to document and communicate the value of their academic libraries primarily in relation to their institution's goals for student learning and success.
- Goal 2: Build and strengthen collaborative relationships with higher education stakeholders around the issue of library value.
- Goal 3: Contribute to higher education assessment work by creating approaches, strategies, and practices that document the contribution of academic libraries to the overall goals and missions of their institutions.

The AiA program design pursued these goals through two frameworks that informed the instructional design of the program: community of practice and action research.

AiA facilitators[3] worked with Etienne Wenger-Trayner and Bev Wenger-Trayner in designing the AiA program, drawing on the concept of communities of practice. They define communities of practice as "groups of people who share a concern or a passion for something they do and learn how to do it better as they interact regularly."[4] Unlike other educational models that spotlight an instructor's central role as the "sage on the stage" with primary authority and content expertise, the AiA blended learning model emphasized the facilitative role of instructors (i.e., "guide on the side"). AiA participants worked collaboratively in face-to-face sessions, webcasts, and asynchronous online environments to create, share, and build content and products. This network supported collective learning, shared competence, sustained interaction, and a climate of mutuality and trust. In the process, a strong community of practice developed. The focus on active learning also led to a deeper understanding of what happens when knowledge and skills are applied in practice.

The design of AiA also drew on the concept of action research.[5] Action research is understood as "a participatory, democratic process concerned with developing practical knowing in the pursuit of worthwhile human purposes.... it seeks to bring together action and reflection, theory and practice, in participation with others, in the pursuit of practical solutions to issues of pressing concern to people, and more generally the flourishing of individual persons and their communities."[6] Key concepts in this definition that were emphasized in the curriculum of AiA are participatory, democratic, and practical solutions. AiA aimed to identify important questions about library impact on student learning and success, to design assessments that reveal information about library contributions, and to take action based on what has been discovered. Action research challenged AiA participants to go beyond library use and satisfaction and examine questions of impact and outcomes. It was understood that not all projects would demonstrate that there is in fact a library impact but that developing and implementing a project as part of the AiA program would engender learning, spur action, and build capacity for continued work.

Achievements of Assessment in Action

AiA generated a body of evidence about the academic library impact on student learning and success, collaborative and team-based approaches to assessment, and leadership for campus assessment work.

AiA projects provide compelling evidence that students benefit from library instruction in their initial coursework, library use increases student success, collaborative academic programs and services involving the library enhance student learning, information literacy instruction strengthens general education outcomes, and library research consultation services boost student learning. There is an evidence base developing to demonstrate that student retention improves with library instructional services, library instruction adds value to a student's long-term academic experience, the library promotes academic rapport and student engagement, and use of library space relates positively to student learning and success.

AiA reports also reveal that a team-based approach to assessment leads to meaningful collaboration and problem solving. Each team, consisting of members from different campus departments and units, engaged in important conversations about the attributes of student learning and success. A collaborative approach also builds understanding of the functions and roles of different campus constituents in advancing the institution's academic priorities. In addition, the assessment work tends to promote sustainable organizational change and move beyond a single project because a team-based effort recognizes the multifaceted nature of student learning. Compelling findings about student learning and success emerge that have campus-wide significance.

For librarians leading campus teams, analysis of AiA reports provides insight into emergent leadership practices for collaborative assessment, including the ability to achieve common understanding about definitions and attributes of academic success, produce meaningful measures of student learning, keep collaborative assessment activities aligned with institutional priorities, and create a unified campus message about student learning and success. Many AiA projects modeled these types of collaborative leadership approaches to conducting assessment and used the results to create transformative and sustainable change.

Building on Assessment in Action

As the three-year AiA project came to a close and the IMLS grant concluded, the success of the AiA projects motivated ACRL to identify next steps that would build on the AiA program. In order to continue to align ACRL's efforts with both member needs and higher education at large, AiA project leaders conducted exploratory interviews with the executive directors of twelve higher education and research organizations in fall/winter 2015.[7] In each case, the project leaders shared the findings of the AiA program and then held a semi-structured discussion with the higher education leaders in order to gather input for planning next steps.

Four themes emerged from these conversations regarding key trends in higher education related to the assessment of student learning and students' academic experiences that inform library leadership and engagement with campus constituents:

1. *Astute use of data:* Significant effort within the higher education arena has been focused on collecting, analyzing, and interpreting data, but we now need to know if the yield in student learning improvements is proportional to the effort. Energy is now being directed toward better use of evidence to make improvements rather than conducting new research.

2. *Leadership as advocacy:* It is essential to have leadership using evidence to make improvements at the program director level. Higher education institutions need individuals who know how to identify and use the appropriate data in collaboration with others on campus; think of these leaders as ambassadors and advocates.

3. *Contextual nature of the educational experience:* Emphasis is shifting to how students achieve general learning outcomes related to critical thinking across disciplines and through experiences in and out of the classroom. How do different educational experiences correlate to learning? Many students need a rich array of learning experiences to complete their degrees.

4. *Role of higher education:* New questions are emerging: How does higher education contribute to an individual's lifelong learning for careers and general life satisfaction? What is the role of higher education in our national life? If higher education associations can show the impact of colleges and universities on the education of students broadly, then members of these associations will benefit.

The findings from AiA were well-received by higher education leaders in this context, and ACRL was encouraged to focus its efforts on communicating these findings and supporting librarians in using the findings to advocate for libraries.

As a result of these recommendations, as well as input from the ACRL Board of Directors and the ACRL Value of Academic Libraries Committee, two new programs are being developed on the basis of the AiA design and findings.

The first program supports the need for an ongoing professional development program for libraries to continue to develop their assessment skills and competencies. This daylong workshop, Assessment in Action: Demonstrating and Communicating Library Contributions to Student Learning and Success, was first offered at the ACRL 2017 Conference as a preconference and has since been available for contracted delivery onsite in a region, state, or institution. Focusing on strategic and sustainable assessment, participants in the workshop identify institutional priorities and campus partners, design an assessment project grounded in action research, and prepare a plan for communicating the project results. All attendees in this workshop become members of the ACRL Assessment in Action participants email list (acrl-aia-participants@lists.ala.org), the virtual community of practice that includes librarian team leaders from the original AiA program as well.

The second program is still in development and aimed at supporting librarians in using the findings for evidence-based advocacy for academic libraries. A draft design of such a program was offered at the ACRL 2017 Conference and was open to directors of those libraries that participated in the AiA program. The Value of Academic Libraries Committee is working to design future opportunities based on the assessment of that program.

Conclusion

AiA was a highly successful program that achieved its goals to strengthen the competencies of librarians in campus leadership and data-informed advocacy, to foster collaborative campus relationships around assessment, to build an evidence base about the impact of academic libraries on student learning and success, and to document effective assessment practices and strategies. AiA also demonstrated that meaningful and sustained assessment is best achieved when the academic library takes a collaborative leadership role on campus. From these results, ACRL continues to develop its Value of Academic Libraries Initiative, meeting library needs and responding to the needs of higher education at large.

Biography

Lisa Janicke Hinchliffe is Professor and Coordinator for Information Literacy Services and Instruction in the University Library at the University of Illinois at Urbana-Champaign. She is also an affiliate faculty member in the University's School of Information Sciences. Lisa served as the 2010–2011 President of the Association of College and Research Libraries, which launched the Value of Academic Libraries Initiative during her presidency. Lisa has consulted, presented, and published widely on information literacy, teaching and learning, the value of libraries, library assessment, program evaluation, and organizational innovation. Lisa received her Master of Education in Educational Psychology and Master of Library and Information Science degrees from the University of Illinois at Urbana-Champaign and earned her Bachelor of Arts degree in philosophy from the University of St. Thomas in Minnesota. Reach her at ljanicke@illinois.edu.

Notes

1. Association of College and Research Libraries, *The Value of Academic Libraries: A Comprehensive Review and Report*, prepared by Megan Oakleaf (Chicago: Association of College and Research Libraries, 2010).
2. Association of College and Research Libraries, *Connect, Collaborate, and Communicate: A Report from the Value of Academic Libraries Summits*, prepared by Karen Brown and Kara J. Malenfant (Chicago: Association of College and Research Libraries, 2012). Reprinted as appendix B.
3. AiA design/facilitation team was led by Debra Gilchrist, Vice President for Learning and Student Success, Pierce College, WA; Lisa Janicke Hinchliffe, Coordinator for Information Literacy and Professor, University of Illinois at Urbana-Champaign; and Kara Malenfant, Senior Strategist for Special Initiatives, Association of College and Research Libraries. Additional designers/facilitators participated throughout the length of the project: April Cunningham, Library Instruction Coordinator at Saddleback College in Mission Viejo, CA; Carrie Donovan, Head of Teaching & Learning for the Indiana University Libraries in Bloomington, IN; Eric Resnis, Organizational Effectiveness Specialist in the Libraries at Miami University in Oxford, OH; and John Watts, Undergraduate Learning Librarian at University of Nevada Las Vegas. Libby Miles, Associate Professor of Writing & Rhetoric in the Harrington School of Communication and Media at the University of Rhode Island in Kingston, RI, was part of the facilitation team for the first 18 months of the program. Project analyst Karen Brown, Professor at the Graduate School of Library and Information Science at Dominican University, IL, worked with the team to document replicable action learning projects undertaken by the institutional teams.
4. Etienne Wenger-Trayner and Beverly Wenger-Trayner, "Introduction to Communities of Practice: A Brief Overview of the Concept and Its Uses," Wenger-Trayner website, 2015. http://wenger-trayner.com/introduction-to-communities-of-practice/.

5. Kara J. Malenfant, Lisa Janicke Hinchliffe, and Debra Gilchrist, "Assessment as Action Research: Bridging Academic Scholarship and Everyday Practice," *College and Research Libraries* 77, no. 2(March 2016): 140–43, https://doi.org/10.5860/crl.77.2.140.

6. Peter Reason and Hilary Bradbury, eds., *The SAGE Handbook of Action Research*, 2nd ed. (London: SAGE 2006), 1.

7. The higher education and research organizations are Achieving the Dream, American Association of State Colleges and Universities, Association for Institutional Research, Association of American Colleges and Universities, Association of Public and Land-grant Universities, Center of Inquiry in the Liberal Arts (Wabash College), Community College Research Center (Columbia University), Council of Independent Colleges, National Institute for Learning Outcomes Assessment, National Survey of Student Engagement, Pew Research Center, and Student Affairs Administrators of Higher Education.

APPENDIX A

Program Contributors and Participating Institutions

THE ACRL PROGRAM ASSESSMENT IN ACTION: Academic Libraries and Student Success relied on a large number of dedicated individuals.

The design/facilitation team was led by Debra Gilchrist, Vice President for Learning and Student Success, Pierce College, WA; Lisa Janicke Hinchliffe, Coordinator for Information Literacy and Professor, University of Illinois at Urbana-Champaign; and Kara Malenfant, Senior Strategist for Special Initiatives, Association of College and Research Libraries. Additional designers/facilitators participated during the program and are listed with their titles and institutional affiliation at the time: April Cunningham, Library Instruction Coordinator at Saddleback College in Mission Viejo, CA; Carrie Donovan, Head of Teaching and Learning for the Indiana University Libraries in Bloomington, IN; Eric Resnis, Assessment Coordinator in the Center for Teaching, Learning, and University Assessment and Organizational Effectiveness Specialist in the Libraries at Miami University in Oxford, OH; and John Watts, Undergraduate Learning Librarian at University of Nevada, Las Vegas.

Community of practice experts Etienne and Beverley Wenger-Trayner advised the team during the early design process. Libby Miles, Associate Professor of Writing and Rhetoric in the Harrington School of Communication and Media at the University of Rhode Island in Kingston, RI, was part of the facilitation team for the first eighteen months of the program. Project analyst Karen Brown, Professor at the School of Information Studies at Dominican University, IL, worked with the team to prepare an analysis and synthesis of the program results each year.

The AiA grant advisory team included ACRL member leaders Steven Bell, President of ACRL 2012–13 and then Associate University Librarian for Research and Instructional Services, Temple University; Megan Oakleaf, then Assistant Professor, School of Information Studies, Syracuse University; and Joyce Ogburn, President of ACRL 2011–12 and then Dean, J. Willard Marriott Library and University Librarian, University of Utah.

AiA was made possible by a grant from the Institute of Museum and Library Services (IMLS). Our grant partners were helpful at key junctures, in particular at Association of Public and Land-grant Universities, Christine Keller, then Vice President of Research and Policy Analysis and Executive Director of the Voluntary System of Accountability and Student Achievement Measure; and at the Association for Institutional Research, Randy Swing, then Executive Director.

ACRL members who chaired the Value of Academic Libraries Committee during the years of the AiA program were Teresa Fishel, Library Director, Macalaster College; Lynn Silipigni Connaway, Senior Research Scientist and Director of User Research, OCLC Research; Melissa Bowles-Terry, Head of Educational Initiatives, University of Nevada, Las Vegas; Debbie Malone, Library Director, DeSales University; and Jaime Corris Hammond, Director of Library Services, Naugatuck Valley Community College.

Participating Institutions

In each year of the AiA program, institutions applied to participate. An institutional team was required to have a librarian team leader as well as faculty and assessment campus representatives. Additional team members were at the institution's discretion.

First-Year Teams: In April 2013, ACRL selected seventy-five institutional teams to participate in the first year of the AiA program. The selected teams, representing all types of institutions from twenty-nine states and three Canadian provinces, were

- Alverno College (Milwaukee, WI)
- Anne Arundel Community College (Arnold, MD)
- Appalachian State University (Boone, NC)
- Arizona State University (Tempe, AZ)
- Augustana College (Rock Island, IL)
- Brown University (Providence, RI)
- Bucks County Community College (Newtown, PA)
- California Lutheran University (Thousand Oaks, CA)
- Central Washington University (Ellensburg, WA)
- The Citadel (Charleston, SC)
- Claremont Colleges (Claremont, CA)
- The College at Brockport, State University of New York (Brockport, NY)
- Dakota State University (Madison, SD)
- Dalhousie University (Halifax, NS)
- DePaul University (Chicago, IL)
- Elizabethtown College (Elizabethtown, PA)
- Fairfield University (Fairfield, CT)
- George Mason University (Fairfax, VA)
- Grand Valley State University (Allendale, MI)
- Greenfield Community College (Greenfield, MA)
- Grinnell College (Grinnell, IA)
- Hofstra University (Hempstead, NY)
- Howard University (Washington, DC)
- Illinois Central College (East Peoria, IL)
- Indiana University of Pennsylvania (Indiana, PA)
- Institute of American Indian Arts (Santa Fe, NM)
- Kapiolani Community College (Honolulu, HI)
- Lakeland Community College (Kirtland, OH)
- Lasell College (Newton, MA)
- Le Moyne College (Syracuse, NY)
- Los Angeles Trade Technical College (Los Angeles, CA)
- Medaille College (Buffalo, NY)
- Mercy College (Dobbs Ferry, NY)
- Miami University (Oxford, OH)
- Michigan Technological University (Houghton, MI)
- Middlesex Community College (Bedford, MA)
- Montana State University (Bozeman, MT)
- Muhlenberg College (Allentown, PA)
- Murray State University (Murray, KY)

- North Carolina Central University (Durham, NC)
- Northeastern Illinois University (Chicago, IL)
- The Ohio State University (Columbus, OH)
- Pacific Lutheran University (Tacoma, WA)
- Radford University (Radford, VA)
- Rockhurst University (Kansas City, MO)
- Rollins College (Winter Park, FL)
- Saint Mary's College of California (Moraga, CA)
- Salem State University (Salem, MA)
- Santa Barbara City College (Santa Barbara, CA)
- South Texas College (McAllen, TX)
- Southern Connecticut State University (New Haven, CT)
- St. Mary's College of Maryland (St. Mary's City, MD)
- Stonehill College (Easton, MA)
- Towson University (Towson, MD)
- UNC Charlotte (Charlotte, NC)
- University of Baltimore (Baltimore, MD)
- University of Connecticut Health Center (Farmington, CT)
- University of Guelph (Guelph, ON)
- University of Idaho (Moscow, ID)
- University of Manitoba (Winnipeg, MB)
- University of Maryland University College (Adelphi, MD)
- University of Massachusetts Dartmouth (North Dartmouth, MA)
- University of Michigan (Ann Arbor, MI)
- University of Nebraska Kearney (Kearney, NE)
- University of Northern Colorado (Greeley, CO)
- University of Redlands (Redlands, CA)
- University of South Florida (Tampa, FL)
- University of Texas at El Paso (El Paso, TX)
- University of Wisconsin-Eau Claire (Eau Claire, WI)
- University of Wisconsin-Green Bay (Green Bay, WI)
- University of Wisconsin-Milwaukee (Milwaukee, WI)
- Virginia Tech (Blacksburg, VA)
- Webster University (St. Louis, MO)
- Western University of Health Sciences (Pomona, CA)
- York University (Toronto, ON)

Second-Year Teams: In April 2014, ACRL selected seventy-three additional institutional teams to participate in the second year of the program. The selected teams, representing all types of institutions from thirty-four states and one Canadian province, were:

- A. T. Still University (Mesa, AZ)
- Arkansas Tech University (Russellville, AR)
- Becker College (Worcester, MA)
- Benedictine College (Atchison, KS)
- Champlain College (Burlington, VT)
- City University of Seattle (Seattle, WA)
- The College of Saint Scholastica (Duluth, MN)

- College of Southern Nevada (Las Vegas, NV)
- Colorado Mesa University (Grand Junction, CO)
- Culinary Institute of America (Hyde Park, NY)
- CUNY Borough of Manhattan Community College (New York, NY)
- Defiance College (Defiance, OH)
- Des Moines Area Community College (Des Moines, IA)
- Eastern Kentucky University (Richmond, KY)
- Eastern Mennonite University (Harrisonburg, VA)
- Florida International University (Miami, FL)
- Fulton-Montgomery Community College (Johnstown, NY)
- Georgia College and State University (Milledgeville, GA)
- Georgia Institute of Technology-Main Campus (Atlanta, GA)
- Georgia Southern University (Statesboro, GA)
- Illinois of Institute of Technology (Chicago, IL)
- Joliet Junior College (Joliet, IL)
- Kalamazoo College (Kalamazoo, MI)
- Knox College (Galesburg, IL)
- Kutztown University of Pennsylvania (Kutztown, PA)
- Lone Star College System (Houston, TX)
- Luther Seminary (St. Paul, MN)
- Macalester College (St. Paul, MN)
- Marquette University (Milwaukee, WI)
- Massachusetts College of Liberal Arts (North Adams, MA)
- McDaniel College (Westminster, MD)
- Michigan State University (East Lansing, MI)
- Montclair State University (Montclair, NJ)
- Naugatuck Valley Community College (Waterbury, CT)
- Northwest Arkansas Community College (Bentonville, AR)
- Northwest Vista College (San Antonio, TX)
- Nova Southeastern University (Fort Lauderdale, FL)
- Otero Junior College (La Junta, CO)
- Our Lady of the Lake University (San Antonio, TX)
- Peninsula College (Port Angeles, WA)
- Pierce College at Fort Steilacoom (Lakewood, WA)
- Point Park University (Pittsburgh, PA)
- Purdue University (West Lafayette, IN)
- Rutgers, The State University of New Jersey (Piscataway, NJ)
- Samuel Merritt University (Oakland, CA)
- South Dakota State University (Brookings, SD)
- Southern Methodist University (Dallas, TX)
- Southwestern Indian Polytechnic Institute (Albuquerque, NM)
- Temple University (Philadelphia, PA)
- The University of Akron-Main Campus (Akron, OH)
- University of Alberta (Edmonton and Camrose, AB)
- University of California, Merced (Merced, CA)
- University of California-San Francisco (San Francisco, CA)

- University of Iowa (Iowa City, IA)
- University of Minnesota-Morris (Morris, MN)
- University of Mississippi (University, MS)
- University of Mississippi Medical Center (Jackson, MS)
- University of Nebraska Omaha (Omaha, NE)
- University of North Carolina Wilmington (Wilmington, NC)
- University of Pittsburgh-Pittsburgh Campus (Pittsburgh, PA)
- University of South Dakota (Vermillion, SD)
- University of West Georgia (Carrollton, GA)
- University of Wisconsin-Stevens Point (Stevens Point, WI)
- Utah State University (Logan, UT)
- Utah Valley University (Orem, UT)
- Virginia Wesleyan College (Norfolk, VA)
- Wake Forest University (Winston-Salem, NC)
- Wake Technical Community College (Raleigh, NC)
- Washington University in St. Louis (St. Louis, MO)
- Wayne State University (Detroit, MI)
- West Virginia State University (Institute, WV)
- Western Michigan University (Kalamazoo, MI)
- Yeshiva University (New York, NY)

Third-Year Teams: In April 2015, ACRL selected fifty-five additional institutional teams to participate in the third year of the program. The selected teams, representing all types of institutions from twenty-four states, the District of Columbia, and Australia, were:

- Arcadia University (Glenside, PA)
- Bentley University (Waltham, MA)
- Blue Mountain Community College (Pendleton, OR)
- Boston University (Boston, MA)
- Brandeis University (Waltham, MA)
- Brigham Young University-Provo (Provo, UT)
- California State University-East Bay (Hayward, CA)
- California State University-Fullerton (Fullerton, CA)
- California State University-San Marcos (San Marcos, CA)
- Catawba College (Salisbury, NC)
- College of DuPage (Glen Ellyn, IL)
- College of the Holy Cross (Worcester, MA)
- CUNY Hunter College (New York, NY)
- Davidson College (Davidson, NC)
- DeSales University (Center Valley, PA)
- Drexel University (Philadelphia, PA)
- Edward Via College of Osteopathic Medicine (Blacksburg, VA)
- Elmhurst College (Elmhurst, IL)
- Emerson College (Boston, MA)
- Franklin University (Columbus, OH)
- Georgetown University (Washington, DC)
- Georgia Regents University (Augusta, GA)
- Gettysburg College (Gettysburg, PA)

- Guilford College (Greensboro, NC)
- Hawaii Pacific University (Honolulu, HI)
- John Carroll University (Cleveland, OH)
- Lincoln University (Jefferson City, MO)
- Midwestern State University (Wichita Falls, TX)
- Nevada State College (Henderson, NV)
- Northeastern State University (Tahlequah, OK)
- Northern Michigan University (Marquette, MI)
- Queensland University of Technology (Brisbane, Queensland)
- Seattle University (Seattle, WA)
- Southern Illinois University-Carbondale (Carbondale, IL)
- St. Catherine University (St. Paul, MN)
- SUNY at Fredonia (Fredonia, NY)
- Swarthmore College (Swarthmore, PA)
- Tulsa Community College (Tulsa, OK)
- University of California-Santa Cruz (Santa Cruz, CA)
- University of Illinois at Urbana-Champaign (Urbana, IL)
- University of Iowa (Iowa City, IA)
- University of Kansas (Lawrence, KS)
- University of Massachusetts-Boston (Boston, MA)
- University of Miami (Coral Gables, FL)
- University of Minnesota-Duluth (Duluth, MN)
- University of Nevada-Las Vegas (Las Vegas, NV)
- University of New Mexico (Albuquerque, NM)
- University of New Mexico-Main Campus (Albuquerque, NM)
- University of North Carolina at Greensboro (Greensboro, NC)
- University of Pittsburgh-Greensburg (Greensburg, PA)
- University of Southern California (Los Angeles, CA)
- University of St. Thomas (St. Paul, MN)
- The University of Texas at San Antonio (San Antonio, TX)
- University of Wyoming (Laramie, WY)
- Virginia Polytechnic Institute and State University (Blacksburg, VA)

Connect, Collaborate, and Communicate:

A Report from the Value of Academic Libraries Summits*

---

* Reprinted with permission from Association of College and Research Libraries, *Connect, Collaborate, and Communicate: A Report from the Value of Academic Libraries Summit*, prepared by Karen Brown and Kara J. Malenfant (Chicago: Association of College and Research Libraries, 2012).

Citation:
Association of College and Research Libraries. *Connect, Collaborate, and Communicate: A Report from the Value of Academic Libraries Summits*. Prepared by Karen Brown and Kara J. Malenfant. Chicago: Association of College and Research Libraries, 2012.

Published online at www.acrl.ala.org/value

About the Authors

Karen Brown is an associate professor at Dominican University (River Forest, IL) in the Graduate School of Library and Information Science and teaches in the areas of collection management, foundations of the profession, and literacy and learning. Prior to joining Dominican University's faculty in 2000, she developed and coordinated continuing education programs for the Chicago Library System, one of Illinois's former regional library systems. She has also held positions focusing on collection development, reference, and instruction at the University of Wisconsin, University of Maryland, Columbia University, and Bard College. She holds a PhD in media studies from New York University and master's degrees in library science and adult education from the University of Wisconsin.

Kara J. Malenfant is a senior staff member at ACRL, where she coordinates government relations advocacy and scholarly communication activities and is the lead staff member on the Value of Academic Libraries initiative. She provides consulting services on organizational development and use of ACRL's standards for libraries in higher education. Kara began her position at ACRL in fall of 2005, after working for six years at DePaul University Libraries in Chicago. She holds a PhD in leadership and change from Antioch University and an MS in library science from the University of Illinois at Urbana-Champaign.

Table of Contents

Executive Summary

As part of ACRL's Value of Academic Libraries Initiative, a multiyear project designed to assist academic librarians in demonstrating library value, ACRL joined with three partners—the Association for Institutional Research, the Association of Public and Land-grant Universities, and the Council of Independent Colleges—to sponsor two national summits held November 29–December 1, 2011, in Chicago. The summits convened representatives from twenty-two postsecondary institutions, including senior librarians, chief academic administrators, and institutional researchers, for discussions about library impact. Fifteen representatives from higher education organizations and associations also participated in the summits.

The summits were initiated in response to the 2010 ACRL publication *The Value of Academic Libraries: A Comprehensive Research Review and Report*. As one of its recommendations, the report called on the association to create a professional development program to build librarians' capacity to document, demonstrate, and communicate library value in advancing the mission and goals of their colleges and universities. The two summits formed the basis of "Building Capacity for Demonstrating the Value of Academic Libraries," a project made possible by a National Leadership Collaborative Planning Grant from the Institute of Museum and Library Services.

Five overarching recommendations for the library profession emerged from the discussions, presentations, and facilitated small group work at the summits:

1. *Increase librarians' understanding of library value and impact in relation to various dimensions of student learning and success.*
   Summit participants noted the complexity of determining the library's impact on student learning and success in relation to multiple variables and data sources. They emphasized a need to define standards for evidence and approaches for data collection, analysis, and interpretation.

2. *Articulate and promote the importance of assessment competencies necessary for documenting and communicating library impact on student learning and success.*
   Even though library assessment activities should be tailored to the unique context of an academic institution, there is a set of core competencies essential to designing and implementing effective assessment practices (e.g., outcomes-based evaluation, data analysis and interpretation). At the summits, the participants stressed the importance of librarians recognizing and acquiring these competencies.

3. *Create professional development opportunities for librarians to learn how to initiate and design assessment that demonstrates the library's contributions to advancing institutional mission and strategic goals.*
   Participants encouraged the creation of professional development activities that bring librarians together to learn about and share assessment practices, strategies, and resources. While identifying a single generic assessment approach that can be used by all academic libraries is not realistic and multiple approaches are needed, librarians (and their campus constituents) recognized the need for a community of practice to share best practices and develop standardized measures and metrics as appropriate to advance library value in higher education contexts.

4. *Expand partnerships for assessment activities with higher education constituent groups and related stakeholders.*
   Participants emphasized the value of bringing together individuals with different roles in the assessment process for discussion. Participants additionally stressed the need to sustain these kinds of discussions and promote partnerships between librarians and constituent groups on their campuses and within the broader higher education community.

5. *Integrate the use of existing ACRL resources with library value initiatives.*
   ACRL has developed several resources for advancing assessment practices in libraries. Librarians at the summits frequently mentioned three resources in particular: *Standards for Libraries in Higher Education, Information Literacy Competency Standards for Higher Education*, and ACRL Metrics. Although these three resources provide rich information and data, discussions revealed that many librarians do not always know how best to use them.

This report discusses these recommendations and articulates a framework for future action. It serves as a resource for academic librarians along with library and higher education groups involved with helping institutions to assess and advance their missions. In preparing this report, all participants—planning partners, speakers, and invited participants from the twenty-two colleges and universities—were provided with the opportunity to react and comment on drafts to ensure that the findings are accurate and complete.

Introduction

Academic librarians recognize the need to be part of the larger national dialogue about higher education effectiveness and quality. In ACRL's 2012 membership survey, demonstrating library relevance within this context was listed as the top issue of concern, and it has become one of the association's strategic priorities. [1]

Recent articles in the *Chronicle of Higher Education* and *Inside Higher Ed*, as well as Congressional hearings and initiatives like the Voluntary System of Accountability, highlight the increased attention to issues of accountability. [2] Leading higher education organizations are responding in various ways to the growing pressure to document the quality and value of colleges and universities, particularly in relation to student learning, achievement, and success. The six higher education accreditation commissions are changing the language of their accreditation standards to encompass a more holistic approach for assessing student learning outcomes, a paradigm shift from the largely prescriptive guidelines used in the past. In its 2012

---

[1] ACRL, *ACRL Plan for Excellence* (Chicago: ACRL: 2011), www.ala.org/acrl/aboutacrl/strategicplan/stratplan.

[2] Paul Basken, "Quest for Campus Accountability Produces Demand for Yet More Student Data," *Chronicle of Higher Education*, May 17, 2012, corrected May 25, 2012, chronicle.com/article/Quest-for-College/131910; Doug Lederman, "Raising the Bar on Quality Assurance," *Inside Higher Ed*, November 18, 2011, www.insidehighered.com/news/2011/11/18/western-accreditor-pushes-boundaries-quality-assurance; "Governors Say It Again: Higher Ed Needs Accountability," *The Ticker* (blog), *Chronicle of Higher Education*, July 15, 2011, chronicle.com/blogs/ticker/governors-say-it-again-higher-ed-needs-accountability/34644; *Keeping College within Reach: Discussing Ways Institutions Can Streamline Costs and Reduce Tuition, Before the Subcommittee on Higher Education and Workforce Training,* 112th Cong. (November 30, 2011); L. Johnson, S. Adams, and M. Cummins, *NMC Horizon Report: 2012 Higher Education Edition* (Austin, TX: New Media Consortium, 2012), net.educause.edu/ir/library/pdf/HR2012.pdf.

Horizon Report, EDUCAUSE notes the increased focus on individual students through use of learning analytics, which are early intervention systems that gather a wide range of data produced by students to assess academic progress. As the report notes, "Learning analytics responds to calls for accountability on campuses and aims to leverage the vast amount of data produced by students in academic activities."[3] Moreover, the Gates Foundation is currently funding a broad-based data mining research initiative focused on increasing higher education's understanding of factors leading to student success.[4]

ACRL has long been concerned with accountability, assessment, and student learning. In the early 1980s, ACRL led the way with a publication on assessment to "stimulate librarians' interest in performance measures and to provide practical assistance."[5] The association is the national authority for developing standards and guidelines to enhance library effectiveness and is the authority to which the higher education community looks for standards and guidelines on all aspects of academic libraries. The summits provided an opportunity to stimulate innovative and strategic thinking within the library profession and among higher education constituent groups about the ways academic libraries contribute to institutional mission.

Overview of Summits

Building on the association's work on assessment issues and student learning, ACRL's Value of Academic Libraries Initiative is a multiyear initiative designed to provide academic librarians with competencies and methods for demonstrating library impact relative to the mission and goals of postsecondary institutions. As part of the effort, ACRL commissioned a report on existing research and literature on assessing and documenting library value: *The Value of Academic Libraries: A Comprehensive Research Review and Report.*[6] As one of its recommendations, the report suggests that ACRL create a professional development program to build the profession's capacity to document, demonstrate, and communicate library value in alignment with institutional goals, and the content of the report served as a framework for much of the discussion that occurred during the summits.

ACRL's 2011 IMLS National Leadership Collaborative Planning Grant provided funding to partner with three influential higher education groups experienced with education assessment and institutional effectiveness—the Association for Institutional Research, the Association of Public and Land-Grant Universities, and the Council of Independent Colleges—to plan and carry out two national summits, "Demonstrating Library Value: A National Conversation." The summits, held November 29–December 1, 2011, in Chicago, brought together representatives from a broad spectrum of twenty-two postsecondary institutions, including senior librarians, chief academic administrators, and institutional researchers, for discussions about library impact. Fifteen representatives from higher education organizations and associations also participated in the summits. Megan Oakleaf, assistant professor at Syracuse University and author of ACRL's

---

[3] Johnson, Adams, and Cummins, *NMC Horizon Report,* 22.

[4] Paul Fain, "Big Data's Arrival," *Inside Higher Ed*, February 1, 2012, www.insidehighered.com/news/2012/02/01/using-big-data-predict-online-student-success.

[5] Nancy A. Van House, Beth Weil, and Charles R. McClure, *Measuring Academic Library Performance: A Practical Approach* (Chicago: ALA, 1990.

[6] ACRL, *The Value of Academic Libraries: A Comprehensive Research Review and Report, prepared by Megan Oakleaf* (Chicago: ACRL, 2010), www.ala.org/acrl/sites/ala.org.acrl/files/content/issues/value/val_report.pdf.

Value of Academic Libraries report, facilitated the summit activities (for roster of participants, see Appendix A).

The combination of provocative speakers, panel presentations, and facilitated small group sessions at the summits stimulated participants' thinking, generated lively discussions, and resulted in recommendations on leveraging collaborative efforts with campus stakeholders, investigating and articulating various dimensions of library impact, and building the profession's capacity to demonstrate and communicate library value. Even though faculty productivity and research are integral to discussions of library value, the primary focus of these summits was on student learning and success, an issue facing increasing public scrutiny. The accreditation agency representatives at Summit One affirmed the importance of addressing the issue of student learning and success as a growing concern.

Several broad questions framed the conversations throughout the summits:
- *Library value*: What is library value? How should academic libraries position themselves in relation to issues of library value?

- *Stakeholders*: Given the variety of stakeholders, how should academic librarians leverage their efforts? What do our stakeholders know about library impact, and what do they expect of us?

- *Student learning and success*: How are student learning and success defined in different higher education settings and contexts? What is the library's impact on student learning and success? How should we frame discussions about the library's impact on student learning and success?

- *Data*: What existing sources of evidence and data could document library impact? What data are missing? How should the data be analyzed and interpreted? What data elements could best be integrated to tell the story of the library's contribution to institutional mission?

- *Library value competencies*: What competencies and skill sets are needed to demonstrate library value? How might librarians develop these competencies?

Summit One
The full body of participants gathered for the first summit to discuss the increased attention of accrediting bodies on documenting student learning and success and to identify the data needed by campus administrators from librarians in order to further institutional goals (for Summit One agenda, see Appendix B).

Two opening presentations set the stage for the facilitated discussions and panel sessions that unfolded during the summits. Megan Oakleaf highlighted the findings covered in ACRL's *Value of Academic Libraries: A Comprehensive Research Review and Report*. A central goal of the report was to review the literature to determine what we already know about library value (in all types of libraries) and to look at higher education in terms of value. Oakleaf noted that libraries are often viewed as the heart of the institution, but attention is typically directed toward library spaces and collections. She encouraged the attendees to consider the library in relation to their institution's most pressing needs or areas of greatest strengths and referenced Sarah Pritchard, the current Dean of Libraries at Northwestern University, who noted that, "Few libraries exist in a vacuum, accountable only to themselves. There is always a larger context for assessing library quality, that is, what and how well does the library contribute to achieving the overall goals of the parent constituencies?"[7]

Charles Blaich, Director of the Center of Inquiry at Wabash College and the Higher Education Data Sharing Consortium, responded to Oakleaf's presentation, discussing his experience with a national study of the net effects of liberal arts colleges on nineteen measures of quality teaching and learning practices. The first lesson learned from the study was that no singular effect could be identified. The study highlighted the importance of positioning assessment within the context of an institution's mission and campus culture and the importance of broad campus conversations around assessment issues. At liberal arts colleges, it was important for traditional-age students to develop relationships with caring adults—whether faculty or otherwise—and to develop "academic intimacy."

> Reports of assessment efforts are often a stumbling block. It usually works better to get people together in conversation with basic data (not a report). It's the process of reflecting on the data that's important. – Charles Blaich, Director, Center of Inquiry at Wabash College and the Higher Education Data Sharing Consortium

Blaich emphasized that good teaching and learning practices are essentially about relationships, not data. In other words, data do not force change and reports do not force action. He urged participants to create communities of action and break down silos across departments and disciplines.

He also noted the dual challenge of customizing assessment to align with an institution's unique campus environment and identifying common assessment practices that promote sharing among institutions. Blaich acknowledged the enormous pressure, both external and internal, at higher education institutions to provide evidence about how they meet their missions in respect to student learning and success. Collecting data and reporting for national policy and external accountability, however, are very different from collecting, analyzing, and interpreting data for local campus improvement.

The following day, as Summit One continued, participants engaged in small and large group sessions which yielded rich discussions of their views on the most pressing needs of higher education institutions. These discussions were interspersed with panel presentations by chief academic officers and representatives of accreditation agencies. It quickly became clear that continuing the dialogue among librarians, the staff of regional and disciplinary accrediting bodies, and campus administrators about the evolving perspectives on the value of libraries and its attendant criteria is essential. The mix of perspectives stimulated productive conversations about the kinds of data and collaborative assessment efforts that might address these needs.

Summit Two

The librarian participants continued the discussion in Summit Two by examining the needs identified in Summit One and recommending strategic approaches that leverage the library's

---

[7] ACRL, *Value of Academic Libraries,* 11.

contributions to addressing these needs (for Summit Two agenda, see Appendix C). The work was carried out largely in guided small group deliberations, followed by full group reactions. These deliberations were stimulated and informed by the experiences of a panel of librarians who have implemented different approaches for demonstrating library value on their campuses. Participants considered various dimensions of student learning and success in relation to sources and types of data that have the potential to demonstrate library impact. In addition, the librarians generated ideas and suggestions for professional development opportunities that will advance librarians' competencies to implement and promote library value initiatives on their campuses.

Mapping the Territory

Broad themes about the dynamic nature of higher education assessment emerged from the discussions and collaborative work at each summit. To capture these themes, summit organizers relied on detailed field notes, flip charts created during the event, recorded interviews during the summits, written participant comments gathered from a recording tool used by librarians and facilitators (see Appendix D), a summit reflection form completed by academic administrators and institutional researchers (see Appendix E), and an online survey administered after the summit, asking participants to evaluate their experience (see report in Appendix F). These themes, discussed below, provide the context for the recommendations and action steps outlined in this report.

Accountability drives higher education discussions.

Issues of accountability are in the spotlight for postsecondary institutions, particularly in relation to concerns about the quality of higher education, its affordability, career preparedness, the value of a college degree, and higher education's contribution to workforce development. There is increased pressure to open up the accrediting process to public scrutiny, and these pressures bring into question core higher education notions of self-regulation, institutional autonomy, and peer review. Questions about accountability come from numerous stakeholders:

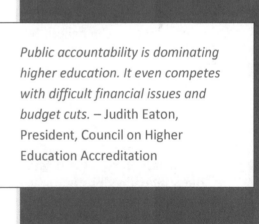

Public accountability is dominating higher education. It even competes with difficult financial issues and budget cuts. – Judith Eaton, President, Council on Higher Education Accreditation

- *Government*: National, state, and regional agencies often require reporting, and individual legislators focus attention on higher education accountability through conversations with constituents, the media, and legislative action.
- *Accrediting agencies*: There are eighty recognized accrediting agencies, and most postsecondary education institutions have multiple accreditations as part of their academic and administrative oversight.
- *Trustees and boards*: Whether appointed or elected, higher education trustees and board members see themselves as the liaison between institutions and the communities they serve and may raise accountability questions in response to the concerns of the stakeholders they represent.
- *Employers*: Employers of graduates are demanding improved levels and quality of career preparedness.

- *Students*: Although students have always been part of the conversation about the value of a higher education degree, the difficult economic situation has raised the volume of this discussion as tuition increases and the job market becomes tighter.
- *Parents*: Parents seek assurances that the funds they and their children expend for tuition (or encumber through loans) will be well spent.
- *The public*: As taxpayers, the public wants to know about the use and impact of public funds to support educational institutions and agencies.

A unified approach to institutional assessment is essential.

To address growing public scrutiny of higher education, colleges and universities find that institutional assessment is most effective when the efforts of various campus units are aligned toward common goals and communicate a unified message. Collaborative discussions with administrators, academic staff, and faculty from across the institution generate a cohesive, shared approach to documenting student learning and institutional effectiveness. Creating a unified approach, however, does not come without its challenges. The summits' participants raised significant issues related to these challenges:

> *Partner, partner, partner; be visible and demonstrate value of libraries as campus partners in the student and faculty learning process.* – Academic administrator at summit

- *Multiple campus constituents*: At universities and colleges across the country, individual campus units find that they are wrestling with how best to demonstrate their value. The library should recognize that it is but one constituent group among many and must articulate its unique contribution to the institution's goals in a compelling way. Libraries can benefit by partnering with other campus units and developing assessment activities in tandem with existing campus systems and data centers.
- *Competing priorities*: Academic administrators face competing priorities in relation to the pressing needs of their institution, a situation further exacerbated by current economic constraints. As a result, library goals should clearly and visibly align with the institution's goals and priorities.
- *Different stakeholders, different perspectives*: Perspectives on the library vary depending on the stakeholder, both across a campus and in the public arena. Some disciplines value the print collections in libraries, whereas others may rely more heavily on the electronic resources. Likewise, graduate students tend to want a quiet place to study, while other students seek a collaborative working environment. Campus administrators, on the other hand, often focus on return on investment and budget issues when considering the library's contributions to the institution. Librarians need to be active participants in campus conversations to increase awareness and a shared understanding about the diverse and multiple ways that the library contributes to the institution's mission.
- *Isolated pockets of institutional data*: As more departments and divisions on a campus participate in assessment activities, data often reside in different locations and on separate servers. Library data are enriched and strengthened when combined with other academic and student service data sources to document and demonstrate student learning and success.

Student learning and success are the primary focus of higher education assessment.

Throughout the summits, speakers and participants emphasized the importance of documenting student learning and success at all types of postsecondary institutions. In fact, a central question permeated many of the discussions: What constitutes student learning and success, and how should it be defined? The definition and parameters that guide an institution's assessment activities often differ at community colleges, four-year colleges, and research universities. In addition, several issues come into play when looking at factors that contribute to student learning and success. Numerous indicators, for example, need to be considered, and assessment should account for different levels and types of student progress and achievement. Rather than analyzing individual elements, skills, or competencies, it is more advantageous to see student learning outcomes as an ecosystem and the library's impact as likely multifaceted. Different areas of library impact were noted at the summits, as follows:

The focus has shifted more to outcomes and away from library as a place. You need to see your role as key players in this outcomes process. – Ralph Wolff, President and Executive Director, Western Association of Schools and Colleges

Although I think we all know that faculty members, largely, should control the curriculum and content of what goes on in their courses, I think it's absolutely vital to think of librarians as partners in that learning process. – Andrew Lootens-White, Vice President for Accreditation Relations, Higher Learning Commission

- *Impact of information literacy*: The value of information literacy to student learning and success continues to gain recognition in higher education and accreditation communities. During the summit, chief academic officers, institutional researchers, and accrediting agency representatives affirmed that information literacy competencies are integral, and increasingly essential, to student achievement and success. What librarians are doing matters and should be infused even more extensively into academic activities across the campus.
- *Core proficiencies*: Throughout the higher education community, there is a growing movement to establish core student proficiencies for workforce readiness. Information literacy and fluency is one of the five proficiency areas most often noted.
- *Beyond borders*: Learning is becoming more multidisciplinary, extending beyond the borders of any one discipline. Information literacy competencies, which span the disciplines, increasingly become a means for students and faculty to enhance and integrate content.
- *Student/faculty interactions*: Student/faculty interactions are important on many levels. For example, members of the campus community often provide meaningful academic connections for students. The library is one of the places on campus where students have

opportunities for quality interactions through such activities as reference exchanges, instructional sessions, and student employment.

- *Learning outside the classroom*: Growing recognition of the multiple factors that contribute to student learning and success has placed more attention on situations and settings outside the classroom that foster learning. Academic administrators noted that they are in a position to reframe perspectives on the library as both a physical and virtual learning space—not merely a warehouse, as it was often viewed in the past.
- *New programs*: When new academic programs are developed, administrators seek broad input from across the campus to ensure a cohesive and comprehensive planning approach. Library involvement and support are central to this process.
- *Curriculum design*: While the faculty of a discipline typically oversees curriculum content, there is growing support for stronger integration of information literacy in curriculum design and course development.

Academic administrators and accreditors seek evidence-based reports of measureable impact.

As issues of accountability move to the forefront, colleges and universities look to means of assessment that document student learning and success in ways that are clear, specific, and based on multiple data points. Such efforts call for the strategic collection, analysis, and interpretation of data. Numerous sources of data from across the campus must be identified and marshaled to align with, and contribute to, the institution's assessment activities. A data-informed approach to assessment requires attention to the following issues:

- *Outcomes*: Assessment efforts at colleges and universities are now shaped largely in terms of the impact of the institution's programs on constituent groups. Rather than focus on outputs (e.g., number of students in a degree program, number of courses offered, etc.), postsecondary institutions are interested in documenting what students have learned. In a similar manner, assessment of library programs, services, and collections should document and demonstrate impact on student learning and success.

> *Being able to use the data that we already have, the rich resources that we're already surrounded with, to more robustly connect the individual student experience in the library to some of our existing database of information about student learning, would be very, very valuable to us and something I'm sure we'll be looking at doing.* – Richard Ray, Provost, Hope College [◄ ►] PLAY

- *External versus internal assessment*: Postsecondary institutions conduct assessment for external and internal purposes. National and state educational reporting and accreditation reviews focus on external assessment activities, while assessment data that inform budget allocations and campus improvement address internal needs. Library assessment efforts also require data for both external and internal reporting purposes, and there are differences in collecting and using data for these two purposes.
- *Accreditation standards*: National, regional, and academic program accreditation standards drive much of the assessment conducted by higher education institutions.

Academic librarians need to be cognizant of these multiple standards in relation to potential areas for contributing library data and impact statements.

- *Existing data, new data*: Higher education institutions often find themselves swimming in data and need to differentiate when existing data streams can be used and when new data are needed. First and foremost, librarians should identify what data are needed to advance the institution's mission and strategic goals before determining whether to use existing data or collect new data. The library, for example, may already have data that contribute to the assessment of student learning and success. Common sources of library data include reference and research consultations, circulation counts, database usage statistics, and the number and types of instruction sessions. Collaboration with institutional research staff will help to determine the best way to leverage library data with other campus data sets or how to shape the data to communicate library value. For campuses that have institutional researchers, librarians can partner with them for their expertise in research question design, data collection methods, and data analysis techniques.

- *Qualitative and quantitative data*: Although quantitative data have traditionally been the most common type of assessment data, the value of qualitative data for understanding the various dimensions of student learning and success is gaining recognition. In addition, triangulation of quantitative, qualitative, and anecdotal data shows promise for powerful and meaningful statements about library impact.

- *Privacy issues*: As more and more data are collected, legal statutes and ethical policies are increasingly important considerations. Collecting individual student–level data could rub up against deeply held values and longstanding policies in the library profession. With data collection for assessment purposes, anonymity differs from confidentiality, and this difference needs further discussion and articulation as it relates to library data. While librarians should be cognizant of confidentiality and privacy restrictions, these need not unnecessarily inhibit the collection of data important to communicating library value and impact.

- *Institutional review boards*: Most data collection activities require clearance by an institutional review board (IRB) prior to gathering, sharing, or publishing the data. To promote discussions on a campus and among postsecondary institutions at conferences or to report assessment results in publications, IRB approval is essential.

Charting a Course: Recommendations and Next Steps

The themes detailed in the preceding section paint a backdrop of intensified attention to assessment and accountability issues in the higher education sector. Against this backdrop, five overarching recommendations for the academic library profession emerged. Each recommendation is followed by proposed action steps.

Recommendation 1: Increase librarians' understanding of library value and impact in relation to various dimensions of student learning and success.

The assessment of student learning in general needs to take into account multiple variables, including demographics, learning styles, educational goals, motivations, and instructional format, to name just a few. Sources of quantitative and qualitative data are numerous as well (e.g., surveys, testing, comparative data, course materials, interviews, etc.). Summit participants noted the complexity of determining the library's impact on student learning and success in relation to these variables and data sources. The need to define standards for evidence and approaches for data collection, analysis, and interpretation, in particular, was emphasized in the discussions.

Research on student retention, for example, reveals the importance of academic intimacy in the student's academic experience. Instructors and coaches are often cited as examples of adults who contribute to academic intimacy. Librarians have frequent one-on-one exchanges with students, and possible correlations between this type of contact and student learning deserves further exploration. Some assessment efforts will require data about individuals, while other assessment work can rely on aggregate data. Additional assessment strategies that demonstrate the influence of library information literacy programs on aspects of student learning also need consideration and articulation.

Actions for the profession, based on recommendation 1:

1.1. Develop a research agenda that considers key questions raised by Megan Oakleaf at the summits: How can we increase library impact? How can we document this impact? How can we partner to increase and document impact?

1.2. Review accreditation standards to determine the extent to which information literacy competencies are represented.

1.3. Continue development of information literacy rubrics that address the unique content areas and knowledge domains of different disciplines.

1.4. Identify common data sources on campuses that can be shared and leveraged with library data to document student learning and success.

1.5. Identify, describe, and publicize data collection and management tools and systems to advance library assessment activities.

1.6. Develop strategies to advance library participation in learning analytics initiatives, which use technology applications to monitor student learning and achievement.

Recommendation 2: Articulate and promote the importance of assessment competencies necessary for documenting and communicating library impact on student learning and success.

Even though library assessment activities should be tailored to the unique context of an academic institution, there is a set of core competencies essential to designing and implementing effective assessment practices. The summit participants identified many of the skills sets integrating these competencies, including the following:

- *Outcomes*: Incorporating outcomes into library planning and evaluation.
- *Data*: Applying knowledge of assessment data, including the different roles of quantitative and qualitative data, sources of data, and the analysis and interpretation of data.

There's a tremendous need for training in libraries for outcomes assessment. That's not just in the area of student learning outcomes but programmatic outcomes assessment. Especially since our new standards, the frame is totally dependent upon outcomes assessment; we have a significant need for training in that area. – Patricia Iannuzzi, Dean of University Libraries, University of Nevada, Las Vegas `◄ ► PLAY`

- *Leadership*: Demonstrating the ability to initiate and facilitate campus conversations about assessment.

These competencies are not necessarily limited to senior-level administrative positions; they should be included to some degree in the responsibilities of most librarian positions.

Actions for the profession, based on recommendation 2:

2.1   Identify and articulate the core competencies necessary to demonstrate academic library value.

2.2   Promote the need for assessment librarian positions, as well as clearly defined library value responsibilities across all library positions.

2.3   Encourage the integration of assessment competencies in graduate library and information science curricula.

2.4   Include library value competencies in professional development programs and resources as appropriate.

Recommendation 3: Create professional development opportunities for librarians to learn how to initiate and design assessment that demonstrates the library's contribution to institutional mission and strategic goals.

"One size does not fit all" was a consistent and recurring theme at the summits. When an academic library develops an assessment plan, it should be aligned with the institution's mission and strategic goals and should take into consideration the campus environment unique to that particular college or university. The mission and campus culture varies from institution to institution. Sources of existing data and the resources (i.e., staff and funds) to collect new data are also different at each institution. As a result, developing a single generic assessment approach is not realistic; multiple approaches are needed. Professional development opportunities for librarians (and their campus constituents) to learn about and share best practices would advance efforts to demonstrate library value within higher education contexts. These opportunities would likely stimulate discussion and collaboration with campus stakeholders in ways that are critical to effective assessment initiatives. Librarians could also develop a set of common practices needed by the wider library community when working on internal and external assessment efforts.

> *We need to reinforce that one size does not fit all. Students succeed for many different reasons.* – April Mason, Provost and Senior Vice President, Kansas State University

Actions for the profession, based on recommendation 3:

3.1   Create professional development opportunities that bring together librarians with representatives from their institutions to develop library value and assessment plans and activities.

3.2 Develop multiple replicable approaches for documenting and demonstrating library impact on student learning and success.

3.3 Build a community of practice to engage and sustain professional dialogue about library value.

Recommendation 4: Expand partnerships for assessment activities with higher education constituent groups and related stakeholders.

During the summits, the librarians, academic administrators, institutional researchers, and representatives of higher education organizations had numerous opportunities to exchange perspectives and ideas about assessment. Comments on the evaluation forms emphasized the value of bringing together individuals with different roles in the assessment process for collaborative discussions. The presentations and breakout sessions promoted awareness, deepened understanding, and resulted in recommendations about the unique contribution of libraries to advancing the overall goals and missions of higher education institutions. All of the representative groups highlighted the need to sustain these kinds of discussions and promote partnerships between librarians and constituent groups on their campuses.

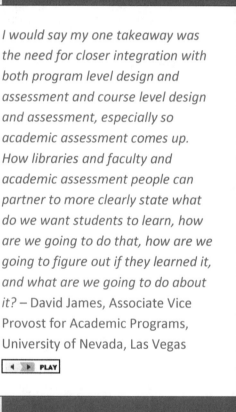

I would say my one takeaway was the need for closer integration with both program level design and assessment and course level design and assessment, especially so academic assessment comes up. How libraries and faculty and academic assessment people can partner to more clearly state what do we want students to learn, how are we going to do that, how are we going to figure out if they learned it, and what are we going to do about it? – David James, Associate Vice Provost for Academic Programs, University of Nevada, Las Vegas

Actions for the profession, based on recommendation 4:

4.1. Build on the partnerships established with external higher education stakeholders to develop assessment initiatives and embed library outcomes.

4.2. Identify higher education organizations and accreditation groups to collaborate on library impact activities and explore potential partnerships.

4.3. Articulate strategies for librarians to initiate, partner in (for example, by working with IR staff), and facilitate campus conversations about institutional assessment.

4.4. Develop guidelines and promote models that expand and integrate multiple academic and student service units in library spaces.

4.5. Encourage library and related vendors to incorporate learning analytics features in their products to advance library assessment work.

Recommendation 5: Integrate the use of existing ACRL resources with library value initiatives.

ACRL has developed a variety of tools that can be used to advance assessment practices in libraries. Librarians at the summits frequently mentioned three tools in particular. *Standards for Libraries in Higher Education* uses an outcomes-based approach to guide librarians in advancing and sustaining their role as partners in educating students, achieving their institution's mission, and positioning libraries as leaders in assessment and continuous improvement on their campuses. *Information Literacy Competency Standards for Higher Education* articulates a set of abilities that students should acquire to identify, evaluate, manage, and use information effectively and efficiently. These standards provide a framework for librarians as they consider the library's contribution to improving learning and institutional effectiveness. Finally, ACRL recently created an online resource, ACRL Metrics, providing access to academic library data collected by ACRL and the National Center for Education Statistics. Although these three tools, along with others, provide rich information and data essential to assessment activities, discussions at the summits revealed that many librarians do not always know how to best use these resources.

Actions for the profession, based on recommendation 5:

5.1. Review ACRL resources to identify complementary content about how the library contributes to institutional mission.

5.2. Create and publicize strategies for using ACRL resources to increase awareness and recognition of library contributions to college and university campuses.

5.3. Investigate the potential incorporation and application of learning analytics practices in conjunction with ACRL resources.

Mile Markers: An ACRL Update

Since the summits, ACRL has already taken several steps to move several of the recommendations forward.

As a direct result of the collaborative planning grant, the association submitted a follow-up proposal to IMLS in early 2012. If funded, a professional development program to strengthen the competencies of librarians in campus leadership and data-informed advocacy will be designed, implemented, and evaluated. Three hundred postsecondary institutions would participate in the three-year project. Each participating institution would identify a team consisting of a librarian and at least two additional team members as determined by the campus (e.g., faculty member, student affairs representative, institutional researchers, academic administrator). The librarians would participate as cohorts in a one-year professional

Assessment and demonstrating value will be a topic of conversation with all librarians next semester. We will start by having our IR person give us an overview of assessment activities on campus and which instruments collect data that we might tap into. We will use the Standards for Libraries in Higher Education to set our next set of priorities. – Senior librarian at the summit

development program that includes team-based assessment activities carried out on their campuses. Supported by a blended learning environment and a peer-to-peer network, the librarians would lead their campus team in the development and implementation of an action-learning project designed to examine and document the impact of the library on student success and to contribute data to assessment activities on their campus.

In June 2012, ACRL will hold a half-day invitational working session to articulate and develop a specific, multiyear research agenda that the library research community could pursue and that would serve as the basis for potential grant funding to support library value research. *The Value of Academic Libraries: A Comprehensive Research Review and Report* outlines numerous research questions on a range of topics and provides a foundation for discussion at the meeting. Working session participants will include leading researchers in the area of library value, as well as individuals who have engaged in conversations with ACRL about the research agenda proposed in the report. Through a series of structured discussions, participants will contribute to establishing priorities and defining directions for a focused research agenda, which will then be vetted with the academic library community in fall 2012.

ACRL's Value of Academic Libraries Committee, in collaboration with the ACRL staff, will have primary responsibility for reviewing the proposed activities of the working session report. The committee will create a work plan and implementation timeline, in consultation with the ACRL Board of Directors, to provide a means for monitoring progress in achieving the recommendations.

Conclusion

Through the discussion at the summits, it became increasingly clear that the external push for greater accountability in higher education will continue. As demonstrated by the enthusiasm of their team members, participating institutions expressed deep interest in, and commitment to, improving the ways they meet their mission to provide high-quality environments and experiences so that teaching, learning, and research activities can flourish.

The higher education assessment movement provides a unique opportunity for library leadership. Academic librarians can serve as connectors and integrators, promoting a unified approach to assessment. As a neutral and well-regarded place on campus, the academic library can help break down traditional institutional silos and foster increased communication across the institutional community. Librarians can bring together people from a wide variety of constituencies for focused conversations and spark communities of action that advance institutional mission.

I find it all amazingly invigorating that many smart people are thinking about some of the same problems that we're trying to deal with, and also very frightening, because I don't know if anyone's really figured it out in a home-run kind of way. I think that's the challenge of what we're dealing with. – Troy Swanson, library department chair, Moraine Valley Community College in Palos Hills, IL

◀ ▶ PLAY

The recommendations of this report complement other ongoing ACRL Value of Academic Libraries activities and have the potential to move the academic library profession towards new areas of collaborative assessment designed to document the library's impact on student learning and success. They also serve as a framework and resource for other library and higher education groups involved with helping institutions to assess and advance their missions.

As proven by the energetic and collaborative discussions at the summits, the road to demonstrating library value may just be starting, but academic librarians and their campus partners are prepared to make the journey together.

Appendix A: Roster of Participants

EVENT ORGANIZERS

Association of College and Research Libraries (ACRL)

Karen Brown, Associate Professor, Dominican University Graduate School of Library and Information Science

Mary Ellen Davis, ACRL Executive Director

Steve Hiller, Director of Assessment and Planning, University of Washington Libraries

Lisa Janicke Hinchliffe, ACRL Past-President and Associate Professor/Coordinator for Information Literacy Services and Instruction, University of Illinois at Urbana-Champaign

Kara Malenfant, ACRL Scholarly Communications and Government Relations Specialist

Megan Oakleaf, Assistant Professor, Syracuse University School of Information Services

Joyce Ogburn, ACRL President, Dean, J. Willard Marriott Library and University Librarian, University of Utah

Mary Jane Petrowski, ACRL Associate Director

Association for Institutional Research (AIR)

Trudy Bers, AIR Past-President and Executive Director, Research, Curriculum and Planning, Oakton Community College

Randy Swing, AIR Executive Director

Association of Public and Land-grant Universities (APLU)

Christine Keller, APLU Director of Research Policy & Analysis and Executive Director, Voluntary System of Accountability

David Shulenburger, APLU Senior Fellow

Council of Independent Colleges (CIC)

Richard Ekman, CIC President

Stephen Gibson, CIC Director of Programs

SPEAKERS

Charles Blaich, Director, Center of Inquiry at Wabash College and the Higher Education Data Sharing Consortium

Judith Eaton, President, Council on Higher Education Accreditation

Andrew Lootens-White, Vice President for Accreditation Relations, Higher Learning Commission of the North Central Association

Ralph Wolff, President and Executive Director, Western Association of Schools and Colleges

INSTITUTIONAL TEAMS

Bellarmine University, Louisville, KY

David Mahan, Director of Institutional Research

John Stemmer, Director of Library Services

Doris Tegart, Provost

Berea College, Berea, KY
Anne Chase, Director of Library Services
Scott Steele, Dean of Curriculum and Student Learning
Judith Weckman, Director of Institutional Research and Assessment

California State University, Fresno, CA
Bill Covino, Provost and VP for Academic Affairs
Tina Leimer, Associate Vice President for Institutional Effectiveness
Peter McDonald, Dean of Library Services

Drexel University, Philadelphia, PA
Jan Biros, Vice Provost for Budget, Planning, and Administration
Danuta Nitecki, Dean of Libraries and Professor, College of Information Science & Technology

Grinnell College, Grinnell, IA
Richard Fyffe, Rosenthal Librarian of the College
Mark Schneider, Associate Dean of the College and Professor of Physics

Hope College, Holland, MI
Kelly Jacobsma, Director of Libraries
Richard Ray, Provost
Scott VanderStoep, Professor of Psychology and Chair of Assessment Committee

Hostos Community College/CUNY, Bronx, NY
Carmen Coballes-Vega, Provost and Vice-President for Academic Affairs
Madeline Ford, Interim Chief Librarian
Richard Gampert, Director of Institutional Research and Student Assessment

Kansas State University, Manhattan, KS
Lori Goetsch, Dean of Libraries
April Mason, Provost and Senior Vice President
Brian Niehoff, Associate Provost for Institutional Effectiveness

Linfield College, McMinnville, OR
Susan Agre-Kippenhan, Dean of Faculty/Vice President of Academic Affairs
Jennifer Ballard, Director of Institutional Research
Susan Barnes Whyte, Library Director

Moraine Valley Community College, Palos Hills, IL
Gabe Estill, Director of Academic Assessment
Sylvia Jenkins, Vice President, Academic Affairs
Troy Swanson, Library Department Chair

Mount Holyoke College, South Hadley, MA
Lenore Carlisle, Coordinator of Educational Programs and Assistant Professor of Education
Matt McKeever, Associate Professor of Sociology and Associate Dean
Alex Wirth-Cauchon, Director of Research and Instructional Support

North Carolina Agricultural & Technical State University, Greensboro, NC
Winser Alexander, Interim Provost and Vice Chancellor for Academic Affairs
Vicki Coleman, Dean of Library Services
Scott Jenkins, Director of Institutional Research

Oakton Community College, IL
Trudy Bers, Executive Director, Research, Curriculum and Planning
Sherill Weaver, Professor of Library Services

Pennsylvania State University, PA
Loanne Snavely, Librarian and Head, Library Learning Services, University Libraries

Pierce College, Lakewood & Puyallup, WA
Debra Gilchrist, Dean of Libraries and Institutional Effectiveness
Denise Yochum, President, Pierce College Fort Steilacoom

Rio Salado College, Tempe, AZ
Hazel Davis, Faculty Chair, Library Services
Daniel Huston, Coordinator of Strategic Systems
Vernon Smith, Vice President, Academic Affairs

San Diego State University, San Diego, CA
Carolyn Baber, Instructional Services Librarian
Nancy Marlin, Provost
Reynaldo Monzon, Director, Student Testing, Assessment & Research

Santa Barbara City College, Santa Barbara, CA
Robert Else, Senior Director Institutional Assessment, Research and Planning
Kenley Neufeld, Library Director
Alice Scharper, Dean, Educational Programs, Humanities

The University of West Florida, Pensacola, FL
Bob Dugan, Dean of University Libraries
George Ellenberg, Vice Provost for Academic Affairs
Chula King, Provost and Vice President for Academic Affairs

University of Cincinnati, Cincinnati, OH
Gisela Escoe, Vice Provost for Undergraduate Affairs
Victoria Montavon, Dean and University Librarian
Lee Mortimer, Director, Institutional Research

University of Nevada, Las Vegas, Las Vegas, NV
Kari Coburn, Assistant Vice Provost, Institutional Analysis and Planning
Patricia Iannuzzi, Dean of Libraries
David James, Associate Vice Provost for Academic Programs

Utah State University, Logan, UT
Richard Clement, Dean of Libraries
Raymond Coward, Executive Vice President and Provost
Michael Torrens, Director of Analysis, Assessment & Accreditation

Appendix B: Agenda for Summit One

Tuesday, November 29, 2011

5:00 p.m.	Opening Reception
5:45 p.m.	Welcome *Joyce Ogburn, ACRL President, Dean, J. Willard Marriott Library and University Librarian, University of Utah*
5:55 p.m.	Dinner
6:10 p.m.	Introduction *Mary Ellen Davis, ACRL Executive Director*
6:15 p.m.	Overview of "The Value of Academic Libraries: A Comprehensive Research Review and Report" *Megan Oakleaf, Assistant Professor, Syracuse University School of Information Services*
7:15 p.m.	Reaction and Response: Improving Student Learning Outcomes *Charlie Blaich, Director, Center of Inquiry at Wabash College and the Higher Education Data Sharing Consortium*
8:00 p.m.	Questions and Answers *Lisa Hinchliffe, ACRL Past-President and Associate Professor/Coordinator for Information Literacy Services and Instruction, Univ. of Illinois at Urbana-Champaign*
8:30 p.m.	Adjourn

Wednesday, November 30, 2011

7:30 a.m.	Continental Breakfast (optional)
9:00 a.m.	Agenda for the Day *Megan Oakleaf, Assistant Professor, Syracuse University School of Information Services*
9:15 a.m.	View from Chief Academic Officers *April Mason, Provost and Senior Vice President, Kansas State University* *Richard Ray, Provost, Hope College* *Deb Gilchrist, Dean of Libraries and Institutional Effectiveness, Pierce College Fort Steilacoom**
9:45 a.m.	Questions and Answers
10:10 a.m.	Student Learning/Faculty Productivity: Confronting the Essential Questions *Institutional teams, small group discussion*
10:50 a.m.	Break
11:05 a.m.	Debrief of Student Learning/Faculty Productivity: Confronting the Essential Questions *Large group discussion*
12:00 p.m.	Lunch – Louvre Ballroom

---

* On-site substitution for Denise Yochum, President, Pierce College Fort Steilacoom.

Wednesday, November 30, 2011

1:00 p.m.	Reconvene – Montrose Room
1:00 p.m.	View from Accreditors
	Judith Eaton, President, Council on Higher Education Accreditation
	Andrew Lootens-White, Vice President for Accreditation Relations, Higher Learning Commission of the North Central Association
	Ralph Wolff, President and Executive Director, Western Association of Schools and Colleges
1:40 p.m.	Questions and Answers
2:00 p.m.	Innovations and Best Practices: Case Studies
	Megan Oakleaf, Assistant Professor, Syracuse University School of Information Services
2:20 p.m.	What's Next? Your Suggestions
	Affinity groups by profession, small group discussion
2:50 p.m.	Debrief of What's Next? Your Suggestions
	Large group discussion
3:20 p.m.	Summit One Wrap Up
	Mary Ellen Davis, ACRL Executive Director
3:30 p.m.	Adjourn
4:00 p.m.	Art Gallery Tour – Lobby (optional)

Appendix C: Agenda for Summit Two

Wednesday, November 30, 2011

5:50 p.m.	Dinner – Meet in Lobby (optional)

Thursday, December 1, 2011

7:30 a.m.	Continental Breakfast (optional)
9:00 a.m.	Agenda for the Day *Megan Oakleaf, Assistant Professor, Syracuse University School of Information Services*
9:15 a.m.	Library's Contributions to Institutional Focus Areas *Small group activity and large group discussion*
10:15 a.m.	Break
10:30 a.m.	Evidence and Partnerships *Steve Hiller, Director of Assessment and Planning, University of Washington*
11:00 a.m.	Questions and Answers
11:15 a.m.	What Do We Need to Learn? How Can We Learn It? *Small group discussion*
12:00 p.m.	Lunch
1:00 p.m.	Debrief of What Do We Need to Learn? How Can We Learn It? *Large group discussion*
2:00 p.m.	Perspectives on the Summits *Bob Dugan, Dean of University Libraries, The University of West Florida* *Deb Gilchrist, Dean of Libraries and Institutional Effectiveness, Pierce College* *Steve Hiller, Director of Assessment and Planning, University of Washington*
2:30 p.m.	Questions and Answers
2:45 p.m.	Break
3:00 p.m.	Campus Assessment Projects *Silent brainstorming and report out*
3:15 p.m.	Take Aways *Individual report out*
3:45 p.m.	Summit Two Wrap Up *Mary Ellen Davis, ACRL Executive Director* *Joyce Ogburn, ACRL President, Dean, J. Willard Marriott Library and University Librarian, University of Utah*
4:00 p.m.	Adjourn

Appendix D: Recording Tool for Librarians/Facilitators

Instructions

Please use this recording tool* to take notes throughout the first summit, "Demonstrating Library Value: A National Conversation."

Purpose: This tool is intended to **facilitate the documentation of ideas** you encounter during our first summit, both through the **comments of the groups** you are seated with as well as **your own thinking** and reflection. Please consider it as "parking space" for brainstormed ideas—a way not to lose track of them. Because you are recording brainstormed comments and thoughts, **you do not need to evaluate** the quality of what you record. The important thing is to capture as many as possible so that we can reflect on them later, in the second summit and beyond.

You may also find this tool helpful as a guide to conversation. Should table conversations stray off track, some of the questions below may be of assistance in getting the conversation back on task.

This recording tool will be collected Wednesday afternoon at the close of the first summit and used to prepare materials for the second summit on Thursday. It may also be used to inform the white paper that ACRL will produce after the close of both summits.

Facilitators will also be recording information during the first summit. If you are at a table with more than one person recording, please take your own notes and do not worry about duplication with others. However, we do need you to record your Wednesday morning table number and your Wednesday afternoon table number. You do not need to identify yourself by name. However, if you would like this recording tool returned to you, please include your name and indicate so below.

Morning table number: _____   Name (optional): _____

Afternoon table number: _____   Please return to me: ___Yes   ___No

---

*Developed by summit facilitator, Megan Oakleaf, including portions of her past work.

FOCUS AREAS
What are the major institutional focus areas (IFAs) libraries can/do contribute to?

LIBRARY CONTRIBUTIONS
In what ways can/do libraries contribute to IFAs?

EVIDENCE/DATA
What evidence/data do librarians need to show the library's contribution to IFAs?
(including data *we* have that *they* need, and data *they* have that *we* need)

PARTNERSHIPS/COLLABORATIONS
What partnerships/collaborations do librarians need to establish/expand to contribute to IFAs?

SKILLS & STRATEGIES
What do librarians need to learn in order to contribute to IFAs?

LEARNING SKILLS/STRATEGIES
How would you like to learn these things? For example, what formats or types of professional development might be helpful? What tools would be most useful?

ACRL
What would you like ACRL to do to support the effort to demonstrate library contributions to IFAs?

PROJECT IDEAS
Did any ideas emerge about research/assessment projects that demonstrate library contributions to IFAs?

What final thoughts do you have about what you've heard or considered during Summit #1?

CHALLENGES
What, if anything, concerns you about demonstrating library contribution to IFAs? What challenges do you perceive?

EXCITEMENT
What, if anything, excites you about demonstrating library contributions to IFAs? What opportunities do you perceive?

Appendix E: Reflection Form for Academic Administrators/Institutional Researchers

I am an:

_____ Academic administrator

_____ Institutional researcher

_____ Other: _____

Please take a few minutes to respond to the following questions about what you've heard or considered during this summit. You may leave this sheet at your table.

CHALLENGES What, if anything, concerns you about libraries working to demonstrate their contributions to institutional focus areas? What challenges do you perceive?
EXCITEMENT What, if anything, excites you about libraries working to demonstrate their contributions to institutional focus areas? What opportunities do you perceive?
OTHER What else would you like us to know?

If you would be willing to participate in a follow-up interview or focus group, please provide your contact information.

Name: _____

Institution: _____

Contact phone/email: _____

Appendix F: Report of Participant Evaluations

ACRL's IMLS 2011 National Leadership Collaborative Planning Grant provided funding to convene two national summits. ACRL teamed with three influential higher education groups experienced with education assessment and institutional effectiveness—the Association for Institutional Research, the Association of Public and Land-grant Universities, and the Council of Independent Colleges—to plan and carry out the two summits, "Demonstrating Library Value: A National Conversation," held November 29–December 1, 2011, in Chicago. The summits brought together representatives from 22 postsecondary institutions, including senior librarians, chief academic administrators, and institutional researchers, for discussions about library impact. Fifteen representatives from higher education organizations and associations also participated in the summits, which combined plenary presentations and facilitated discussion sessions.

Summit organizers sent a brief survey to the 59 members of institutional teams who attended the summits. Just over half responded (35 total, broken down as follows: 10 academic administrators, 6 institutional researchers and 19 librarian/library administrators). Participants were asked why they chose to attend and they reported:

Please select the factors that most influenced your desire to attend this summit:	Response Percent	Response Count
Because I was invited by ACRL or someone on campus	77%	26
Program topic	50%	17
Involvement of multiple higher education associations	35%	12
Grant funded (i.e., no direct cost to participate)	29%	10
Demonstrate my clear support for the library	29%	10
Influence national conversation about assessment of student learning	41%	14
Demonstrate institutional commitment to/investment in larger topic of accountability/assessment	44%	15

Participants were asked to self-assess their knowledge and understanding, prior to and after the summits, of several areas which are project grant goals. Participants scored themselves on a scale of 1-6 (where 6 is the highest). Every goal area saw an increase when comparing pre- and post summit self-assessment (with increases anywhere from 20 to 46 percentage points) as follows:

Statement of project goal:	Response Percent	Percent Change
"PRIOR to attending this summit, I would rate my awareness and understanding about how academic libraries contribute to the overall goals and missions of their institutions as:" a 5 or 6 (where 6 is the highest).	71%	20% increase
"AFTER attending this summit, I would rate my awareness and understanding about how academic libraries contribute to the overall goals and missions of their institutions as:" a 5 or 6 (where 6 is the highest).	91%	

"PRIOR to attending this summit, I would rate my awareness and understanding of the value of collaborative relationships with others on campus around the issue of library value and institutional success as:" a 5 or 6 (where 6 is the highest).	62%	26% increase
"AFTER attending this summit, I would rate my awareness and understanding of the value of collaborative relationships with others on campus around the issue of library value and institutional success as:" a 5 or 6 (where 6 is the highest).	88%	
"PRIOR to attending this summit, I would rate my knowledge of available data that my institution currently tracks with respect to library contributions to student learning as:" a 5 or 6 (where 6 is the highest).	32%	35% increase
"AFTER attending this summit, I would rate my knowledge of available data that my institution currently tracks with respect to library contributions to student learning as:" a 5 or 6 (where 6 is the highest).	67%	
"PRIOR to attending this summit, I would rate my knowledge of data about library performance that higher education administrators need to advance institutional mission and goals as:" a 5 or 6 (where 6 is the highest).	27%	46% increase
"AFTER attending this summit, I would rate my knowledge of data about library performance that higher education administrators need to advance institutional mission and goals as:" a 5 or 6 (where 6 is the highest).	73%	

Participants were asked "How was the experience of participating in the summit valuable to you?" Selected replies follow:

- I learned a great deal from other administrators and Library personnel attending. I think attending as a team from our campus was a great asset to the summit.
- Helping to develop ideas regarding collaboration between administration and library staff regarding institutional goals.
- Although my awareness was high before, it was very valuable to participate in conversations across multiple institutions of different types and to consider how practices can be implemented in institution-specific ways.
- Confirming that there are no golden rings out there which our institution has not found … it's an interesting time to explore this topic
- It helped to broaden my knowledge and expose me to perspectives I don't ordinarily get the chance to hear.
- It made me more aware of how important it is to help create an assessment plan for the library.
- Listening to the advice of IR people and some academic administrators about being judicious in deciding to collect new data and instead, reviewing the value of data that is already captured at our institutions. Recognizing that sometimes qualitative assessments are superior to quantitative measures.
- Always invaluable to spend time with one's dean. Having the IR people there was an unanticipated pleasure. Good to hear from the accreditation people too. Really good having my new dean hear about the good work that academic libraries do already in assessment.
- It got my Provost's juices flowing and will jumpstart conversations about the library being included in all forms of assessment activities on campus.
- Exchange of ideas; reinforced how central a role the library plays in student retention, achievement, and success

- A good chance to have some general conversations with our librarian and our academic officer. It also gave me some insight into some of the challenges libraries are facing. And it challenged me to figure out how to incorporate 'non-traditional' library measures (beyond # of books, circulation, etc.) into existing systems.
- I gained some insight as to how librarians look at what their mission and position is in the overall student learning outcomes of the university. Also leaving the notion of output volume and beginning to think about the process of measuring value added to the learning outcomes university-wide.
- The summit immediately helped me recognize that understanding library value is not about justifying the existence of a library in an institution of higher education, but how valuing libraries impacts on students, faculty, staff, and administration.
- First, It was very valuable to travel with and discuss with my colleagues from campus. While I have served on many committees with them, we never have had a chance to think specifically about the library in those settings. It also was very valuable to hear the perspective of accrediting agencies and to then look at what we are doing in light of their questions. Finally, it was helpful to have time to work with colleagues from other libraries to explore ways we might collaborate on this effort.

While the summits were designed to elicit advice and recommendations from attendees (and were not an educational event or aimed at program planning), many participants discussed plans for when they returned to their home campuses. Therefore, the evaluation included the question "What steps are you likely to take at your institution given what you learned at the summit?" Selected replies follow:

- I have scheduled a follow-up meeting involving both the team that attended with me and others on campus for whom this is relevant.
- We will engage the Library personnel in our discussions of retention.
- Share information with other deans. Organize conversation/discussion with library faculty. Identify first projects to begin a library impact data study.
- Institute more collaboration between administration and library staff regarding institutional goals, especially around effectiveness and assessment.
- More involvement of library in student success initiatives, Dev[elopement] ed., etc.
- Have conversations with library middle managers regarding documenting measures that show the library's impact and value. Learn to talk the same language as senior level campus administrators so that I can better convey the library's contributions to them (in their language).
- We will begin a more proactive and robust effort to quantify our contribution to the overall academic mission of our university, in consort with our IR person.
- Delve more deeply into how information literacy is incorporated into coursework based on the priority regional accrediting agencies have given to this topic
- Assessment and demonstrating value will be a topic of conversation with all librarians next semester. We will start by having our IR person give us an overview of assessment activities on campus and which instruments collect data that we might tap into. We will use the *Standards for Libraries in Higher Education* to set our next set of priorities.
- Include a library faculty member (discipline specialist) on each academic program review committee.
- Work to create actionable data that librarians and library administrators can use to make decisions. Work on ways to more effectively communicate the library's contribution to the intuition and ensure that all library staff are able to articulate this contribution.

- The first step is that I will confer with our librarians to figure out what data they have, how it is stored, and how I might gain access to it to link to other information we have in other databases. The answers to those questions will guide following steps.
- Meeting with Dean of Libraries and working on gathering information about what her objectives/outcomes she is working on to submit as part of the ongoing strategic planning process on campus.
- Joint meetings with IR and Libraries to achieve better understanding of data collection and availability from both parties. Follow-up meeting with Provost and IR person to debrief and determine next steps. Take a closer look at our draft HLC self-study for treatment of the library.
- Work with the library to make visible (through data collection and reporting strategies) their impact on university goals and priorities. For example, there are a number of ways we can track the library's impact on retention, including using data on the integration of the library into the curriculum and syllabi.
- Work with one of our departments to assess the impact of mentors and library instruction on student performance. Recognized the importance of focusing on a smaller number of areas on which the library has the most direct impact.
- Work more closely with IR to determine the type of data that we should be collecting. Identify collaborative opportunities outside of the libraries that demonstrate library value. Identify within the library the value it adds to the institution and develop a strategy for collecting information. Use the information that is collected to enhance what the library provides to college community.

Participants were asked "Is there anything else you'd like to share?" Selected replies follow:
- I thought the program was excellent and would hope the conversation will continue.
- Loved the list of possible ways that libraries can support institution's mission.
- The meeting itself was very well run and just the right size.
- Enjoyed the exchange of ideas and the well-organized agenda.
- This was of very high value to me to get my provost involved. He is already a library supporter, but I can't help but think that the provosts who really need to participate are those who don't give much thought to libraries. How can we get them involved in these kinds of discussions, particularly with other provosts who value academic libraries?
- I'd like to see dean of students-type person brought into the conversation. We plan to do that here.

Applying for the Assessment in Action Program

Editor's note: This appendix preserves unique content about the application process for the ACRL program Assessment in Action: Academic Libraries and Student Success (AiA). ACRL sought applications from all types of higher education institutions to participate in AiA. The following information excerpt describes how applicants should have prepared to apply to participate in the third year, from April 2015 to June 2016, as exemplar of the application process for the program; however, it is important to note that there was no fee to participate in the first or second year due to the subsidy provided through the IMLS grant.

THE AIA PROGRAM, part of ACRL's Value of Academic Libraries initiative, employs a blended learning environment and a peer-to-peer network over the course of the fourteen-month-long program, which—during the third year—runs from April 2015 to June 2016. In order to apply, each prospective institution must identify a team consisting of a librarian and at least two additional team members from other campus units (e.g., faculty member, student affairs representative, institutional researcher, assessment officer, or academic administrator). The application requires two essays—the first describes the team's project goals, and the second describes the goals of the librarian team leader—and statements of support from the library dean/director and campus chief academic officer.

Learn more about the AiA program from the recording/presentation slides of an online open forum held February 10, 2015, for prospective applicants. It provided background on AiA and details on how to apply for the third year plus featured two AiA librarian team leaders who talked about their experiences participating in the first year.

Selection
Program Goals
About the Action Learning Projects
Expectations of Librarians as Team Leaders
Expectations of Librarians as Members of a Community of Practice
Expectations of Campus Team Members
Timeline
Costs
Scholarships
Preparing Applications
Application Instructions and Deadline
Application FAQs

Selection

An important component of the AiA program, part of ACRL's Value of Academic Libraries initiative, is to establish a learning community in which all team leaders contribute to the success of the program through active engagement. Participation is limited to 125 teams to ensure an environment that fosters group interaction and active participation.

The institutional teams for AiA will be selected through a competitive application process designed to ensure representation from an array of geographic regions and postsecondary institutions (i.e., community colleges, colleges, and universities). Other criteria considered are demonstrated need, evidence of team readiness, and institutional support for a library-led assessment project. The review team consists of ACRL member leaders, grant partner organizations, and representatives of higher education organizations who serve on the grant advisory panel. AiA program design team members are excluded from the review process. All the applications will be reviewed at once after the application deadline.

Application reviewers will seek evidence that:

- The team and proposed project topic have the potential to contribute to the greater library and higher education community.
- The team and institution demonstrate the commitment of resources and support to enthusiastically sustain the project to completion.
- The librarian team leader, as an individual, demonstrates potential for sustained growth as a campus leader and shows evidence of positive skills and attitude to contribute to a collaborative learning experience.

Program Goals

The AiA program has three broad goals:

- GOAL 1: Develop the professional competencies of librarians to document and communicate the value of their academic libraries primarily in relation to their institution's goals for student learning and success.
- GOAL 2: Build and strengthen collaborative relationships with higher education stakeholders around the issue of library value.
- GOAL 3: Contribute to higher education assessment work by creating approaches, strategies, and practices that document the contribution of academic libraries to the overall goals and missions of their institutions.

About the Action Learning Projects

The AiA program focuses on assessment, which we believe is rooted in identifying important questions about student learning/success, designing assessments that yield information about library contributions, and taking action based on what has been uncovered. All action learning projects should go beyond use and satisfaction and examine questions of *impact* and *outcomes*. For some teams the projects may be a first step in examining what impact the library may have on student learning and success. Work will represent an initial step or pilot project through which teams will learn more, move to action, and take a deeper look at a particular area of interest. Teams undertaking "seed" projects of this type will begin an effort that will result in a longer-term commitment on campus in the future. For other teams, a previous assessment activity may have raised questions for further exploration. Therefore, some projects will move beyond describing *what* type of impact is occurring (or not occurring) and take a deeper look into *how* the library creates an impact on students. Not all projects will demonstrate that there is in fact a library impact, and key criteria for "success" will be different. Developing and implementing a project as part of the AiA program will engender learning, spur action, and build capacity for continued work in this area.

Action learning projects should be realistic, and applications should propose the best project for the team in the context of campus priorities and available resources. Ideally this project will fit into current planning and goals, and data-gathering processes (if existing data from surveys, swipe cards, database logins, instruction sessions, etc., will not be used) will be part of the regular workflow of students. To increase the likelihood of successful completion, it is important that this project be intrinsic to day-to-day work. It should be integrated into the work of the team leader, library, or institution in order to maintain commitment to this type of work into the future. Finding a topic that truly piques interest and satisfies a need on campus will allow sustainability for the length of the AiA program.

Projects can consider any aspect of the library (e.g., collections, space, instruction, reference, etc.) but must ultimately be tied to student learning (e.g., course, program, degree) or success (e.g., retention, completion, persistence). The project organizers do not expect that all projects will be designed to yield generalizable results as you would expect of findings from social science research conducted from a positivist perspective or determine meaning or relevance as in qualitative social science research methods. However, many projects will be replicable at other libraries or contain elements that will be transferable to other settings. Two ACRL resources may help stimulate thinking about potential project topics: *Standards for Libraries in Higher Education* (see principle 3, Educational Role) and *The Value of Academic Libraries: A Comprehensive Research Review and Report* (see research agenda, beginning on p. 101).

When applying to the AiA program, some of the successful past applicants stated their central inquiry questions as:

- Do students who attend information or media literacy sessions attain higher grades than students who did not?
- How does students' work with special collections materials affect their ability to think critically and develop intellectual curiosity?
- Do re-admitted students (who have appealed dismissal) improve their academic performance and persist at a higher rate due to mandatory meetings with a librarian for research assistance?
- Does our new library/learning resource center facility have an impact on the student community, contributing to student enrollment and excitement about completing skills sessions and library orientations?
- How does information literacy immersion (credit-bearing online information literacy course) compare to point-of-need ("one-shot") research instruction in helping students achieve information competencies (general education outcomes)?
- What impact does the use of library resources and Open Educational Resources as primary instructional material have on student learning?

Other potential action learning project topics that applicants may propose could include:

- What is the relationship between use of library-provided electronic journals and the rate/speed of degree completion for chemistry graduate students?
- Do students in selected presentation-intensive courses who practice in library presentation rooms have better learning outcomes, as measured by course grade?

- Our optional library instruction sessions are well-attended by those students who have some of the lowest GPAs on campus. Why is that? What could this suggest about better supporting these students?
- On our campus, transfer students taking a course with an assigned reference librarian consultant during their first semester have a much higher retention rate. What factors are contributing? What can we learn about continuing to help transfer students succeed?
- History majors at our college who use primary sources from our campus special collections during their junior year persist at a higher rate than those who use primary source materials from other archives and collections. To what extent is this attributed to qualities of faculty members who are more likely to partner with the library? To what extent can we claim an impact due to student use of materials and interactions with staff members in our library special collections?
- We have a grant program for faculty and librarians to collaborate on the redesign of courses that incorporate the research process as a central element. What is the impact of this program on student learning?

Librarian team leaders from past years of the AiA program shared their advice on how to define a project:

- *"We came up with a project for AiA; I think things would have worked out better if we had already had a project, or at least a research question that we wanted answered."*
- *"I would have created a SWOT analysis ahead of time in an effort to identify my problem areas before starting the (application) process."*
- *"Don't worry about not knowing much about assessment… the program guides you through getting some sort of assessment off the ground. Have a project (topic) really thought out so you aren't scrambling to implement."*
- *"It's important to get a big picture of the overall planning and implementation before rushing into designing a project. Learning to be a leader is definitely part of the process."*
- *"Use ACRL and AiA to leverage resources you need for your project on campus. We have been able to use the national aspects of this project to generate interest among some faculty members and get things moving that would have never gotten moving without the leverage."*
- *"Be flexible and realize that you may have to change your methods and goals as you move forward because there may be a better way to move forward with the project."*
- *"Go ahead and initiate conversations on-campus about the project, and what you would like to do, until you find at least one other person who is almost as enthusiastic as you are."*

Expectations of Librarians as Team Leaders

Being a librarian team leader in the AiA program will help develop professional skills by applying the program learning outcomes in a real-world context, while building more effective campus collaborations in the process. Librarians who participate will improve their skills as effective leaders through facilitating their campus team toward the completion of an action learning project. Furthermore, librarian team leaders will dedicate themselves to engaging with each other as a learning community, as described in the following section on being members of a community of practice.

"My primary take away is a combination of increased confidence in my abilities and an assessment worldview. There are a number of smaller skills that I developed over the course of the 14 months, but this shift in the way I look at the work I do and the knowledge that I can do it will stay with me into future projects."

Participants should understand that being part of the AiA learning community is a continuous year-round commitment, including the summer. During the middle phase of gathering and analyzing evidence, an intensive effort is expected. At other points during the program, approximately two to five hours of project-related work per week are anticipated. Librarians who participate in the program will both actively contribute to a community of practice by providing peer support to each other and lead their campus teams to facilitate the execution of an action learning project.

"You don't have to be the library dean/chair/director to do this. This is a great opportunity to lead a big project."

Librarian team leaders will participate in a fourteen-month-long professional development program, with sequenced learning events and activities at key junctures. The AiA program includes team-based activities carried out on participant's campuses. Librarian participants will submit a final project report at the conclusion of the program and prepare and deliver a poster and brief report describing their projects and their learning. Team leaders will engage in activities on campus such as:

- Creating a project timeline and goals, monitoring progress, and adjusting as needed.
- Facilitating the team's work by drafting agendas and scheduling regular meetings with team members and allies.
- Securing funding, if any, for project activities (e.g., incentives for survey completion, printing of poster).
- Assuming responsibility for ensuring application to institutional review board, if necessary.
- Enlisting others to provide specific skills/expertise if the team needs additional support to complete the project.
- Effectively communicating about the project, its goals, and accomplishments to library leaders, the campus community, and possibly external stakeholders.
- Serving as the main point of contact for the institution to the AiA design team and ACRL staff for the duration of the program.

While the bulk of the support for the AiA learning community will take place virtually through an online asynchronous classroom, live online meetings, and webcasts, librarian team leaders are expected to attend three in-person events and must secure funding as the terms of the IMLS grant to ACRL do not include participant travel. The three events are scheduled in conjunction with the ALA Midwinter Meeting and Annual Conferences as follows:

- Thursday, June 25, 2015, 1–5 p.m., and Friday, June 26, 2015, 8:30 a.m.–12:30 p.m.: San Francisco, CA. Cohort 3, first meeting.
- Thursday, January 7, 2016, 1–5 p.m., and Friday, January 8, 2016, 8:30 a.m.–12:30 p.m.: Boston, MA. Cohort 3, second meeting.
- June 23–28, 2016: Orlando, FL. Cohort 3, poster session (two slots to choose from, dates TBD).

By submitting an application, librarian team leaders agree to meet these expectations to the best of their ability if the application is accepted. New or substitute team leaders may be identified only in extreme cases and team leader replacements are permanent.

Librarians from past years of the AiA program shared their advice on leading team projects:

- *"It's a lot more work than you think…. Pick something small to start."*
- *"Be flexible and [have] patience with the process. If you are not currently working at a campus where libraries drive assessment campus-wide, be prepared for the struggle of trying to break the barriers of inclusion and proving your relevance to faculty."*

- *"While there is support, a majority of the work and responsibility rests on the team leader. Applicants should sincerely be enthusiastic about the project and receive administration support.... Do you have the time to work on your project? Are you comfortable in creating a team and asking for help?"*
- *"The AiA experience is great; however, it is a significant time commitment, which is important for supervisors/directors to know. If possible, secure 'release time' from supervisors before embarking on this project."*
- *"My greatest challenge was finding balance—balance between the AiA project and my other responsibilities and balance in the distribution of project tasks. In a small library it can be easier to just do things yourself, rather than put the effort into navigating shared responsibilities. This doesn't really work in the community of practice model."*
- *"(Team leaders) should prepare to do a lot of work over the summer so they are ready to go in the Fall. They may need to begin project meetings as soon as they are notified of acceptance, before professors leave town for the summer."*
- *"Set designated time to work on AiA projects, attend webinars, etc., with your supervisor when applying. It can be something flexible such as 3 hours per week. My institution was very supportive for me to apply (but it has been a challenge) to actually do the work for my project."*
- *"The responsibility falls mainly on the team leader. But that responsibility is easier because the Provost's support makes the many collaborations more possible."*
- *"Communicate regularly with relevant constituencies and keep track of who you tell what. Even if it's brief, such as 2–3 sentences."*

Expectations of Librarians as Members of a Community of Practice

The AiA program is designed so that librarian team leaders learn together and actively support each other, providing insight and perspective. Through a peer-to-peer collegial network, the librarian team leaders will support collective learning, shared competence, sustained interaction, and a climate of mutuality and trust. In the process, a "community of practice" will develop. As Etienne Wenger-Trayner explains, "Communities of practice are groups of people who share a concern or a passion for something they do and learn how to do it better as they interact regularly."[1] Find out more about the AiA approach to developing a peer-to-peer collegial network and community of practice on the program homepage (http://www.ala.org/acrl/AiA).

Librarian team leaders in past years of the AiA program stressed the importance of their active roles in supporting each other:

- *"Think of this program as truly about developing a community of practice with your AiA cohort and on your campuses. The AiA facilitators provide excellent learning opportunities but cohort members need to be self-directed and responsible to each other for learning and developing their projects."*
- *"Expect to be active participants in the learning community—i.e., participation in the project not only results in a campus-specific assessment project but also in the creation of a professional community of practice. (Your) participation in the learning activities is critical to the development of this community of practice."*
- *"You need to devote time to (regular online) work every week because others (librarian team leaders) are depending on you, even if your campus is very busy that week.... The online environment is where (you) will interact the most."*

Expectations of Campus Team Members

Being part of the AiA learning community is a continuous year-round commitment. The involvement of team members will vary depending on project role.

All team members will engage in a peer-review process, providing feedback about projects being developed by other participating teams. The projects will be documented and disseminated, via poster session and in online project reports via the ACRL website, for use by the wider academic library and higher education communities.

Librarian team leaders from past years of the AiA program shared their advice on finding team members who can commit to being involved:

- *"Make sure to have campus buy-in and teammates who are focused on assessment. Having an Institutional Researcher or someone from the Assessment Office on the team would be a good idea."*
- *"It is imperative to choose campus partners wisely; those individuals who can make significant contributions to a team project."*
- *"Mak(e) sure your campus partners have a good understanding of time commitment going in, and recogniz(e) how much work and planning there will be on your part to keep the campus partners engaged."*
- *"Make sure that others on your team are committed to helping out with work, rather than seeing themselves in only an advisory role."*
- *"Be very clear with those you invite to be part of your campus team that it will require some level of work/communication over the summer. As someone in a 12-month position, it can be easy to overlook the fact that teaching faculty may be away and less likely to engage during the summer months. Strategically planning for this would have been helpful—creating designated 'email check-in' dates or something like that."*
- *"Build on established relationships. There may be more glamorous projects out there, but when you (and your campus) are new to assessment, it is wise to work with individuals you know well and who already support the work that you do. This allows you to build your skills in a supportive environment. As an added bonus, they are more likely to go out and 'testify' about your findings—you can't buy that kind of PR."*
- *"Communication between team members, especially with members outside of the Library, is crucial to the success of the project."*

Timeline

As a general guide, librarian team leaders who are selected for the third year of the AiA program can expect to participate in a range of activities as follows:

ACTIVITY	2014									2015					
	A	M	J	J	A	S	O	N	D	J	F	M	A	M	J
Receive notification of AiA acceptance	▓														
Agree to participate, pay registration fee	▓														
Receive and provide AiA peer support in online learning community	▓	▓	▓	▓	▓	▓	▓	▓	▓	▓	▓	▓	▓	▓	▓
Attend AiA webcasts on assessment (i.e., project outcomes and criteria, methods, tools, analysis, interpretation)		▓		▓							▓	▓			
Project planning: define outcomes and set criteria			▓	▓											
Act: perform actions and gather evidence					▓	▓	▓	▓							
Reflect: analyze evidence and interpret results										▓	▓				
Share: plan changes in order to improve												▓	▓	▓	
Participate during in person AiA mtgs			▓												
Present AiA project poster															▓
Submit AiA project report															▓

This timeline is just one way of illustrating a team leader's involvement in the AiA learning community and how a project could be executed. Because individual action learning projects vary greatly according to institutional needs and priorities, the AiA program offers flexibility. For example, some teams may gather and analyze evidence at a later time than others.

ACRL will use this third year of the AiA grant to inform how it can best support the community in developing and carrying out assessment projects going forward. A grant from the Institute of Museum and Library Services covered the majority of the costs for developing the AiA program and for delivering it the first two years. The third year of the grant marks a transition year to determine if this program is sustainable or if other models better address the needs of the community.

Costs

There is a registration fee of $1,200 for participating in the third year of the AiA program. For the first two years, the IMLS grant covered the majority of the costs for developing and delivering the AiA program. In the third year, the IMLS grant will subsidize only part of the costs, and ACRL is implementing a registration fee as the program transitions to a cost-recovery model. Full payment due in April 2015, upon acceptance.

Librarian team leaders need to secure their own funding for travel to three in-person events: June 2015 (full-day meeting), January 2016 (full-day meeting), and June 2016 (poster session). Librarian team leaders who are attending only AiA meetings in June 2015 and January 2016 do not have to register for the full ALA conference. In order to present their posters, librarian team leaders must register and pay for attending the 2016 ALA Annual Conference.

Other costs to develop and implement projects will be carried by the institution (e.g., incentives for survey completion, printing of poster, etc.).

On the application form, applicants will be asked to affirm that, if their team is accepted, the institution will provide full financial support for registration in addition to travel funding for the librarian team leader to attend three in-person events.

Scholarships

ACRL is now offering up to 20 scholarships that would underwrite half of the $1200 registration fee. Scholarships will be awarded to institutions that have demonstrated the strongest commitment to support the team's project over the course of the AiA program and the clearest connection between the team's project goals and institutional priorities.

On the application form, each applicant will be asked to indicate whether their institution is seeking a scholarship.

Preparing Applications

ACRL will use this third year of the AiA grant to inform how it can best support the community in developing and carrying out assessment projects going forward. A grant from the Institute of Museum and Library Services covered the majority of the costs for developing the AiA program and for delivering it the first two years. The third year of the grant marks a transition year to determine if this program is sustainable or if other models better address the needs of the community. The following information describes how applicants should have prepared to apply to participate in the third year, from April 2015 to June 2016.

Begin the application process early and prepare and submit materials as soon as possible. It takes time to consult with colleagues in the library, meet with prospective team members across campus, secure commitment, scope out an area of interest for the team's project, write the essays, arrange for travel funding, and request statements of support. The application requires two essays—the first describes the team's project goals and the second describes the goals of the librarian team leader—and statements of support from the library dean/director and campus chief academic officer. Each piece is described in detail below.

Essay #1 on the team's project goals may be up to 300 words long. The essay should clearly explain the central question that would be investigated through this project, the goals the college/university has established for carrying out a project as part of the AiA program, and how the central question and the contributions of the library align with those goals. If the team has a particular method in mind for collecting data, include that briefly. Explain the ways in which the proposed project has the potential to make a contribution to assessment work in other libraries or higher education. Given what you know about existing assessment endeavors in other academic libraries, what is distinctive or unique about your proposed project? What could others learn? Some of the questions you may want to consider addressing in your essay could include things such as: What aspects of student learning or student success are most important at the institution? Has your college or university developed student learning outcomes/goals across the institution that the library has potential to impact? What aspects of the library (e.g., collections, space, instruction, reference, etc.) are related to the project? What connections would be explored as the basis for the action learning project? How has the library been involved in past assessment efforts? Why is this the right time for the institution to take on this project? Why are the chosen team members the right mix of people given the team's area of interest? What do their positions and experience bring to this project? (Campus team members are identified fully by name and title/position elsewhere in the application.) These questions are simply a few examples; you do not need to answer each explicitly, but use them for guidance as you write your essay.

Institutions that participated previously in AiA may apply to participate a second time, or institutions applying for the first time may submit two applications for two teams and projects. In this first essay describing the proposed project, they should explain briefly why a second team/project would be helpful to their institution.

Essay #2 on the goals of the librarian team leader may be up to 300 words long. The essay should briefly explain the team leader's professional background for undertaking the work described in essay #1 (e.g., attended conferences, webinars, presented papers, etc.) and length of time in the profession (newer and less experienced librarians will not be penalized). Explain the strengths, skills, and attitude the team leader will bring to the collaborative learning community and to the role as team leader on campus. The essay should briefly state personal goals for professional growth in assessment competency and leadership acumen.

Statement of Support #1 from the library dean or director may be up to 500 words long and should address the commitment of the library to assessment, including the dean or director's role in that process, and indicate how the institution will support the team's project over the course of the AiA program. The statement does not need to be uploaded or faxed on formal letterhead. Simply copy and paste the final text of the statement provided by the dean/director into the online application form.

Statement of Support #2 from the campus chief academic officer (i.e., provost or vice president for academic affairs) may be up to 500 words and should address how the team's project goals are connected to institutional priorities. The statement does not need to be uploaded or faxed on formal letterhead. Simply copy and paste the final text of the statement provided by the chief academic officer into the online application form.

Application Instructions

The online application to participate in the third year of AiA is no longer available as it was due by March 25, 2015.

1. Each application must identify a librarian team leader who will receive notification of the team's acceptance or rejection. If the team's application is accepted, the librarian team leader will serve as the main point of contact for the ACRL design team and staff for the duration of the program.
2. Once the online application process has begun, statements can be revised as many times as needed until they are complete and ready to submit. No deadline exceptions will be granted.
3. Have the following information prepared before beginning the online application form:
    a. Names, titles, affiliations (i.e., department, office, or school), and contact information for all team members.
    b. Two essays.
    c. Two statements of support.
    d. Whether your institution is seeking a scholarship.
    e. Whether your institution will provide full financial support for registration in addition to travel funding or only if a scholarship is awarded.
4. Incomplete applications can be saved and edited or additional information can be added before the submission deadline date. An ID number and password will be assigned when the proposal is submitted. Be sure to print the ID number and password and keep them in a safe place; these will be needed in order to edit the proposal at a future time.
5. Please note that this is a team application process and acceptance into the program is based, in part, on who is identified as members of the team.

Application Deadline

Applications were due by Wednesday, March 25, 2015, 5 p.m. Central.

ACRL will use this third year of the AiA grant to inform how it can best support the community in developing and carrying out assessment projects going forward. A grant from the Institute of Museum and Library Services covered the majority of the costs for developing the AiA program and for delivering it the first two years. The third year of the grant marks a transition year to determine if this program is sustainable or if other models better address the needs of the community.

Notifications

The librarian team leader listed on the application will be ACRL's primary contact. All applicants were notified of their status via email by Friday, April 17, 2015, 5 p.m. Central.

See the application frequently asked questions for more details about applying. Questions may be directed to ACRL Senior Strategist for Special Initiatives Kara Malenfant at kmalenfant@ala.org or 312-280-2510.

Assessment in Action: Application FAQs

Below are frequently asked questions by prospective applicants. The online application to participate in the third year of Assessment in Action: Academic Libraries and Student Success, made possible by the Institute of Museum and Library Services, was due by Wednesday, March 25, 2015, 5 p.m. Central.

Are you offering AiA in 2016–17?

ACRL will use this third year of the AiA grant to inform how it can best support the community in developing and carrying out assessment projects going forward. A grant from the Institute of Museum and Library Services covered the majority of the costs for developing the AiA program and for delivering it the first two years. The third year of the grant marks a transition year to determine if this program is sustainable or if other models better address the needs of the community. ACRL remains committed to supporting academic librarians as they work to document and communicate the value of their academic libraries. However, at this time there is not a commitment to offer the specific AiA cohort-based fourteen-month-long program in 2016–17. While we will continue to support the community, the format for doing so may look quite different, based on community needs.

What made for strong applications in past years?

We can characterize the strongest applications in several ways:

- They were distinguished by the team composition and their readiness.
- They contained clear project goals with specific topics to investigate and close alignment with institutional priorities.
- They had the most potential to contribute to the greater library and higher education community.
- They contained statements of specific institutional support to help the teams see their projects through to completion.
- Librarian team leaders of the most robust applications provided evidence of how they would contribute to a collaborative learning experience for the good of all.

Can institutions that participated in year one or year two apply to participate again in the third year? Or could an institution submit two applications for two teams and projects?

Yes. Institutions that participated previously in AiA may apply to participate a second time, or institutions applying for the first time may submit two applications for two teams and projects. In the first essay describing the proposed project, they should explain briefly why a second team/project would be helpful to their institution.

How do we apply for a scholarship? Is there a separate form?

No, there is no separate form; simply indicate "yes" on your application. Reviewers will base the awards off of information presented on the application through the essays and letters of support. Scholarships will be awarded to institutions that have demonstrated the strongest commitment to support the team's project over the course of the AiA program and the clearest connection between the team's project goals and institutional priorities.

I am the library director and my supervisor is the Associate Vice President for Academic Affairs. She works closely with the chief academic officer, the Vice President for Academic Affairs. For the second statement of support, is something by the AVP sufficient for the application?

You could do this; however, your application may not appear as strong as others. One option would be to have a statement from your AVP indicating she has discussed this with the VP and has received full support. It could explain why you feel a statement from the AVP is stronger/more pertinent than one from the VP. That being said, it is possible that the review team may not rate your institutional application as highly as other applications that do have a letter of support from the chief academic officer.

I know that I have a conflict with some of the in-person meetings but see that librarian team leaders can identify a substitute in extreme cases. Can you say a little more?

Being a librarian team leader is a serious commitment to both leading your team and actively providing peer support for the other librarians in the AiA learning community. This is a continuous year-round commitment, including the summer. That being said, we understand that during the fourteen-month long program unexpected events may occur; a librarian team leader may leave for a job at another institution, experience a medical emergency, or have a family crisis. It is only in cases such as these that it should be necessary to identify a substitute. If you know in assembling your application that you are not able to meet all of the expectations of librarian team leaders and expectations of librarians as members of a community of practice, then you should find another person who can do so.

I am the library director and would like to submit an application as the team leader. But I see that the statement of support must come from the library director. Does this mean that the librarian team leader should be someone other than the library director, or are library directors eligible to participate as team leaders?

You certainly are eligible, as the library director, to be a team leader. We expect a number of applications from institutions where the library director will both apply as team leader and provide a letter of support. We would suggest that you write each of the pieces (the essays and the letter) from the particular perspectives required at that moment. Another way to say this is that you should put on a different "hat" and write from that place.

I am an assessment librarian and we already have a program at our library. I have a good project in mind and feel like I would benefit by being part of the AiA community. But I wonder if I should save space for smaller institutions that are just getting started?

You should most certainly apply. While some teams will undertake projects that are a first step toward assessing the impact of the library on student learning and success, we encourage applications from teams that have undertaken previous assessment projects. It is important to have a diversity of experiences, projects, and perspectives as this will make the entire AiA community stronger. As a more seasoned practitioner, you will have much to offer as you provide peer support to other librarian leaders in the program.

Our proposed project will be to assess the impact of a yet-to-be-formed program, which won't be underway until the fall. Is that OK for the purposes of the AiA program?

Perhaps. Is your program definitely going to happen or still a tentative idea being formed? Will you accomplish enough during the time of the AiA program to actually assess the impact of your work? We expect the middle phase of gathering and analyzing evidence to take place August 2015–February 2016. If you feel confident that your library's program will be up and running and that you will have evidence to gather/analyze, then you should make your case in essay #1.

I have a question about the monetary support that IMLS is providing for the program. Is ACRL sub-granting to the participating institutions? Should we be including a budget for our action learning projects in our application?

IMLS provided a grant to ACRL to develop the AiA program. The grant funds cover our expenses for items such as a modest stipend to our design team, honorarium for expert speakers, the software to support the application process, the technology for the webcasts, meeting room rental, a.v. during the meetings, refreshment for librarian team leaders during working breaks, etc. ACRL also is funding part of the AiA program by providing a one-third match to the IMLS grant funding. This is not a pass-through grant, however, and participating institutions do not receive direct funding from ACRL. For the first two years selected team members receive access to the educational program and learning community at no charge. In the third year of the AiA program, we are making a transition to cost recovery and began charging a registration fee of $1,200.

If we are not a research library, will our team be at a disadvantage in applying for the AiA program?

Absolutely not. The institutional teams for AiA are being selected through a competitive application process designed to ensure representation from an array of postsecondary institutions (i.e., community colleges, colleges, and universities).

My library consortium is considering applying. Would you accept a consortial team?

The intention of the program is to support librarians in leading campus teams as they develop and implement a project on their campuses. This is not an individual professional development experience, per se, for academic librarians. Therefore, we would expect that the review team would rate a consortial team of librarians at different institutions much lower than a single institutional team. Individual colleges/universities within a single consortium should apply, but applications won't be given higher priority based on consortial affiliation.

We are a branch campus of a US university in another country and are interested in participating. Would we qualify to apply?

Yes; however, you should have conversations with your home institution as others in the library may also be interested in applying. It could be difficult to secure support for more than one application from the library dean and provost. Also, it is not likely that reviewers would accept two applications from the same university.

Will we need to have a project formulated prior to applying, or is that something the team establishes during the program?

While you do not need to have your project formulated in full, you should explain in the first essay what you are thinking, based on the conversations you had with your team in preparing the application. You should describe the direction you plan on taking because applicant readiness is a criterion for selection.

Do we need to have team members selected prior to applying? Or is the idea really to coach the librarians through the process of coming up with the question and forming a team?

In order to have the strongest possible application, we recommend you have all team members on board before applying. Reviewers will not rate an incomplete application, with a team member yet to be determined, as highly as a complete application.

Can my additional team members be librarians?

Many teams may rely on additional librarians and library staff members to provide specific skills/expertise over the course of completing the projects. However, for the purposes of this application you should indicate only one librarian team leader. This person will be our main contact, and there is only one seat available per team at the in-person meetings. On this application you should indicate at least two team members from other campus units. Reviewers will not rate an application with more than one librarian on a team as highly as an application with team members from other campus units.

How do we decide who should be applying from our institution?

Every institution will have different priorities, needs, and skills. The AiA facilitation team is committed to creating an experience that allows people with varied expertise to explore issues together. The goal is to have the cohort represent a wide range of professional backgrounds, types and sizes of institutions, and roles within the institutions. For the librarian team leader, examples of institutional roles include:
- Librarians who work directly with students on campus.
- Library administrators.
- Librarians responsible for information literacy programs.
- Librarians with assessment responsibilities.
- Librarians with responsibility for faculty development via Centers for Faculty Development, Writing Centers, or other similar campus units.

The additional team members will vary widely, based on the area of focus for the project. Some potential teammates may be faculty members, student affairs representatives, institutional researchers, or academic administrators. Be sure to read the advice from first-year librarian team leaders in the section on expectations of campus team members.

Who will be the facilitating the AiA learning community?

The AiA program design team is led by project leaders Debra Gilchrist, Vice President for Learning and Student Success, Pierce College, WA; Lisa Janicke Hinchliffe, Coordinator for Information Literacy and Professor, University of Illinois at Urbana-Champaign; and Kara Malenfant, Senior Strategist for Special Initiatives, Association of College and Research Libraries. Additional designers/facilitators will participate throughout the length of the project: April Cunningham, Instruction/Information Literacy Librarian at Palomar College in San Marcos, CA; and Carrie Donovan, Head of Teaching and Learning for the Indiana University Libraries in Bloomington, IN. Two new facilitators joined the team in February 2015: Eric Resnis, who currently serves in a dual appointment at Miami University as Assessment Coordinator in the Center for Teaching, Learning, and University Assessment (CELTUA) and as Organizational Effectiveness Specialist in the Libraries at Miami University in Oxford, OH; and John Watts, an Undergraduate Learning Librarian at the University of Nevada, Las Vegas. A community of practice expert advised the team during the early design process. Project analyst Karen Brown, Professor at the Graduate School of Library and Information Science at Dominican University, IL, is working with the team to document projects. Expert speakers, selected to augment the program, will present briefly at key junctures. Read more about the design team members in their biographies.

What topics will be covered over the course of the year-long AiA program?

While we will be presenting material on value and assessment (i.e., outcomes and criteria, methods, tools, analysis, and interpretation), being part of the AiA learning community is much more than learning new content. Librarians who participate will improve their skills as effective leaders when they facilitate their campus team in completing an action learning project. Furthermore, librarian team leaders will dedicate themselves to engaging with each other as a learning community and providing one another peer support.

How many people will be accepted for the AiA program?

We aimed to select three hundred colleges and universities of all types to participate in the AiA learning community (Year 1: 75 institutions; Year 2: 100 institutions; Year 3: 125 institutions). Each participating institution will identify a team consisting of a librarian and at least two additional team members as determined by the campus (e.g., faculty member, student affairs representative, institutional researchers, or academic administrator). AiA will result in training for approximately 300 librarians, along with instructional engagement and resources for an additional 600–900 campus representatives on the teams.

Why are these termed "action learning projects" and not "research projects"?

The program focuses on assessment, which we believe is rooted in identifying important questions about student learning/success, designing assessments that yield information about library contributions, and taking action based on what has been uncovered. We do not expect that all projects will be designed to yield generalizable results as you would expect of findings from social science research conducted from a positivist perspective or determine meaning or relevance as in qualitative social science research methods. We do expect that projects will be important to their institutions and that many projects will be replicable at other libraries or contain elements that will be transferable to other settings. Additionally, while not all projects will demonstrate that there is in fact a library impact, our key criteria for "success" are a bit different. Developing and implementing a project as part of the AiA program will engender learning, spur action, and build capacity for continued work in this area. For those reasons, we are intentional in describing the work you will undertake as "action learning projects" and not "research projects."

Will the AiA program support only projects with a quantitative focus? Using survey data?

No. We do expect some projects will use quantitative data and may connect existing library data (from surveys, swipe cards, database logins, instruction sessions, or the like) with institutional data on GPA, retention, or other measures. However, we welcome projects that explore questions best answered with qualitative data from focus groups, interviews, and other means.

Do the projects all have to be on a topic related to information literacy?

Not at all. We welcome projects that consider any aspect of the library (e.g., collections, space, instruction, reference, etc.) as long as they are tied to student learning (e.g., course, program, degree) or success (e.g., retention, completion, persistence).

We are interested in focusing on graduate students. Do you expect the projects to be focused on undergraduate students only?

No. We advise that you explain why you've chosen a particular student group for your project's focus, in the context of your institution's priorities, as that will help make a stronger application.

We are interested in looking at library impact on faculty. Will that fit for a project focus?

For the AiA program, we are focusing on student learning outcomes and student success, in direct response to the needs we heard articulated during our planning grant (see more about the genesis of the AiA program and its scope on the program homepage). Reviewers may look favorably on a project that would consider the impact of the library on faculty interactions with students or the ways in which faculty engagement with the library is related to student learning outcomes or student success.

Why do we need to provide two statements of support?

One key to a successful campus-wide project is organizational support and engagement. We require that your institution make a strong commitment to your team and demonstrate that in two statements of support.

Where should I fax my two statements of support? Or should I email PDFs instead?

You do not need to include statements of support on formal letterhead. Simply copy and paste the final text of the statements provided to you into the online application form.

Are there any restrictions on the application?

Yes. Please note that each of the essay fields will accept up to 300 words and each of the statement of support fields will accept up to 500 words.

What can we do to improve our chances of being accepted for the AiA program?

Submit a *complete* application before the published deadline. Offer clear, succinct, and thoughtful statements regarding your team's goals for participating and your personal goals as a librarian team leader. Make sure your statements of support are included and explicitly address the evaluation criteria listed.

Will you accept participation from outside the US?

As you might guess, because the AiA project is funded by IMLS, the majority of participation and benefit must be by and for US citizens. However, because international and diverse perspectives are valuable, a limited number of teams from outside the US may be selected.

What will I need to do, as a librarian team leader, to prepare for the program if our team's application is accepted?

The kickoff webcast to be held in May will be particularly useful for asking questions and seeking clarification about participating in the AiA program.

Notes

1. Etienne and Beverly Wenger-Trayner, "Introduction to Communities of Practice," *Wenger-Trayner*, 2015 accessed January 8, 2018, http://wenger-trayner.com/introduction-to-communities-of-practice.

First Interim Narrative Report to Institute of Museum and Library Services

PROJECT TITLE: Assessment in Action: Academic Libraries and Student Success

PARTNERS: Association for Institutional Research (AIR) and the Association of Public and Land-grant Universities (APLU)

Overview

As part of its Value of Academic Libraries Initiative, a multiyear project designed to assist academic librarians in demonstrating library value, the Association of College and Research Libraries (ACRL) began work in October 2012 on "Assessment in Action: Academic Libraries and Student Success" (AiA). A National Leadership Demonstration Grant of $249,330 from the Institute of Museum and Library Services (IMLS) funds the AiA program for three years. The AiA program builds on the outcomes of an IMLS 2011 National Leadership Collaborative Planning grant (LG-62-11-0216-11) by designing, implementing, and evaluating a professional development program to build the competencies of librarians for demonstrating library value.

In the first year of the AiA program, ACRL made progress toward achieving all three stated goals:
1. develop the professional competencies of librarians to assess, document, and communicate the value of their academic libraries primarily in relation to their institution's goals for student learning and success,
2. build and strengthen collaborative relationships with higher education stakeholders around the issue of library value, and
3. contribute to higher education assessment work by creating approaches, strategies, and practices that document the contribution of academic libraries to the overall goals and missions of their institutions.

Project Activities

In the grant proposal narrative, the primary activities that would meet each goal were listed as:
- Goal 1 activity: Librarians participate in professional development activities and apply the learning to a library value project on their campus.
- Goal 2 activity: Librarians will lead their institutional teams in the design and implementation of a library value project.
- Goal 3 activity: Institutional teams led by their participating campus librarian will design, implement, and evaluate library value projects on their campus, resulting in multiple ap-

proaches, strategies, and practices for documenting the library's impact on student learning and success.

We made significant progress on each of these activities, as described more fully below.

Facilitation/Design Team

As planned, in fall 2012, we conducted an open search and application process to identify three facilitators to join those identified in the grant proposal as lead facilitators—Lisa Hinchliffe, Deb Gilchrist, and staff program lead Kara Malenfant. The three additional facilitators selected are April Cunningham, library instruction coordinator at Pomona College in Claremont, California; Carrie Donovan, head of teaching and learning for the Indiana University Libraries in Bloomington, Indiana; and Libby Miles, associate professor of writing and rhetoric in the Harrington School of Communication and Media at the University of Rhode Island in Kingston, Rhode Island.

We actively recruited applicants both inside and outside the library profession. Our selection of Miles, who is not a librarian but serves as disciplinary faculty member, provides complementary strength for the facilitation team. With a solid team of designer/facilitators in place, work began in earnest in January 2013 to develop the professional development curriculum for the librarian team leaders. We have used a variety of techniques and tools to maintain our momentum and connection, including in person meetings, regular phone calls, and online tools to test out approaches we are considering implementing within the program.

Teams Selected

In mid-January 2013 the online application was available and was promoted broadly by ACRL and our partners. We received 99 applications for the 75 available slots by the early March deadline, and a review panel of ACRL member leaders selected the 75 teams in early April. (AiA facilitators were excluded from the review process.) The institutional teams for AiA were selected through a competitive application process designed to ensure representation from an array of geographic regions and postsecondary institutions (i.e., community colleges, colleges, and universities).

The teams come from 29 U.S. states and 3 Canadian provinces spanning 7 time zones (from Hawaii to Nova Scotia). The colleges and universities these teams represent are accredited by the full spectrum of regional accrediting bodies: 15 by Middle States Association of Colleges and Schools, Middle States Commission on Higher Education; 9 by New England Association of Schools and Colleges, Commission on Institutions of Higher Education; 21 by North Central Association of Colleges and Schools, The Higher Learning Commission; 4 by Northwest Commission on Colleges and Universities; 12 by Southern Association of Colleges and Schools, Commission on Colleges; 3 by Western Association of Schools and Colleges, Accrediting Commission for Community and Junior Colleges; and 6 by Western Association of Schools and Colleges, Accrediting Commission for Senior Colleges and Universities. There are also four accredited by Canadian bodies, and one institution is accredited by a medical accreditor.

In addition to geographic diversity, the selected teams represent all types of postsecondary institutions, as follows: 10 are two-year/technical colleges, 9 are four-year/baccalaureate-granting colleges, 31 are comprehensive (undergraduate/graduate) institutions, and 25 are universities (research/doctoral granting).

The strongest applications can be characterized in several ways:

- They were distinguished by the team composition and their readiness.

- They contained clear project goals with specific topics to investigate and close alignment with institutional priorities.
- They had the most potential to contribute to the greater library and higher education community.
- They contained statements of specific institutional support to help the teams see their projects through to completion.
- Librarian team leaders of the most robust applications provided evidence of how they would contribute to a collaborative learning experience for the good of all.

The application process required prospective participants to list a librarian team leader and at least two team members from campus units other than the library. It required applicants to explain the composition of their team and why it was appropriate in light of their proposed inquiry areas. Team members come from a variety of campus units such as: assessment office, institutional research, teaching faculty, writing center, information technology, academic technology, student affairs, residence life, and campus administration. Many teams include additional librarians or library administrators.

Scope of Action Learning Projects

These 75 teams are investigating questions related to student learning and student success that matter to their institutions. They are examining the impact of a variety of library factors, such as: instruction (games, tutorials, single/multiple session, and course embedded), reference and individual research assistance, physical space, discovery of library resources through institutional web or library-based resource guides, collections, and personnel.

The AiA program creates space and support for teams to use a variety of tools and methods, gathering both direct and indirect data. In this way teams choose the means of assessment that are most credible, trustworthy, and practical given their institutional context. Some methods and tools being used include surveys, interviews, focus groups, observations, and pre/post tests. Evidence is gathered from many sources including rubrics, student portfolios, research papers/projects, other class assignments, test scores, GPA, degree completion rate, and retention rate.

There is a wide range of inquiry questions, which are refined and reworked in the early stages of the AiA program. A few examples from application essays follow:

- Do students who attend information or media literacy sessions attain higher grades than students who did not?
- How does students' work with special collections materials affect their ability to think critically and develop intellectual curiosity?
- Do re-admitted students (who have appealed dismissal) improve their academic performance and persist at a higher rate due to mandatory meetings with a librarian for research assistance?
- Does our new library/learning resource center facility have an impact on the student community, contributing to student enrollment and excitement about completing skills sessions and library orientations?

We do not expect that all projects will yield generalizable results as one would expect of findings from social science research conducted from a positivist perspective. However, many projects will be replicable at other libraries or contain elements that will be transferable to other settings. While not all projects will demonstrate that there is in fact a library impact, our key criteria for success are a bit different. Developing and implementing a project as part of the AiA program will engender learning, spur action, and build capacity for continued assessment work. For those reasons, we are intentional in describing the work institutional teams undertake as "action learning projects" and not "research projects."

Building a Community of Practice

The AiA project design includes a sequenced set of experiences to promote and support the creation of a community of practice. The facilitators are strongly committed to establishing an environment that supports collective learning, shared competence, and sustained interaction. Etienne Wenger-Trayner, who pioneered the concept with Jean Lave, explains, "A community of practice is a group of people who share a concern or a passion for something they do, and learn how to do it better as they interact regularly."*

We broke down the 75 teams into small cohort groups of 5 to foster a climate of mutuality and trust. The facilitation team was very fortunate to be advised by Wenger-Trayner and Beverly Wenger-Trayner. While we initially proposed in the grant that we would seek advice from a community of practice expert for a brief initial phase, we sought a more extensive period of engagement. The Wenger-Trayners provided coaching to the facilitation team over six months. They attended the first in-person meeting of the 75 librarian team leaders, held in conjunction with the American Library Association (ALA) Annual Conference and described more fully below, in order to provide richer, better-informed guidance to the facilitators.

Engaging With Librarian Team Leaders

To create a dynamic, authentic learning experience, the AiA program uses blended learning, peer-to-peer collegial relationships, and action learning projects. The librarians are leading their campus teams in the development and implementation of a library value project that is informed by the skill-building activities and designed to contribute to assessment activities on their campus. Details on the particular activities participants have experienced in the first five months of their 14-month experience follow.

Webcasts

To formally kick off the program, and at key junctures throughout, the facilitators present live 90-minute webcasts using the Blackboard Collaborate online meeting software. We ask team leaders to gather their full AiA project team at one location on campus and watch together. The webcasts typically include presentation on a topic, time for breakout conversations by teams, reporting back to the full group, and a closing question-and-answer period. The webcasts thus far have been:
- April 18: Assessment Cycle
- August 5: Design
- September 5: Instruments/Evidence

In Person

Librarian team leaders met in person for the first time in conjunction with the ALA Annual Conference. The meetings lasted for four hours on Thursday, June 27, and four hours on Friday, June

---

* **Source** http://wenger-trayner.com/resources/what-is-a-community-of-practice.

28. Participants built a community of practice and developed knowledge and skills in the areas of assessment and leadership through a variety of in-person activities:
- Cohort Poster Creation
- Gallery Walk of the Posters
- Generating Themes and the Learning Agenda
- Direct Instruction on Community of Practice
- Cohort Leadership Roles
- Direct Instruction on the Assessment Cycle
- Direct Instruction on Writing Outcomes
- Developing Outcomes from the Case Study
- Developing an Outcome for Your Own Project
- Getting Cohort Feedback on Your Outcome
- Giving Cohort Feedback on Their Outcomes
- Direct Instruction on Writing Criteria
- Developing Criteria with Your Cohort

Asynchronous Forums

Using the Moodle elearning platform, facilitators regularly post questions, resources, and exercises for the AiA librarian team leaders. The bulk of the threaded discussions take place within each cohort of five librarian team leaders, but some open general discussion forums are posted for broader sharing. Sometimes facilitators present a reading, video, or set of questions to prompt discussion, other times members of the cohort lead and facilitate discussion on key concepts. The discussion topics follow.

Cohort based threaded discussion topics

Campus Team Overviews (Due April 23)
Campus Team Project Description (Due April 26)
Key Concepts (Complete Discussion by May 3)
Background Research Reflection (Due May 10)
Local Information Gathering (Due May 17)
Research Ethics Exploration (Due May 24)
Project Commonalities and Differences across the Cohort (Due June 7)
Inquiry Questions (Due June 14)
Mapping Your Project (Due June 21)
Leading a Team (Due June 21)
Discussion Post-Chicago
The AiA Workshop Experience and Your Leadership Role
Developing a Community of Practice
Setting Criteria and Getting Feedback (Due August 14)
Leadership and Communication—Big Picture (Due September 13 and 27)

Cross cohort threaded discussion topics

Getting to Know Each Other
Librarian as Team Leader
Sharing Resources for Background Research

Jam Sessions

In July, we introduced optional Jam Sessions, which are live events, held in an Adobe Connect online meeting room with audio, text chat, and document sharing. These are intended to give team leaders another chance to talk through a topic and to engage in shared discussion and exploration with interested fellow team leaders and one facilitator. Topics have included the outcomes and criteria concepts in the assessment cycle and correlation/causation, which included discussion of commonalities and differences of assessment and research. Jam Sessions are approximately 45 minutes in length, depending on the number of participants and depth of discussion.

Informal Meet Ups

To foster collegial relationships and increase the ability to easily connect, we organized several informal (pay on your own) opportunities for participants to connect with one another during conferences, as follows:

- We invited newly admitted librarian team leaders to a "meet and greet" on April 12, held in conjunction with ACRL 2013 in Indianapolis, Indiana. Facilitators were present as were the ACRL president, executive director, and other member leaders.
- We asked librarian team leaders to tell institutional researchers from their teams to join in an informal dinner meet up on May 19, held in conjunction with the AIR annual conference in Long Beach, California. One facilitator was present, and our AIR partners helped us secure space and include the event in their schedule.
- We asked librarian team leaders to tell assessment officers from their teams to join in an informal dinner meet up on June 4, held in conjunction with the Association for the Assessment of Learning in Higher Education in Lexington, Kentucky. One facilitator was present.
- We organized optional "dine around" opportunities for librarian team leaders on June 27, held in conjunction with the ALA Annual Conference in Chicago, Illinois. By making reservations for tables of eight at several local restaurants and providing sign-up sheets on site, we encouraged groups to continue connecting and supporting each other by cohort, type of institution, project topic, or assessment method.

Analyzing Progress

Although ACRL has a long history of initiating and sponsoring innovative training, an approach that focuses on blended, peer-to-peer learning is an enhancement to the existing models. The AiA professional development program differs from other ACRL training by involving librarians in a 14-month long series of activities that merge learning with application and the opportunity for reflective practice.

Focus Group

We notified applicants of their status on April 3, and just a few days later, on April 11, held a focus group with 14 of the selected librarian team leaders during ACRL 2013 in Indianapolis. An outside facilitator met with newly selected team leaders, who reported a high level of early, proactive interest and support from campus partners. A report on the focus findings yielded information about the hopes and concerns of the team leaders, which was of immediate use to the AiA facilitators in further designing the curriculum.

Survey

In July, the facilitators asked all librarian team leaders to reflect on the first two-and-a-half months of the program and provide feedback. We asked team leaders how well specific aspects of the AiA program matched their learning and leadership styles. We invited comments on how the way the program is organized has helped their development. We asked about the extent to which particular resources and activities (webinars, Moodle prompts, and in-person activities) had helped team leaders to develop knowledge and skills. We asked about particular elements in the AiA program and which had most affected participants' perspectives on assessment and on leadership. As with the focus group report, this direct participant feedback was of immediate use to the facilitation team in refining our planned activities over the following months.

Through this feedback from librarian team leaders and our own observations, the facilitation team has begun to clearly identify program strengths as well as areas for growth and improvement. We have navigated challenges as librarian team leaders have resigned from their institutions and passed the reigns to new librarian team leaders. We have seen that the wide variety of action learning projects not only requires the program to be flexible enough to support differing student learning and success impact areas, library factors, assessment methods, and tools, but also to support differing timelines for the campus-based action learning projects. We have seen that forming cohorts to be highly diverse by institution type has advantages, but that affiliation around topic (inquiry area or library factor examined) may be more meaningful.

The facilitation team has been regularly reflecting on the strengths and areas for growth and improvement. We expect to modify the program design for the second group of teams, which will start the program in April 2014. Accordingly, the facilitators will hold an additional intensive planning session in conjunction with the ALA Midwinter Meeting in January 2014.

Communicating Broadly

As expected, ACRL and its grant partners AIR and APLU have used their well-established communication channels to promote the AiA program and encourage teams to apply. In addition, ACRL member leaders and senior staff members have presented at many conferences to raise awareness about the program. Presentations and poster sessions have been offered at the following library and higher education conferences:

- Library Assessment Conference (Charlottesville, Virginia, October 29, 2012)
- Coalition for Networked Information Fall Membership Meeting (Washington, D.C., December 11, 2012)
- ALA Midwinter Meeting (Seattle, Washington, January 27, 2013)
- Michigan Academic Library Council 2013 Spring Workshop on Imperatives of Library Leadership (Flint, Michigan, March 15, 2013)
- ACRL 2013 (Indianapolis, Indiana, April 12, 2013)
- Association for the Assessment of Learning in Higher Education Third Annual Assessment Conference (Lexington, Kentucky, June 3–5, 2013)
- ALA Annual Conference (Chicago, Illinois, June 30)
- 7th International Evidence Based Library and Information Practice Conference (Saskatoon, Saskatchewan, July 15–18, 2013)
- International Federation of Library Associations World Library and Information Congress (Singapore, August 17–23, 2013)

Next Steps

Our first 75 teams are nearly halfway through the 14-month long AiA program. We are still facilitating the team leaders in their learning, supporting them in carrying out their projects and fostering growth of the community of practice. As one example of how the program continues to be responsive, in October 2013 we will introduce Case Connections. Communities of practice often learn together by helping one member think through his or her project, coming together to problem-solve from different perspectives and with different experiences. Doing so not only helps solve the immediate challenge, but also allows others to contribute their own stories, experiences, and insights, further enriching their expertise.

On the near horizon, the facilitation team is designing the in-person experience for librarian team leaders to be held January 2014 in conjunction with the ALA Midwinter Meeting in Philadelphia, Pennsylvania. This includes planning the prompts for the online component this fall that will build up to and best prepare team leaders for using this in-person time effectively. We are also beginning to plan for the end of the participants' 14-month long experience in June 2014 when team leaders will present posters describing the team's project and their learning in conjunction with the ALA Annual Conference in Las Vegas, Nevada.

In addition to presenting a poster, institutional teams will prepare a final project report, which ACRL will analyze and disseminate. As they prepare those reports, all team members will participate in peer review and provide feedback about projects by other teams. We have begun working with our project analyst Karen Brown, associate professor in the Graduate School of Library and Information Science at Dominican University. She will compile a collection of replicable library value approaches and is working with the facilitation team to integrate this into the program design. In the months ahead, we will refine the project report framework, poster session guidelines and templates, and set in motion the peer review process.

At the same time that the facilitators are supporting the current 75 teams, we are working to improve the information about the AiA program for prospective applicants for year two so it is as clear and accurate as possible. In December, we will update the website with information about how to apply at www.ala.org/acrl/AiAapplication and the FAQs for prospective applicants at www.ala.org/acrl/AiAapplicationfaq. We expect to follow the same schedule for year two: the online application will be available in mid-January 2014 and due in early March 2014, reviewers will select an additional 100 institutional teams, and we will notify applicants in early April of their status.

ACRL, AIR, and APLU will continue to communicate about the opportunity to apply for the second year as one of the additional 100 institutional teams. In summer 2014, we will also promote the analysis of project reports, which Brown will be producing. Sharing the results of the AiA projects widely will contribute to grant goal 3 of contributing to higher education assessment work by creating approaches, strategies, and practices that document the contribution of academic libraries to the overall goals and missions of their institution.

Second Interim Narrative Report to Institute of Museum and Library Services

PROJECT TITLE: Assessment in Action: Academic Libraries and Student Success

PARTNERS: Association for Institutional Research (AIR) and the Association of Public and Land-grant Universities (APLU)

Overview

As part of its Value of Academic Libraries Initiative, a multiyear project designed to assist academic librarians in demonstrating library value, the Association of College and Research Libraries (ACRL) began work in October 2012 on "Assessment in Action: Academic Libraries and Student Success" (AiA). A National Leadership Demonstration Grant of $249,330 from the Institute of Museum and Library Services (IMLS) funds the AiA program for three years. The AiA program builds on the outcomes of an IMLS 2011 National Leadership Collaborative Planning grant (LG-62-11-0216-11) by designing, implementing, and evaluating a professional development program to build the competencies of librarians for demonstrating library value.

In the second year of the AiA program, ACRL made progress toward achieving all three stated goals:
1. develop the professional competencies of librarians to assess, document, and communicate the value of their academic libraries primarily in relation to their institution's goals for student learning and success,
2. build and strengthen collaborative relationships with higher education stakeholders around the issue of library value, and
3. contribute to higher education assessment work by creating approaches, strategies, and practices that document the contribution of academic libraries to the overall goals and missions of their institutions.

Project Activities

In the grant proposal narrative, the primary activities that would meet each goal were listed as:
- Goal 1 activity: Librarians participate in professional development activities and apply the learning to a library value project on their campus.
- Goal 2 activity: Librarians will lead their institutional teams in the design and implementation of a library value project.
- Goal 3 activity: Institutional teams led by their participating campus librarian will design, implement, and evaluate library value projects on their campus, resulting in multiple ap-

proaches, strategies, and practices for documenting the library's impact on student learning and success.

We made significant progress on each of these activities, as described more fully below.

First Year Teams

Remaining Curriculum

The first group of 75 AiA teams began in April 2013 and concluded their participation in the program in June 2014. During the last nine months of their experience (covered by this reporting period) the AiA program continued using blended learning, peer-to-peer collegial relationships, and action learning projects. The librarians lead their campus teams in the development and implementation of a library value project that is informed by the skill-building activities and designed to contribute to assessment activities on their campus. Details on the particular activities participants in the first year of the program experienced in the remaining nine months of their 14-month experience follow.

Webcasts

At key junctures throughout the facilitators present live 90-minute webcasts using online meeting software (Adobe Connect or BlackBoard Collaborate). The webcasts typically were one hour in length and included presentation on a topic and a closing question-and-answer period. The final two webcasts (of five) were:
- Visualizing Data and Poster Design—April 2, 2014
- Communicating Your Results—May 5, 2014

In Person

Librarian team leaders met in person for the second time in conjunction with the 2014 ALA Midwinter Meeting in January. As with the first meeting in June 2013, this second meeting lasted for four hours on Thursday and four hours on Friday. Participants continued to foster a community of practice and developed knowledge and skills in the areas of assessment and leadership through a variety of in-person activities:
- Taking stock of progress (cohort)
- Data analysis (break out)
- Evaluating assessment results (affinity groups)
- Using your results (plenary)
- Planning the 'ask' (affinity groups)
- Makings of a great elevator speech (plenary)
- Deliver elevator speech (cohort)
- Consolidating learning and reflection (plenary)

Asynchronous Forums

Using the Moodle elearning platform, facilitators continued to regularly post questions, resources, and exercises for the AiA librarian team leaders. The bulk of the threaded discussions took place within each cohort of five librarian team leaders, but some open general discussion forums were posted for broader sharing. Sometimes facilitators presented a reading, video, or set of questions to prompt discussion, other times members of the cohort lead and facilitated discussion on key concepts. The discussion topics follow.

Preparation for In-Person: Sustaining Our Community of Practice—January 2014
> Reading Bolman and Gallos Chapter on Academic Leadership
> Revisiting Relevant Resources
> Data Analysis: Jumpstart Your Thinking
> Qualitative Data Analysis Recording and Handout
> Quantitative Data Analysis Recording and Handout

Cross cohort threaded discussion topics
> Sharing your AiA project at conferences, list of relevant conferences and deadlines
> Questions about the Poster Development and Feedback Process
> Final report questions
> Pay It Forward—Recommended Readings for Year 2 AiA Participants

Case Connections

To ensure the program was responsive to the needs of participants, in October 2013 we introduced Case Connections. Communities of practice often learn together by helping one member think through his or her project, coming together to problem-solve from different perspectives and with different experiences. Doing so not only helps solve the immediate challenge, but also allows others to contribute their own stories, experiences, and insights, further enriching their expertise.

During each Case Connection, one team leader's project became the focus. The leader provided a one-page scenario describing the dilemma and ending with 1–3 "burning" questions s/he would like fellow AiA Team Leaders (from all cohorts) to take up. Everyone who chose to participate was asked to read the case in advance of the live session. During an online synchronous work time, the team leader told the story in his/her own words in the first 5 minutes. The next 5 minutes were for fellow AiA Team Leaders to ask clarifying questions so they understood the situation and the team leader's questions. Fellow AiA team leaders then provided insight, perspectives of how they have dealt with the issue, or prompted with questions to consider. Case Connections lasted 30–60 minutes total length depending on the depth of each "question."

We invited all team leaders to be the focus of a Case Connection and facilitated them for all who sought out this opportunity. From November–January we held six Case Connections on these topics:

- Assessing student learning of evaluation of sources; benchmarking.
- Developing an instrument to assess student learning; best way to report qualitative data.
- Research design and challenges with correlation/causation.
- Strengthening research design so as to demonstrate library impact.
- Working with a biased faculty member; models of information literacy others are using.
- Swaying the naysayers; grant sources; how to talk about the project when the results are not what was expected.

Informal Meet Ups

To foster collegial relationships and increase the ability to easily connect, team leaders organized their own informal meet up to connect with one another during the ALA Annual Conference in June 2014 and invited the second year AiA team leaders to join.

Disseminating First Year Project Results

Participants' 14-month long experience culminated in June 2014 when 74 of the selected 75 teams presented posters in conjunction with the ALA Annual Conference in Las Vegas, Nevada. The posters described each team's project and their learning. Most often these were presented by the librarian team leaders, but in some cases another campus team members joined in making the poster presentation. Half the teams presented on Friday afternoon and half on Saturday morning. The timing was purposeful to ensure many newly selected AiA librarian team leaders for year two of the program could attend. They had only just completed their first in-person session mid-day Friday.

In spring 2014, we focused on supporting AiA librarian team leaders as they prepared to disseminate project results. We started in March by providing a complete timeline for poster development, cohort peer feedback, cross cohort peer view, and final project reporting. To support the team leaders in every step of this dissemination process, we provided concrete guidelines for developing a poster, including information on poster design. A cross-cohort threaded discussion allowed team leaders from any cohort to pose questions and provide answers about the poster development and feedback process. Poster abstracts were June 2 and a public PDF was released on June 10 as part of our promotion of the sessions.

In addition to presenting a poster, institutional teams prepared final project reports, which are being analyzed by Karen Brown. Her synthesis will be disseminated later in 2014 together with a searchable online collection of individual project reports. In our initial grant narrative, we did not include this searchable online collection, but we realized how valuable it would be for others in the community to find reports of assessment projects by type of institution, method used, focus area etc. Final project reports were due via an online form June 23 (see Appendix A for reporting questions). Developing this online reporting tool was an addition not included in the grant narrative. After fully defining the scope and issuing a competitive RFP process, we chose an internal partner in another ALA office to develop the report input form and search interface. The cost for these professional services was nominal and covered by grant funding which had initially been allocated for another professional service that was no longer needed.

As they prepared those posters and reports throughout the spring, AiA librarian team leaders supported one another through a structured process which started with peer feedback, within each cohort. Once team leaders made revisions, they undertook peer review across cohorts so each team leader, with fresh eyes, provided feedback about two projects outside their cohort. Again, team leaders made appropriate revisions based on this feedback. This iterative process ensured that final posters and project reports were robust and clear.

In addition to these formal mechanisms supported by the AiA program, ACRL is using its other platforms to promote the results of AiA projects in other ways. ACRL's Value of Academic Libraries Committee has invited AiA team leaders and their projects to be featured on the ACRL VAL blog. They asked interested team leaders to answer three questions:

1. What was your greatest challenge during the course of your Assessment in Action project?
2. What is your #1 recommendation for other librarians who want to conduct an assessment project on student learning and success?
3. What is the #1 thing you gained through your participation in Assessment in Action?

In October, our first team leader was featured in the spotlight on the ACRL VAL blog, see http://www.acrl.ala.org/value/?paged=2. ACRL is also working to publish a book on assessment methods with one AiA team leader as editor and other team leaders as contributors. Lastly AiA facilitators are working with ACRL's premier scholarly journal *College and Research Libraries* to consider publishing a special issue focused exclusively on AiA projects as action research in spring 2016.

And librarian team leaders are finding their own ways to disseminate their findings on campus and locally. At the national level, in August, several AiA year one librarian team leaders presented at the Library Assessment Conference in Seattle, WA.

Bridging First and Second Year AiA Experience

As mentioned above under the section on curriculum, we created a discussion thread to encourage the year one AiA librarian team leaders to "pay it forward" by sharing their favorite readings and sources for year two AiA participants. The first year team leaders planned an informal get together at the ALA Annual Conference and invited the second year team leaders. Many second year team leaders were able to attend poster sessions by the first year team leaders and commented on how helpful it was to see completed projects. We posted rosters for each year in the other year's Moodle online course to further encourage connections across years.

In late October, we asked first year AiA team leaders to help us improve information about the AiA program for prospective applicants for year two. We asked them, specifically, to review the information about how to apply at http://www.ala.org/acrl/AiAapplication and the FAQs for prospective applicants at http://www.ala.org/acrl/AiAapplicationfaq. Then we asked the year one team leaders to give us feedback in three areas:

1. What should we change or emphasize more so that applicants have the clearest possible understanding of the AiA program?
2. What advice would you give to others who are thinking about applying?
3. Looking back on it, now that you are actually in the middle of carrying out your project, what do you wish you had known from the beginning? What would you have done differently at the outset?

The information the team leaders provided was invaluable in improving the webpages about how to apply, and we were able to weave in direct quotes to let their voices be heard. This gave prospective applicants a more fulsome understanding of what it takes to be part of the AiA community and to lead a team based assessment project on campus.

Librarian team leaders in the 2013–14 AiA program shared their advice on how to define a project:

- *"We came up with a project for AiA; I think things would have worked out better if we had already had a project, or at least a research question that we wanted answered."*
- *"I would have created a SWOT analysis ahead of time in an effort to identify my problem areas before starting the (application) process."*
- *"Don't worry about not knowing much about assessment…the program guides you through getting some sort-of assessment off the ground. Have a project (topic) really thought out so you aren't scrambling to implement."*
- *"It's important to get a big picture of the overall planning and implementation before rushing into designing a project. Learning to be a leader is definitely part of the process."*
- *"Use ACRL and AiA to leverage resources you need for your project on campus. We have been able to use the national aspects of this project to generate interest among some faculty members and get things moving that would have never gotten moving without the leverage."*

Librarians in the 2013–14 AiA program shared their advice on leading team projects:

- *"It's a lot more work than you think…Pick something small to start."*
- *"Be flexible and [have] patience with the process. If you are not currently working at a campus where libraries drive assessment campus wide be prepared for the struggle of trying to break the barriers of inclusion and providing your relevance to faculty."*

- *"While there is support, a majority of the work and responsibility rests on the team leader. Applicants should sincerely be enthusiastic about the project and receive administration support...Do you have the time to work on your project? Are you comfortable in creating a team and asking for help?"*
- *"The AiA experience is great; however it is a significant time commitment, which is important for supervisors/directors to know. If possible, secure 'release time' from supervisors before embarking on this project."*

Librarian team leaders in the 2013–14 AiA program stressed the importance of their active roles in supporting each other:

- *"Think of this program as truly about developing a community of practice with your AiA cohort and on your campuses. The AiA facilitators provide excellent learning opportunities but cohort members need to be self-directed and responsible to each other for learning and developing their projects."*
- *"Expect to be active participants in the learning community—i.e., participation in the project not only results in a campus-specific assessment project but also the creation of a professional community of practice. (Your) participation in the learning activities is critical to the development of this community of practice."*
- *"You need to devote time to (regular online) work every week because others (librarian team leaders) are depending on you, even if your campus is very busy that week… The online environment is where (you) will interact the most."*

Librarian team leaders in the 2013–14 AiA program shared their advice on finding team members who can commit to being involved:

- *"Make sure to have campus buy-in and teammates who are focused on assessment. Having an Institutional Researcher or someone from the Assessment Office on the team would be a good idea."*
- *"It is imperative to choose campus partners wisely; those individuals who can make significant contributions to a team project."*
- *"Mak(e) sure your campus partners have a good understanding of time commitment going in, and recogniz(e) how much work and planning there will be on your part to keep the campus partners engaged."*
- *"Make sure that others on your team are committed to helping out with work, rather than seeing themselves in only an advisory role."*
- *"Be very clear with those you invite to be part of your campus team that it will require some level of work/communication over the summer. As someone in a 12-month position, it can be easy to overlook the fact that teaching faculty may be away and less likely to engage during the summer months. Strategically planning for this would have been helpful—creating designated 'email check in' dates or something like that."*

The information these first year team leaders provided had the added benefit of helping the AiA facilitators understand how team leaders were doing. Their comments reinforced some of the design choices we had made and helped us refine other areas where more support seemed necessary.

Second Year Teams
Teams Selected

We updated our website in late fall 2013 and offered an online open forum for prospective applicants to learn more about the program on December 9, 2013. In mid-January 2014 the online application was available and promoted broadly by ACRL and our partners. We extended the deadline two weeks from March 7 to March 21 in an effort to increase the number of applications. Our grant partners, APLU and AIR promoted the opportunity to apply using their considerable communication networks both with the initial and extended deadlines. While our grant narrative indicated we would grow the program and have 100 teams in the second year, a review panel of ACRL member leaders selected 73 qualified teams in early April. (AiA facilitators were excluded from the review process.) The institutional teams for AiA were selected through a competitive application process designed to ensure representation from an array of geographic regions and postsecondary institutions (i.e., community colleges, colleges, and universities).

The teams come from 34 U.S. states and 1 Canadian province. The colleges and universities these teams represent are accredited by the full spectrum of regional accrediting bodies: 11 by Middle States Association of Colleges and Schools, Middle States Commission on Higher Education; 4 by New England Association of Schools and Colleges, Commission on Institutions of Higher Education; 30 by North Central Association of Colleges and Schools, The Higher Learning Commission; 6 by Northwest Commission on Colleges and Universities; 18 by Southern Association of Colleges and Schools, Commission on Colleges; and 3 by Western Association of Schools and Colleges, Accrediting Commission for Senior Colleges and Universities. There is also one accredited by a Canadian body.

In addition to geographic diversity, the selected teams represent all types of postsecondary institutions, as follows: 13 are two-year/technical colleges, 15 are four-year/baccalaureate-granting colleges, 11 are comprehensive (undergraduate/graduate) institutions, 27 are universities (research/doctoral granting), 6 are special focus institutions (medical, culinary, theological) and one is a tribal college.

The application process continued the same requirements as the first year. It required prospective participants to list a librarian team leader and at least two team members from campus units other than the library. It required applicants to explain the composition of their team and why it was appropriate in light of their proposed inquiry areas. Team members come from a variety of campus units such as: assessment office, institutional research, teaching faculty, writing center, information technology, academic technology, student affairs, residence life, and campus administration. Many teams include additional librarians or library administrators.

Scope of Action Learning Projects

As with participants of the first year, this second group of 73 teams are investigating questions related to student learning and student success that matter to their institutions. They are examining the impact of a variety of library factors, such as: instruction (games, tutorials, single/multiple session, and course embedded), reference and individual research assistance, physical space, discovery of library resources through institutional web or library-based resource guides, collections, and personnel. There is a wide range of inquiry questions, which are refined and reworked in the early stages of the AiA program.

The AiA program creates space and support for teams to use a variety of tools and methods, gathering both direct and indirect data. In this way teams choose the means of assessment that are most credible, trustworthy, and practical given their institutional context. Some methods and tools being used include surveys, interviews, focus groups, observations, and pre/post tests. Evidence is gathered from many sources including rubrics, student portfolios, research papers/projects, other class assignments, test scores, GPA, degree completion rate, and retention rate.

We continue our expectation that not all projects will yield generalizable results as one would expect of findings from social science research conducted from a positivist perspective. However, many projects will be replicable at other libraries or contain elements that will be transferable to other settings. While not all projects will demonstrate that there is in fact a library impact, our key criteria for success are a bit different. Developing and implementing a project as part of the AiA program will engender learning, spur action, and build capacity for continued assessment work. For those reasons, we are intentional in describing the work institutional teams undertake as "action learning projects" and not "research projects."

Community of Practice

The AiA project design includes a sequenced set of experiences to promote and support the creation of a community of practice. The facilitators are strongly committed to establishing an environment that supports collective learning, shared competence, and sustained interaction. Etienne Wenger-Trayner, who pioneered the concept with Jean Lave, explains, "A community of practice is a group of people who share a concern or a passion for something they do, and learn how to do it better as they interact regularly."*

While in the first year, we created small cohort groups of 5, we learned that size was too small to ensure the sustained interaction. For this second group's librarian team leaders, we have four cohorts of 18–20 each which is still intimate enough to foster a climate of mutuality and trust, but allows for a more diverse range of interactions. We grouped the four larger cohorts around timing, asking when they plan to collect their data.

In addition to the cohort groupings, we helped participants form affinity groupings during our first in person even at the ALA Annual Conference in June 2014, Las Vegas Nevada. The affinity groupings they chose are numerous and varied, as follows:

- Institution Type: Community Colleges, Medical Schools, Small Liberal Arts Colleges, Research Universities , Primarily Hispanic-Serving Institutions, Religious, and Mid-size Universities
- What-ifs: Workload, Project Failure, Campus Team, Engaging the Expertise of Campus Team, Timeline, Faculty Buy-in, Imposter Syndrome, Transition to New Team Leader, Team Dynamics
- Professional Role: Library Administration, Instruction Librarian, Instruction Coordinator, Technical Services, Public Services, Instructional Designer, Systems & IT, Researcher and Department Head.
- Project Type: Correlation/Causation, Campus Partnerships, Non-Instructional Services, and Instruction & Information Literacy.

Engaging With Librarian Team Leaders

The AiA program continues to use blended learning, peer-to-peer collegial relationships, and action learning projects. The librarians lead their campus teams in the development and implementation of a library value project that is informed by the skill-building activities and designed to contribute to assessment activities on their campus. Details on the particular activities participants in the second year of the program experienced in their first five months of their 14-month experience follow.

---

* **Source** http://wenger-trayner.com/resources/what-is-a-community-of-practice

Webcasts

We no longer ask team leaders to gather their full AiA project team at one location on campus and watch together. Now the webcasts are designed specifically for a librarian audience exclusively. Some leaders may choose to invite team members, but it is not an expectation. Instead, we offered a recorded introduction for Campus Teams, just after the live introductory webcast for librarians. In this way, they could choose to bring their teams together to watch a short overview of the AiA program and hear our expectations, then lead their teams in a discussion about their particular projects. Webcasts for the librarian team leaders were:

- Introduction for Librarian Team Leaders (May 7, 2014)
- Assessment Cycle (July 31, 2014)
- Project Design (August 28, 2014)
- Designing with Data (to be held October 2, 2014)

Jam Sessions

We will again hold optional Jam Sessions, which are live events, held in an Adobe Connect online meeting room with audio, text chat, and document sharing. These are intended to give team leaders another chance to talk through a topic and to engage in shared discussion and exploration with interested fellow team leaders and one facilitator. Topics will include ethnographic practices in September and correlation/causation in October, which included discussion of commonalities and differences of assessment and research. Jam Sessions are approximately 45 minutes in length, depending on the number of participants and depth of discussion.

Case Connections

We will again facilitate optional Case Connections in winter so that individual team leaders can pose burning questions and be the focus of concentrated help from other AiA team leaders.

Asynchronous Forums

Continuing our use of the Moodle elearning platform, facilitators regularly post questions, resources, and exercises for the AiA librarian team leaders. The bulk of the threaded discussions take place within each cohort of 18–20 librarian team leaders, but some open general discussion forums are posted for broader sharing. Sometimes facilitators present a reading, video, or set of questions to prompt discussion, other times members of the cohort lead and facilitate discussion on key concepts. The discussion topics follow.

Cohort threaded discussion topics
Team Introduction (May 23)
Project Overview (May 23)
Experience Hosting Team Meeting with Recorded Webinar (May 19–30)
Concepts (May 28)
Background Research (June 4)
Gather Local Documents (June 13)
Local Information Reflection (June 20)
Research Ethics (July 25)
Criteria (August 6)

Outcomes and Criteria Alignment Check-in (September 10)
Leadership (September 30th)

Cross cohort threaded discussion topics
Self Introduction (Due May 14)
Open Discussion and General Networking
Recommended Readings—Share Your Favorite Sources!

In Person

Librarian team leaders met in person for the first time in conjunction with the ALA Annual Conference. The meetings lasted for four hours on Thursday, June 27, and four hours on Friday, June 28. Participants built a community of practice and developed knowledge and skills in the areas of assessment and leadership through a variety of in-person activities:
- Welcome and Introductions
- Institutional Alignment
- Inquiry Questions
- Assessment Cycle
- Outcomes
- Criteria
- Focus on Your Project
- Revisit Outcomes & Criteria (in cohorts)
- Leadership
- Alignment
- Wrap-up

Analyzing Progress

Although ACRL has a long history of initiating and sponsoring innovative training, this particular approach focusing on blended, peer-to-peer learning over a 14-month period is an enhancement to our existing models. The facilitation team has been regularly reflecting on the strengths and areas for growth and improvement. The facilitators held an additional intensive planning session in conjunction with the ALA Midwinter Meeting in January 2014.From this came modifications to the program design for the second group of teams, such as larger cohort groupings, changing the webcast audience to librarians only, and altering the pacing and flow for the first two months of the program.

Brown facilitated two focus groups of AiA year one team leaders in June, in part to assist with her analysis and synthesis of the final project reports. The results also helped facilitators netter understand program elements that should be retained, strengthened or softened.

Through the various forms of feedback from librarian team leaders and our own observations, the facilitation team continues to identify program strengths as well as areas for growth and improvement. We continue to navigate challenges as librarian team leaders have resigned from their institutions and passed the reigns to new librarian team leaders. We continue to see that the wide variety of action learning projects not only requires the program to be flexible enough to support differing student learning and success impact areas, library factors, assessment methods, and tools, but also to support differing timelines for the campus-based action learning projects.

Communicating Broadly

As expected, ACRL and its grant partners AIR and APLU have used their well-established communication channels to promote the AiA program and encourage teams to apply. In addition, ACRL member leaders and senior staff members have presented at many conferences to raise awareness about the program. Presentations and poster sessions have been offered at the following library and higher education conferences:

- 2013 Illinois Library Association (Chicago, IL, October 15–17, 2013)
- Library 2.013 (Online, October 19, 2013)
- Southeastern Library Assessment Conference (Atlanta, GA, October 21–22, 2013)
- 2013 Assessment Institute (Indianapolis, IN, October 27–29, 2013)
- Professional and Organizational Development Network in Higher Education Conference (Pittsburgh, PA, November 6–10, 2013)
- ACRL Assessment in Action Program Open Online Forum (Online, December 9, 2013)
- ALA Midwinter Meeting (Philadelphia, PA, January 26, 2014)
- Academic Library Association of Ohio, Assessment Interest Group Spring Workshop. (Dublin, OH, April 24, 2014)
- 2014 WASC Academic Resource Conference. (Los Angeles, CA, April 24, 2014)
- ALA Annual Conference (Las Vegas, NV, June 29, 2014)
- Library Assessment Conference. (Seattle, WA, August 4–6, 2014)

Next Steps

Our second year team leaders are nearly halfway through the 14-month long AiA program. We are still facilitating them in their learning, supporting them in carrying out their projects and fostering growth of the community of practice. At the same time we are preparing to promote the analysis of the first year's project reports, which Brown will be producing. Sharing the results of the AiA projects widely will contribute to grant goal 3 of contributing to higher education assessment work by creating approaches, strategies, and practices that document the contribution of academic libraries to the overall goals and missions of their institution.

APPENDIX A: Final report template for AiA team leaders

DOCUMENT 1: *Institutional and Library Profile*

Note to Team Leaders: *This section will be pre-populated for you with information from NCES and other existing public data sources. Team leaders will not be able to edit this section.*

1. Name of institution
2. Basic classification
3. FTE enrollment
4. U.S. Regional Accrediting organization
5. Sector Affiliation
6. Fiscal Affiliation
7. Information literacy is student learning outcome for institution
8. Total librarians and other professional staff
9. Total library expenditures (salaries and wages, materials and operating)

DOCUMENT 2: *AiA Project Description*

Directions to Team Leaders: *Please tell us about your project. All the information in this project description section will be publicly searchable. Be sure to proofread/spell check before you submit. We will be publishing the information exactly as you enter it, without review. You can start the report, save, then come back and complete it later. You have **until June 23** to complete this section of the report.*

1. Primary outcome examined (select one or more)
   - ○ student learning: assignment
   - ○ student learning: course
   - ○ student learning: major
   - ○ student learning: degree
   - ○ student engagement
   - ○ student experience
   - ○ student success
   - ○ academic intimacy/rapport
   - ○ enrollment
   - ○ retention
   - ○ completion
   - ○ graduation
   - ○ articulation
   - ○ graduates' career success
   - ○ testing (e.g., GRE, MCAT, LSAT, CAAP, CLA, MAPP)
   - ○ Other (please describe) : _____

2. Primary library factor examined (select one or more)
   - ○ instruction
   - ○ instruction: games
   - ○ instruction: one shot

○ instruction: course embedded
○ instruction: self-paced tutorials
○ reference
○ educational role (other than reference or instruction)
○ space, physical
○ discovery (library resources integrated in institutional web and other information portals)
○ discovery (library resource guides)
○ discovery (from preferred user starting points)
○ collections (quality, depth, diversity, format, or currency)
○ personnel (number and quality)
○ Other (please describe) : _____

3. Student population (select one or more)
○ undergraduate
○ graduate
○ incoming
○ graduating
○ pre-college/developmental/basic skills
○ Other (please describe) : _____

4. Discipline (select one or more)
○ Arts
○ Humanities
○ Social sciences
○ Natural sciences (i.e., space, earth, life, chemistry, or physics)
○ Formal sciences (i.e., computer sciences, logic, mathematics, statistics, or systems science)
○ Professions/applied sciences
○ English composition
○ General education
○ Information literacy credit course
○ Other (please describe) : _____

5. AiA team members (select one or more)
○ assessment office
○ institutional research
○ teaching faculty
○ writing center
○ information/academic technology
○ student affairs
○ campus administrator
○ library administrator
○ other librarian
○ Other (please describe) : _____

6. Methods and tools (select one or more)
○ survey
○ interviews
○ focus group(s)
○ observation

○ pre/post test
○ rubric
○ Other (please describe) : _____

7. Direct data type (artifact) (select one or more)
   ○ student portfolio
   ○ research paper/project
   ○ class assignment (other than research paper/project)
   ○ Other (please describe)

8. Indirect data type (select one or more)
   ○ test scores
   ○ GPA
   ○ degree completion rate
   ○ retention rate
   ○ Other (please describe) : _____

9. Executive Summary
   (150 words open)
   Prompts:
   • How does the project align with your institution's priorities and needs?
   • Why did you choose the outcome and library factor as areas to examine?
   • What was the project's primary inquiry question?
   • Why was the team composition appropriate?

10. Contribution
    (150 words open)
    Prompts:
    • What are the significant contributions of your project?
    • What was learned about assessing the library's impact on student learning and success?
    • What was learned about creating or contributing to a culture of assessment on campus?
    • What, if any, are the significant findings of your project?

11. Conclusions, Implications, and Recommendations
    (150 words open)
    Prompts:
    • What will you change as a result of what you learned (e.g., institutional activities, library functions or practices, personal/professional practice, other)?
    • How does this project contribute to current, past, or future assessment activities on your campus?

12. PDF of poster (Permitted file types: pdf, doc, docx, rtf, xls, xlsx, csv, jpg, jpeg, png, gif, tif, tiff, ppt. Maximum file size is 5 megabytes.)
    (upload)

13. More information
    (150 words open)
    Prompts: Please list any articles published, presentations given, URL of project website, and team leader contact details.

DOCUMENT 3: *Reflective Report*

Directions to Team Leaders: *Please tell us about your experiences working on your project and being part of the AiA learning community. The information for this reflective section of the report remains confidential and will never be public or searchable. Karen Brown, our project analyst, will analyze this section across the entire AiA team leader group to see if there are patterns by type of institution, type of outcome examined, type of method/tool used, etc. She will synthesize and report without any identifying information. You can start the report, save, then come back and complete it later. You have **until June 23** to complete this section of the report.*

Project Experiences

1. What contributed to the success of the project?
2. What problems or delays did you encounter? How did you address or resolve these problems?
3. How has the project contributed to assessment activities on your campus?
4. Thinking about your campus assessment team, what factors contributed to a positive experience for the team members?
5. Did your campus assessment team encounter challenges during the project as a result of group dynamics, roles, assumptions, expectations, or other issues? Please explain and indicate how you or other group members addressed the challenge(s).
6. How has your campus assessment project changed administrators', faculty, and/or students' perceptions of the value of the library?
7. What have been the reactions of other library staff to your involvement in this project?
8. How will your library and institution use the results of the project?
9. How will the assessment activity created through the project be sustained on your campus?

AiA Cohort and Community of Practice Experiences

10. Describe 2–3 meaningful experiences within AiA that contributed in significant ways to your action learning project (e.g., your cohort, Moodle activities, in person meetings, other means). Why were they significant?
11. What specific competencies or insights have you gained as a result of the AiA experience?
12. What information or resources were particularly useful to you during the project?
13. How have your AiA experiences influenced your professional practice? What difference has it made to your performance? What has it enabled that would not have happened otherwise?
14. How prepared are you now to lead similar projects?
15. How have your learning and experiences contributed to and enriched the AiA community of practice?
16. If you had had an opportunity within AiA to focus more deeply on one more element, theory or concept, what would that have been?

Final Narrative Report to Institute of Museum and Library Services

PROJECT TITLE: Assessment in Action: Academic Libraries and Student Success

PARTNERS: Association for Institutional Research (AIR) and the Association of Public and Land-grant Universities (APLU)

Overview

As part of its Value of Academic Libraries Initiative, a multiyear project designed to assist academic librarians in demonstrating library value, the Association of College and Research Libraries (ACRL) began work in October 2012 on "Assessment in Action: Academic Libraries and Student Success" (AiA). A National Leadership Demonstration Grant of $249,330 from the Institute of Museum and Library Services (IMLS) funds the AiA program for three years. The AiA program builds on the outcomes of an IMLS 2011 National Leadership Collaborative Planning grant (LG-62-11-0216-11) by designing, implementing, and evaluating a professional development program to build the competencies of librarians for demonstrating library value.

Over the course of the three-year AiA program, ACRL achieved all three stated goals:

1. develop the professional competencies of librarians to assess, document, and communicate the value of their academic libraries primarily in relation to their institution's goals for student learning and success,
2. build and strengthen collaborative relationships with higher education stakeholders around the issue of library value, and
3. contribute to higher education assessment work by creating approaches, strategies, and practices that document the contribution of academic libraries to the overall goals and missions of their institutions.

Project Activities

In the grant proposal narrative, the primary activities that would meet each goal were listed as:

- Goal 1 activity: Librarians participate in professional development activities and apply the learning to a library value project on their campus.
- Goal 2 activity: Librarians will lead their institutional teams in the design and implementation of a library value project.

> To date, our project has significantly increased the library's role in assessment of General Education.... This helps establish the library as an integral part of the campus culture of assessment of student learning outcomes, rather than an auxiliary unit assessing its own objectives.
>
> – University of Idaho

- Goal 3 activity: Institutional teams led by their participating campus librarian will design, implement, and evaluate library value projects on their campus, resulting in multiple approaches, strategies, and practices for documenting the library's impact on student learning and success.

We made significant progress on each of these activities during the three-year program, as described more fully below.

Participating Teams

Over the course of the three years, we have selected 203 institutions to participate (75 in the first year, 73 in the second year, and 55 in the third year). They represented all types of institutions from 41 states, the District of Columbia, 4 Canadian provinces, and Australia. The colleges and universities are accredited by the full spectrum of regional accrediting bodies, as seen below.

TABLE 1. REGIONAL ACCREDITING AGENCIES FOR SELECTED AIA TEAMS

REGIONAL ACCREDITING AGENCY	AIA TEAMS 2013–14	AIA TEAMS 2014–15	AIA TEAMS 2015–16	TOTAL
MSCHE (Middle States Association of Colleges and Schools, Middle States Commission on Higher Education)	15	11	9	35
NEASC-CIHE (New England Association of Schools and Colleges, Commission on Institutions of Higher Education)	9	4	6	19
NCA-HLC (North Central Association of Colleges and Schools, The Higher Learning Commission)	21	30	18	69
NWCCU (Northwest Commission on Colleges and Universities)	4	6	5	15
SACS (Southern Association of Colleges and Schools, Commission on Colleges)	12	18	9	39
WASC-ACCJC (Western Association of Schools and Colleges, Accrediting Commission for Community and Junior Colleges)	3	0	0	3
WASC-ACSCU (Western Association of Schools and Colleges, Accrediting Commission for Senior Colleges and Universities)	6	3	6	15
Other (Medical, Theological, Canadian)	5	1	2	8
TOTAL	**75**	**73**	**55**	**203**

In addition to geographic diversity, the selected teams represent all types of postsecondary institutions, as shown in the following table.

TABLE 2. INSTITUTION TYPE FOR SELECTED AIA TEAMS (verified in National Center for Education Statistics Integrated Postsecondary Education Data System)

INSTITUTION TYPE	AIA TEAMS 2013–14	AIA TEAMS 2014–15	AIA TEAMS 2015–16	TOTAL
Associate Colleges	10	13	3	26
Baccalaureate Colleges	7	15	10	32
Masters Colleges and Universities	32	11	18	61
Doctoral/Research Universities	6	4	1	11
Research Universities (High/Very High Research Activity)	18	23	20	61
Special Focus Institutions—Medical, Culinary, Theological Seminary)	1	6	1	8
Tribal college	1	1	0	2
Not available	0	0	2	2
TOTAL	75	73	55	203

In the first year, one team dropped out, and in the second year five teams dropped before completing the 14-month long program, reflecting a high completion rate.

Third Year Teams

As planned, the IMLS grant covered the majority of the costs for developing the AiA program and for delivering it in the first two years. The third year of the grant marked a transition year as the grant subsidized only part of the costs. As we had described in our original grant proposal, ACRL implemented a registration fee as the program transitioned to determine if a cost-recovery model was sustainable. There was a registration fee of $1,200 for participating in the third year of the AiA program.

We updated our website in December 2014 to reflect the fee and promoted this change broadly, noting that the online application itself would be available in early January. In early January 2015, the online application was available and promoted widely by ACRL and our partners. We offered an online open forum for prospective applicants to learn more about the program on February 10, 2015. Given the low number of applicants, we decided in late February to extend the deadline three weeks from March 4 to March 25. Our grant partners, APLU and AIR promoted the opportunity to apply using their considerable communication networks both with the initial and extended deadlines. In an effort to increase applications, ACRL also announced in late February that criteria were amended so that institutions that participated previously in AiA could apply to participate a second time, or institutions applying for the first time could submit two applications for two teams and projects.

Additionally in the late February announcement, ACRL offered up to 20 scholarships to underwrite half of the $1,200 registration fee. Scholarships were awarded to institutions that demonstrated the strongest commitment to support the team's project over the course of the AiA program and the clearest connection between the team's project goals and institutional priorities.

While our grant narrative indicated we would grow the program and have 125 teams in the third year, in early April, a review panel of ACRL member leaders accepted all of the 55 qualified teams that applied. (AiA facilitators were excluded from the review process.)

Curriculum

Each group of AiA teams began in April and concluded their participation in the program the following June, for a 14 month-long experience. The AiA program used blended learning, peer-to-peer collegial relationships, and action learning projects. The librarians led their campus teams in the development and implementation of a library value project that is informed by the skill-building activities and designed to contribute to assessment activities on their campus. Participants experienced a range of activities, as seen in the syllabus for participants in the third year of the program (see Appendix A).

The AiA project design includes a sequenced set of experiences to promote and support the creation of a community of practice. The facilitators are strongly committed to establishing an environment that supports collective learning, shared competence, and sustained interaction. While in the first year, we created small cohort groups of five, we learned that size was too small to ensure sustained interaction. For the second year, we had four cohorts of 18–20 each which we believed would still be intimate enough to foster a climate of mutuality and trust, but allow for a more diverse range of interactions. We grouped the four larger cohorts around timing, asking when they planned to collect their data. In the third year, we shifted strategies again, creating six cohorts of approximately nine members.

> The most rewarding experience for me is the process of learning the different components of project planning and management. The cohort model is really effective in cultivating a sense of belonging and communities of practice as the cohort grew together intellectually.
>
> – Elise Wong, St. Mary's College of California

As described in our grant proposal, we issued a call for an additional facilitator in mid December 2013. Applicants wishing to join the design/facilitation team must have engaged with the AiA program during the first or second year in some capacity (e.g., team leader, team member, library dean/director, researcher, etc.). We had a very strong pool of applicants and, in February 2014, we announced two new facilitators: Eric Resnis, who serves in a dual appointment as Assessment Coordinator in the Center for Teaching, Learning, and University Assessment and as Organizational Effectiveness Specialist in the Libraries at Miami University in Oxford, Ohio, and John Watts, Undergraduate Learning Librarian at University of Nevada Las Vegas. Because one of our initial facilitators did not continue past her first year, we had need and funding to add a second facilitator. Both Eric and John had been AiA team leaders in the first year of the program and each brought valuable knowledge to complement the existing facilitation team.

Disseminating Project Results

The more than 200 participating AiA teams are contributing to innovation in higher education assessment by creating approaches, strategies, and practices that document the contribution of academic libraries to the overall goals and missions of their institutions.

AiA teams continue to show very promising results about which aspects of the library (e.g., collections, space, instruction, reference, etc.) have the strongest positive effect on student learning or success (e.g., retention, completion, persistence). The AiA librarian team leaders are also mastering the skills and capacity needed to assume leadership roles on campus for local data-informed and evidence-based decision making.

In January 2015, ACRL released the report "Academic Library Contributions to Student Success: Documented Practices from the Field" which synthesizes results from over 70 higher education institutions from across North America which had completed team-based assessment projects. These projects, from the first year of AiA, resulted in promising and effective approaches to demonstrating the library's value to students' academic success.

The findings from the assessment work of the first two years of AiA campus teams are impressive. By demonstrating the variety of ways that libraries contribute to student learning and success, academic librarians are establishing connections between such academic success outcomes as student retention, persistence, GPA, engagement, graduation, career preparedness, and different aspects of the library (e.g., instruction, reference, space and facilities, and collections). Many of the projects are replicable at other academic libraries or contain elements that can be adapted to a college or university's unique institutional context. Libraries can learn about ideas and strategies that promote evidence-based demonstrations of an academic library's contributions to student learning and success through the wide variety of projects.

Additionally, at the same time ACRL released a database of individual AiA team project reports, poster abstracts and images, and it includes detailed information about the projects of first and second year teams. This database, available at https://apply.ala.org/aia/public contains library value approaches, practices, and tools that can be replicated in a variety of higher education settings.

A report synthesizing the second year AiA projects and leadership of campus assessment teams will be issued in early 2016. In addition to the synthesis report and individual campus project reports and posters, there are numerous other ways that ACRL is disseminating AiA results to the broader academic library community:

AiA Librarian Team Leader Profiles: ACRL's Value of Libraries (VAL) Committee regularly profiles AiA team leaders on the VAL blog. Read reflections on challenges, greatest learning, and recommendations for others at http://www.acrl.ala.org/value/?cat=25.

Comprehensive Bibliography: Late in 2015, ACRL issued a comprehensive listing of dozens of journal articles, conference presentations and other public reports about the AiA program and campus-based projects by AiA campus team members, facilitators, and ACRL staff. See Appendix B for full bibliography, also available online at http://www.acrl.ala.org/value/?page_id=980.

Putting Assessment into Action: Selected Projects from the First Cohort of the Assessment in Action Grant: This forthcoming ACRL case book, edited by Eric Ackerman, will showcase

> Sharing the results of this project with the liaison librarians showed them how keeping accurate statistics can help us demonstrate our own role in student success, as well as helping position them as assessment partners with their assigned colleges and departments.
>
> – University of North Carolina-Charlotte

> Rockhurst's AiA project facilitated collaboration between departments and schools at the university and serves as a great example of a cross-campus assessment project.
>
> – Rockhurst University

> I must also thank you—and ALA, IMLS, ACRL—for the opportunity to participate in the AiA initiative. I have done so very much, professionally, with the results of this project, that I am now well-positioned to go up for Full Professor at my University Library. This level of productivity would not have happened without the excellent support and incentive that AiA provided to me. Thank you!
>
> – AiA team leader

27 short reflections by first year AiA team leaders on the inquiry methods they used in their assessment projects. Assembled into three groupings—Assessing Information Literacy and Library Instruction; Assessing Outreach, Services, and Spaces; and Longitudinal Assessment—the cases describe assessment methods used and the successes and/or failures of these methods along with lessons learned.

College and Research Libraries: The March 2016 special issue of ACRL's scholarly journal will proudly features a selection of 7 action research studies by AiA teams, along with an introductory essay. The aim of the special issue is to help *C&RL* readers learn more about action research as an approach to scholarship and showcase examples of fruitful action research studies undertaken by AiA teams.

Communicating Broadly

As expected, ACRL and its grant partners, AIR and APLU, have used their well-established communication channels to promote the AiA program and encourage teams to apply. In addition, ACRL member leaders and senior staff members have presented at many conferences to raise awareness about the program. Presentations and poster sessions have been offered at the following library and higher education conferences during the past year:

- 2014 Assessment Institute (Indianapolis, IN, October 2014)
- ACRL Assessment in Action Program Open Online Forum (Online, February 10, 2015)
- ALA Midwinter Meeting (Chicago, IL, February 1, 2015)
- Association for the Assessment of Learning in Higher Education Fifth Annual Assessment Conference: Actionable Assessment (Lexington, KY, June 2015)
- IMLS Focus Conference (New Orleans, LA, November 2015)
- Chicago Area Assessment Group (Chicago, IL, December 2015)

Achievement of Project Goals

In our grant proposal narrative, we described these three AiA project goals:

1. develop the professional competencies of librarians to assess, document, and communicate the value of their academic libraries primarily in relation to their institution's goals for student learning and success,
2. build and strengthen collaborative relationships with higher education stakeholders around the issue of library value, and
3. contribute to higher education assessment work by creating approaches, strategies, and practices that document the contribution of academic libraries to the overall goals and missions of their institutions.

The program has been very successful in meeting all three of these goals. A cadre of academic librarians have developed their

> My confidence level for working on assessment projects has soared as a result of participating in AiA. As part of the project, our team designed a rubric and survey. Not only did I collect feedback from colleagues at my institution, but also from AiA cohort members. I received valuable training on analyzing data, which I was able to put into practice. All of these experiences have made me feel more comfortable designing assessment metrics, which I have done since the completion of the AiA project.
>
> – Elizabeth Young Miller, Elizabethtown College

professional competencies. Campus teams strengthened their relationships as did ACRL with our higher education grant partners and others. Through AiA, librarians have made significant contributions to higher education assessment work.

Although ACRL has a long history of initiating and sponsoring innovative training, this particular approach focusing on blended, peer-to-peer learning over a 14-month period is an enhancement to our existing models. The AiA program facilitators successfully navigated a variety of challenges as librarian team leaders have resigned from their institutions and passed the reigns to new librarian team leaders. The wide variety of action learning projects not only required the program to be flexible enough to support differing student learning and success impact areas, library factors, assessment methods, and tools, but also to support differing timelines for the campus-based action learning projects.

While the AiA program yielded very positive outcomes for participating librarian team leaders, team members, libraries, and institutions, it required a sustained investment of time and energy for participants. Although the IMLS grant covered the majority of the costs for delivering the AiA program for the first two years, team leaders needed to secure travel funding for three in-person events, and this was a barrier for some potential applicants. Based on feedback from focus groups and lower than expected application numbers, we have concluded that this particular format (a cohort-based 14-month long blended program) is not sustainable on an annual basis under a cost-recovery model.

> The campus is seeking re-accreditation by the National Association of Schools of Art and Design (NASAD). During the re-accreditation visit process, the NASAD team highlighted the library's assessment project and recommended it as a model for other academic departments on campus.
>
> — Institute of American Indian Arts

The need to articulate and demonstrate library relevance and value remains of vital importance to the community, however. Responses to ACRL's 2015 membership survey reinforce this imperative. We asked members to select the top three issues facing academic and research libraries today and the number one issue was "demonstrating the relevance and value of academic libraries" with 58% followed by "declining financial support and increasing costs for academic/research libraries" at 56%.

Next Steps

Our third year team leaders are nearly halfway through the 14-month long AiA program. We are still facilitating them in their learning, supporting them in carrying out their projects and fostering growth of the community of practice. In addition, we are actively planning ways to help the community of practice flourish outside of the AiA program structure and to continue independent of AiA facilitator support. By working with team leaders from all three years in an intentional way, we will help them assume leadership for continuing their own community of practice.

ACRL remains committed to supporting academic librarians as they work to document and communicate the value and relevance of academic libraries. ACRL does not plan to offer the specific AiA cohort-based 14-month long program in 2016–17. We are considering offering it every three years and, in the interim, offering shorter, discrete development experiences such as a webcast series, a multi-week online course, and an in-person boot camp/immersive event of a few days length. AiA facilitators are actively seeking ways to rework the curriculum in a modular way to maximize its reuse.

To better inform our next steps, this fall we began seeking input beyond our own experience with AiA and what we know of the needs of the broader academic library community. We reached out to expert thinkers outside of libraries in order to clarify our own rationale about future directions. We identified higher education associations and researchers of interest and invited them to have conversations; our invitations were all received enthusiastically. We held a dozen conversations over fall and winter 2015, taking careful notes during each conversation. By analyzing these notes, we were able to discern recurrent patterns and heard the following broad themes emerge regarding key trends in higher education related to data, assessment, and research:

- **Astute use of evidence**: Significant effort within the higher education arena has been focused on collecting, analyzing, and interpreting data, but we now need to know if the yield in student learning improvements is proportional to the effort. Energy is now being directed towards better use of evidence to make improvements rather than conducting new research.
- **Leadership as advocacy**: It's essential to have leadership in using evidence to make improvements at the program director level; Higher education institutions need individuals who know how to identify and use the appropriate data in collaboration with others on campus; Think of these leaders as ambassadors and advocates.
- **Contextual nature of the educational experience:** The emphasis is now shifting to how students are achieving general learning outcomes related to critical thinking across disciplines and through experiences in and out of the classroom; How do different educational experiences correlate to learning? Many students need a rich array of learning experiences to complete degree.
- **Role of higher education in our national life**: New questions are emerging: How does higher education contribute to an individual's lifelong learning for careers and general life satisfaction? What is the role of higher education in our national life? If higher education associations can show impact of colleges and universities on the education of students broadly, then members of these associations will benefit.

The results of these conversations have stimulated our thinking about future directions as well as how to present the findings of the AiA program to a broader higher education audience. Given all we now know from AiA teams about their astute use of evidence and what it takes to lead on campus, we are preparing to disseminate AiA results to new audiences and through new channels next fall, after our third year participants complete the program in late June. We are working to articulate findings in such a way that they will resonate strongly with the broader higher education community and what matters most to colleges and institutions.

APPENDIX A: **Assessment in Action Syllabus 2015 – 2016**

Last updated 4/16/15

Dates and other details included in this syllabus may be adjusted in response to participant needs and logistics. Please refer to the Moodle newsfeed to check for additional details and any changes to dates or content

Description:

Assessment in Action (AiA) is a 14-month long curriculum of collaborative learning to support team leaders' work on assessment projects at their institutions.

Delivery:

This program is delivered in a blended format with a few face-to-face meetings and it relies heavily on webinars and discussion forums. These will be available through the Moodle site. In order to sustain your engagement online throughout the duration of AiA, you will be part of a cohort of team leaders.

This cohort is one of your communities of practice (others include your campus team and past years of AiA team leaders) and is essential to getting the most out of AiA. The work you do with members of your cohort to build, test, and apply your knowledge of assessment will result in better project outcomes. The relationships you form also have the potential to support your ongoing assessment in the years to come and can lead to collaborations on professional publications and presentations.

Outcomes:

Through participation in Assessment in Action, Team Leaders will be able to...

1. Develop professional competencies needed to document and communicate the value of the academic library in relation to an institution's goals.

2. Strengthen collaborative relationships with higher education stakeholders, including campus faculty, academic administrators, and assessment officers.

3. Contribute to higher education assessment by creating approaches, strategies, and practices that document the contribution of academic libraries.

Expectations and Recommendations:

Recommendations, including best practices for interacting on Moodle

Check Moodle at least twice a week. If you are concerned about remembering to check, ensure that you receive e-mail notifications for new content. You can double check your settings by clicking on 'Profile' in the left hand side of Moodle, under 'Administration'. Then click on the 'Edit Profile' tab in the middle of the page.

Ask those lingering questions! Remember that others may be pondering the same question, and that other team leaders may have prior experience with your questions. Use the forum to ask these questions, and be sure to offer help and guidance to fellow team leaders when you can!

Devise a way to communicate with your fellow cohort members. Past cohorts have used Moodle, as well as Google Hangouts, or simple e-mail communication.

Carve out a few hours each week to engage with the community and your campus team. Mark it on your calendar. You may not need all the hours every week, but this will ensure you do have time available during periods of very high activity.

General Expectations

Being part of the AiA learning community is a continuous year-round commitment, with approximately 2-5 hours per week anticipated.

Complete the reading and writing that is requested of you and meet the deadlines provided.

Dedicate yourself to engaging with other librarian team leaders and actively contribute to a community of practice by providing peer-to-peer collegial support.

Facilitate your campus team in completing an action learning project, and communicate program expectations with team mates as necessary.

Specific Expectations

A final project report will be submitted at the conclusion of the program.

A poster describing my team's project and our learning will be presented at ALA Annual Conference in Orlando (June, 2016).

You are expected to attend to following in-person events:

ALA Annual 2015 San Francisco: June 26, 1-5pm; June 27 8:30am-12:30 pm

ALA Midwinter 2016 Boston: January 7, 1-5pm; January 8 8:30am-12:30pm

ALA Annual 2016 Orlando: Poster Session

Elements of the Curriculum Designed to Foster a Community of Practice:

Cohorts – You will be assigned to a cohort that will be your support throughout your time in AiA. The purpose of the cohort is to provide a community that will challenge and encourage you by building in accountability for the process and progression of your assessment project.

Webinars – These are synchronous online sessions where the facilitators present content to support your assessment project progress. The webinars are scheduled throughout the year to coincide with your stages of assessment and your preparations for presenting and reporting your results. The goal of these webinars is to anticipate your learning needs and provide a foundation for your projects. You will have at least two weeks advance notice about the dates and times of all scheduled webinars. All webinars are recorded and available in Moodle.

Forums – These are online discussion threads in Moodle. Often, these forums will be your chance to share your progress with your cohort, give feedback and support, and get advice. Other forums will be open to all team leaders and will allow you to make connections across cohorts. There will be instructions posted in Moodle to guide your forum posts throughout the year. The forum assignments are designed to coincide with the stages of your assessment project. The goal is to guide your work and create a space for reflection and accountability to your cohort. Facilitators will set due dates for forum participation in order to establish clear expectations for participation and support sustained discussions within cohorts. Forum descriptions, goals, and instructions will be posted at least two weeks before scheduled due dates.

Jam Sessions – These are synchronous online sessions that are scheduled as needed. The content of the jam sessions is determined by team leaders' learning needs as they emerge throughout the year. They are focused on particular elements of assessment and communication. They are different from webinars because they are not intended to be relevant to all team leaders. Instead, they are meant to address needs that are specific to your assessment design and provide further depth on topics like rubric design or correlation. The dates and times for jam sessions will be posted in Moodle as they become available. All jam sessions are recorded and available in Moodle.

Case Connections – These are synchronous online session that are led by team leaders. The purpose of these sessions is to give team leaders a chance to share the details of their assessment projects and get advice or feedback from fellow team leaders. They capitalize on your experiences and collective expertise. Opportunities to lead case connections will be posted in Moodle and AiA facilitators will work with team leaders to schedule and plan these sessions. The dates and times for jam sessions will be posted in Moodle as they become available. All jam sessions are recorded and available in Moodle.

In-person Meetings – These are scheduled to coincide with ALA Annual 2015 and Midwinter 2016. At these sessions the facilitators present content designed to provide a foundation for your assessment projects and the presentation of your results. In addition to direct instruction, the in-person meetings include group learning activities, hands-on practice with assessment concepts, and informal discussion with your fellow team leaders. The goal of these in-person meetings is to generate commonplaces that will sustain the community of practice during periods of online-only interaction.

Poster Feedback and Peer Review – Prior to the poster presentation at ALA Annual 2016, team leaders will share their posters electronically through Moodle. The first round of feedback will come from cohort members. The second round will be structured peer review. In the peer review you will review the posters of team leaders from outside of your cohort and receive peer reviews from outside of your cohort as well. The purpose of this process is to strengthen your final reports and posters because they will be available online.

Poster Presentation – At ALA Annual 2016, you will present your poster reporting on the results of your assessment project. This poster session will be promoted to ALA attendees and will be your opportunity to share your project with the wider library community. The goal is to expand the discussion about assessment in academic libraries

Schedule:

2015

May 15 – Kick-off **Webinar**

> Description – 1-hour. Provides an overview of the AiA program including the timeline, your role as a team leader, and immediate next steps.

Goals – 1) Describe AiA plans and expectations. 2) Support team leaders' work with campus team members. 3) Answer team leaders' questions.

May – Team Leaders meet with their campus teams and draft a timeline for assessment projects.

Forums:

Team Overviews
Team Projects
Background Research
Local Information Gathering
Research Ethics/Institutional Review Board

June – Team leaders prepare for the in-person meeting at ALA by participating in cohort forums.

Forums:

Project Commonalities and Differences
Inquiry Questions

June 25-26 – **In-Person Meeting**

Description – Two half-day workshops. Facilitators will introduce the assessment cycle and project management strategies. Team leaders will draft learning outcomes and begin planning for the alignment among their outcomes, actions, and criteria.

Goals – 1) Establish connections among cohort-members and facilitators. 2) Initiate team leaders' assessment cycles. 3) Develop team leaders' project management strategies.

July & August – Team leaders prepare for assessment. Team leaders submit materials for Institutional Review Board (IRB) approval.

July – Assessment Cycle and Project Design **Webinar**

Description – 1 hr. Builds on the assessment cycle foundation you received at the in-person meeting by going in-depth and emphasizing the value of connecting your assessment project to institutional accountability efforts.

Goals – 1) Emphasize the importance of defining an inquiry question. 2) Challenge team leaders to further refine outcomes and clarify the alignment among library actions, student outcomes, and institutional goals.

Forums:

Research Ethics & IRB
Writing Outcomes, Identifying Actions, & Getting Feedback

August – Assessment Instruments and Project Design **Webinar**

Description – 1 hr. Introduces assessment instrument and method considerations including instrument types, techniques for creating instruments, and methodological concepts.

Goals – 1) Prepare team leaders to make informed decisions about their assessment methods and instruments. 2) Distinguish between direct and indirect assessment methods. 3) Weigh the strengths and weaknesses of common assessment instruments.

Forum:

Setting Criteria & Getting Feedback

September – Team leaders are drawing upon their campus team members' expertise to finalize plans for assessment.

Forums:

Checking for Alignment among Criteria, Outcomes, and Actions
Leadership

Early October – Designing with Data **Webinar**

Description – 1 hr. Emphasizes the value of using a mixture of assessment methods to collect data that gives insight into student outcomes from multiple perspectives. Also includes guest speakers from previous AiA teams to share their experiences designing mixed methods assessment projects and working with their campus teams.

Goals – 1) Encourage team leaders to consider adding one or more complementary data collection methods to their assessment designs. 2) Provide insight from successful AiA teams. 3) Inspire creativity and perseverance in team leaders' approach to their projects.

Jam Sessions and **Case Connections** will be scheduled as needed in the summer, fall, and winter.

2016

January 7-8 – **In-Person Meeting**

Description: Two half-day in-person workshops focusing on data collection, analysis, and reporting.

Goals: 1) prioritize next steps for data collection and result analysis. 2) Select an approach for sharing results with stakeholders.

April – Data Visualization **Webinar**

Description: A one-hour webinar to discuss data visualization, visualization tools, and poster best practices, and introduces the timeline for poster presentation at ALA Annual.

Goals: 1) Introduce ways to transform data into graphics 2) Discuss poster design elements 3) Introduce poster schedule and expectations

April & May – Team leaders prepare their posters.

May – Poster Creation & Reporting **Webinar**

Description: A one-hour webinar to explain best practices and requirements for developing posters for ALA Annual as well as guidelines for reporting project findings to campus stakeholders.

Goals: 1) Review best practices for data visualization and general poster design 2) Discuss options for communicating project results 3) Introduce final report and instructions for submission

May – **Feedback and Peer Review**

Description: In Moodle, Team leaders will first give feedback to and get feedback from cohort-members. Team leaders are then assigned 3 posters to review outside of their cohorts

Goal: Provide and receive constructive feedback on poster content and design.

June 22 – Deadline for Report

Description: Team leaders will submit a final report documenting projects and providing reflection on their AiA experience.

Goals 1) Contribute project descriptions to a searchable database of all AiA projects. 2) Reflect on the process and outcome of individual projects as well as the overall AiA experience.

June – **Poster Presentation at ALA Annual Conference in Orlando**

Description: Team Leaders are assigned to present at one of two poster sessions at ALA Annual.

Goals: 1) Share project results with the greater library community 2) Celebrate a job well done!

Technology Requirements:

Computer Requirements

- Reliable internet access

- The latest version of <u>Java</u>
- The latest version of <u>QuickTime</u>
- The latest version of <u>Adobe Reader</u>
- A current word processing software
- A Web-enabled video camera for optional online meetings with cohort members

Browser requirements

- Most recent versions of the following:
- Internet Explorer, Chrome or Firefox for Windows computers
- Firefox, Chrome or Safari for Apple computers

Who Do I Ask?

While you are encouraged to consult with the members of your cohort or your own cohort facilitators when you seek guidance on issues related to your projects, there are facilitators who have particular expertise in the following areas. Please feel free to contact the designated facilitator with questions regarding these topics.

Topic	Facilitator
AiA Program Participation Logistics	Kara Malenfant
Campus Team Dynamics	Carrie Donovan
Classroom Assessment Design	Eric Resnis
Correlation vs. Causation	Lisa Hinchliffe
Focus Groups	April Cunningham
Interviews	April Cunningham
Institutional Review Board (IRB)	Eric Resnis
Mixed Methods	John Watts, April Cunningham
Norming	Eric Resnis
Rubrics	Deb Gilchrist, Lisa Hinchliffe, John Watts
Student Self-Reporting	Deb Gilchrist
Survey Design	April Cunningham

Arc of the AiA Year

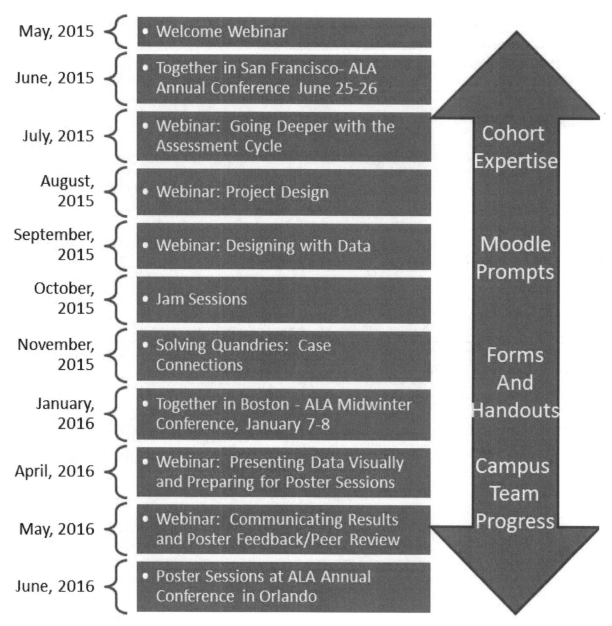

May, 2015	• Welcome Webinar
June, 2015	• Together in San Francisco- ALA Annual Conference June 25-26
July, 2015	• Webinar: Going Deeper with the Assessment Cycle
August, 2015	• Webinar: Project Design
September, 2015	• Webinar: Designing with Data
October, 2015	• Jam Sessions
November, 2015	• Solving Quandries: Case Connections
January, 2016	• Together in Boston - ALA Midwinter Conference, January 7-8
April, 2016	• Webinar: Presenting Data Visually and Preparing for Poster Sessions
May, 2016	• Webinar: Communicating Results and Poster Feedback/Peer Review
June, 2016	• Poster Sessions at ALA Annual Conference in Orlando

Cohort Expertise

Moodle Prompts

Forms And Handouts

Campus Team Progress

APPENDIX B: **Assessment in Action Bibliography**

Last updated 12/31/15
Available online at http://www.acrl.ala.org/value/?page_id=980

This bibliography aims to be comprehensive, capturing all scholarly and practice-based literature and presentations about ACRLs' program "Assessment in Action: Academic Libraries and Student Success" (AiA) and campus projects conducted as part of the AiA program by staff, facilitators, and participants.

Assessment in Action Bibliography:
Introduction
ACRL Reports
Journal Articles
Books/Book Chapters
Conference Presentations
Conference Posters

Introduction
In September 2012, ACRL was awarded a National Leadership Demonstration Grant by the Institute of Museum and Library Services (IMLS) for the program "Assessment in Action: Academic Libraries and Student Success" (AiA). Part of ACRL's Value of Academic Libraries initiative, AiA was undertaken in partnership with the Association for Institutional Research (AIR) and the Association of Public and Land-grant Universities (APLU). The grant supported the design, implementation and evaluation of a program to strengthen the competencies of librarians in campus leadership and data-informed advocacy.

Librarian-led teams carried out assessment projects over 14 months at their community colleges, colleges and universities. The projects examined the impact of the library (instruction, reference, collections, space, and more) on student learning/success. Over the course of the three-year program, teams from more than 200 institutions have participated in AiA. They represent all types of institutions from 41 states, the District of Columbia, 4 Canadian provinces and Australia.

Upon completing the 14-month program, each AiA team presented a poster at the ALA Annual Conference in June 2014, 2015 or 2016; find poster abstracts, images and full project descriptions in a searchable online collection. Additionally, the Value of Academic Libraries blog profiled selected AiA team leaders.

This bibliography aims to be comprehensive, capturing all scholarly and practice-based literature and presentations about AiA and campus projects conducted as part of the AiA program by staff, facilitators, and participants.

ACRL Reports
Association of College and Research Libraries. *Academic Library Contributions to Student Success: Documented Practices from the Field.* Prepared by Karen Brown. Contributions by Kara J. Malenfant. Chicago: Association of College and Research Libraries, 2015.
Read the full report synthesizing the first year AiA projects and executive summary to share broadly with campus stakeholders.

Second year synthesis (forthcoming, 2016)

First interim narrative report submitted to IMLS describes the first year of grant activities, 10/01/12-09/30/13 (October 2013).

Second interim narrative report submitted to IMLS describes the second year of grant activities, 10/01/13-09/30/14 (December 2014).

Final narrative report submitted to IMLS describes completion of the project (10/01/14-09/30/15 (December 2015).

Journal Articles

College & Research Libraries 77, no. 2 (2016).
Special issue of ACRL's scholarly journal on action research from the Assessment in Action program. Contents:

- Malenfant, Kara J., Lisa Janicke Hinchliffe, and Debra Gilchrist. "Assessment as Action Research: Bridging Academic Scholarship and Everyday Practice."
- Arellano Douglas, Veronica and Celia Rabinowitz. "Why Collaborate? Examining the Relationship Between Faculty-Librarian Collaboration and First Year Students' Information Literacy Abilities."
- Davidson Squibb, Sara, and Susan Mikkelsen. "Assessing the Value of Course-Embedded Information Literacy on Student Learning and Achievement."
- Goebel, Nancy and Jérôme Melançon. "Personal Librarian for Aboriginal Students: A Programmatic Assessment."
- Jones, Phil, Julia Bauder and Kevin Engel. "Mixed or Complementary Messages: Making the Most of Unexpected Assessment Results."
- Lundstrom, Kacy, Pamela Martin and Dory Cochran. "Making Strategic Decisions: Conducting and Using Research on the Impact of Sequenced Library Instruction."
- Massengale, Lisa, Pattie Piotrowski and Devin Savage. "Identifying and Articulating Library Connections to Student Success."
- Whitlock, Brandy and Nassim Ebrahimi. "Beyond the Library: Using Multiple, Mixed Measures Simultaneously in a College-Wide Assessment of Information Literacy."

Francis, Mary. "Assessing varied instructional approaches in the instruction of online graduate students."*Library & Information Research* 38, no. 119 (2014): 3-12.

Hinchliffe, Lisa Janicke. "Professional Development for Assessment: Lessons from Reflective Practice," *The Journal of Academic Librarianship* 41, no. 6 (2015): 850–852. http://dx.doi.org/10.1016/j.acalib.2015.10.004

Kiel, Stephen "Mike," Natalie Burclaff, and Catherine Johnson. "Learning by Doing: Developing a Baseline Information Literacy Assessment," *portal: Libraries and the Academy* 15, no. 4 (2015): 747-766.http://muse.jhu.edu/journals/portal_libraries_and_the_academy/v015/15.4.kiel.html

Lowe, M. Sara, Char Booth, Sean Stone, and Natalie Tagge. "Impacting Information Literacy Learning in First-Year Seminars: A Rubric-Based Evaluation," *portal: Libraries and the Academy* 15, no. 3 (2015): 489–512.https://www.press.jhu.edu/journals/portal_libraries_and_the_academy/portal_pre_print/articles/15.3lowe.pdf

McPherson, Patricia. "Paired Proficiencies: Incorporating Information Literacy into Language Instruction," *The Language Educator* 10, no. 2 (2015): 45-49.

Montgomery, Susan E. and Suzanne D. Robertshaw. "From Co-Location to Collaboration: Working Together to Improve Student Learning," *Behavioral & Social Sciences Librarian* 34, no. 2 (2015): 55-69. DOI: 10.1080/01639269.2015.1047728

Murray, Adam, Ashley Ireland, and Jana Hackathorn, "The Value of Academic Libraries: Library Services as a Predictor of Student Retention," *College & Research Libraries* 77, no.6 (2016). Preprinthttp://crl.acrl.org/content/early/2015/11/05/crl15-837.full.pdf+html

Radcliff, Sharon and Elise Y. Wong, "Evaluation of sources: a new sustainable approach," *Reference Services Review* 43, no. 2 (2015): 231-250. http://www.emeraldinsight.com/doi/pdfplus/10.1108/RSR-09-2014-0041

Young, Scott W. H., Angela Tate, Doralyn Rossmann, and Mary Anne Hansen, "The Social Media Toll Road: The Promise and Peril of Facebook Advertising," *College & Research Libraries News* 75.8 (2014): 427-434. Available at http://crln.acrl.org/content/75/8/427.full.

Whelan, Jennifer L.A., "Personal Research Sessions: A Consultation-Based Program for Research Support," *Library Connect* 13.7 (2015). http://libraryconnect.elsevier.com/articles/personal-research-sessions-consultation-based-program-research-support

Whitlock, Brandy and Julie Nanavati, "A Systematic Approach to Performative and Authentic Assessment," *Reference Services Review* 41.1 (2013): 32-48.http://www.emeraldinsight.com/doi/abs/10.1108/00907321311300866

Books/Book Chapters

Putting Assessment into Action: Selected Projects from the First Cohort of the Assessment in Action Grant Edited by Eric Ackermann. Chicago: Association of College and Research Libraries, 2016. Contents:

Part 1: Assessing Information Literacy/Library Instruction
First Year Students/First Year Experience
- Jagman, Heather. "'I felt Like Such a Freshman': Reflections on DePaul University Library's Assessment in Action Project."
- Kremer, Jacalyn. "Honor Bound: Assessing Library Interventions into the Complex Problem of Academic Integrity."
- Nye, Valerie. "Cite Me! What Sources are Students Using for Research?"
- Delevan, Kelly. "Employing Multiple Methods to Assess Information Literacy in a New Core Curriculum."
- Douglas, Veronica Arellano. "Assessing Student Learning and Faculty-Librarian Collaboration with a Mixed-Methods Approach."
- Prorak, Diane. "Assessment of Library Instruction within General Education Learning Outcomes and Academic Support Programs: Determining Impact on Student Research Skills, Confidence, and Retention."
- Allen, Maryellen. "Impact of Information Literacy Instruction on the Success of First Year Composition Students."
- Miller, Robin E. "Information Literacy Learning in First Year Composition: A Rubric-Based Approach to Assessment."
- DeBose, Kyrille Goldbeck and Carolyn Meier. "Comparing Apples and Oranges: Putting Virginia Tech's FYE Inquiry Assessment Program into Perspective."

Second to Fourth Year Undergraduates

- Mondschein, Henri. "Assessment in Action Case Study: Do Online Learning Modules Have a Role in Information Literacy Instruction?"
- Jones, Phil. "Complementary, Not Conflicting Data: Using Citation Analysis and NVivo to Explore Student Learning."
- Catalano, Amy. "Predictors of Information Literacy Competencies at a Large University: A Reflection on Testing Methods."
- Shoemaker, Jill S. "Assessing Graduating Seniors' Information Literacy Skills."
- Watts, John. "Using Single-Case Research Design to Assess Course-Embedded Research Consultations."

Graduate Students
- Francis, Mary. "Assessing Online Graduate Students."
- Crea, Kathleen. "In Their Own Words: Evolution of Effective Search Behaviors by Medical Students and Residents at the University of Connecticut Health Center."

Institutional
- Whitlock, Brandy. "Finding the Cocked Hat: Triangulating Assessment of Information Literacy as a College-Wide Core Competency."

Part 2: Assessing Outreach, Services and Spaces
Outreach
- McDevitt, Theresa. "Get by with a Little Help from Your Friends: Working with Student Affairs to Engage and Assess College Students."

Services
- Paddick, Courtney. "ARC to Success: Linking the "Commons" Model to Academic Success at Central Washington University."
- O'Kelly, M. "Library research consultants: Measuring a new service."
- Resnis, Eric. "Dedicated Technology Facilities: Impacts, Success, and Implications."
- Montgomery, Susan E. and Suzanne D. Robertshaw. "Filling in the Venn Diagram: Second Year Students, Research, Writing."
- Bedwell, Linda. "Research Assistance Linked to Student Retention."

Spaces
- Epperson, Annie. "Methodological Issues: Assessing the Impact of Using the Library on Student Success at the University of Northern Colorado."

Part 3: Longitudinal Assessment
- Ireland, Ashley. "Known Library Use and Student Retention: A Methods Case Study."
- Bradley, Alison and Stephanie Otis. "Assessment Archaeology: Digging up Old Data for Longitudinal Assessments."
- Lupton, Aaron. "Impact of Library Usage on Student Success: Exploring New Territory."

Mikkelsen, Susan and Elizabeth McMunn-Tetangco, "Think Like a Researcher: Integrating the Research Process in the Introductory Composition Curriculum," in *The New Information Literacy Instruction: Best Practices*, eds. Patrick Ragains and Sandra Wood. (New York: Roman and Littlefield, 2015): 3-26.

Conference Presentations

Alexander, David. "Telling the Library Story: Assessment Activities in an Academic Library." Presentation at the joint conference of the Wyoming Library Association and Mountain Plains Library Association, Cheyenne, WY, September 2015.

Allen, Maryellen, Sarah Bordac, Lorraine Hefferman, Jennifer Jarson, and Eric Resnis. "Sustainably Supporting Assessment Work with Communities of Practice." 2015 ACRL Conference, Portland, OR, March 2015.

Bartholomew, Jennifer. "Cultivating a Culture of Assessment Using Multiple Collaborative Assignments to Teach Information Literacy Skills." Presentation at the American Theological Library Association Annual Conference, Denver, CO, June 13, 2015.

Bishop, Katie. "Collaboration that Works: How to Build and Assess Partnerships with Student Support Services Groups." Presentation at the Nebraska C&U/Kansas CULS Joint Spring Meeting, Crete, NE, May 2015.

Blank, Michelle. "Planning the 'Ask': Effective Strategies to Use the Story that Data Tells to Shape Your Message." Presentation at OhioNET Dive into Data Conference Worthington, OH, July 2015.

Blank, Michelle. "Planning the 'Ask': Effective Strategies to Use the Story that Data Tells to Shape Your Message." Presentation at the Ohio Private Academic Libraries Annual Conference, Findlay, OH, August 2015.

Blank, Michelle and Alex Hauser. "I've a Feeling We're Not in High School Anymore: Information Literacy as a Bridge for Transitioning First-Year Students." Presentation at OhioNET Dive into Data Conference, Worthington, OH, July 2015.

Blank, Michelle and Alex Hauser. "Project redesign: Using the ACRL Framework for Information Literacy for Higher Education to bridge the CORE Curriculum." Presentation at the LOEX Fall Focus, Ypsilanti, MI, November 2015.

Bowman, Elizabeth, Liza Harrington, Thomas Hyland, Annie Keola Kaukahi Thomas, and Brandy Whitlock. "Sustaining Success: Creating Community College Assessment Methods." Presentation at the 2015 ACRL Conference, Portland, OR, March 2015.

Brown, Karen and Kara Malenfant. "Academic Library Contributions to Student Success: Documented Practices from the Field." Presentation at the Association for the Assessment of Learning in Higher EducationFifth Annual Assessment Conference: Actionable Assessment, Lexington, KY, June 1-3, 2015.

Brown, Karen and Kara Malenfant. "Assessment in Action: High Impact Practices in Academic Libraries." Presentation at the Library Assessment Conference, Seattle, WA, August 4-6, 2014.

Brown, Karen and Kara Malenfant. "Academic Libraries and Student Success: Findings and Applications from 70 Campus Teams." Presentation at the 2014 Assessment Institute, Indianapolis, IN, October 2014.

Brown, Karen, Kara Malenfant, Kristin Johnson, Elizabeth Killingsworth, and Steven Wise. "Assessment in Action: Academic Libraries and Student Success." Presentation at the Texas Library Association Conference, Houston, TX, April 2016.

Cantwell, Laureen. "Does What We Do Matter?: Intensive Ask-a-Librarian Statistics Tracking and Doubling-Down on Professional Librarian Expertise." Presentation at the Library 2.015 Conference, online, October 2015.

Cobb, Mike, Gretchen Rings, Doralyn Rossmann, and Tara Wood. "Understanding Social Media and the Library User Experience: Be Interesting, Be Interested." Presentation at the Electronic Resources & Libraries Conference, Austin, TX, March 2014.

Davis, Mary Ellen K. and Kara Malenfant. "Assessment in Action: ACRL's Newest IMLS Grant-Funded Project." Presentation at the CNI Fall Membership Meeting, Washington, DC, December 11, 2012.

Davis, Mary Ellen K. and Kara Malenfant. "Assessment in Action: Academic Libraries and Student Success." Presentation at the Library 2.013, online, October 19, 2013.

DeBose, K., C. Meier, R.K. Miller, and P. Tomlin. "Get thee to the library! Incorporating inquiry into first year programs." Presentation at the 2012 Conference on Higher Education Pedagogy, Blacksburg, VA, February 2012.

Donohue, Mary and JeanMarie Reinke. "Building Bridges: Crossing Silos to Inspire Student Success." Presentation at the Assessment Network of New York conference, Dobbs Ferry, NY, April 2015.

Douglas, Veronica Arellano. "Why collaborate? Examining the impact of faculty-librarian collaboration on students' information literacy skill development in the First Year Seminar." Presentation at the Congress of Academic Library Directors of Maryland Spring Meeting, Columbia, MD, April 23, 2015.

Epperson, Annie. "Quickly Collect Qualitative Data with a Video Booth!" 7th Qualitative and Quantitative Methods in Libraries International Conference (QQML2015), Paris, France, May 26-29, 2015.

Epperson, Annie. "True Confessions: A New Method for Gathering Qualitative Data." Colorado Council of Medical Librarians Membership Meeting, Aurora, CO, September 11, 2015.

Epperson, Annie, James Henderson, and Evan Welch. "Designed and Furnished for Success: Fostering an 'Academically Social' Campus Space!" 2015 University of Northern Colorado Assessment Fair, Greeley, CO, March 31, 2015.

Francis, Mary. "Assessing Student Learning: Lessons Learned from the ACRL 'Assessment in Action: Academic Libraries and Student Success' Program." Presentation at the South Dakota Library Association Annual Conference, Pierre, SD, October 2014.

Garwood, K., K. Nicholson, M. Parlette-Stewart, and T. Tucker. "Evaluating the Effectiveness of Face-to-Face, Online, and Blended Learning Approaches in Teaching Research and Referencing Strategies to First-Year Students." Presentation at the Canadian Writing Centres Conference, St. Catharines, ON, May 2014.

Gersch, Beate and Joe Salem. "Who's Afraid of … Assessment?" Presentation/Workshop at the Institute of Teaching and Learning, Akron, OH, February 16, 2015.

Goebel, Nancy. "Considerations for Implementing a Personal Librarian Program." Presentation at the Texas Library Association, Austin, TX, April 2015.

Goebel, Nancy. "Personal Librarian for Aboriginal Students." Presentation at the Council of Pacific and Prairie University Libraries meeting, Edmonton, AB, September 2014.

Gregory, Lua, Shana Higgins, Sara Lowe, Robin Miller, and Danielle Theiss. "We've Only Just Begun: Determining the Value of Information Literacy Instruction in the First Year." Panel presentation at the 2015 ACRL Conference, Portland, OR, March 27, 2015.

Gregory, Lua and Shana Higgins. "Information Literacy and First-year Students: What Do They Know, What Do They Learn, and What Do We Learn?" Presentation at the European Conference on Information Literacy, Dubrovnik, Croatia, October 21, 2014.

Grimwood, Karen, Sofi King, and Paula Perez. "Assessment in Action: Academic Libraries and Student Success at NCCU." Presentation at the 6th Annual Technology Institute for Educators, Raleigh, NC, April 2014.

Harrington, Liza and Amanda Hyde. "Collaborating to Assess Science Information Literacy: An Assessment in Action Project." Presentation at the Massachusetts Community College Teaching, Learning, and Student Development Conference, Fall River, MA, April 10, 2015.

Hauser, Alex. "Research Consultations: Creating Personalized, One-on-one, Library Instruction." Presentation at the Ohio Private Academic Libraries Annual Conference, Findlay, OH, August 2015.

Higgins, Shana. "Panel on Assessing Core Competencies in General Education." Presentation at the WASC Academic Resource Conference, Los Angeles, CA, April 23-25, 2014.

Hinchliffe, Lisa and Kara Malenfant. "Assessment in Action: Academic Libraries and Student Success." Presentation at the Southeastern Library Assessment Conference, Atlanta, GA, October 21-22, 2013.

Hinchliffe, Lisa and Kara Malenfant. "The Endless Possibilities for Professional Development for Continuous Improvement and Demonstrating Library Value: a Case Report of an Initial Project." Presentation at the 7th International Evidence Based Library and Information Practice Conference, Saskatoon, SK, July 15-18, 2013.

Hinchliffe, Lisa, Sarah Horowitz, Amy Glass, Heather Jagman, and Mary Thill. "CARLI Libraries Assessing Library Impact: Engaging a National Initiative." Presentation at the CARLI Annual Meeting, Champaign, IL, November 2013.

Hyland, Thomas. "One Shot at Success? Assessing the Effectiveness of Single Session Instruction on Student Attainment of Information Literacy Skills." Presentation at the 2015 Academic Library Association of Ohio Annual Conference, Lewis Center, Ohio, November 20, 2015.

Johnson, Catherine, Stephen Kiel, and Natalie Burclaff. "Measuring Students' Information Literacy Skills: An Assessment Strategy." Presentation at the Maryland Library Association/Delaware Library Association Joint Library Conference, Ocean City, MD, May 2014.

Killingsworth, E. and H. Gardner. "Curriculum Mapping to Support Information Literacy Instruction." Presentation at the Cross Timbers Library Collaborative Conference, Commerce, TX, August 2015.

Kopecky, Linda, Robin Miller, Eau Claire, and Mitchell Scott. "Assessment in Action Initiative: The Wisconsin Connection." Presentation at the Council of University of Wisconsin Libraries (CUWL) Summer Conference, Madison, WI, June 2014.

Lockaby, D. C., S. L. Hazel, B. M. Usher, and P. West. "Embedded library instruction in undergraduate research classes: Assessing the impact." Presentation at the CUR Conference, Washington, DC, 2014.

Lowe, Sarah, Lua Gregory, Shana Higgins, and April Cunningham. "Information Literacy and Student Success: Assessing a Core Competency." Presentation at the Western

Association of Schools & Colleges (WASC) Academic Resource Conference, Los Angeles, CA, April 2014.

Malenfant, Kara. "Assessment in Action: Academic Libraries and Student Success." Presentation at the Association for the Assessment of Learning in Higher Education Third Annual Assessment Conference, Lexington, KY, June 3-5, 2013.

Martinez, Josie U. "Embedding Information Literacy in Multi-Section Composition Courses to Improve First Year Student Success." Presentation at the Georgia International Conference on Information Literacy, Savannah, GA, October 2014.

Martinez, Josie U. "Information Literacy and the First Year Experience: A case-study of the embedded librarian." Presentation at the NMLA Annual Conference, Albuquerque, NM, April 2013.

Massengale, L., S. Bluemie, A. Glass, and H. Jagman. "Success! Assessment in Action and its Impact on Four Academic Libraries." Presentation at the Illinois Library Association Conference, Peoria, IL, October 2015.

Meier, C. "Assessing Inquiry in Virginia Tech's First Year Experience Program." Presentation at the First Year Experience & Personal Librarian Conference, Cleveland, OH, April 2014.

Meier, C. and P. Tomlin. "Fostering Innovation, Expanding Librarian Roles: The Challenges and Opportunities of First Year Experience Programs." Roundtable discussion at the ACRL 2013 Conference, Indianapolis, IN, April 2013.

Mikkelsen, Susan and Heather Devrick. "Think Like a Researcher!: A Library/Faculty Collaboration to Improve Student Success." Presentation at the LOEX Conference, Denver, CO, May 2015.

Mikkelsen, Susan and Matt Moberly. "TRAIL: Teaching Research and Information Literacy." Presentation at the Assessment as Research Symposium, Merced, CA, March 2015.

Miles, Linda. "Investigating Student-Staff Interactions." Presentation at the New York Metropolitan Area Library Council (METRO) Reference Special Interest Group, November 2014.

Miller, Rebecca K., Kiri Goldbeck Debose, and Margaret Merrill. "Stewarding our first year students into the information ecosystem." Presentation at the 14th USAIN Biennial Conference, Burlington, VT, May 2014.

Mondschein, Henri. "Do Online Learning Modules Have a Role in Information Literacy Instruction?" Presentation at the Western Association of Schools & Colleges (WASC) Academic Resource Conference, Los Angeles, CA, April 2013.

Montgomery, Susan and Suzanne Robertshaw. "Finding and filling the gaps: Assessment for new neighbors in the library." Presentation at the International Writing Centers Association & National Conference on Peer Tutoring in Writing, Orlando, FL, October 31, 2014.

Parlette- Stewart, M., K. Nicholson, K. Garwood, and T. Tucker. "Evaluating the Impact of Face-to-Face and Online Information Literacy and Writing Skills Instruction Using a Mixed Methods Research Design." Presentation at the WILU 2014 Conference, London, ON, May 2014.

Philips, Margaret. "Tales from an AiA Project: Demonstrating the Value of Faculty Collaboration and Library Instruction on Student Learning and Confidence." Presentation at the Northwoods Library Symposium, Marquette, MI, August 13, 2014.

Phillips, Margaret and Rebecca Miller. "Assessment in Action – Tales from Two AiA Projects." Presentation at the ACRL STS-IL Chat, online, February 2014.

Radcliff, S. and E. Wong. "Evaluation of sources: a new sustainable approach using argument analysis and critical thinking." Presentation at the Library Instruction West 2014 Conference, Portland, OR, July 2014.

Radcliff, S. and E. Wong. "Assessing Argument, Critical Thinking and Information Literacy Learning Outcomes." Presentation at the Library Assessment Conference, Seattle, WA, August 2014.

Resnis, Eric and Jennifer Natale. "Using Visual Literacy to Demonstrate the Impact of Technological Space." Presentation at the Academic Library Association of Ohio Assessment Interest Group Spring Workshop, Columbus, OH, April 2015.

Rolls, L. and D. Sachs. "I Want You to Want Me! Demonstrating Value by Integrating Information Literacy into the Curriculum." Presentation at the Michigan Library Association Academic Libraries Conference, East Lansing, MI, May 29, 2014.

Rossmann, Doralyn and Scott Young. "Online Community Building in an Academic Context: A University Library Case Study." Presentation at the Social Media & Society Conference, Halifax, Nova Scotia, September 2013.

Sachs, Diana. "Integrating Information Literacy in the Health Sciences Curriculum: Successful Library/Faculty Collaboration." Presentation at the European Conference on Information Literacy, Dubrovnik, Croatia, October 2014.

Selberg-Eaton, R., C. Wood, R.K. Miller, and C. McConnell. "Six departments, two hundred students and six learning outcomes in one credit first year seminar." Presentation at the Annual Conferencing of the International Society for Exploring Teaching and Learning, Orlando, FL, October 2013.

Shanley, Caitlin. "Building Capacity, Measuring Success: Assessment in Action at Temple University Libraries." Lightning Talk presentation at the Philadelphia Library Assessment Discussion Group, Philadelphia, PA, April 2015.

Smith, Tyler Scott. "Steering Student Workers into Success." Presentation at the CUWL Annual Conference, Madison, WI, June 2014.

Statkus, Daryl and Pamela Graham. "Improving Student Learning Outcomes Through Embedded Information Literacy Instruction." Presentation at the NERCOMP workshop, Providence, RI, March 2014.

Steward-Mailhiot, A., M. O'Kelly, and D. Theiss. "Assessment in Action: A Journey Through Campus Collaboration, a Learning Community and Research Design." Presentation at the ARL Library Assessment Conference, Seattle, WA, August 2014.

Sweeper, Darren. "The ACRL Assessment in Action Project: the Montclair State University Experience." Presentation at the Virtual Academic Library Environment (VALE) Assessment Fair, New Brunswick, NJ, July 2014.

Sweeper, Darren. "Finding the Right Public Health Data: f(Librarians + Students) = Success." Presentation at the Virtual Academic Library Environment (VALE) Assessment Fair, New Brunswick, NJ, July 2014.

Tagge, Natalie. "More = Better: A Rubric-Based Evaluation of Librarian Course Collaborations at the First Year." Presentation at Library Instruction West, Portland, OR, July 2014.

Tate, Angela, Doralyn Rossmann, Mary Anne Hansen, and Scott Young. "Social Media with a Strategy: Connecting with Library Users." Presentation at the LITA Preconference Workshop at the ALA Midwinter Meeting, Philadelphia, PA, January 2014.

Tharp, Julie and Kate Frost. "The Power of Partnerships: Assessing the Impact of Information Literacy on Student Success." Presentation at the GWLA Student Learning Outcomes Conference, Las Vegas, NV, November 2013.

Theiss, Danielle, Mary O'Kelly, Amy Stewart-Mailhiot, and Leo Lo. "Assessment in Action: A Journey through Campus Collaboration, a Learning Community and Research Design." Presentation at the 2014 Library Assessment Conference, Seattle, WA, August 2014.

Thomas, Annie. "Assessment in Action: a Community of Practice." Presentation at the Hawai'i Library Association Annual Conference, Honolulu, HI, December 2014.

Watts, John. "Assessing Library Research Consultations: A Mixed-Method Approach." Lighting Talk presentation at the Library Assessment Conference 2014, Seattle, WA, August 2014.

Whitlock, Brandy and Julie Nanavati. "Coming Face-to-Face with the Future of IL Assessment: Why and How to Use Authentic and Performative Measures to Assess Student Learning." Presentation at the IFLA Information Literacy Satellite Meeting, Limerick, Ireland, August 2014.

Whitlock, Brandy. "Measuring Information Literacy Skills of Transferring Students." Presentation at the Join Fall Program of ACRL MD and MILEX, Columbia, MD, November 2015.

Young, Brian. "Assessing Faculty Perceptions and Use of Open Education Resources (OERs)." Presentation at the 2015 ACRL Conference, Portland, Oregon, March 2015.

Young, Scott and Doralyn Rossmann. "Transforming Community with a Strategic Social Media Program." Presentation at the CNI Spring meeting, St. Louis, MO, April 2014.

Conference Posters

Upon completing the 14-month program, each AiA team presented a poster at the ALA Annual Conference in June 2014, 2015 or 2016; find poster abstracts, images and full project descriptions in a searchable online collection. In addition many team members presented posters at other conferences, listed below.

Bird, Kenton, Diane Prorak, and Rodney Frey. "Assessment of General Education and Information Literacy Learning Outcomes at the University of Idaho." Poster presentation at AAC&U Network for Academic Renewal Conference, New Orleans, LA, February 2016.

Charles, L.H. and J. Wiley. "R U up for the challenge? A Partnership to Measure Library Impact on Student Learning: Rutgers University Libraries and the Ronald E. McNair Post Baccalaureate Degree Achievement Program." Poster presentation at the Virtual Academic Library Environment (VALE) Assessment Fair, Piscataway, NJ, July 2015.

Crea, Kathleen and Brian Benson. "In Their Own Words: Surveying UConn Students About Developing Effective Search Behaviors and Use of Clinical Information – including mobile apps – During Medical School." Poster presentation at Northeast Group on Educational Affairs (NEGEA) Conference, Worcester, MA, April 17, 2015.

Chu, Frances, Rudy R. Barreras, and Elizabeth Hoppe. "Librarians Collaborating with Faculty to Develop and Deliver an Evidence-Based Eye Care Course." Poster presentation at the Medical Library Group of Southern California and Arizona conference, 2012.

Chu, Frances, Rudy R. Barreras, and Elizabeth Hoppe. "Librarians Collaborating with Faculty to Develop and Deliver an Evidence-Based Eye Care Course." Poster presentation at the California Academic & Research Libraries conference, 2012.

Chu, Frances, Rudy R. Barreras, and Elizabeth Hoppe. "Librarians Collaborating with Faculty to Develop and Deliver an Evidence-Based Eye Care Course." Poster presentation at the Medical Library Association conference, 2013.

Dempsey, Paula R. and Heather Jagman. "'I Felt Like Such a Freshman': Integrating First-Year Student Identities Through Collaborative Reflective Learning." Poster presentation at the Library Research Seminar VI: The Engaged Librarian: Libraries Partnering with Campus and Community, University of Illinois at Urbana-Champaign, Urbana, IL. October 2014.

Epperson, Annie and Valerie Nye. "Diverse Roles of the Library in Student Success." Poster presentation at the Colorado Academic Library Association Summit, online, June 2014.

Gregory, Lua and Shana Higgins. "Assessment in Action: Information Literacy in the First-Year Seminar." Poster session at the Annual Conference on the First-Year Experience, San Diego, CA, February 15-18, 2014.

Hinchliffe, Lisa and Kara Malenfant. "Assessment in Action: Academic Libraries and Student Success." Poster presentation at the 2013 Assessment Institute, Indianapolis, IN, October 27-29, 2013.

Hinchliffe, Lisa and Kara Malenfant. "Assessment in Action: Inquiry and Discovery Connecting Libraries and Students." Poster presentation at the Professional and Organizational Development Network in Higher Education Conference, Pittsburgh, PA, November 6-10, 2013.

Jarson, Jennifer. "Information Literacy and Student Learning at a Liberal Arts College: An Assessment in Action Project." Poster presentation at the CUNY Assessment Conference, New York, NY, June 2014.

Knox, Joshua, Tara Baillargeon, Martha Jerme, and Sharron Ronco. "Flipped Learning and Evidence Based Medicine Skills." Poster presentation at the Physician Assistant Education Association (PAEA) Education Forum, Washington, DC, November 13, 2015.

Lowe, Sara and Sean Stone. "Librarian Impact on First-Year Students' Information Literacy Skills across Multiple Liberal Arts Colleges." Poster presentation at the CUNY Assessment Conference, New York, NY, June 2014.

Lowe, Sara, Char Booth, Sean Stone, and Natalie Tagge. "Librarians Matter! Librarian Impact on First-Year Student Information Literacy Skills at Five Liberal Arts Colleges." Poster presentation at the 2014 Library Assessment Conference, Seattle, WA, August 4-6, 2014.

Mix, Vickie L. "Collaboration in Learning: Partnering Academic Support Services for ESL Student Information Literacy." Poster presentation at the South Dakota Library Association Conference, Rapid City, SD, September 24, 2015.

Nye, Valerie. "Cite Me!" Poster presentation at the Tribal College Library Institute, Bozeman, MT, June 2, 2014.

Resnis, Eric. "Assessing Technological Self-Efficacy to Support Student Learning." Poster presentation at the Lilly International Conference on College Teaching, Oxford, OH, November 2014.

Resnis, Eric, Jennifer Natale, and Laura Birkenhauer. "Visual Literacy Assessment: Engaging Students to Improve Success." Poster presentation at the Academic Library Association of Ohio Annual Conference, Sandusky, OH, October 2014.

Stinson, Willette F. "On the Journey: Leveraging Information Literacy Instruction to Impact First-Year College Student Success." Poster presentation at the Christian Women United Conference, Charleston, WV, November 6, 2015.

Assessment in Action Syllabus 2015–2016

Last updated 4/16/15

Dates and other details included in this syllabus may be adjusted in response to participant needs and logistics. Please refer to the Moodle newsfeed to check for additional details and any changes to dates or content.

Description

Assessment in Action (AiA) is a 14-month long curriculum of collaborative learning to support team leaders' work on assessment projects at their institutions.

Delivery

This program is delivered in a blended format with a few face-to-face meetings and it relies heavily on webinars and discussion forums. These will be available through the Moodle site. In order to sustain your engagement online throughout the duration of AiA, you will be part of a cohort of team leaders.

This cohort is one of your communities of practice (others include your campus team and past years of AiA team leaders) and is essential to getting the most out of AiA. The work you do with members of your cohort to build, test, and apply your knowledge of assessment will result in better project outcomes. The relationships you form also have the potential to support your ongoing assessment in the years to come and can lead to collaborations on professional publications and presentations.

Outcomes

Through participation in Assessment in Action, Team Leaders will be able to…
1. Develop professional competencies needed to document and communicate the value of the academic library in relation to an institution's goals.
2. Strengthen collaborative relationships with higher education stakeholders, including campus faculty, academic administrators, and assessment officers.
3. Contribute to higher education assessment by creating approaches, strategies, and practices that document the contribution of academic libraries.

Expectations and Recommendations:
Recommendations, including best practices for interacting on Moodle

Check Moodle at least twice a week. If you are concerned about remembering to check, ensure that you receive e-mail notifications for new content. You can double check your settings by clicking on 'Profile' in the left hand side of Moodle, under 'Administration'. Then click on the 'Edit Profile' tab in the middle of the page.

Ask those lingering questions! Remember that others may be pondering the same question, and that other team leaders may have prior experience with your questions. Use the forum to ask these questions, and be sure to offer help and guidance to fellow team leaders when you can!

Devise a way to communicate with your fellow cohort members. Past cohorts have used Moodle, as well as Google Hangouts, or simple e-mail communication.

Carve out a few hours each week to engage with the community and your campus team. Mark it on your calendar. You may not need all the hours every week, but this will ensure you do have time available during periods of very high activity.

General Expectations

Being part of the AiA learning community is a continuous year-round commitment, with approximately 2–5 hours per week anticipated.

Complete the reading and writing that is requested of you and meet the deadlines provided.

Dedicate yourself to engaging with other librarian team leaders and actively contribute to a community of practice by providing peer-to-peer collegial support.

Facilitate your campus team in completing an action learning project, and communicate program expectations with team mates as necessary.

Specific Expectations

A final project report will be submitted at the conclusion of the program.

A poster describing my team's project and our learning will be presented at ALA Annual Conference in Orlando (June, 2016).

You are expected to attend to following in-person events:
    ALA Annual 2015 San Francisco: June 26, 1–5pm; June 27 8:30 am–12:30 pm
    ALA Midwinter 2016 Boston: January 7, 1–5pm; January 8 8:30 am–12:30 pm
    ALA Annual 2016 Orlando: Poster Session

Elements of the Curriculum Designed to Foster a Community of Practice:

Cohorts—You will be assigned to a cohort that will be your support throughout your time in AiA. The purpose of the cohort is to provide a community that will challenge and encourage you by building in accountability for the process and progression of your assessment project.

Webinars—These are synchronous online sessions where the facilitators present content to support your assessment project progress. The webinars are scheduled throughout the year to coincide with your stages of assessment and your preparations for presenting and reporting your results. The goal of these webinars is to anticipate your learning needs and provide a foundation for your projects. You will have at least two weeks advance notice about the dates and times of all scheduled webinars. All webinars are recorded and available in Moodle.

Forums—These are online discussion threads in Moodle. Often, these forums will be your chance to share your progress with your cohort, give feedback and support, and get advice. Other forums will be open to all team leaders and will allow you to make connections across cohorts. There will be instructions posted in Moodle to guide your forum posts throughout the year. The forum assignments are designed to coincide with the stages of your assessment project. The goal is to guide your work and create a space for reflection and accountability to your cohort. Facilitators will set due dates for forum participation in order to establish clear expectations for participation and support sustained discussions within cohorts. Forum descriptions, goals, and instructions will be posted at least two weeks before scheduled due dates.

Jam Sessions—These are synchronous online sessions that are scheduled as needed. The content of the jam sessions is determined by team leaders' learning needs as they emerge throughout the year. They are focused on particular elements of assessment and communication. They are different from webinars because they are not intended to be relevant to all team leaders. Instead, they are meant to address needs that are specific to your assessment design and provide further depth on topics like rubric design or correlation. The dates and times for jam sessions will be posted in Moodle as they become available. All jam sessions are recorded and available in Moodle.

Case Connections—These are synchronous online session that are led by team leaders. The purpose of these sessions is to give team leaders a chance to share the details of their assessment projects and get advice or feedback from fellow team leaders. They capitalize on your experiences and collective expertise. Opportunities to lead case connections will be posted in Moodle and AiA facilitators will work with team leaders to schedule and plan these sessions. The dates and times for jam sessions will be posted in Moodle as they become available. All jam sessions are recorded and available in Moodle.

In-person Meetings—These are scheduled to coincide with ALA Annual 2015 and Midwinter 2016. At these sessions the facilitators present content designed to provide a foundation for your assessment projects and the presentation of your results. In addition to direct instruction, the in-person meetings include group learning activities, hands-on practice with assessment concepts, and informal discussion with your fellow team leaders. The goal of these in-person meetings is to generate commonplaces that will sustain the community of practice during periods of online-only interaction.

Poster Feedback and Peer Review—Prior to the poster presentation at ALA Annual 2016, team leaders will share their posters electronically through Moodle. The first round of feedback will come from cohort members. The second round will be structured peer review. In the peer review you will review the posters of team leaders from outside of your cohort and receive peer reviews from outside of your cohort as well. The purpose of this process is to strengthen your final reports and posters because they will be available online.

Poster Presentation—At ALA Annual 2016, you will present your poster reporting on the results of your assessment project. This poster session will be promoted to ALA attendees and will be your opportunity to share your project with the wider library community. The goal is to expand the discussion about assessment in academic libraries

Schedule
2015

May 15—Kick-off **Webinar**

> Description—1-hour. Provides an overview of the AiA program including the timeline, your role as a team leader, and immediate next steps.

> Goals—1) Describe AiA plans and expectations. 2) Support team leaders' work with campus team members. 3) Answer team leaders' questions.

May—Team Leaders meet with their campus teams and draft a timeline for assessment projects.

Forums:

Team Overviews
Team Projects
Background Research
Local Information Gathering
Research Ethics/Institutional Review Board

June—Team leaders prepare for the in-person meeting at ALA by participating in cohort forums.

Forums:

Project Commonalities and Differences
Inquiry Questions

June 25–26—In-Person Meeting

Description—Two half-day workshops. Facilitators will introduce the assessment cycle and project management strategies. Team leaders will draft learning outcomes and begin planning for the alignment among their outcomes, actions, and criteria.

Goals—1) Establish connections among cohort-members and facilitators. 2) Initiate team leaders' assessment cycles. 3) Develop team leaders' project management strategies.

July & August—Team leaders prepare for assessment. Team leaders submit materials for Institutional Review Board (IRB) approval.

July—Assessment Cycle and Project Design **Webinar**

Description—1 hr. Builds on the assessment cycle foundation you received at the in-person meeting by going in-depth and emphasizing the value of connecting your assessment project to institutional accountability efforts.

Goals—1) Emphasize the importance of defining an inquiry question. 2) Challenge team leaders to further refine outcomes and clarify the alignment among library actions, student outcomes, and institutional goals.

Forums:

Research Ethics & IRB
Writing Outcomes, Identifying Actions, & Getting Feedback

August—Assessment Instruments and Project Design **Webinar**

Description—1 hr. Introduces assessment instrument and method considerations including instrument types, techniques for creating instruments, and methodological concepts.

Goals—1) Prepare team leaders to make informed decisions about their assessment methods and instruments. 2) Distinguish between direct and indirect assessment methods. 3) Weigh the strengths and weaknesses of common assessment instruments.

Forum:

Setting Criteria & Getting Feedback

September—Team leaders are drawing upon their campus team members' expertise to finalize plans for assessment.

Forums:

Checking for Alignment among Criteria, Outcomes, and Actions
Leadership

Early October—Designing with Data **Webinar**

Description—1 hr. Emphasizes the value of using a mixture of assessment methods to collect data that gives insight into student outcomes from multiple perspectives. Also includes guest speakers from previous AiA teams to share their experiences designing mixed methods assessment projects and working with their campus teams.

Goals—1) Encourage team leaders to consider adding one or more complementary data collection methods to their assessment designs. 2) Provide insight from successful AiA teams. 3) Inspire creativity and perseverance in team leaders' approach to their projects.

Jam Sessions and **Case Connections** will be scheduled as needed in the summer, fall, and winter.

2016

January 7–8—**In-Person Meeting**

Description: Two half-day in-person workshops focusing on data collection, analysis, and reporting.

Goals: 1) prioritize next steps for data collection and result analysis. 2) Select an approach for sharing results with stakeholders.

April—Data Visualization **Webinar**

Description: A one-hour webinar to discuss data visualization, visualization tools, and poster best practices, and introduces the timeline for poster presentation at ALA Annual.

Goals: 1) Introduce ways to transform data into graphics 2) Discuss poster design elements 3) Introduce poster schedule and expectations

April & May—Team leaders prepare their posters.

May—Poster Creation & Reporting **Webinar**

Description: A one-hour webinar to explain best practices and requirements for developing posters for ALA Annual as well as guidelines for reporting project findings to campus stakeholders.

Goals: 1) Review best practices for data visualization and general poster design 2) Discuss options for communicating project results 3) Introduce final report and instructions for submission

May—**Feedback and Peer Review**
Description: In Moodle, Team leaders will first give feedback to and get feedback from cohort-members. Team leaders are then assigned 3 posters to review outside of their cohorts

Goal: Provide and receive constructive feedback on poster content and design.

June 22—Deadline for Report

Description: Team leaders will submit a final report documenting projects and providing reflection on their AiA experience.

Goals 1) Contribute project descriptions to a searchable database of all AiA projects. 2) Reflect on the process and outcome of individual projects as well as the overall AiA experience.

June—**Poster Presentation at ALA Annual Conference in Orlando**

Description: Team Leaders are assigned to present at one of two poster sessions at ALA Annual.

Goals: 1) Share project results with the greater library community 2) Celebrate a job well done!

Technology Requirements:

Computer Requirements
- Reliable internet access
- The latest version of Java
- The latest version of QuickTime
- The latest version of Adobe Reader
- A current word processing software
- A Web-enabled video camera for optional online meetings with cohort members

Browser requirements
- Most recent versions of the following:
- Internet Explorer, Chrome or Firefox for Windows computers
- Firefox, Chrome or Safari for Apple computers

Who Do I Ask?

While you are encouraged to consult with the members of your cohort or your own cohort facilitators when you seek guidance on issues related to your projects, there are facilitators who have particular expertise in the following areas. Please feel free to contact the designated facilitator with questions regarding these topics.

TOPIC	FACILITATOR
AiA Program Participation Logistics	Kara Malenfant
Campus Team Dynamics	Carrie Donovan
Classroom Assessment Design	Eric Resnis
Correlation vs. Causation	Lisa Hinchliffe
Focus Groups	April Cunningham
Interviews	April Cunningham
Institutional Review Board (IRB)	Eric Resnis
Mixed Methods	John Watts, April Cunningham
Norming	Eric Resnis
Rubrics	Deb Gilchrist, Lisa Hinchliffe, John Watts
Student Self-Reporting	Deb Gilchrist
Survey Design	April Cunningham

Arc of the AiA Year

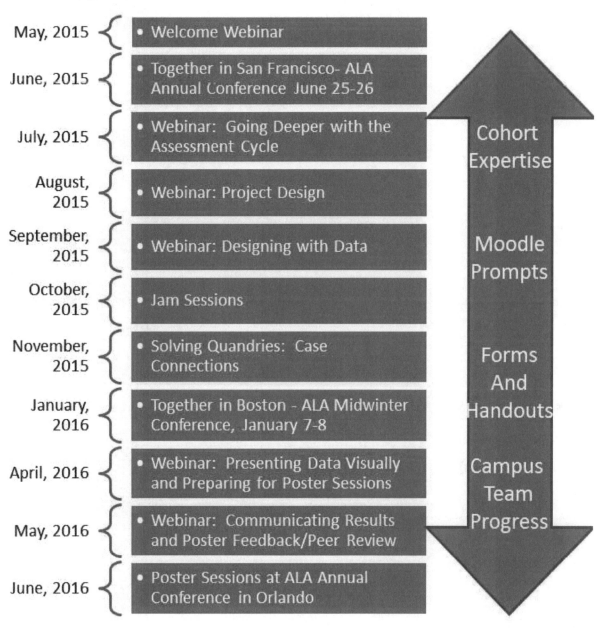

May, 2015 — • Welcome Webinar

June, 2015 — • Together in San Francisco- ALA Annual Conference June 25-26

July, 2015 — • Webinar: Going Deeper with the Assessment Cycle

August, 2015 — • Webinar: Project Design

September, 2015 — • Webinar: Designing with Data

October, 2015 — • Jam Sessions

November, 2015 — • Solving Quandries: Case Connections

January, 2016 — • Together in Boston - ALA Midwinter Conference, January 7-8

April, 2016 — • Webinar: Presenting Data Visually and Preparing for Poster Sessions

May, 2016 — • Webinar: Communicating Results and Poster Feedback/Peer Review

June, 2016 — • Poster Sessions at ALA Annual Conference in Orlando

Cohort Expertise

Moodle Prompts

Forms And Handouts

Campus Team Progress

Assessment in Action Team Report Index by Regional Accrediting Agency

A SEARCHABLE ONLINE COLLECTION of all three years of individual Assessment in Action (AiA) team project reports, poster abstracts, and images is freely available at https://apply.ala.org/aia/public. AiA team projects can be sorted by a number of options, including institution type, geographic location, expenditures, and more.

AiA participating institutions are sorted below by accreditation body as an example of how librarians might engage with the online collection. Institutions that are soon facing accreditation review may find it valuable to see how similar institutions demonstrated library value and student success.

Commission on Osteopathic College Accreditation (COCA)
- Edward Via College of Osteopathic Medicine, Virginia, Medical School and Medical Center

Middle States Commission on Higher Education (MSCHE)
- Anne Arundel Community College, Maryland, Associate's College
- Arcadia University, Pennsylvania, Master's College and University
- Bucks County Community College, Pennsylvania, Associate's College
- CUNY Borough of Manhattan Community College, New York, Associate's College
- CUNY Hunter College, New York, Master's College and University
- DeSales University, Pennsylvania, Master's College and University
- Drexel University, Pennsylvania, Research University
- Elizabethtown College, Pennsylvania, Baccalaureate College
- Fulton-Montgomery Community College, New York, Associate's College
- Georgetown University, Washington, DC, Research University
- Gettysburg College, Pennsylvania, Baccalaureate College
- Hofstra University, New York, Doctoral/Research University
- Howard University, Washington, DC, Research University
- Indiana University of Pennsylvania, Pennsylvania, Doctoral/Research University
- Kutztown University of Pennsylvania, Pennsylvania, Master's College and University
- Le Moyne College, New York, Master's College and University
- McDaniel College, Maryland, Baccalaureate College
- Medaille College, New York, Master's College and University
- Mercy College, New York, Master's College and University
- Montclair State University, New Jersey, Master's College and University

- Muhlenberg College, Pennsylvania, Baccalaureate College
- Point Park University, Pennsylvania, Master's College and University
- Rutgers University-New Brunswick, New Jersey, Research University

St. Mary's College of Maryland, Maryland, Baccalaureate College
SUNY College at Brockport, New York, Master's College and University
Swarthmore College, Pennsylvania, Baccalaureate College
Temple University, Pennsylvania, Research University
The State University of New York at Fredonia, New York, Master's College and University
Towson University, Maryland, Master's College and University
University of Baltimore, Maryland, Master's College and University
University of Maryland-University College, Maryland, Master's College and University
University of Pittsburgh-Greensburg, Pennsylvania, Baccalaureate College
University of Pittsburgh-Pittsburgh Campus, Pennsylvania, Research University
Yeshiva University, New York, Research University

North Central Region-Higher Learning Commission (NCA-HLC)

- A.T. Still University of Health Sciences, Arizona, Special Focus Institution
- Alverno College, Wisconsin, Master's College and University
- Arizona State University, Arizona, Research University
- Arkansas Tech University, Arkansas, Master's College and University
- Augustana College, Illinois, Baccalaureate College
- Benedictine College, Kansas, Baccalaureate College
- College of DuPage, Illinois, Associate's College Colleges
- Colorado Mesa University, Colorado, Baccalaureate College
- Dakota State University, South Dakota, Master's College and University
- Defiance College, Ohio, Baccalaureate College
- DePaul University, Illinois, Doctoral/Research University
- Des Moines Area Community College, Iowa, Associate's College
- Elmhurst College, Illinois, Master's College and University
- Franklin University, Ohio, Schools of business and management
- Grand Valley State University, Michigan, Master's College and University
- Grinnell College, Iowa, Baccalaureate College
- Illinois Central College, Illinois, Associate's College
- Illinois Institute of Technology, Illinois, Research University
- Institute of American Indian Arts, New Mexico, Tribal
- John Carroll University, Ohio, Master's College and University
- Joliet Junior College, Illinois, Associate's College
- Kalamazoo College, Michigan, Baccalaureate College
- Knox College, Illinois, Baccalaureate College
- Lakeland Community College, Ohio, Associate's College
- Lincoln University, Missouri, Master's College and University
- Luther Seminary, Minnesota, Special Focus Institution
- Macalester College, Minnesota, Baccalaureate College
- Marquette University, Wisconsin, Doctoral/Research University
- Miami University, Ohio, Research University

- Michigan State University, Michigan, Research University
- Michigan Technological University, Michigan, Research University
- Northeastern Illinois University, Illinois, Master's College and University
- Northeastern State University, Oklahoma, Master's College and University
- Northern Michigan University, Michigan, Master's College and University
- NorthWest Arkansas Community College, Arkansas, Associate's College
- Ohio State University, Ohio, Research University
- Otero Junior College, Colorado, Associate's College
- Purdue University, Indiana, Research University
- Rockhurst University, Missouri, Master's College and University
- South Dakota State University, South Dakota, Research University
- Southern Illinois University Carbondale, Illinois, Research University
- Southwestern Indian Polytechnic Institute, New Mexico, Tribal
- St Catherine University, Minnesota, Master's College and University
- The College of Saint Scholastica, Minnesota, Master's College and University
- Tulsa Community College, Oklahoma, Associate's College Colleges
- University of Akron Main Campus, Ohio, Research University
- University of Illinois at Urbana, Illinois, Research University
- University of Iowa, Iowa, Research University
- University of Kansas, Kansas, Research University
- University of Michigan, Michigan, Research University
- University of Minnesota-Duluth, Minnesota, Master's College and University
- University of Minnesota-Morris, Minnesota, Baccalaureate College
- University of Nebraska at Kearney, Nebraska, Master's College and University
- University of Nebraska at Omaha, Nebraska, Doctoral/Research University
- University of New Mexico-Main Campus, New Mexico, Research University
- University of New Mexico-Main Campus, New Mexico, Research University
- University of Northern Colorado, Colorado, Doctoral/Research University
- University of South Dakota, South Dakota, Research University
- University of St Thomas, Minnesota, Doctoral/Research University
- University of Wisconsin-Eau Claire, Wisconsin, Master's College and University
- University of Wisconsin-Green Bay, Wisconsin, Master's College and University
- University of Wisconsin-Milwaukee, Wisconsin, Research University
- University of Wisconsin-Stevens Point, Wisconsin, Master's College and University
- University of Wyoming, WY, Research University
- Washington University in St. Louis, Missouri, Research University
- Wayne State University, Michigan, Research University
- Webster University, Missouri, Master's College and University
- West Virginia State University, West Virginia, Baccalaureate College
- Western Michigan University, Michigan, Research University

New England Association of Schools and Colleges-Commission on Institutions of Higher Education (NEASC-CIHE)

- Becker College, Massachusetts, Baccalaureate College
- Bentley University, Massachusetts, Master's College and University

- Boston University, Massachusetts, Research University
- Brandeis University, Massachusetts, Research University
- Brown University, Rhode Island, Research University
- Champlain College, Vermont, Baccalaureate College
- College of the Holy Cross, Massachusetts, Baccalaureate College
- Emerson College, Massachusetts, Master's College and University
- Fairfield University, Connecticut, Master's College and University
- Greenfield Community College, Massachusetts, Associate's College
- Lasell College, Massachusetts, Baccalaureate College
- Massachusetts College of Liberal Arts, Massachusetts, Baccalaureate College
- Middlesex Community College, Massachusetts, Associate's College
- Naugatuck Valley Community College, Connecticut, Associate's College
- Salem State University, Massachusetts, Master's College and University
- Southern Connecticut State University, Connecticut, Master's College and University
- Stonehill College, Massachusetts, Baccalaureate College
- University of Connecticut Health Center, Connecticut, Research University
- University of Massachusetts-Boston, Massachusetts, Research University
- University of Massachusetts-Dartmouth, Massachusetts, Master's College and University

Northwest Commission on Colleges and Universities (NWCCU)

- Blue Mountain Community College, Oregon, Associate's College Colleges
- Brigham Young University-Provo, Utah, Research University
- Central Washington University, Washington, Master's College and University
- City University of Seattle, Washington, Master's College and University
- College of Southern Nevada, Nevada, Associate's College
- Montana State University, Montana, Research University
- Nevada State College, Nevada, Baccalaureate College
- Pacific Lutheran University, Washington, Master's College and University
- Peninsula College, Washington, Associate's College
- Pierce College at Fort Steilacoom, Washington, Associate's College
- Seattle University, Washington, Master's College and University
- University of Idaho, Idaho, Research University
- University of Nevada-Las Vegas, Nevada, Research University
- Utah State University, Utah, Research University
- Utah Valley University, Utah, Baccalaureate College

Southern Association of Colleges and Schools (SACS)

- Appalachian State University, North Carolina, Master's College and University
- Augusta University, Georgia, Doctoral/Research University
- Catawba College, North Carolina, Baccalaureate College
- Davidson College, North Carolina, Baccalaureate College
- Eastern Kentucky University, Kentucky, Master's College and University
- Eastern Mennonite University, Virginia, Baccalaureate College
- Florida International University, Florida, Research University
- George Mason University, Virginia, Research University

- Georgia College and State University, Georgia, Master's College and University
- Georgia Institute of Technology-Main Campus, Georgia, Research University
- Guilford College, North Carolina, Baccalaureate College
- Lone Star College System, Texas, Associate's College
- Midwestern State University, Texas, Master's College and University
- Murray State University, Kentucky, Master's College and University
- North Carolina Central University, North Carolina, Master's College and University
- Northwest Vista College, Texas, Associate's College
- Nova Southeastern University, Florida, Research University
- Our Lady of the Lake University, Texas, Doctoral/Research University
- Radford University, Virginia, Master's College and University
- Rollins College, Florida, Master's College and University
- South Texas College, Texas, Associate's College
- Southern Methodist University, Texas, Research University
- The University of Texas at San Antonio, Texas, Research University
- University of Miami, Florida, Research University
- University of Mississippi, Mississippi, Research University
- University of Mississippi Medical Center, Mississippi, Special Focus Institution
- University of North Carolina at Charlotte, North Carolina, Doctoral/Research University
- University of North Carolina at Greensboro, North Carolina, Research University
- University of North Carolina Wilmington, North Carolina, Master's College and University
- University of South Florida, Florida, Research University
- University of Texas at El Paso, Texas, Research University
- University of West Georgia, Georgia, Master's College and University
- Virginia Polytechnic Institute and State University, Virginia, Research University
- Virginia Polytechnic Institute and State University, Virginia, Research University
- Virginia Wesleyan College, Virginia, Baccalaureate College
- Wake Forest University, North Carolina, Research University
- Wake Technical Community College, North Carolina, Associate's College

Western Association of Schools and Colleges-Accrediting Commission for Community and Junior Colleges (WASC-ACCJC)

- Kapi'olani Community College, Hawaii, Associate's College
- Los Angeles Trade Technical College, California, Associate's College
- Santa Barbara City College, California, Associate's College
- California Lutheran University, California, Master's College and University
- California State University-East Bay, California, Master's College and University
- California State University-Fullerton, California, Master's College and University
- California State University-San Marcos, California, Master's College and University
- Claremont Colleges, California, Research University
- Hawaii Pacific University, Hawaii, Master's College and University
- Saint Mary's College of California, California, Master's College and University
- University of California-Merced, California, Research University
- University of California-Santa Cruz, California, Research University
- University of Redlands, California, Master's College and University

- University of Southern California, California, Research University
- Western University of Health Sciences, California, Special Focus Institution

International Accrediting Agencies

- Dalhousie University, Halifax, Nova Scotia
- Queensland University of Technology, Brisbane, Queensland
- University of Alberta, Edmonton and Camrose, Alberta
- University of Guelph, Guelph, Ontario
- University of Manitoba, Winnipeg, Manitoba

Assessment in Action Comprehensive Bibliography

The three-year Assessment in Action (AiA) program resulted in a wide array of scholarly and prac-tice-based literature and presentations advancing the conversation of the library's contributions to student success. An open call to AiA librarian team leaders was issued for contributions to this bibliography in fall 2015, and again in summer 2017. This bibliography aims to be comprehensive in capturing all scholarly and practice-based literature and presentations about the AiA program and campus projects conducted as part of AiA by staff, facilitators, and participants.

An electronic version of this bibliography, with links to many publications and presentations, is also available on the ACRL Value of Academic Libraries website at www.acrl.ala.org/value.

Journal Articles

College & Research Libraries 77, no. 2 (2016).

Special issue on Action Research from the Assessment in Action program (Contents):
    Malenfant, Kara J., Lisa Janicke Hinchliffe, and Debra Gilchrist. "Assessment as Action Research: Bridging Academic Scholarship and Everyday Practice."

    Arellano Douglas, Veronica, and Celia Rabinowitz. "Why Collaborate? Examining the Relationship between Faculty-Librarian Collaboration and First Year Students' Information Literacy Abilities."

    Davidson Squibb, Sara, and Susan Mikkelsen. "Assessing the Value of Course-Embedded Information Literacy on Student Learning and Achievement."

    Goebel, Nancy, and Jérôme Melançon. "Personal Librarian for Aboriginal Students: A Programmatic Assessment."

    Jones, Phil, Julia Bauder, and Kevin Engel. "Mixed or Complementary Messages: Making the Most of Unexpected Assessment Results."

    Lundstrom, Kacy, Pamela Martin, and Dory Cochran. "Making Strategic Decisions: Con-ducting and Using Research on the Impact of Sequenced Library Instruction."

    Massengale, Lisa, Pattie Piotrowski, and Devin Savage. "Identifying and Articulating Li-brary Connections to Student Success."

    Whitlock, Brandy, and Nassim Ebrahimi. "Beyond the Library: Using Multiple, Mixed Measures Simultaneously in a College-wide Assessment of Information Literacy."

Brown, Robin. "Lifting the Veil: Analyzing Collaborative Virtual Reference Transcripts to Demonstrate Value and Make Recommendations for Practice." *Reference & User Services Quarterly* 57, no. 1 (2017): 264–70.

Francis, Mary. "Assessing Varied Instructional Approaches in the Instruction of Online Graduate Students." *Library and Information Research* 38, no. 119 (2014): 3–12.

Hinchliffe, Lisa Janicke. "Professional Development for Assessment: Lessons from Reflective Practice." *The Journal of Academic Librarianship* 41, no. 6 (2015): 850–852.

Kiel, Stephen "Mike," Natalie Burclaff, and Catherine Johnson. "Learning by Doing: Developing a Baseline Information Literacy Assessment." *portal: Libraries and the Academy* 15, no. 4 (2015): 747–66.

Lowe, M. Sara, Char Booth, Sean Stone, and Natalie Tagge. "Impacting Information Literacy Learning in First-Year Seminars: A Rubric-Based Evaluation." *portal: Libraries and the Academy* 15, no. 3 (2015): 489–512.

McPherson, Patricia. "Paired Proficiencies: Incorporating Information Literacy into Language Instruction." *The Language Educator* 10, no. 2 (2015): 45–49.

Montgomery, Susan E., and Suzanne D. Robertshaw. "From Co-location to Collaboration: Working Together to Improve Student Learning." *Behavioral & Social Sciences Librarian* 34, no. 2 (2015): 55–69. https://doi.org/10.1080/01639269.2015.1047728.

Murray, Adam, Ashley Ireland, and Jana Hackathorn. "The Value of Academic Libraries: Library Services as a Predictor of Student Retention." *College & Research Libraries* 77, no. 5 (2016): 631–42.

Radcliff, Sharon, and Elise Y. Wong. "Evaluation of Sources: A New Sustainable Approach." *Reference Services Review* 43, no. 2 (2015): 231–50.

Saunders, Laura. "Academic Libraries' Strategic Plans: Top Trends and Under-recognized Areas." *The Journal of Academic Librarianship* 41, no. 3 (2015): 285–91.

Whelan, Jennifer L. A. "Personal Research Sessions: A Consultation-Based Program for Research Support." *Library Connect* 13, no. 7 (2015).

Whitlock, Brandy, and Julie Nanavati. "A Systematic Approach to Performative and Authentic Assessment." *Reference Services Review* 41, no. 1 (2013): 32–48.

Young, Scott W. H., Angela Tate, Doralyn Rossmann, and Mary Anne Hansen. "The Social Media Toll Road: The Promise and Peril of Facebook Advertising." *College & Research Libraries News* 75, no. 8 (2014): 427–34.

Books and Book Chapters

Ackermann, Eric, ed. Putting Assessment into Action: Selected Projects from the First Cohort of the Assessment in Action Grant. Chicago: Association of College and Research Libraries, 2015. Contents:

Part 1: Assessing Information Literacy/Library Instruction

FIRST YEAR STUDENTS/FIRST YEAR EXPERIENCE

Jagman, Heather. "'I Felt like Such a Freshman': Reflections on DePaul University Library's Assessment in Action Project."

Kremer, Jacalyn. "Honor Bound: Assessing Library Interventions into the Complex Problem of Academic Integrity."

Nye, Valerie. "Cite Me! What Sources Are Students Using for Research?"

Delevan, Kelly. "Employing Multiple Methods to Assess Information Literacy in a New Core Curriculum."

Douglas, Veronica Arellano. "Assessing Student Learning and Faculty-Librarian Collaboration with a Mixed-Methods Approach."

Prorak, Diane. "Assessment of Library Instruction within General Education Learning Outcomes and Academic Support Programs: Determining Impact on Student Research Skills, Confidence, and Retention."

Allen, Maryellen. "Impact of Information Literacy Instruction on the Success of First Year Composition Students."

Miller, Robin E. "Information Literacy Learning in First Year Composition: A Rubric-Based Approach to Assessment."

DeBose, Kyrille Goldbeck, and Carolyn Meier. "Comparing Apples and Oranges: Putting Virginia Tech's FYE Inquiry Assessment Program into Perspective."

SECOND TO FOURTH YEAR UNDERGRADUATES
Mondschein, Henri. "Assessment in Action Case Study: Do Online Learning Modules Have a Role in Information Literacy Instruction?"

Jones, Phil. "Complementary, Not Conflicting Data: Using Citation Analysis and NVivo to Explore Student Learning."

Catalano, Amy. "Predictors of Information Literacy Competencies at a Large University: A Reflection on Testing Methods."

Shoemaker, Jill S. "Assessing Graduating Seniors' Information Literacy Skills."

Watts, John. "Using Single-Case Research Design to Assess Course-Embedded Research Consultations."

GRADUATE STUDENTS
Francis, Mary. "Assessing Online Graduate Students."

Crea, Kathleen. "In Their Own Words: Evolution of Effective Search Behaviors by Medical Students and Residents at the University of Connecticut Health Center."

INSTITUTIONAL
Whitlock, Brandy. "Finding the Cocked Hat: Triangulating Assessment of Information Literacy as a College-wide Core Competency."

Part 2: Assessing Outreach, Services, and Spaces

OUTREACH
McDevitt, Theresa. "Get by with a Little Help from Your Friends: Working with Student Affairs to Engage and Assess College Students."

SERVICES

Paddick, Courtney. "ARC to Success: Linking the 'Commons' Model to Academic Success at Central Washington University."

O'Kelly, M. "Library Research Consultants: Measuring a New Service."

Resnis, Eric. "Dedicated Technology Facilities: Impacts, Success, and Implications."

Montgomery, Susan E., and Suzanne D. Robertshaw. "Filling In the Venn Diagram: Second Year Students, Research, Writing."

Bedwell, Linda. "Research Assistance Linked to Student Retention."

SPACES

Epperson, Annie. "Methodological Issues: Assessing the Impact of Using the Library on Student Success at the University of Northern Colorado."

Part 3: Longitudinal Assessment

Ireland, Ashley. "Known Library Use and Student Retention: A Methods Case Study."

Bradley, Alison, and Stephanie Otis. "Assessment Archaeology: Digging Up Old Data for Longitudinal Assessments."

Lupton, Aaron. "Impact of Library Usage on Student Success: Exploring New Territory."

Gersch, Beate, and Joseph A. Salem Jr. "Cooking with Information Resources in the Online Kitchen." In *The Library Assessment Cookbook*. Edited by Aaron Dobbs, 53–54. Chicago: Association of College and Research Libraries, 2017.

Mikkelsen, Susan, and Elizabeth McMunn-Tetangco. "Think like a Researcher: Integrating the Research Process in the Introductory Composition Curriculum." In *The New Information Literacy Instruction: Best Practices*. Edited by Patrick Ragains and Sandra Wood, 3–26. New York: Roman and Littlefield, 2015.

Penner, Katherine J., and Sarah Clark. "Assessing an Event: Mixin' It Up with the Long Night Against Procrastination." In *The Library Assessment Cookbook*. Edited by Aaron Dobbs, 85–86. Chicago: Association of College and Research Libraries, 2017.

Conference Presentations

Alexander, David. "Telling the Library Story: Assessment Activities in an Academic Library." Presentation at the joint conference of the Wyoming Library Association and Mountain Plains Library Association, Cheyenne, WY, September 23–25, 2015. Conference program at https://wyla.memberclicks.net/assets/docs/Conference/ConferenceCommittee/wla_mpla program_2015ed 2 1.pdf.

Allen, Maryellen, Sarah Bordac, Lorraine Hefferman, Jennifer Jarson, and Eric Resnis. "Sustainably Supporting Assessment Work with Communities of Practice." Presentation at the 2015 ACRL Conference, Portland, OR, March 25–28, 2015.

Avery, Susan, and Kirsten Feist. "Assessing International Students in the Library Instruction Classroom." Presentation at the 2016 Library Assessment Conference, Arlington, VA, October 31–November 2, 2016.

Avery, Susan, and Kirsten Feist. "Growing Your Instruction as the World Becomes Smaller: International Students and the Academic Library." Presentation at the Forty-Fourth National LOEX Library Conference, Pittsburgh, PA, May 5–7, 2016.

Bartholomew, Jennifer. "Cultivating a Culture of Assessment Using Multiple Collaborative Assignments to Teach Information Literacy Skills." Presentation at the American Theological Library Association Annual Conference, Denver, CO, June 13, 2015.

Bishop, Katie. "Collaboration That Works: How to Build and Assess Partnerships with Student Support Services Groups." Presentation at the Nebraska C&U/Kansas CULS Joint Spring Meeting, Crete, NE, May 29, 2015. Conference program at https://drive.google.com/file/d/0B_JAA7qxzEWHZ3RBZmNpeG9MTUk/view.

Blank, Michelle. "Planning the 'Ask': Effective Strategies to Use the Story That Data Tells to Shape Your Message." Presentation at OhioNET Dive into Data Conference Worthington, OH, July 17, 2015. https://www.ohionet.org/sites/default/files/Blank Planning the Ask.pdf.

Blank, Michelle. "Planning the 'Ask': Effective Strategies to Use the Story that Data Tells to Shape Your Message." Presentation at the Ohio Private Academic Libraries Annual Conference, Findlay, OH, August 2015. https://www.ohionet.org/sites/default/files/Blank Planning the Ask.pdf.

Blank, Michelle, and Alex Hauser. "I've a Feeling We're Not in High School Anymore: Information Literacy as a Bridge for Transitioning First-Year Students." Presentation at OhioNET Dive into Data Conference, Worthington, OH, July 17, 2015. https://www.ohionet.org/sites/default/files/Blank Hauser Not In High School Anymore.pdf.

Blank, Michelle and Alex Hauser. "Project Redesign: Using the ACRL Framework for Information Literacy for Higher Education to Bridge the CORE Curriculum." Presentation at the LOEX Fall Focus, Ypsilanti, MI, November 13–14, 2015.

Bowman, Elizabeth, Liza Harrington, Thomas Hyland, Annie Keola Kaukahi Thomas, and Brandy Whitlock. "Sustaining Success: Creating Community College Assessment Methods." Presentation at the 2015 ACRL Conference, Portland, OR, March 25–28, 2015.

Brown, Karen, and Lisa Janicke Hinchliffe. "Team-Based Assessment: Collaborating for a Campus Message about Student Learning." Presentation at the Leading Change: American Association of State Colleges and Universities Academic Affairs Summer Meeting, Denver, CO, July 21–23, 2016.

Brown, Karen, Lisa Janicke Hinchliffe, and Kara Malenfant. "Leveraging the Campus Message about Student Learning through Collaborative Assessment with Faculty." Presentation at the 2016 Assessment Institute, Indianapolis, IN, October 16–18, 2016.

Brown, Karen, and Kara Malenfant. "Academic Libraries and Student Success: Findings and Applications from 70 Campus Teams." Presentation at the 2014 Assessment Institute, Indianapolis, IN, October 19–21, 2014.

Brown, Karen, and Kara Malenfant. "Academic Library Contributions to Student Success: Documented Practices from the Field." Presentation at the Association for the Assessment of Learning in Higher Education Fifth Annual Assessment Conference: Actionable Assessment, Lexington, KY, June 1–3, 2015.

Brown, Karen, and Kara Malenfant. "Assessment in Action: High Impact Practices in Academic Libraries." Presentation at the Library Assessment Conference, Seattle, WA, August 4–6, 2014. Conference program at http://libraryassessment.org/index.shtml.

Brown, Karen, and Kara Malenfant. "Team-Based Assessment: Collaborating for a Campus Message about Student Learning." Presentation at the Association for the Assessment of Learning in Higher Education 2016 Annual Conference, Milwaukee, WI, June 6–8, 2016.

Brown, Karen, Kara Malenfant, Hollie Gardner, Kristin Johnson, Linda Reeves, and Steven Wise. "Assessment in Action in Academic Libraries." Presentation at the Texas Library Association Conference, Houston, TX, April 21, 2016.

Brown, Karen, Kara Malenfant, Kristin Johnson, Elizabeth Killingsworth, and Steven Wise. "Assessment in Action: Academic Libraries and Student Success." Presentation at the Texas Library Association Conference, Houston, TX, April 19–22, 2016.

Cantwell, Laureen. "Does What We Do Matter? Intensive Ask-a-Librarian Statistics Tracking and Doubling-Down on Professional Librarian Expertise." Presentation at the Library 2.015 Conference, online, October 2015. http://www.library20.com/forum/topics/does-what-we-do-matter-intensive-ask-a-librarian-statistics.

Careaga, Gregory A., Frank Gravier, Kenneth Lyons, Laura Meriwether, and Deborah A. Murphy. "Measuring Information Literacy Project Outcomes: Process as Value-Added." Presentation at the 12th International Conference on Performance Measurement in Libraries, Oxford, UK, July 31–August 2, 2017.

Charles, Leslin H. "Leveraging Partnerships to Assess Library Impact on Undergraduate Student Learning via a Longitudinal Study." Presentation at the European Conference on Information Literacy (ECIL), St. Malo, France, September 18–21, 2017.

Cobb, Mike, Gretchen Rings, Doralyn Rossmann, and Tara Wood. "Understanding Social Media and the Library User Experience: Be Interesting, Be Interested." Presentation at the Electronic Resources and Libraries Conference, Austin, TX, March 17, 2014. http://erl2014.sched.org/event/44bf10378cfe8970f647d4450242a258#.VjOC20ZWLXs.

Davis, Mary Ellen K., and Kara Malenfant. "Assessment in Action: ACRL's Newest IMLS Grant-Funded Project." Presentation at the CNI Fall Membership Meeting, Washington, DC, December 11, 2012. http://www.cni.org/wp-content/uploads/2012/12/cni_demonstrating_malenfant.pdf.

Davis, Mary Ellen K., and Kara Malenfant. "Assessment in Action: Academic Libraries and Student Success." Presentation at the Library 2.013, online, October 19, 2013. https://sas.elluminate.com/drtbl?sid=2008350&suid=D.EEC984E70D02D71F8272CAD0EE6B08.

DeBose, K., C. Meier, R. K. Miller, and P. Tomlin. "Get Thee to the Library! Incorporating Inquiry into First Year Programs." Presentation at the 2012 Conference on Higher Education Pedagogy, Blacksburg, VA, February 2012.

DeVilbiss, Samantha, Tammy Durant, Michelle Filkins, Kim Pittman, and Elizabethada Wright. "Students in the Information Age: Access, Research, and Persistence." Plenary presentation at Minnesota Writing and English Conference, St. Paul, MN, April 1, 2016.

Donohue, Mary, and JeanMarie Reinke. "Building Bridges: Crossing Silos to Inspire Student Success." Presentation at the Assessment Network of New York conference, Dobbs Ferry, NY, April 29–May 1, 2015. Slides at http://www.slideshare.net/jeanmariereinke/buildingbridgesfmccannypresentation20150430v4.

Douglas, Veronica Arellano. "Why Collaborate? Examining the Impact of Faculty-Librarian Collaboration on Students' Information Literacy Skill Development in the First Year Seminar." Presentation at the Congress of Academic Library Directors of Maryland Spring Meeting, Columbia, MD, April 23, 2015.

Epperson, Annie. "Quickly Collect Qualitative Data with a Video Booth!" Presentation at the 7th Qualitative and Quantitative Methods in Libraries International Conference (QQML2015), Paris, France, May 26–29, 2015. Conference program at http://www.isast.org/images/QQML2015_Program_Final.pdf.

Epperson, Annie. "True Confessions: A New Method for Gathering Qualitative Data." Presentation at the Colorado Council of Medical Librarians Membership Meeting, Aurora, CO, September 11, 2015.

Epperson, Annie, James Henderson, and Evan Welch. "Designed and Furnished for Success: Fostering an 'Academically Social' Campus Space!" Presentation at the 2015 University of Northern Colorado Assessment Fair, Greeley, CO, March 31, 2015. Conference abstracts at https://apply.ala.org/attachments/8881.

Francis, Mary. "Assessing Student Learning: Lessons Learned from the ACRL 'Assessment in Action: Academic Libraries and Student Success' Program." Presentation at the South Dakota Library Association Annual Conference, Pierre, SD, October 3, 2014.

Garwood, K., K. Nicholson, M. Parlette-Stewart, and T. Tucker. "Evaluating the Effectiveness of Face-to-Face, Online, and Blended Learning Approaches in Teaching Research and Referencing Strategies to First-Year Students." Presentation at the Canadian Writing Centres Conference, St. Catharines, ON, May 23, 2014. Conference program at https://cwcaaccr.wordpress.com/past-conferences/cwcaaccr-2014-conference/.

Gersch, Beate, and Joe Salem. "Who's Afraid of… Assessment?" Presentation/Workshop at the Institute of Teaching and Learning, Akron, OH, February 16, 2015. Video of presentation at https://www.youtube.com/watch?v=f65F7xdPE2U&feature=youtu.be.

Goebel, Nancy. "Considerations for Implementing a Personal Librarian Program." Presentation at the Texas Library Association, Austin, TX, April 14–17, 2015. Conference website at http://www.txla.org/TLA2015.

Goebel, Nancy. "Personal Librarian for Aboriginal Students." Presentation at the Council of Pacific and Prairie University Libraries meeting, Edmonton, AB, September 19, 2014.

Gregory, Lua, and Shana Higgins. "Information Literacy and First-Year Students: What Do They Know, What Do They Learn, and What Do We Learn?" Presentation at the European Conference on Information Literacy, Dubrovnik, Croatia, October 21, 2014.

Gregory, Lua, Shana Higgins, Sara Lowe, Robin Miller, and Danielle Theiss. "We've Only Just Begun: Determining the Value of Information Literacy Instruction in the First Year." Panel presentation at the 2015 ACRL Conference, Portland, OR, March 27, 2015.

Grimwood, Karen, Sofi King, and Paula Perez. "Assessment in Action: Academic Libraries and Student Success at NCCU." Presentation at the 6th Annual Technology Institute for Educators, Raleigh, NC, April 25–26. 2014. Conference program at http://www.nccu.edu/formsdocs/proxy.cfm?file_id=3014.

Harrington, Liza, and Amanda Hyde. "Collaborating to Assess Science Information Literacy: An Assessment in Action Project." Presentation at the Massachusetts Community College Teaching, Learning, and Student Development Conference, Fall River, MA, April 10, 2015. https://prezi.com/pod_u4ebdgzo/sustaining-success/.

Hauser, Alex. "Research Consultations: Creating Personalized, One-on-one, Library Instruction." Presentation at the Ohio Private Academic Libraries Annual Conference, Findlay, OH, August 2015.

Higgins, Shana. "Panel on Assessing Core Competencies in General Education." Presentation at the WASC Academic Resource Conference, Los Angeles, CA, April 23–25, 2014.

Hinchliffe, Lisa Janicke (and other panelists). "Lessons from the IMLS Funded Communities of Practice." Presentation at the 2016 ALA Annual Conference, Orlando, FL, June 25, 2016.

Hinchliffe, Lisa, Sarah Horowitz, Amy Glass, Heather Jagman, and Mary Thill. "CARLI Libraries Assessing Library Impact: Engaging a National Initiative." Presentation at the CARLI Annual Meeting, Champaign, IL, November 2013. Slides at http://www.carli.illinois.edu/sites/files/training/131101AssessingLibraryImpact.pptx.

Hinchliffe, Lisa, and Kara Malenfant. "Assessment in Action: Academic Libraries and Student Success." Presentation at the Southeastern Library Assessment Conference, Atlanta, GA, October 21–22, 2013.

Hinchliffe, Lisa, and Kara Malenfant. "The Endless Possibilities for Professional Development for Continuous Improvement and Demonstrating Library Value: A Case Report of an Initial Project." Presentation at the 7th International Evidence Based Library and Information Practice Conference, Saskatoon, SK, July 15–18, 2013. Conference website at http://eblip7.library.usask.ca/.

Hyland, Thomas. "One Shot at Success? Assessing the Effectiveness of Single Session Instruction on Student Attainment of Information Literacy Skills." Presentation at the 2015 Academic Library Association of Ohio Annual Conference, Lewis Center, Ohio, November 20, 2015.

Johnson, Catherine, Stephen Kiel, and Natalie Burclaff. "Measuring Students' Information Literacy Skills: An Assessment Strategy." Presentation at the Maryland Library Association/Delaware Library Association Joint Library Conference, Ocean City, MD, May 8, 2014. http://lanyrd.com/2014/mladla14/scyfhm/.

Kelley, Jennifer. "Program-Level Assessment in the Library: Impact of Information Literacy Instruction on English Composition and Speech Communications Courses at College of DuPage." Presentation at the 20th Annual Illinois Community College Assessment Fair, Palatine, IL, February 24, 2016. http://dc.cod.edu/librarypub/23/.

Killingsworth, E., and H. Gardner. "Curriculum Mapping to Support Information Literacy Instruction." Presentation at the Cross Timbers Library Collaborative Conference, Commerce, TX, August 2015. Conference program at https://ct-lc.org/sites/ct-lc.org/files/CTL-C2015conferenceschedule.pdf.

Kopecky, Linda, Robin Miller, Eau Claire, and Mitchell Scott. "Assessment in Action Initiative: The Wisconsin Connection." Presentation at the Council of University of Wisconsin Libraries (CUWL) Summer Conference, Madison, WI, June 2014.

Lockaby, D. C., S. L. Hazel, B. M. Usher, and P. West. "Embedded Library Instruction in Undergraduate Research Classes: Assessing the Impact." Presentation at the Council on Undergraduate Research Conference, Washington, DC, June 28–July1, 2014. Conference program at https://www.cur.org/assets/1/7/CC14_Program.pdf.

Lowe, Sarah, Lua Gregory, Shana Higgins, and April Cunningham. "Information Literacy and Student Success: Assessing a Core Competency." Presentation at the Western Association of Schools and Colleges (WASC) Academic Resource Conference, Los Angeles, CA, April 23–25, 2014.

Malenfant, Kara. "Academic Libraries and Student Success: Lessons from the Assessment in Action Program." Presentation at the Sharjah International Book Fair and ALA Library Conference, Sharjah, UAE, November 8–10, 2016.

Malenfant, Kara. "Assessment in Action: Academic Libraries and Student Success." Presentation at the Association for the Assessment of Learning in Higher Education Third Annual Assessment Conference, Lexington, KY, June 3–5, 2013.

Martinez, Josie U. "Embedding Information Literacy in Multi-section Composition Courses to Improve First Year Student Success." Presentation at the Georgia International Conference on Information Literacy, Savannah, GA, October 10–11, 2014. http://digitalcommons.georgiasouthern.edu/gaintlit/2014/2014/28/.

Martinez, Josie U. "Information Literacy and the First Year Experience: A Case-Study of the Embedded Librarian." Presentation at the New Mexico Library Association Annual Conference, Albuquerque, NM, April 17–19, 2013.

Massengale, L., S. Bluemie, A. Glass, and H. Jagman. "Success! Assessment in Action and Its Impact on Four Academic Libraries." Presentation at the Illinois Library Association Conference, Peoria, IL, October 22–24, 2015.

Meier, C. "Assessing Inquiry in Virginia Tech's First Year Experience Program." Presentation at the Personal Librarian & First Year Experience Conference, Cleveland, OH, April 2014.

Meier, C., and P. Tomlin. "Fostering Innovation, Expanding Librarian Roles: The Challenges and Opportunities of First Year Experience Programs." Roundtable discussion at the ACRL 2013 Conference, Indianapolis, IN, April 10–13, 2013.

Mikkelsen, Susan, and Heather Devrick. "Think like a Researcher! A Library/Faculty Collaboration to Improve Student Success." Presentation at the LOEX Conference, Denver, CO, April 30–May 2, 2015.

Mikkelsen, Susan, and Matt Moberly. "TRAIL: Teaching Research and Information Literacy." Presentation at the Assessment as Research Symposium, Merced, CA, March 4, 2015.

Miles, Linda. "Investigating Student-Staff Interactions." Presentation at the New York Metropolitan Area Library Council (METRO) Reference Special Interest Group, November 2014.

Miller, Rebecca K., Kiri Goldbeck Debose, and Margaret Merrill. "Stewarding Our First Year Students into the Information Ecosystem." Presentation at the 14th USAIN Biennial Conference, Burlington, VT, May 4–7, 2014.

Mondschein, Henri. "Do Online Learning Modules Have a Role in Information Literacy Instruction?" Presentation at the Western Association of Schools and Colleges (WASC) Academic Resource Conference, Los Angeles, CA, April 2013.

Montgomery, Susan, and Suzanne Robertshaw. "Finding and Filling the Gaps: Assessment for New Neighbors in the Library." Presentation at the International Writing Centers Association and National Conference on Peer Tutoring in Writing, Orlando, FL, October 31, 2014.

Moran, Virginia, Talia Nadir, and Kim Pittman. "Crossing the Unknown Sea: Navigating the Unintended Outcomes of Instruction Assessment." Panel presentation at Association of College and Research Libraries Conference, Baltimore, MD, March 24, 2017.

Murphy, Deborah A. "Dream of a Common Language: Developing a Shared Understanding of Information Literacy Concepts." Presentation at the 2016 Library Assessment Conference, Arlington, VA, October 31–November 2, 2016.

Parlette-Stewart, M., K. Nicholson, K. Garwood, and T. Tucker. "Evaluating the Impact of Face-to-Face and Online Information Literacy and Writing Skills Instruction Using a Mixed Methods Research Design." Presentation at the WILU 2014 Conference, London, ON, May 21–23, 2014.

Phillips, Margaret. "Tales from an AiA Project: Demonstrating the Value of Faculty Collaboration and Library Instruction on Student Learning and Confidence." Presentation at the Northwoods Library Symposium, Marquette, MI, August 13, 2014.

Phillips, Margaret, and Rebecca Miller. "Assessment in Action: Tales from Two AiA Projects." Presentation at the ACRL STS-IL Chat, online, February 2014. http://iue.libguides.com/c.php?g=67118&p=432155.

Radcliff, S., and E. Wong. "Assessing Argument, Critical Thinking and Information Literacy Learning Outcomes." Presentation at the Library Assessment Conference, Seattle, WA, August 4–6, 2014.

Radcliff, S., and E. Wong. "Evaluation of Sources: A New Sustainable Approach Using Argument Analysis and Critical Thinking." Presentation at the Library Instruction West 2014 Conference, Portland, OR, July 23–25, 2014.

Resnis, Eric, and Jennifer Natale. "Using Visual Literacy to Demonstrate the Impact of Technological Space." Presentation at the Academic Library Association of Ohio Assessment Interest Group Spring Workshop, Columbus, OH, April 16, 2015.

Rolls, L., and D. Sachs. "I Want You to Want Me! Demonstrating Value by Integrating Information Literacy into the Curriculum." Presentation at the Michigan Library Association Academic Libraries Conference, East Lansing, MI, May 29, 2014.

Rossmann, Doralyn, and Scott Young. "Online Community Building in an Academic Context: A University Library Case Study." Presentation at the Social Media and Society Conference, Halifax, Nova Scotia, September 14–15. 2013. https://smsociety13.sched.org/event/1a478c6d1aa6f65e07f2bc706ee5f43a#.VjODTUZWLXs.

Sachs, Diana. "Integrating Information Literacy in the Health Sciences Curriculum: Successful Library/Faculty Collaboration." Presentation at the European Conference on Information Literacy, Dubrovnik, Croatia, October 20–23, 2014. http://ecil2014.ilconf.org/wp-content/uploads/2014/11/Sachs.pdf.

Selberg-Eaton, R., C. Wood, R. K. Miller, and C. McConnell. "Six Departments, Two Hundred Students and Six Learning Outcomes in One Credit First Year Seminar." Presentation at the Annual Conference of the International Society for Exploring Teaching and Learning, Orlando, FL, October 2013.

Shanley, Caitlin. "Building Capacity, Measuring Success: Assessment in Action at Temple University Libraries." Lightning Talk presentation at the Philadelphia Library Assessment Discussion Group, Philadelphia, PA, April 2015.

Smith, Tyler Scott. "Steering Student Workers into Success." Presentation at the Council of UW Libraries Annual Conference, Madison, WI, June 2014.

Statkus, Daryl, and Pamela Graham. "Improving Student Learning Outcomes through Embedded Information Literacy Instruction." Presentation at the NERCOMP workshop, Providence, RI, March 2014. https://nercomp.org/uploadFiles/35B100000312.filename.Successful_Faculty_Librarian_Collaborations_-_Pamela_Graham_-_Becker_College_473.pdf.

Stewart-Mailhiot, A., M. O'Kelly, and D. Theiss. "Assessment in Action: A Journey through Campus Collaboration, a Learning Community and Research Design." Presentation at the ARL Library Assessment Conference, Seattle, WA, August 4–6, 2014.

Sweeper, Darren. "The ACRL Assessment in Action Project: The Montclair State University Experience." Presentation at the Virtual Academic Library Environment (VALE) Assessment Fair, New Brunswick, NJ, July 2014.

Sweeper, Darren. "Finding the Right Public Health Data: f(Librarians + Students) = Success." Presentation at the Virtual Academic Library Environment (VALE) Assessment Fair, New Brunswick, NJ, July 2014.

Tagge, Natalie, Sara Lowe, Char Booth, and Sean Stone. "More = Better: A Rubric-Based Evaluation of Librarian Course Collaborations at the First Year." Presentation at Library Instruction West, Portland, OR, July 24, 2014. http://pdxscholar.library.pdx.edu/liw_portland/Presentations/Material/8/.

Tate, Angela, Doralyn Rossmann, Mary Anne Hansen, and Scott Young. "Social Media with a Strategy: Connecting with Library Users." Presentation at the LITA Preconference Workshop at the ALA Midwinter Meeting, Philadelphia, PA, January 2014. http://scott-whyoung.com/talks/social-media-for-libraries-2014/#/.

Tharp, Julie, and Kate Frost. "The Power of Partnerships: Assessing the Impact of Information Literacy on Student Success." Presentation at the GWLA Student Learning Outcomes Conference, Las Vegas, NV, November 2013.

364 Appendix I

Theiss, Danielle, Mary O'Kelly, Amy Stewart-Mailhiot, and Leo Lo. "Assessment in Action: A Journey through Campus Collaboration, a Learning Community and Research Design." Presentation at the 2014 Library Assessment Conference, Seattle, WA, August 4–6. 2014.

Thomas, Annie. "Assessment in Action: A Community of Practice." Presentation at the Hawai'i Library Association Annual Conference, Honolulu, HI, December 5–6. 2014.

Watts, John. "Assessing Library Research Consultations: A Mixed-Method Approach." Lighting Talk presentation at the Library Assessment Conference 2014, Seattle, WA, August 4–6, 2014.

Whitlock, Brandy. "At a Crossroads: After a College-wide Assessment of Information Literacy, Partnering across Campus for Curricular Change." Presentation at the 2016 WILU Conference, Intersections, Vancouver, BC, May 31, 2016.

Whitlock, Brandy. "From Two to Three Dimensions: Leading Institutional Curricular Change by Thinking beyond the Assessment 'Loop.'" Paper Presentation at the 2017 ACRL Conference, At the Helm: Leading Transformation, Baltimore, MD, March 25, 2017.

Whitlock, Brandy. "Measuring Information Literacy Skills of Transferring Students." Presentation at the Joint Fall Program of ACRL MD and MILEX, Columbia, MD, November 2015.

Whitlock, Brandy. "Revitalizing Information Literacy Curricula: Leading to Create Change after a College-wide Assessment." Paper Presentation at the 2016 LOEX Conference, Learning from the Past, Building for the Future, Pittsburgh, PA, May 6, 2016.

Whitlock, Brandy, and Julie Nanavati. "Coming Face-to-Face with the Future of IL Assessment: Why and How to Use Authentic and Performative Measures to Assess Student Learning." Presentation at the IFLA Information Literacy Satellite Meeting, Limerick, Ireland, August 14–15, 2014.

Young, Brian. "Assessing Faculty Perceptions and Use of Open Education Resources (OERs)." Presentation at the 2015 ACRL Conference, Portland, Oregon, March 25–28, 2015.

Young, Scott, and Doralyn Rossmann. "Transforming Community with a Strategic Social Media Program." Presentation at the CNI Spring Meeting, St. Louis, MO, March 31–April 1, 2014. http://scottwhyoung.com/talks/transforming-community-strategic-social-media/.

Conference Posters

Upon completing the fourteen-month program, each AiA team presented a poster at the ALA Annual Conference in June 2014, 2015, or 2016. Poster abstracts, images, and full project descriptions can be found in a searchable online collection at https://apply.ala.org/aia/public. Additionally, many team members presented posters at other conferences, listed below.

Bird, Kenton, Diane Prorak, and Rodney Frey. "Assessment of General Education and Information Literacy Learning Outcomes at the University of Idaho." Poster presentation at AAC&U Network for Academic Renewal Conference, New Orleans, LA, February 18–20, 2016.

Charles, L. H., and J. Wiley. "R U up for the Challenge? A Partnership to Measure Library Impact on Student Learning: Rutgers University Libraries and the Ronald E. McNair Post Baccalaureate Degree Achievement Program." Poster presentation at the Virtual Academic Library Environment (VALE) Assessment Fair, Piscataway, NJ, July 2015.

Crea, Kathleen. "In Their Own Words: Surveying UConn Students about Developing Effective Search Behaviors and Use of Clinical Information—Including Mobile Applications—during Medical School". Poster presentation at ACRL New England Assessment in Action Symposium, Assumption College, Worcester, MA. September 13, 2016. http://guides. masslibsystem.org/c.php?g=570390&p=3930541.

Crea, Kathleen, and Brian Benson. "In Their Own Words: Surveying UConn Students About Developing Effective Search Behaviors and Use of Clinical Information—Including Mobile Apps—during Medical School." Poster presentation at Northeast Group on Educational Affairs (NEGEA) Conference, Worcester, MA, April 17, 2015. https://icollaborative.aamc. org/resource/4129/.

Dempsey, Paula R., and Heather Jagman. "'I Felt Like Such a Freshman': Integrating First-Year Student Identities through Collaborative Reflective Learning." Poster presentation at the Library Research Seminar VI: The Engaged Librarian: Libraries Partnering with Campus and Community, University of Illinois at Urbana-Champaign, Urbana, IL, October 7–9, 2014.

DeVilbiss, Samantha, Patrick Eidsmo, Kim Pittman, and Elizabethada Wright. "A Collaboration toward Persistence: The Impact of Library Instruction on First-Year Writers." Poster presentation at Minnesota Library Association Annual Conference, Duluth, MN, September 29, 2016.

Epperson, Annie, and Valerie Nye. "Diverse Roles of the Library in Student Success." Poster presentation at the Colorado Academic Library Association Summit, online, June 2014.

Gregory, Lua, and Shana Higgins. "Assessment in Action: Information Literacy in the First-Year Seminar." Poster session at the Annual Conference on the First-Year Experience, San Diego, CA, February 15–18, 2014.

Harris, Ruth, Frances Chu, Rudy R. Barreras, and Elizabeth Hoppe. "Librarians Collaborating with Faculty to Develop and Deliver an Evidence-Based Eye Care Course." Poster presentation at the Medical Library Group of Southern California and Arizona Symposium, Los Angeles, CA, March 2, 2012. http://www.mlgsca.mlanet.org/newsletter/?p=4452

Harris, Ruth, Frances Chu, Rudy R. Barreras, and Elizabeth Hoppe. "Librarians Collaborating with Faculty to Develop and Deliver an Evidence-Based Eye Care Course." Poster presentation at the California Academic and Research Libraries conference, San Diego, CA, April 5–7, 2012. Conference proceedings at http://www.carl-acrl.org/conference2012/ 2012ConferenceProceedings.html

Harris, Ruth, Frances Chu, Rudy R. Barreras, and Elizabeth Hoppe. "Librarians Collaborating with Faculty to Develop and Deliver an Evidence-Based Eye Care Course." Poster presentation at the Medical Library Association conference, Boston, MA, May 3–8, 2013.

Hinchliffe, Lisa, and Kara Malenfant. "Assessment in Action: Academic Libraries and Student Success." Poster presentation at the 2013 Assessment Institute, Indianapolis, IN, October 27–29, 2013.

Hinchliffe, Lisa, and Kara Malenfant. "Assessment in Action: Inquiry and Discovery Connecting Libraries and Students." Poster presentation at the Professional and Organizational Development Network in Higher Education Conference, Pittsburgh, PA, November 6–10, 2013.

Jarson, Jennifer. "Information Literacy and Student Learning at a Liberal Arts College: An Assessment in Action Project." Poster presentation at the CUNY Assessment Conference, New York, NY, June 2014.

Knox, Joshua, Tara Baillargeon, Martha Jerme, and Sharron Ronco. "Flipped Learning and Evidence Based Medicine Skills." Poster presentation at the Physician Assistant Education Association (PAEA) Education Forum, Washington, DC, November 13, 2015.

Lowe, Sara, Char Booth, Sean Stone, and Natalie Tagge. "Librarians Matter! Librarian Impact on First-Year Student Information Literacy Skills at Five Liberal Arts Colleges." Poster presentation at the 2014 Library Assessment Conference, Seattle, WA, August 4–6, 2014. http://old.libraryassessment.org/bm~doc/8loweposter.pdf.

Lowe, Sara, and Sean Stone. "Librarian Impact on First-Year Students' Information Literacy Skills across Multiple Liberal Arts Colleges." Poster presentation at the CUNY Assessment Conference, New York, NY, June 2014. http://cuny.edu/libraries/conference/proceedings/CUNYPosterLoewe.pdf.

Mix, Vickie L. "Collaboration in Learning: Partnering Academic Support Services for ESL Student Information Literacy." Poster presentation at the South Dakota Library Association Conference, Rapid City, SD, September 24, 2015.

Nye, Valerie. "Cite Me!" Poster presentation at the Tribal College Library Institute, Bozeman, MT, June 2, 2014.

Resnis, Eric. "Assessing Technological Self-Efficacy to Support Student Learning." Poster presentation at the Lilly International Conference on College Teaching, Oxford, OH, November 2014.

Resnis, Eric, Jennifer Natale, and Laura Birkenhauer. "Visual Literacy Assessment: Engaging Students to Improve Success." Poster presentation at the Academic Library Association of Ohio Annual Conference, Sandusky, OH, October 2014.

Stinson, Willette F. "On the Journey: Leveraging Information Literacy Instruction to Impact First-Year College Student Success." Poster presentation at the Christian Women United Conference, Charleston, WV, November 6, 2015.

APPENDIX J

Assessment in Action Studies with Exemplary Design Elements

THE TEAM FROM OCLC RESEARCH, which developed the ACRL report *Academic Library Impact: Improving Practice and Essential Areas to Research* analyzed a total of 535 documents published between 2010 and 2016, including the AiA project descriptions. As part of that process, and based on feedback from their advisory group, the authors decided that "identifying exemplary studies, or success stories, would also be helpful in suggesting innovative ways that library administrators and staff can align with and impact student-centered outcomes, as well as communicate this impact to higher education stakeholders."* Their intention in designating exemplary studies was so that library administrators, library staff, researchers, practitioners, and students can read more in the details of these effective research designs. In addition to including exemplary studies in the body of the report for each priority area, they included an appendix of AiA studies with exemplary design elements, which follows.

Academic Library Impact
Improving Practice and Essential Areas to Research

---

*Association of College and Research Libraries, *Academic Library Impact: Improving Practice and Essential Areas to Research*, prepared by Lynn Silipigni Connaway, William Harvey, Vanessa Kitzie, and Stephanie Mikitish of OCLC Research (Chicago: Association of College and Research Libraries, 2017), 44.

Context

Balci, Leanna F., Ben Crowder, and Nancy Wentworth. "Lost Library Links: Student's Ignore LMS Library Integration." Assessment in Action. Accessed January 5, 2017. https://apply.ala.org/attachments/26857.

Erickson, Sue, Patty Clark, David Dirlam, Denise Wilkinson, Stephen Leist, and Cathal Woods. "Understanding the Liberal Arts through Book Displays at Hofheimer Library." Assessment in Action. Accessed January 5, 2017. https://apply.ala.org/attachments/20599.

Samuel, Judith, and Sally Romero. "Measuring Information Literacy Success: From One-Shot Basic Skills Workshops to Embedded Librarian in California Acceleration Project." Assessment in Action. Accessed January 5, 2017. https://apply.ala.org/attachments/8871.

Tharp, Julie, Lisa Kammerlocher, Ashley Barckett, Kate Frost, and Jeanne Hanrahan. "Bridging the Critical Thinking Gap: Assessing the Integration of Information Literacy into the Curriculum for At-Risk Students." Assessment in Action. Accessed January 5, 2017. https://apply.ala.org/attachments/8866.

Data Collection

Blank, Michelle, Lisa Crumit-Hancock, Nathan Griggs, and Abigail Taylor. "'I Just Use Google': The Role of Information Literacy Skills in Academic Inquiry." Assessment in Action. Accessed January 5, 2017. https://apply.ala.org/attachments/20474.

Carbery, Alan, Ellen Zeman, Josh Blumberg, and Steve Wehmeyer. "Authentic Assessment: Building a Longitudinal Information Literacy Assessment Model Using Student Research Artifacts." Assessment in Action. Accessed January 5, 2017. https://apply.ala.org/attachments/20610.

Epperson, Anne, James Henderson, and Evan Welch. "Designed and Furnished for Success: Fostering an 'Academically Social' Campus Space." Assessment in Action. Accessed January 5, 2017. https://apply.ala.org/attachments/8881.

Ireland, Ashley, Jana Hackathorn, Jamie Mantooth, Aleeah McGinnis, Adam Murray, and Kelley Wezner. "Predictor of Success: The Relationship between Known Library Use and Student Retention at a Regional Public University." Assessment in Action. Accessed January 5, 2017. https://apply.ala.org/attachments/8986.

Massengale, Lisa, Pattie Piotrowski, and Devin Savage. "Galvin Library Assessment." Assessment in Action. Accessed January 5, 2017. https://apply.ala.org/attachments/20544.

Data Sampling

Alexander, Stephanie, Alexis Alabastro, My-Lan Huynh, and Sharon Radcliff. "Impact of IL Instruction on Transfer Student GPA and Use of Library Resources." Assessment in Action. Accessed January 5, 2017. https://apply.ala.org/attachments/27461.

Caldwell, Lesley, Emma Lausen, Courtney Edwards, Zoe Fisher, Erik Gimness, Rachel Goon, Carly Haddon, Robert Johnson, Krissy Kim, Laurie Shuster, Kathy Twart, Beth Thoms, and Shane Agustin. "Plant More One-Shots? Prune Them Back? Or Plow Them Under?" Assessment in Action. Accessed January 5, 2017. https://apply.ala.org/attachments/20496.

Leung, Sofia, Stephanie Gamble, Ellen Raimond, Anne M. Johnson, and Amalia Monroe-Gulick. "Exploring Undergraduate Student Use of Learning Studio Space at the University of Kansas (KU)." Assessment in Action. Accessed January 5, 2017. https://apply.ala.org/attachments/26824.

Mondschein, Henri, Cia DeMartino, Rodney Reynolds, and Nicole M. Stanoff. "Do Online Learning Modules Have a Role in Information Literacy Instruction?" Assessment in Action. Accessed January 5, 2017. https://apply.ala.org/attachments/8869.

Smith, Kelly, Matthew Irvin, Jens Arneson, Kwan Yi, Todd King, and Chad Adkins. "Library Resource Usage and Student Success at Eastern Kentucky University." Assessment in Action. Accessed January 5, 2017. https://apply.ala.org/attachments/20592.

Data Analysis

Chodock, Ted, Yelena Bailey-Kirby, Courtney Danforth, Shelley Fischer, Linda Foreman, Pamela Gallion, Christopher Perkins, Carrie Preite, Caprice Roberson, and Laura Yavitz. "Attitudes Matter: Student Success beyond Information Literacy." Assessment in Action. Accessed January 5, 2017. https://apply.ala.org/attachments/20460.

Lowe, Sara, Char Booth, Sean Stone, Natalie Tagge, Alexandra Chappell, and Gale Burrow. "Librarians Matter! Impact on First-Year Information Literacy Skills at Five Colleges." Assessment in Action. Accessed January 5, 2017. https://apply.ala.org/attachments/8854.

Resnis, Eric, Carolyn Haynes, Cecilia Shore, Andrea Bakkar, Jennifer Natale, Laura Birkenhauer, Rob Casson, and Mike Bomholt. "Dedicated Technology Facilities: Impacts, Success, and Implications." Assessment in Action. Accessed January 5, 2017. https://apply.ala.org/attachments/8874.

Squibb, Sara D., Susan Mikkelsen, Laura Martin, Matt Moberly, and Anne Zanzucchi. "Assessing an Embedded Information Literacy Emphasis Introductory Writing Class." Assessment in Action. Accessed January 5, 2017. https://apply.ala.org/attachments/20502.

Design

Baillargeon, Tara, Martha Jermé, Josh Know, and Sharron Ronco. "Flipped Learning and Evidence Based Medicine Skills." Assessment in Action. Accessed January 5, 2017. https://apply.ala.org/attachments/20495.

Murphy, Sarah A., Elizabeth L. Black, Sophie Tullier, Emily Slager, and Alexis Collier. "AiA and the Second-Year Transformational Experience Program." Assessment in Action. Accessed January 5, 2017. https://apply.ala.org/attachments/8873.

Nicholson, Karen, Melanie Parlette-Stewart, Kim Garwood, and Trent Tucker. "Evaluating the Impact of Face-to-Face and Online Information Literacy and Writing Skills Instruction Using a Mixed Methods Research Design." Assessment in Action. Accessed January 5, 2017. https://apply.ala.org/attachments/8860.

Ray, Jacquelyn, Cheri Kendrick, and Craig McIntosh. "Expanding Our Reach: Pedagogical Strategies and Information Literacy Learning in an Online versus Traditional Classroom." Assessment in Action. Accessed January 5, 2017. https://apply.ala.org/attachments/26911.

Whitlock, Brandy, Nassim Ebrahimi, and Marjorie Paoletti. "Finding the Cocked Hat: Triangulating Assessment for Information Literacy as a College-wide Core Competency." Assessment in Action. Accessed January 5, 2017. https://apply.ala.org/attachments/8894.

Discussion

Bartholomew, Jennifer, Bruce Eldevik, Michael Chan, Terri Elton, Mark Granquist, Leonard Hummel, Amy Marga, and Laurel Forsgren. "Cultivating a Culture of Assessment Using Multiple Collaborative Assignments to Teach Information Literacy Skills." Assessment in Action. Accessed January 5, 2017. https://apply.ala.org/attachments/20538.

Lock, Mary Beth, Meghan Webb, Glenda Boyles, Le'Ron Byrd, John Champlin, and Ryan Shirey. "What's in It for Me? Success, Motivation, and Gaps." Assessment in Action. Accessed January 5, 2017. https://apply.ala.org/attachments/20513.

Sharpe, Stephanie, Kris Helbling, Carol Mollman, Ted Chaffin, Susan Lowther, and Robert Patterson. "Assessing Research and Writing Support for First-Year Writing." Assessment in Action. Accessed January 5, 2017. https://apply.ala.org/attachments/20520.

Future Work

Burkhardt, Jess, Debbie Malone, Lynne Kvinnesland, Deb Booros, Jim Castagna, and Marc Albanese. "TV or Not TV: Assessing Student Learning of Search as Strategic Exploration." Assessment in Action. Accessed January 5, 2017. https://apply.ala.org/attachments/27096.

Martinez, Josie U., Steven Wise, Brighid Gonzales, Candace Zepeda, Kirsten Komara, Sabrina Zertuche, and Andrew Hale. "Video Killed the One Shot Session: Embedding Online Tutorials in First Year Composition Classes and the Effects on Student Success." Assessment in Action. Accessed January 5, 2017. https://apply.ala.org/attachments/20532.

Reporting

Glass, Amy. "Library Assessment—the Next Frontier! Our Mission for this Project: How Does Library Instruction Impact Student Success within Sections of ENG 111 (Composition II)?" Assessment in Action. Accessed January 5, 2017. https://apply.ala.org/attachments/8765.

Liss, Ken, Tom Casserly, Gwen Kordonowy, Sarah Madsen Hardy, and Gillian Pierce. "Telling Students to 'Get Lost!': Research as Inquiry and Searching as Strategic Exploration." Assessment in Action. Accessed January 5, 2017. https://apply.ala.org/attachments/26789.

Morganelli, H., S. Tonner, L. Driver, S. Doscher, G. Pearson, and K. Perez. "The Influence of Faculty Collaboration on Students' Information Literacy." Assessment in Action. Accessed January 5, 2017. https://apply.ala.org/attachments/20477.

Topic/Problem

Bishop, Katie, Connie Sorensen-Birk, and Derek Boeckner. "Don't Wait for Them to Come to You: Partnering with Student Support Services." Assessment in Action. Accessed January 5, 2017. https://apply.ala.org/attachments/20491.

Lantzy, Tricia, Lea Roberg-Chao, and Melissa Simnett. "How Does It Measure Up? Assessing Student Learning in Online Versus Face-to-Face Instruction." Assessment in Action. Accessed January 5, 2017. https://apply.ala.org/attachments/26823.

Torres, Elizabeth, Timothy Martin, Farris Sanders, Nori Leong, Sheryl Sunia, and Han N. C. Wester. "Assessing Library Instruction for Military Students." Assessment in Action. Accessed January 5, 2017. https://apply.ala.org/attachments/26855.

Progress Report on Planning Multi-Institutional Research on Library Value

To: ACRL Board of Directors

From: Debra Gilchrist and Lisa Janicke Hinchliffe, Lead Facilitators, Assessment in Action (AiA) Program, Karen Brown, AiA Project Analyst, Kara Malenfant, Staff Liaison

Subject: FYI Progress Report on Planning Multi-Institutional Research on Library Value

Date: December 4, 2015

Background

At the ACRL Board meeting I on June 27, 2015, in San Francisco, CA, we met with the Board to discuss a research planning proposal that would build off of the results from the Assessment in Action (AiA) program. We proposed a planning phase to design and develop a research approach in which studies on a small number of key questions would be replicated using the same research methodology at a variety of academic institutions. The profession could then make more informed claims about the contributions of academic libraries to higher education that are specific to a particular institution. The multi-institutional design of such a research project would create unique value for the profession, as no single library could easily pursue such an investigative strategy and ACRL has demonstrated its leadership and capability for supporting collective action.

The Board approved this request for a planning phase to develop a research project focused on library value and designated up to $62,000 in the FY16 budget to support it. The intent was that at the end of this planning work, a full research grant proposal would be developed including research questions, standard protocols, and specific tools for each question to be implemented in multiple academic institutions of different types.

Progress June-December

On June 28, leaders from the AiA program and the VAL committee spent 2 1/2 hours in a joint retreat. During that meeting we updated each other on recent committee discussions and activities, clarified goals, and discussed possibilities for future actions. We were particularly focused on next steps and how to implement the planning proposal the ACRL Board had just funded. We discussed various approaches, particularly how to select the research questions. The group felt that an invitational meeting that brought together library leaders from throughout the country to help hone in on the most impactful and strategic research questions would be a beneficial action.

The AiA leader group holds regular planning calls every other week. Through July and August, we devoted the bulk of our conversation to the research planning project, discussing how to best design the invitational meeting in a manner that would produce the best results and most useful information. We felt it crucial to narrow down and articulate the inquiry questions to some degree prior to convening such a meeting in order to ensure it would be as productive as possible.

After rich discussions of our own, we concluded that an additional step would bring more focus; we believed it was important to pause and check in with expert thinkers outside of libraries in order to clarify our own rationale about the inquiry questions. We identified associations and individuals of interest and reached out with invitations for conversations, which were all received enthusiastically. Over a nine-week period, we held hour-long phone calls with representatives from each of the following organizations:

- Achieving the Dream (11/12): Karen Stout, President and CEO
- Association for Institutional Research (11/12): Randy Swing, Executive Director; Gina Johnson, Strategy Director for IR Capacity Initiatives
- Association of Public and Land-grant Universities (11/10): Christine Keller, Vice President, Research and Policy Analysis, and Executive Director, Voluntary System of Accountability and Student Achievement Measure
- Center of Inquiry in the Liberal Arts—Wabash College (10/13): Charlie Blaich, Director; Kathy Wise, Associate Director
- Community College Research Center—Columbia University (9/25): Shanna Jaggars, Assistant Director; Melinda Karp, Assistant Director for Staff and Institutional Development
- National Survey of Student Engagement (9/25): Alexander C. McCormick, Director; Bob Gonyea, Associate Director of Research and Data Analysis; Kevin Fosnacht, Research Analyst
- National Institute for Learning Outcomes Assessment (10/19): George Kuh, Director and Co-Principal Investigator; Natasha Jankowski, Associate Director; Stan Ikenberry, Co-Principal Investigator
- NASPA—Student Affairs Administrators in Higher Education (11/23): Kevin Kruger, President
- Pew Research Center (10/14): Lee Rainie, Director of Internet, Science and Technology Research

In the near future we have additional calls scheduled with:

- American Association of State Colleges and Universities (12/17): George Mehaffy, Vice President for Academic Leadership and Change)
- Association of American Colleges and Universities (12/17): Debra Humphreys, Vice President for Policy and Public Engagement; Terrel Rhodes, Vice President for Quality, Curriculum, and Assessment
- Council of Independent Colleges (12/18): Richard Ekman,President

We developed a set of guiding questions to help us direct these conversations and each conversation evolved naturally to explore intersections of mutual interest. We asked about key topics or questions each organization is grappling with now, where their research is heading, what they see on the horizon in the larger national conversation regarding factors that impact student learning and success, whether they knew of initiatives where ACRL and librarians could contribute/ complement/ enhance/influence, and about other organizations or individuals with whom we should be talking.

We took careful notes during each conversation. By analyzing these notes, we were able to discern recurrent patterns and are seeing the following broad themes emerging regarding key trends in higher education related to data, assessment, and research:

- **Astute use of evidence:** Significant effort has been focused on collecting, analyzing, and interpreting data, but we now need to know if the yield in student learning improvements is proportional to the effort. Energy is now being directed towards better use of evidence to make improvements rather than conducting newresearch.[1]
- **Leadership as advocacy:** Essential to have leadership at the program director level; Need individuals who know how to identify and use the appropriate data in collaboration with others on campus; Need to think of these leaders as ambassadors and advocates.
- **Contextual nature of the educational experience:** Emphasis on how students are achieving general learning outcomes related to critical thinking across disciplines and through experiences in and out of the classroom; How do different educational experiences correlate to learning? Many students need a rich array of learning experiences to complete degree.
- **Role of higher education in our national life:** How does higher education contribute to an individual's lifelong learning for careers and general life satisfaction? What is the role of higher education in our national life? If higher education associations can show impact on the education broadly, then members will benefit.

An additional in-person meeting allowed us to explore these themes more deeply and solicit feedback with on-the-ground assessment officers. On Thursday, December 3rd, 10:00am–12:00pm, Karen Brown and Kara Malenfant hosted a meeting of the Chicago Area Assessment Group, a professional peer group of assessment officers from 35 area colleges and universities. It provides a forum for sharing good practices, soliciting feedback and creating an open dialogue for gathering information and thinking through ideas. Prior to the meeting, we shared basic information about the AiA program and lessons learned to date from the AiA projects.

During the meeting we provided a 30 minute overview to ACRL's VAL initiative, highlighted key AiA findings, and shared themes which emerged from the fall phone conversations with higher education stakeholders. We asked the assessment officers for their reactions and input about ways that librarians might most effectively and meaningfully contribute to campus assessment activities, particularly in relation to a growing body of findings about library impact, assessment tools and methods used by the AiA campus teams, and collaborative campus approaches to assessment work. They emphasized the value of learning more about collaborative assessment work on campuses, noting that most campuses seem to already have rich sources of evidence to tap, but meaningful use can be problematic.

Our Next Steps

Based on this series of conversations, we deepened our understanding of what is most needed so that libraries can contribute to higher education assessment work in the most meaningful ways possible. We have compiled a lengthy list of recommendations that emerged from the phone conversations and the CAAG meeting. As a result, our thinking has evolved and our immediate next step is to re-engage with the VAL committee to discuss and process all that arose as possible avenues to pursue. We will share the list of recommendations with the VAL Committee and together determine what steps we believe would best serve ACRL and the profession.

Our June proposal to the Board said one intended outcome of the planning phase would be a research grant proposal submitted to IMLS or another funder in February 2016. Given all we now know, we are no longer working towards that goal. We will report back to the Board with specific recommendations for subsequent action in mid-March for discussion at the spring meeting in April.

Notes

1. Indeed, this is the focus of AASCU's February 2016 Academic Affairs Winter Meeting. "A growing body of research suggests that we know a great deal about the most promising practices to dramatically increase student success. Yet student success efforts on too many campuses remain piecemeal, disconnected, or idiosyncratic. We don't have a knowledge problem. We have an implementation problem." See http://www.aascu.org/meetings/aa_winter16.

About the Editors

Karen Brown is a professor at Dominican University (River Forest, Illinois) in the School of Information Studies and teaches in the areas of assessment, collection management, foundations of the profession, and literacy and learning. Prior to joining Dominican University's faculty in 2000, she developed and coordinated continuing education programs for the Chicago Library System, one of Illinois's former regional library systems. She has also held positions focusing on collection development, reference, and instruction at the University of Wisconsin, the University of Maryland, Columbia University, and Bard College. She holds a PhD in media ecology from New York University and master's degrees in library science and adult education from the University of Wisconsin.

Debra Gilchrist is Vice President for Learning and Student Success at Pierce College, Lakewood, Washington. In addition to academic and student affairs, Gilchrist leads efforts focused on accreditation and achieving institutional outcomes. Her scholarship focuses on outcomes assessment as a tool for change; demonstrating the contributions of academic libraries through assessment of both learning and program impact and quality. She is an inaugural member of the ACRL Immersion Program and in 2007 was honored with the Miriam Dudley Award, which recognizes an individual who has made a significant contribution to the advancement of instruction in a college or research library environment. Gilchrist earned her MLS from the University of Denver and her PhD in Higher Education Leadership from Oregon State University. Her doctoral dissertation focused on the leadership role of academic librarians to influence instructional change.

Sara Goek is a Mellon/ACLS Public Fellow at ACRL where she serves as Program Manager contributing to efforts to improve research about academic library contributions to student learning and success. A historian by trade, prior to joining ACRL Sara worked as research faculty at the Illinois Mathematics and Science Academy and as a lecturer, tutor, and post-doctoral researcher at University College Cork (UCC), Ireland. She holds a PhD in History/Digital Arts & Humanities and an MA in Historical Research from UCC, and a BA in History and Irish Studies from Boston College.

Lisa Janicke Hinchliffe is Professor and Coordinator for Information Literacy Services and Instruction in the University Library at the University of Illinois at Urbana-Champaign. She is also an affiliate faculty member in the University's School of Information Sciences. Lisa served as the 2010–2011 President of the Association of College and Research Libraries, which launched the Value of Academic Libraries Initiative during her presidency. Lisa has consulted, presented, and published widely on information literacy, teaching and learning, the value of libraries, library assessment, program evaluation, and organizational innovation. Lisa received her Master of Education in Educational Psychology and Master of Library and Information Science degrees from the University of Illinois at Urbana-Champaign and earned her Bachelor of Arts degree in philosophy from the University of St. Thomas in Minnesota.

Kara Malenfant is a senior staff member at the Association of College and Research Libraries (ACRL, a division of the American Library Association), where she coordinates government relations advocacy and scholarly communication activities and is the lead staff member on the Value of Academic Libraries initiative and Assessment in Action program. She provides consulting services on organization development and use of ACRL's standards for libraries in higher education. Kara began her position at ACRL in fall of 2005 after working for six years at DePaul University

Libraries in Chicago. A former Peace Corps volunteer, she holds a PhD in leadership and change from Antioch University and a master's degree in library science from the University of Illinois at Urbana-Champaign.

Chase Ollis is ACRL's Program Officer for Professional Development. He manages ACRL's Road-Show program, awards program, and Conference scholarship program, and handles logistics and marketing for ACRL's professional development program. Prior to joining ACRL, he worked as a circulation supervisor at Northwestern University's Pritzker Legal Research Center. Chase holds an MS in library and information science from the University of Illinois at Urbana-Champaign and a BA in both English and Communication Studies from Furman University.

Allison Payne is ACRL's Program Officer for Governance. She coordinates activities of the association's Board of Directors and Budget & Finance Committee, prepares and maintains the ACRL budget, and manages division-level appointments. Prior to joining ACRL, Allison has been a library assistant at Kraft Foods Global Research & Development, worked at the University of Iowa Libraries' Preservation Department, and tutored incarcerated youth in Chicago. She holds an MLIS from the University of Wisconsin-Milwaukee and a BA in English with a minor in Psychology from the University of Iowa.